A Precarious Balance

ANTWAIN K. HUNTER

A Precarious Balance

Firearms, Race, and Community
in North Carolina, 1715–1865

The University of North Carolina Press *Chapel Hill*

This book was published with the assistance of the H. Eugene and Lillian Lehman Fund of the University of North Carolina Press.

Set in Arno by codeMantra
Manufactured in the United States of America

Cover art: "A Snipe Shooter" by Alfred Rudolph Waud, 1871.
Courtesy of the Historic New Orleans Collection, 1965.90.61.

Library of Congress Cataloging-in-Publication Data
Names: Hunter, Antwain K., author.
Title: A precarious balance : firearms, race, and community in
North Carolina, 1715–1865 / Antwain K. Hunter.
Description: Chapel Hill : The University of North Carolina Press, [2025] |
Includes bibliographical references and index.
Identifiers: LCCN 2025030395 | ISBN 9781469689883 (cloth ; alk. paper) | ISBN 9781469689890
(paperback ; alk. paper) | ISBN 9781469686615 (epub) | ISBN 9781469689906 (pdf)
Subjects: LCSH: Enslaved persons—North Carolina—Social conditions—History—
18th century. | Enslaved persons—North Carolina—Social conditions—History—
19th century. | Free Black people—North Carolina—Social conditions—History—
18th century. | Free Black people—North Carolina—Social conditions—History—
19th century. | Firearms—Economic aspects. | Firearms—Law and legislation—
North Carolina. | Gun control—North Carolina—History—18th century. |
Gun control—North Carolina—History—19th century. | North Carolina—Race
relations. | BISAC: HISTORY / African American & Black | LAW / Legal History
Classification: LCC F265.B53 H86 2025
LC record available at https://lccn.loc.gov/2025030395

For product safety concerns under the European Union's General Product
Safety Regulation (EU GPSR), please contact gpsr@mare-nostrum.co.uk or
write to the University of North Carolina Press and Mare Nostrum Group
B.V., Mauritskade 21D, 1091 GC Amsterdam, The Netherlands.

For Anthony E. Kaye (1962–2017)

Tony was a generous adviser, an impressively engaged scholar,
and a sharp editor who departed this life far too soon.
Our profession lost an extraordinary talent, and I lost a friend
and mentor with his passing. He was the first person to see the
potential in my scattered thoughts about race, firearms,
and nineteenth-century law. Tony encouraged and, when I needed it,
pushed me through my angsty years as a graduate student.
He continued to support my work through the remainder of
his life. I am deeply indebted to him for that—his mentorship
had an immeasurable impact on my development as a scholar.
In the end, my primary hope for this book is that it stands as
something that Tony would have gotten a kick out of.

Contents

Illustrations

Acknowledgments

This book was a long time in the making, and many people who helped me along the way deserve my deep and heartfelt thanks. The scholarly community at the George and Ann Richards Civil War Era Center at Penn State was instrumental at this project's start. Tony Kaye, Bill Blair, Lori Ginzberg, K. Russell Lohse, and David McBride were patient and generous with their time and comments. Sean Trainor, Tom Brinton, Will Bryan, Bill Cossen, Kathryn Falvo, Leor Golder, David Greenspoon, Chris Hayashida-Knight, Matt Isham, Kelly Knight, Rachel Moran, Andrew Prymak, Evan Rothera, Emily Seitz-Moore, Barby Singer, Will Sturkey, and Alfred Wallace all offered feedback, unwavering support, and friendship.

I am also indebted to many people at Butler University, especially my family in the Department of History, Anthropology, and Classics: Amy Arnold, Bruce Bigelow, Chris Bungard, John Cornell, Viv Deno, Elise Edwards, Nancy Germano, Paul Hanson, Jeana Jorgensen, Lynne Kvapil, Tom Mould, Tom Paradis, John and Mary Ramsbottom, Julie Searcy, Zachary Scarlett, Sholeh Shahrokhi, Ageeth Sluis, Scott Swanson, and Amanda Waterhouse. Their support means everything. I also owe thanks to Terri and Brian Carney, Kaity Creasy, Jim and Bethanie Danko, Janine Frainier, Jay Howard, Terri Jett, Chad Knoderer, Kristen Nichols, Ann Savage, Robin Turner, and Peter Wang, who welcomed me into an extraordinary community that was always much bigger than our scholarship. I also thank my new colleagues at University of North Carolina, Chapel Hill, particularly Kathleen DuVal, Jerma Jackson, Lloyd Kramer, Genna Rae McNeil, Matt Turi, and Ron Williams. Westfield State University's Mara Dodge and Chris Clark at the University of Connecticut offered great support and guidance. Princeton University's Tera W. Hunter was also an irreplaceable source of inspiration, encouragement, and fantastic Thanksgiving dinners.

Further, I am indebted to several organizations and individuals for financial support for my research trips and academic leaves, including the North Caroliniana Society, Penn State's Africana Research Center, and Penn State's College of Liberal Arts. Steven and Janice Brose were also great supporters through the Richards Center. At Butler University, I benefited from an Awards Committee faculty research grant and a sabbatical. At UNC, I enjoyed a Research and Scholarly Activity leave via the College of Arts and Sciences. Armand K. Hunter has been there since we first fell in love with history as little boys and provided timely support at various points—I could not ask for a better twin brother.

I am also grateful to the innumerable archivists, librarians, professional staff, and student workers at the Wilson Library at UNC, the North Carolina Department of Archives and History, the Rubenstein Library at Duke University, the William L. Clements Library at the University of Michigan, the Joyner Library at East Carolina University, the Hargrett Rare Book and Manuscript Library at the University of Georgia, and the Virginia Military Institute Archives who helped me during my research. I also thank several students who worked as research assistants: Maria Rapisarda, Valary Farmer, Eileen Hogan, Brooks Hosfeld, MaryKatherine Klaybor, Andrew Ross, and Megan Ulrich at Butler University; and Andres (Andy) Guillermo Estrella Urrutia at UNC. Additionally, Iris E. Hunter, Auriel K. Hunter, and Caitlin Domagal deserve sainthood for volunteering to read a dizzying number of county court records and letters.

I have also received helpful feedback from so many copanelists, commenters, and audience members during presentations, roundtables, and conference panels through the American Historical Association, the Association of British American Nineteenth Century Historians, the Business History Conference, the Society for Historians of the Early American Republic, the Society of Civil War Historians, the Southern Historical Association, the Association for the Study of African American Life and History, the Indiana Academy of the Social Sciences, the Indiana Association of Historians, the Indianapolis Literary Society, the Midwest Civil War Study Group, and the Center for the Study of Guns and Society at Wesleyan University. I also received useful comments at lectures and workshops at the University of Georgia, the University of North Carolina–Greensboro, Butler University, Wabash College, the Royal Armouries Museum in West Yorkshire, the University of Arkansas–Fort Smith, and Carolina Public Humanities.

I am thankful to Chuck Grench, Debbie Gershenowitz, Alexis Dumain, and everyone else at the University of North Carolina Press for patiently helping me steer this project through the publication process. I would be lost without them. Further, Sally Hadden provided excellent feedback as an outside reader and insightfully introduced me to coroners' reports as useful sources. I thank her and another reader, anonymous to me, for their thoughtful, generous, and helpful comments.

A Precarious Balance's subject matter is often heavy, and the research was mentally and emotionally draining at times. I was fortunately able to find great outlets for momentary escape. The Indianapolis Gaelic Athletic Association provided an awesome community where I could sweat (and occasionally, bleed) out my frustrations on the hurling and Gaelic football pitches and then share a friendly pint or two. I thank Candace Arnold and Risher and Rowen Wortman, who reminded me to take regular breaks to enjoy the sunshine and fresh air—their joie de vivre is infectious and sustaining. Last, but certainly not least, my family has been here since the very beginning; both those who are physically present and those who have already "gone on to glory" are a constant source of unconditional support and love. I am grateful for all of that and more.

.

A Precarious Balance

Reconsidering Historic Black Gun Use

From the colonial era through to the end of the US Civil War, North Carolina faced a conundrum when it came to people of color and firearms. Many of its white residents believed that armed enslaved workers presented a challenge to public safety; but they also recognized that Black people, whom the state and white citizens framed as subordinate, could perform useful labor with guns. Further, both free and enslaved people of color pragmatically used firearms for a range of activities that directly benefited themselves, their families, and their communities, although this use of firearms was sometimes contrary to state law and local customs. Firearms carried a great deal of social weight and violent potential, but this did not change the fact that they were also practical tools in North Carolina's largely agricultural landscape. As such, Black Southerners' firearm use cannot be separated from their labor. Thus equipped, they undertook several different tasks that improved their own lives as well as the lives of the people who hired or enslaved them.

Some bondpeople hunted wild game to provide meat for their enslavers' tables as well as their own. Skilled hunters culled predators that threatened agriculture, and the deerskin trade was also a central part of the colonial economy.[1] As such, enslavers could extract value from their laborers by arming them to kill a range of wild animals. Further, there were a host of other tasks that armed Black workers *might* have engaged in. As quotidian labor was by nature unremarkable, the historic record is often unclear or unspecific about it. Hunting and agricultural work were important, but armed labor stretched to other ventures, too. Armed Black men guarded stores; they probably also protected warehouses, wharves, ships in port, gold mines, and any other spaces that held value. They also likely protected movable property; for instance, during the eighteenth century, large herds of livestock were driven from North Carolina into neighboring Virginia but also as far north as Pennsylvania and New Jersey, or to points southward.[2] Armed Black people also helped to defend the colony from pirates and imperial rivals, groups that sometimes included Black men-at-arms. For example, in 1747, Spanish raiders from St. Augustine came in "several small Sloops & Barcalonjos" to raid along the coast. These vessels were "full of armed men, mostly Mulattoes & Negroes," who plundered Beaufort, killed colonists, destroyed livestock, burned ships, and kidnapped enslaved people.[3] The group of North Carolinians who drove the raiders away included men of color. The triumphant militiamen celebrated that "notwithstanding our ignorance in military affairs," lack or ammunition, slow-to-arrive reinforcements, and smaller numbers, they defeated a "much superior enemy." To further sweeten their victory, one of the white men disparagingly added that of the North Carolinian forces, "many . . . were negroes."[4]

Both the North Carolina General Assembly and local communities used legal mechanisms and local customs to maintain a balance between protecting white citizens from real and imagined Black violence and simultaneously allowing them to use and profit from enslaved workers' armed labor. White North Carolinians were concerned about armed enslaved people, but these anxieties also carried over to free people of color. Free Black people did not have "masters," but after 1841, the assembly nevertheless ensured that white citizens managed their free Black neighbors' gun use as well. The legislators saw free Black people in much the same manner as they did enslaved workers, which contrasts starkly with white people's virtually unrestricted firearm use in this era. This book examines how North Carolinians of different races and socioeconomic statuses understood African-descended people's access to, possession of, and use of firearms during the late colonial and antebellum eras. The state sought a balance between curtailing Black people's gun use and securing the benefits that it offered, despite the persistent threat of violence and the alleged negative influences that free Black persons had on enslaved people. While North Carolina's free Black residents were a complicated group, ranging from wealthy planters and artisans in New Bern to penniless day laborers scattered across rural spaces, these concerns were not wholly unfounded. As Kellie Carter Jackson has argued, "free, literate, and mobile black Americans had the greatest impact" in relaying information to enslaved workers.[5] White Southerners saw armed Black people in several different and often conflicting ways—as a threat to both their physical safety and their property but also as laborers who could work for white people or for themselves. Black North Carolinians capitalized on white people's reliance on their armed labor to access firearms for their own purposes.

The assembly began regulating Black people's firearm use in 1715, and while other legislation was passed well into the nineteenth century, this early law set the tone that North Carolina would pursue through to the Civil War. Historians have pointed out that the Old North State's restrictive laws were based on a 1680 Virginia law that the House of Burgesses passed in the aftermath of Nathaniel Bacon's Rebellion. In the first law in British North America that regulated Black people's firearm use, the Virginians declared that "no Negro or slave may carry arms, such as any club, staff, gun, sword, nor other weapon." It was part of a code that became the "model of repression throughout the South for the next 180 years," not solely for guns but for social, economic, and political issues as well.[6] In 1715, North Carolina's General Assembly sought to keep armed enslaved laborers firmly under white people's supervision by restricting their mobility. The legislators applied these same principles to the armed free Black population in the middle of the nineteenth century, as the assembly assumed control over their gun use, too. These were among the nation's first gun laws.[7]

Free and enslaved Black North Carolinians rejected these restrictions just as they resisted enslavement and a racist legal structure. Their struggles for firearm access took place in localized arenas. The colonial assembly empowered local white communities to manage Black people's access to weapons through their respective county courts. Even though enslaved laborers were completely barred from accessing guns in the early 1830s, the state continued to manage free people of color through the Civil War. This local oversight meant that after 1741, enslavers could arm their workers only with their respective county court's permission. This was part of white North Carolinians' singular and long-standing effort to prevent armed Black people from threatening white citizens' bodies or property. White people worried about physical violence but also lost livestock to armed Black people, especially to maroons and runaways. Despite these persistent and popular concerns about armed Black North Carolinians, many white people viewed firearms as another means through which they might appropriate Black workers' labor, and the assembly made allowances for this until Nat Turner's 1831 rebellion pushed them to ban it altogether.[8]

Enslaved Black North Carolinians took pragmatic approaches to the assembly's firearm laws and their enslavers' controls, both of which curbed their ability to provide for themselves or defend their communities from the brutal system of enslavement. Many of them used firearms—acquired from a range of sources—for their own ends, regardless of the letter of the law. This created tensions in North Carolina's neighborhoods. Some enslaved workers killed white people's livestock. Others fled their enslavers' authority and used firearms to fend off the patrollers and slave catchers who came after them. Further, some enslavers took self-interested approaches to using armed Black labor and deployed their bondpeople in ways that the General Assembly and many other white North Carolinians disproved of.

TABLE I.1 The Population of Select North Carolina Towns and
Their Respective Counties

	1820	1830	1840	1850	1860
Fayetteville	3,532	2,868	4,285	4,646	4,790
Cumberland County	14,446	14,834	15,284	20,610	16,369
Raleigh	2,674	1,700	2,244	4,518	4,780
Wake County	20,102	20,398	21,118	24,888	28,627
New Bern	3,663	3,795	3,690	4,681	5,432
Craven County	13,394	13,734	13,438	14,709	16,268
Wilmington	2,633	3,000	4,268	7,264	9,552
New Hanover County	10,866	10,959	13,312	17,668	15,429

Sources: U.S. Department of Commerce, *Fifteenth Census of the United States: 1830*, 1:780–81.
Wilmington's 1830 and 1840 population statistics are not in the Department of Commerce's
compilation but were printed in newspapers. See *Fayetteville Observer*, December 9, 1840. The
county-level data comes from the University of Virginia's Historical Census Browser, http://
mapserver.lib.virginia.edu/, accessed December 28, 2012. These aggregated statistics show how
small North Carolina's towns were in this era, especially compared with their hinterlands.

The General Assembly passed a law that required free people of color to acquire licenses from their county court before they could bear arms, which essentially put their gun use at the pleasure of their local communities.[9] Additionally, their families and kin were important sources of the social credit they needed to acquire licenses. Free people of color lived in a measured response to the state's demands, however. Many of them chose to ignore the state's firearm laws, which infringed upon their ability to feed their families, threatened their economic independence, or otherwise impeded their ability to live as free people. Black North Carolinians' familial networks extended financial support when an individual was caught in violation of the gun laws, and they could also be used to define an individual person of color's racial heritage. Additionally, a multiracial network of social and professional relationships supplemented the assistance that free people of color gained from their family and kin.

Relatedly, the exploration of race in the eighteenth and nineteenth century is complicated and rests on a host of assumptions around identity. Race was and is constructed, but never in a vacuum. Local and state records, the federal census, and a range of personal correspondences labeled African-descended people as "black," "mulatto," or as a person "of color" and offered no commentary on those people who were *presumed* to be white, although some of them were also, discreetly, multiracial. Some of the people whose racial identity came into question on account of the firearm laws identified as white, despite the state's disagreement. Additionally, by 1860, about 70 percent of North Carolina's free Black residents were mixed-race. Finally, to further complicate things, the term "free people of color" was also applied to the Lumbee and other Indigenous Americans and, as Warren Milteer explains, "an assortment of individuals with a variety of ancestral backgrounds fell into the 'free people of color' category."[10] These categories were imprecise and, in some instances, even the state's "official" designation could be inconsistent with how a person and their neighbors understood their identity; and some people's identities may have shifted over time in their own or others' understanding.

White North Carolinians' use of armed Black laborers continued into the Civil War era, despite the state having banned both free and enslaved Black people's gun use by the war's opening salvo.[11] From the beginning of the conflict, white people used armed Black workers on the home front and unarmed men in military camps. Indeed, they were even more important on North Carolina's plantations when so many enslavers were away with the Confederate army. Nevertheless, the antebellum precedents for military service as the white male's domain led many white North Carolinians to reject the notion of enlisting Black men, though a few Black men saw combat in isolated incidents. White people resisted arming Black men despite their numerous antebellum experiences with armed Black men's labor in other capacities. Some North Carolina enslavers were averse to the idea because they were afraid that they might lose their laborers, at a time when the Confederate government had already put so many of them to work on coastal fortifications. Additionally, many white people were uneasy with the idea of Black soldiers and their society's connections between military service and citizenship.[12]

A Precarious Balance approaches several well-established source bases with some new questions in order to better understand how both Black and white North Carolinians viewed Black people's firearm use and how those views informed their depictions of and interactions with armed people of color. This book relies on an array of newspapers, manuscript collections, municipal records, session laws, congressional debates, legislative petitions, enslaved workers' narratives, coroner's reports, and court records from every level of North Carolina's judiciary. These sources highlight different perspectives on Black people's firearm use. Further, they reveal the struggles between Black and white and free and enslaved people on the issue and how each of these groups navigated the legal terrain. These sources are complicated, however. In the plantation "justice" system, enslavers managed many issues internally, leaving no official record for so many everyday experiences as well as for some exceptional moments, for that matter. For instance, J. A. Stanly insisted that one of his uncle's slaves, who had given pistols to another enslaved man, could be "punished—without the formality of a trial or the interference of the Laws." He had "no doubt, two Gents can not disagree upon such a subject + that it could be arranged without dificulty."[13] The 1858 correspondence is the only record of this illegal interaction. Additionally, the bulk of such records, whether private or public, were produced by white North Carolinians, leaving the historian with the difficult task of carefully gleaning Black people's lives and labors from between the lines, working to preserve their dignity and individuality even as the records offer mere glimpses. Whenever possible, I included their names, ages, occupations, or any other identifying details. While clumsy at times, these details add texture to their lives and share as much as is possible about who these Black North Carolinians were.

This story is influenced by Laura Edwards's view of the centrality of local conditions to the creation and application of antebellum law and legal processes. North Carolina's antebellum legal system was flexible, and the state's efforts to maintain the peace sometimes superseded enslavers' individual rights. Under these circumstances, both free and enslaved Black people had "direct access" to localized legal processes. Some of them used the court or other means to resist their enslavers' and state authorities' claims to their armed labor. Further, this project rests on Max Weber's notion that the state "successfully claims a monopoly over the legitimate physical coercion necessary for the implementation of its laws and decrees." He further argued that all violence within a territory was "ascribed to individuals only to the extent to which the state permits it," which frames the General Assembly's racist laws, the county court's responses to the Black transgressors of those laws, and the ways that these state structures empowered individual white citizens to regulate Black people's actions.[14]

North Carolina provides a useful lens through which to explore Black people's historic firearm use for several reasons. First, the state was home to large numbers of both free and enslaved Black people during the years that this project covers. Combined, they remained about a third of the state's population—averaging about 31 percent for the decades between 1800 and 1860—despite the state's total population doubling. Among the Southern states, this ranked third in total Black population through the 1830s, but it lost ground as enslavers, aided by the federal government, displaced Indigenous people and expanded into the territories that would become Mississippi, Alabama, and Louisiana.[15] Finally, the state also had a substantial population of free people of color, ranking third across the South by 1850. Free and enslaved Black North Carolinians provided abundant samples from which to draw a broader look at Black Southerners' experiences with firearms.[16]

North Carolina holds an interesting place in Southern history. From the start, it was often overshadowed by neighboring Virginia and South Carolina. The colony "lacked the terrain, other than in the extreme northeast and southeast corners, to build and sustain a plantation economy on the scale of the West Indies or of other southern states," although some planters found success.[17] Its beginnings were humble. In the mid-seventeenth century, small subsistence farmers from Virginia headed south for opportunities in the Albemarle region, which would become the northeastern part of North Carolina. The area attracted enslaved and indentured people, religious dissenters, and rebels, all of whom fled or were driven out of Virginia and sought to create new lives for themselves.[18] Early eighteenth-century Virginians blasted their southern neighbors as an "intolerable Lazy" bunch who fled to the Albemarle on account of their "Aversion to Labor." Historian Jonathan Barth describes the early colony as having a "loosely structured political system" which, after 1691, allowed "free blacks, servants, Jews, and lower-class whites" to vote for members of the General Assembly, though this would be curbed in 1715 to deny free Black and Indigenous voters.[19]

In the nineteenth century, some critics derisively referred to North Carolina as "the Rip Van Winkle State," suggesting that it had fallen asleep while the others progressed. This idea that the Old North State was uniquely backward was not lost on Northerners who had relocated to the South or on native Southerners. Sarah Hicks, a New Yorker who married into a Green County, North Carolina, family, wrote to her parents in 1853, "If you call Long Island behind the times, I don't know what you would call North Carolina." Within a year, she would settle into her new home and become critical of abolitionism.[20] Further, in the early 1850s, the famous Southern editor J. D. B. De Bow derisively noted that the state of had "no large towns, and no good seaports." His point was exaggerated, but North Carolina's largest towns were not substantial urban centers, and most of its residents lived in small towns or the countryside.[21] A study of Black people's firearm use in antebellum cities would be enlightening, but in North Carolina, most Black people were in the hinterlands—protecting crops and livestock, hunting, acting in self-defense, or sustaining marronage.[22]

Despite the extensive historical study of free and enslaved Black people in the antebellum era, research on their firearm use, outside of military applications, is still quite slim.[23] This historiographical void is glaring, considering guns' centrality to North Carolina history from the very beginning and the myriad ways Black people's firearm use appears in the historical records. At the end of their terms, early eighteenth-century indentures were entitled to a few barrels of corn, two new sets of clothes, and "in lieu of one suit of Apparrell a good well-fixed Gun, if he be a Manservant."[24] Also, consider the state-level legislation spanning from the colonial era through to the Civil War, the decisions at every level of the state's courts, and the innumerable private actions on Black North Carolinians' access to and use of firearms. Much of the existing scholarship has focused on the role that hunting played in Black communities, a larger conversation about Second Amendment rights, and the law. This historiography is better understood thematically rather than chronology, despite the larger historiographical shifts in the study of slavery.

Antebellum Black people's relationship to guns is briefly mentioned in several comprehensive works on slavery in the United States, dating back through several generations. Classic studies, like Eugene Genovese's *Roll, Jordan, Roll: The World the Slaves Made*; Peter H. Wood's *Black Majority: Negroes in Colonial South Carolina from 1670 through the Stono Rebellion*; Ira Berlin's *Many Thousand Gone: The First Two Centuries of Slavery in North America* and *Generations of Captivity*; and Philip D. Morgan's *Slave Counterpoint: Black Culture in the Eighteenth-Century Chesapeake and Lowcountry* have offered comment. These works, and several others like them, note that enslaved people sometimes used firearms to hunt for themselves or their enslavers and that the states' laws and local labor practices maintained some allowance for this. Morgan's *Slave Counterpoint*, one of the most thorough of these, is primarily concerned with firearm's utility for hunters and maroons, and how both enslavers and the enslaved pragmatically approached their respective state governments' firearm laws.[25]

Studies that examine antebellum hunting practices, like Stuart A. Marks's *Southern Hunting in Black and White: Nature, History, and Ritual in a Carolina Community* and Nicolas Proctor's *Bathed in Blood: Hunting and Mastery in the Old South*, demonstrate that hunting could supplement enslaved people's often-meager diets but also, of equal importance, that it was a community building and masculinity affirming activity. Guns are not central to these works because, as they show, antebellum Black Southerners hunted through several methods and firearms were a rarer, though not wholly uncommon tool. Scott Giltner continues these conversations in *Hunting and Fishing in the New South: Black Labor and White Leisure after the Civil War*. He argues that for Black Southerners, fishing and hunting were "vivid symbols of an economic, cultural, and spatial separation from whites that reflected the struggle for control over their own lives and labors" and a "key marker of racial and class status." White hunters increasingly pushed for stronger regulations as they framed Black hunters as "bad, even dangerous, sportsmen" over whom the state needed to reassert control in the post-emancipation era. The South was awash with firearms after the war, and while many were in far from pristine condition, Black hunters made the most of them.[26]

Scholarship on the Second Amendment examines the racially restrictive colonial and antebellum laws as part of a long pattern of government regulation of firearms. Robert J. Cottrol, Clayton Cramer, Stephen P. Halbrook, Adam Winkler, and others have focused on the broader history of firearm rights in the United States. They offer useful commentary on the antebellum restrictions placed on armed people of color, but much like many of the other texts herein referenced, they do not generally explore what firearm use meant to people of color.[27] These scholars use the past to contextualize their present. For instance, Winkler's entry point is the political debate over firearms in the wake of the massacre at the Sandy Hook Elementary School, but he lays out how extremists on both ends miss that "a reasonable right to bear arms has always been available to Americans—one that balances gun rights with gun control."[28] Carol Anderson boldly argues that the Second Amendment "was designed and has consistently been constructed to keep African Americans powerless and vulnerable" regardless of their position—whether they were "enslaved, free Black, denizen, Jim Crowed citizen, or citizen of 'post-racial America.'" Black people faced a great deal of violence when they carried arms, as their "military uniforms angered. Their self-defense enraged. Their right to bear arms triggered. Their claims to citizenship lynched."[29] Some other projects have framed their antebellum firearm use in the broader context of Southern slave codes. In his look at the country's legal system, A. Leon Higginbotham argues that much of the slave code was modeled on Virginia's 1680 regulations, which covered enslaved people's use of weapons.[30]

Black people's firearm use was very closely connected to resistance but is not examined with much depth in works that have otherwise made strong historiographical contributions in this area. One of the earliest works in this field, Herbert Aptheker's *American Negro Slave Revolts*, offered a sweeping survey of violent resistance but did not explore the broader implications of firearm use. Kenneth Stampp's *The Peculiar Institution* demonstrated that enslaved laborers actively resisted their imposed condition "with great eagerness" and mentioned that some of them were "well armed," although without further exploration of this recognized occurrence. Similarly, in John Blassingame's early examination of the enslaved community, he notes that "a gun or knife ... were essential" tools for those who fled. He also describes how groups of maroons undertook "guerilla-like activities" and that if they "obtained enough arms" they could "terrorize" local white farmers and planters.[31] Despite framing how useful firearms were, especially for outlaws, Blassingame does not further probe this use.

John Hope Franklin and Loren Schweninger's insightful work portrays fleeing enslaved people as "rebels on the plantation." Like Blassingame, they highlight firearms' utility but stress that fugitives were "only occasionally armed with guns," and they do not pursue a more rigorous study. Other historians have argued that small-scale acts of resistance served as a sort of "safety valve" that prevented more dramatic attempts to overthrow enslavement.[32] North Carolina's enslaved people used their guns to defend and feed themselves and to carve out autonomous space in the region's swamps and forests. This book argues that Black North Carolinians' firearm-based resistance, particularly that which fell short of armed rebellion, improved their lives and forced both individual white citizens and the General Assembly to take a cautious and balanced approach to armed Black laborers.

Firearms are also inherently linked to violence, and some scholars have explored Black people's gun use through this lens. Kellie Carter Jackson's *Force and Freedom* highlights "the complex and varied ways violence was deployed by antebellum black activists," particularly in the decade before the Civil War. She explains that "the 1830s and '40s were made up of black leaders seeking and securing white allies," but that "by the 1850s, black leaders took up a position of armed resistance regardless of white support."[33] Jeff Forret's comprehensive work on acts of violence between enslaved people is far more interested in other modes of violence because, as he explains, they "rarely committed acts of gun violence upon one another." In *Slave against Slave*, he recognizes that the intraracial firearm violence that did occur was caused by Southern white folks' failure to "exercise due vigilance" in enforcing their local gun laws. Forret contextualizes the object of the firearm as a powerful physical representation of manhood and a multifaceted tool for fugitives.[34] My work here is interested in what those acts of gun violence, however limited, meant within the broader slave society (and not merely among enslaved workers); but more importantly, *A Precarious Balance* pushes firearms beyond tools of interpersonal violence.

Historians have also explored free people of color's gun use. A few studies, like Ira Berlin's *Slaves without Masters: The Free Negro in the Antebellum South* and *Many Thousand Gone: The First Two Centuries of Slavery in North America*, and Adam Rothman's *Slave Country: American Expansion and the Origins of the Deep South*, briefly mention the laws restricting their firearm use.[35] Further, Melvin Ely's work on the free Black community at Prince Edward County, Virginia, highlights how those free people of color's firearm rights were restricted in the aftermath of Nat Turner's rebellion. Ely shows that many of the county's white residents, including the constables, were quite comfortable with Black gun owners prior to Turner and that even after that violent episode, they remained lackadaisical about enforcing their legislature's ban on Black people's gun use. Further, Ely shows that the county court sought to treat Black gun owners fairly under the circumstances.[36] Much like the works on armed enslaved laborers, Ely does not do much to interrogate the social implications of this gun use.

Additionally, some scholars specifically focused on North Carolina's Black population. John Hope Franklin's work sees the increased restrictions on their gun use as part of a larger trend toward curtailing their rights. He is careful to not overstate these restrictions, noting that "nothing less than the imminence of a civil war could force . . . such a drastic move as to forbid free Negroes to possess arms of any kind." Warren Milteer continues this legendary thread in *North Carolina's Free People of Color, 1715–1885,* where he frames the laws against free Black people's firearm use as part of an effort by radical proslavery legislators. Free people of color were themselves the "antithesis of the argument that the promises of life, liberty, and the pursuit of happiness did not belong to persons of color." Further, he highlights that the state supreme court cases revolving around free men of color's firearm use were important legal benchmarks beyond the immediate question of gun use. For instance, Milteer notes that *State v. Chavers* "displayed the illogic and intellectual limitations encoded in some of the state's discriminatory legislation."[37]

In her broader discussion about Reconstruction violence in *Beyond Redemption,* Carole Emberton argues that during the years directly following the Civil War, "freedpeople viewed gun possession as a symbol of freedom and independence." As a continuation of the antebellum dynamic, Black Southerners relied on their firearms to feed and protect themselves and their communities. In that post-emancipation era, however, they increasingly viewed firearm access as a constitutional right to which they were entitled. Emberton also devotes significant space to the Black soldiers, militiamen, and veterans whose armed service informed their self-positioning as men and citizens. Finally, she notes that in the face of the period's rampant anti-Black violence, even Black Southerners' white allies expected that their violence "had to be tightly controlled by white authorities and channeled into discrete expressions on the battlefield."[38]

Several important books that explore Black life in the late nineteenth century through to the Civil Rights Movement also provide a look at firearm use. David F. Krugler's *1919, The Year of Racial Violence: How African Americans Fought Back* examines how, in the United States' post–World War I wave of anti-Black violence, Black people, especially veterans, armed themselves. Krugler also explains how the federal, state, and local governments as well as individual white people partnered to disarm them "because of fears that they were plotting violent uprisings."[39] Nicholas Johnson's *Negroes and the Gun: The*

Black Tradition of Arms, offers a sweeping survey of Black firearm use through the nineteenth and twentieth centuries. He covers both military and civilian aspects but focuses on the latter. Johnson presents "a tradition of church folk, merchants, and strivers, the very best people in the community, armed and committed to the principle of individual self-defense." He is also interested in where antebellum Black people acquired their firearms; and further, Johnson describes a "budding culture of gun ownership and a commitment to self-defense" among them.[40]

Akinyele Omowale Umoja's *We Will Shoot Back*, Lance Hill's *The Deacons for Defense*, and Charles E. Cobb Jr.'s *This Nonviolent Stuff'll Get You Killed*, each highlight armed resistance during the Civil Rights and Black Power Movements, which Umoja explains as "two related but distinct periods of social movement."[41] Like Johnson, these scholars challenge popular framings of the Civil Rights Movement as wholly pacifist. Umoja roots the precursor of this resistance in Mississippi's violent Reconstruction, which foreshadowed the federal government's inability to protect Black people from white terror. He argues that "without armed resistance . . . activists would not have been able to organize in Mississippi."[42] Similarly, Hill frames the Deacons for Defense's armed resistance as "an implicit claim to social and civil equality." He notes that the Black community took up arms because they could not get redress from the law and that the Deacons transformed an older tradition of armed defense into "a public and wide-ranging organization." This defensive violence is contextual—as Cobb points out, "the prevailing system of white supremacy in the South was enforced by violence, and black people sometimes used the threat to survive." For many Black Southerners, "shotguns and pistols were an ordinary part of everyday southern life," defensive safeguards that they kept on hand.[43] These studies offer little on the antebellum precedent for armed Black resistance, as they are more interested in a later era. Nonetheless, they make strong contributions to the longer arc of Black people's arms use.

Many of these forementioned works examine people of color's firearm use at the margins of their central subject matter. They are far more interested in other aspects of free and enslaved Black Southerners' lives or the laws that governed them. They generally do not explore where the weapons came from, what broad purposes they were used for, or many of the social implications that this particular gun use had on the South. This dearth of intensive scholarship minimizes how productive the lens of firearms can be. Further, it stands out starkly against a rich backdrop of primary sources that showcase how people of color's firearms were so incredibly useful, for both creative and destructive purposes. The story of Black Southerners' firearm use is very much centered on the relationships between Black and white people and their shared communities. This book builds on these glimpses offered by the aforementioned scholars but blazes new pathways by focusing on armed Black North Carolinians at both the individual and community levels and by considering just what this armed labor meant within the bounds of the enslavers' society.

Violence is an integral part of discussions on both slavery and firearms. After serious consideration, I chose to include a few period descriptions of shootings in which North Carolinians—most of whom were Black and enslaved—suffered horrific injuries. These are predominately located in chapter three. Writing about traumatic historic violence is a serious endeavor, and scholars have a responsibility to our subjects and our readers to do so without further extending that trauma. This is challenging in this book, as the violence that armed people inflicted on each other and themselves is part of the story that it tells. Black people living in the Slave South knew it intimately. Its ugliness often hung over their heads, a threat wielded by the state and by white civilians who sought to control them. Violence also emanated from other Black people, those who were strangers as well as familiar members of the community. This violence was often recorded by white newspaper editors or coroners for white audiences, most of whom were detached from the Black victims. The coroner's or editor's commentary is often the only extant record of an individual's life, but we must remember that the subjects of these commentaries were much more than victims of violence. Each was a member of a family and a community that cared about them and was affected by their death. In *A Precarious Balance*, I have tried to present this part of the story of firearm use with respect and historic empathy, which I hope carries through.

This book has some notable limitations. First, it does not offer a quantitative survey of Black North Carolinians gun use. The abundance of examples shows the phenomena as commonplace, but how many people had access to firearms and how often they used them in any given period is immeasurable. Further, this book is focused on Black people's gun use; but long before the English arrived and forced enslaved Africans to the region that they called Carolina, it was home to many Indigenous peoples, including the ancestors of the Coharie Indian Tribe, the Eastern Band of Cherokee Indians, the Haliwa-Saponi Indian Tribe, the Lumbee Tribe of North Carolina, the Meherrin Indian Tribe, the Sappony Tribe, the Occaneechi Band of the Saponi Nation, and the Waccamaw Siouan Tribe. The farms, plantations, and towns in this book were built on lands that the English and Americans dispossessed them of. Further, Indigenous people were sometimes enslaved in the colonial era and, for a time, "nowhere in the English empire . . . was the enslavement of Indians undertaken on such a large scale as in Carolina."[44] Although *A Precarious Balance* is focused on Black North Carolinians, there is an overlapping history with the state's efforts to regulate Indigenous communities' firearm access.[45]

Additionally, while this book is primarily interested in the eastern and central parts of the state, this does not suggest that there were not armed free and enslaved Black people in the state's western counties; rather, it reflects my interest in the plantation districts and larger towns of the eastern and central parts of the state. John Inscoe challenged historians of North Carolina to reject the long-disproven assumption about slavery's marginalized position in the state's western reaches.[46] Additionally, Darin Waters shows that slavery was the "primary impetus" behind the Black population's explosive growth in Asheville, in Buncombe County, which saw a 576 percent increase in its Black population between 1800 and 1860, and that racism abounded there. He also explains that some enslaved workers in the west traveled long distances on business for their enslavers, sometimes transporting valuable goods by themselves.[47] One wonders if these Black men were armed to protect these items. There is a need for further scholarship in these areas and hopefully this project encourages some of it.

A Precarious Balance is divided into five thematic chapters. Chapter 1 examines how the colonial and antebellum legislatures established racially specific gun laws to control Black people. It explains that these laws were often instigated at the local level, legislated by the North Carolina General Assembly, and again interpreted and applied at the local level with input from white members of the community. I argue that these laws, which impacted both free and enslaved Black people, should be understood as a singular and long-standing effort to limit Black people's contact with white citizens and their property. Nonetheless, despite the persistent and popular concerns about armed Black North Carolinians, many white citizens viewed Black people's firearm use as another means to appropriate Black labor, and the assembly made allowances for this until Nat Turner's rebellion made it untenable.

Chapter 2 explores how and why unfree Black people—those who were enslaved and those who fled their enslavement and lived as outlaws—disregarded the Old North State's racist firearm laws. I examine their legal transgressions with a broad approach to the notion of crime, which in this volume suggests only a violation of the state's legal code. One might ask to what extent enslaved North Carolinians, or free people of color for that matter, owed obedience to the state in the first place, and I do not frame their ignoring the law as inherently negative. Black people pragmatically approached the laws that limited their ability to live independently. They found illegal ways to acquire guns for a range of purposes, and while they sometimes robbed or murdered, they also fed and defended themselves. Additionally, armed Black people could force dialogue with any white person who might otherwise simply have used force against them. Black people's guns could be an effective counterweight to enslavers' power. This chapter also describes how some enslavers themselves also used armed Black laborers in ways that both the state and other white citizens disproved of.

The third chapter conceptualizes firearms as tools that free and enslaved Black North Carolinians used in their work for themselves, their families, or broader communities. Further, enslavers and local governments also harnessed this labor—they centered Black people's existence in work. Stephanie McCurry reminds us that white Southerners "had great difficulty shaking an instrumentalist view of African American people even when confronted with evidence to the contrary."[48] Firearms' utility and potential danger exacerbated tensions over who could command this labor and how it should be effectively controlled. The friction between enslavers, bondpeople, and state lawmakers was divisive at times, but it also highlighted how important Black people's firearm use was for these interested parties. Ultimately, Black North Carolinians' armed labor allowed them to create lives for themselves, their families, and their communities that were more independent of overbearing white people than would otherwise have been possible.

Chapter 4 focuses on armed free Black North Carolinians' experiences in a legal and social landscape that marked them as second-class citizens. I argue that free Black people's families and communities offered support, which was crucial for gun access after 1840, when the legislature passed a license mandate. Family relationships helped these individuals acquire the invaluable social credit and, in some instances, the character witnesses that one needed before a court would issue a license. Also, some free people of color used their lineage to challenge how the courts framed their racial identity. Family and kin also extended financial support to those who broke the gun laws. These needs were also met by a multiracial network of social and professional contacts that free people of color relied on. Finally, free Black North Carolinians took a measured response to the state's regulatory efforts. Many decided not to follow the gun laws that infringed upon their ability to feed their families, threatened their economic independence, or otherwise impeded the limited liberties that they enjoyed as second-class citizens in a society built on racial slavery.

The final chapter highlights how Black and white North Carolinians and the state balanced the utility and threat of armed Black people during the Civil War. I argue that while Black people's armed labor was instrumental to wartime productivity at the local level, many white North Carolinians were vehemently opposed to enlisting Black men for armed military service. This remained true even after the Confederate government embraced a plan for "negro soldiers" as a last resort in the war's final months. This popular opposition in the state was rooted in the belief that militarized armed labor would undermine the long-standing racial system of firearm use. In contrast, some armed Black men's labor was instrumental on the Southern home front. In limited instances, white men left home for military service and turned over the management of their farms to enslaved men whom they trusted. This included, in some instances, using a firearm to protect the plantation from the wartime threats posed by both Black and white outsiders. These armed Black laborers both challenged and bolstered the Confederate nation, regardless of their personal intentions.

A Precarious Balance frames firearms as an instrumental part of Black North Carolinians' lives and labor from the late colonial era through to the Civil War. Oftentimes, this created contentious legal and social dynamics, as the General Assembly, local courts, free and enslaved Black people, and a range of white North Carolinians struggled against each other over the issue as they pursued their individual interests. Enslavers armed Black workers for labor and put them to several different tasks in support of white people's agricultural interests. Alternatively, Black people across the state picked up arms for their own purposes, which occasionally meant resistance but, more importantly, was often for labor that materially improved their lives. That quotidian firearm use—whether at the direction of enslavers or of Black people's own volition—is the central piece of this story.

CHAPTER ONE

The Law in Theory and Practice

In antebellum North Carolina, the county courts interpreted and enforced the General Assembly's laws at the local level. This was by design, as the legislators gave the counties wide discretion to apply the laws to their specific local circumstances. Further, as Laura Edwards's scholarship has shown, many white people in the period rejected the idea that the assembly's laws should "control local practice, define the needs of the peace in local areas, or constitute a definitive body of law uniformly applicable throughout the state." They saw Raleigh's dictates as "laws generated in a different place—the state level," but they did not understand these as coming from a necessarily higher legal authority. They believed that the law was intended to resolve conflicts at the local level and was therefore best "defined and applied locally." The county courts tailored enforcement to fit local circumstances.[1] In this respect, the values of a particular community and its residents' interpersonal relationships influenced how the courts enforced the law. Black people's gun access also fit into this local structure. White citizens, who were divided on their Black neighbors' possessing firearms, came together with their respective county courts to manage local free and enslaved Black people's firearm use.

This management was not an easy task. The state legislature, the county courts, and individual white people believed that there were potential dangers in Black people's firearm use but sought to balance these dangers with the benefits that they could glean from it. Reflecting on these concerns, Raleigh's city commissioners saw the state's law against enslaved workers "going armed, or hunting with a gun" as part of a larger plan to "to secure subordination amongst our slave population."[2] The assembly tried to limit Black gun users' contact with white people and their property while still allowing both Black and white North Carolinians to benefit from Black people's armed labor, which was useful in a number of applications. The legislators relied on the county courts to interpret and enforce the law according to their respective communities' needs and concerns. The people constituting the body politic were the final but most important piece of this legal and judicial landscape. North Carolinians—whether Black or white, free or enslaved, male or female—did not always agree with the assembly or with their local county officials. These disagreements meant that the legal code, while thematically consistent throughout the state, could be shaped by local communities to fit their specific social contexts.

North Carolina's legislators began facilitating localized gun regulation in the colonial era, mandating that all enslavers receive their respective county court's permission before they could legally arm their enslaved workers, thereby empowering the county courts with local oversight. This process relied on white men in the community to cosign the enslavers' bonds for their armed workers' good behavior.[3] One hundred years later, the state's General Assembly would extend this control into the lives of free people of color by requiring that they get authorization from their county court before they could carry arms. The applicants were supported by their white neighbors who could vouch for their good character.[4] Effectively, white locals' perceptions of their Black neighbors' character were crucial to people of color's legal access to firearms from the very beginning. Further, the state's nervousness about Black gun users echoed earlier responses to Indigenous nations. In the colonial era, the General Assembly also sought to regulate Indigenous people's access to firearms but was hampered by the South Carolinians and Virginians who continued to sell arms to them within North Carolina despite the laws against it. Some merchants complained to the Lord Commissioners of Trade and Plantations that "private Indian Traders will have more regard to their own gain, than the security of their distressed Neighbors, or the Publick good: and will endeavor to make their advantages by selling arms and ammunition to our Indian Enemies."[5]

White citizens' desire to police Black people's firearm use was rooted in a perception that such use threatened white families' physical and economic well-being. Rumored and actual rebellions by enslaved people in neighboring states coupled with whispers of domestic revolts encouraged the legislature and local communities to restrict Black North Carolinians' firearm access. During the colonial period, the assembly empowered individual enslavers to control their armed bondpeople, but this loose regulation proved insufficient to assuage public concerns. The legislature addressed this by authorizing the county courts to play an active role in deciding *which* Black workers could be trusted to use firearms. The assembly's limits on when and where an enslaver could arm his or her laborers were an important aspect of the firearm law, but individual actors were always central to these processes. Individuals sought to harness enslaved people's armed labor, but their efforts to do so were frustrated by both the General Assembly's dictates and enslaved people's decision-making.

With North Carolina's slow population growth, relatively small numbers of enslaved people, and the colony's early instability, the colonial leadership saw little need for an extensive slave code until 1715.[6] Black and white people did not live on equal terms, but in the late seventeenth and early eighteenth centuries, some Virginians frowned upon North Carolinians' relative poverty, interracial social interactions, perceived laziness, and their "'excessive drinking' and 'extreme looseness.'"[7] Many Carolinians, however, wanted nothing to do with Virginia's more hierarchical structures, and Virginia elites, in turn, frowned on their neighbors' government as inefficient.[8] The 1715 law, an "Act concerning Servants and Slaves," criminalized enslaved people's unauthorized and unsupervised weapons use and set the precedent for the next century's gun laws. It was intended to ensure that armed subordinates were supervised by trustworthy members of the body politic. The assembly understood that these laborers' mobility and firearm use combined to present a singular threat to public safety and property. Black people's armed status only sharpened the aggressive attitudes that some white landowners held against them when they crossed onto others' property. In 1795, John Fooks told another white man that he would kill one of his neighbor's enslaved laborers "or any body elses negros that he found on his Land" by the river. He added that he thought "no more of killing of a Negro" than he did "a Brute Beast." Later, Fooks very likely shot and mortally wounded an enslaved man named Frank.[9]

The 1715 law sought to confine armed laborers by encouraging all persons to "use their utmost endeavours" to capture any enslaved person or servant who was "seen off his Master's ground Arm'd with any Gun, Sword or any other weapon of defence or offence" unless his enslaver had given his or her permission. This law, which was directed at both Black and white subordinate laborers, defined any laborer who was armed and roaming the countryside without permission as a rebel. It made a distinction between these groups, however—anyone who saw a "Runaway Slave that hath lyen out two months" could kill them if they could not be apprehended.[10] This 1715 law did not make an explicit link between errant subordinate laborers and the property damage that they might cause, but the assembly was concerned that such laborers might be roaming without the consent of their master, here understood as either an enslaver or indenture holder. This early effort to boost supervision was supposed to limit injury to white people or damage to their property. It required masters' oversight over armed subordinate laborers, whether on or off their property. Further, the law relied on "all persons" to help manage the laborers if their masters failed to do so. This call for citizens' assistance hearkened back to the "hue and cry" English Common Law and reiterated to white men that they had a responsibility to help maintain the law in their communities.[11] As New Bern's "Rules, Regulations and Ordinances" stated in 1811, it was the town sergeant's job to "keep a watchful eye on all persons" who broke the law, but that "all good citizens are invited to aid and assist him in bringing offenders to justice."[12]

The 1715 law was applicable to both Black and white members of the servile classes, but the legislature strengthened this legal code and made it racially specific in 1729. At that juncture, the assembly decided that it needed to devote its attention to enslaved Black people.[13] This was in part due to the colony's trouble in attracting indentured servants and its "disadvantageous competitive position" compared to Virginia. Bradford J. Wood and Larry E. Tise's scholarship highlights that in the late seventeenth and early eighteenth centuries, North Carolina landowners used Black, white, and Indigenous laborers who often worked alongside each other.[14] By 1730, the colony's population consisted of 30,000 white people and some 6,000 people of color. The legislature's worries about subordinate workers continued into the next century. The 1729 law noted that "great damages are frequently done, by slaves being permitted to hunt or range with dogs and guns," and that it would thereafter be illegal for them to go hunting on lands belonging to anyone other than their enslaver, unless they were overseen by a white man. The law threatened a twenty-shilling fine against the enslaver, which would be paid to the person upon whose land the armed enslaved person was found. Further, when traveling, enslaved laborers were required to stay on the "most usual and accustomed Road," and any landowner who caught them on his or her property was permitted to give them a "severe whipping, not exceeding Forty Lashes."[15] This law did not prevent enslaved people from accessing guns, nor was it intended to, as the assembly recognized enslaved people's utility to themselves and their enslavers when they were armed. Instead, it restricted enslaved people's movement and ensured that they were supervised.

In 1741, the assembly took an even greater role in restricting enslaved Black people's gun use. It empowered the county courts to certify which local enslavers could arm specific laborers. Enslavers were no longer able to arm their laborers at their own discretion; instead, they would first need local officials' consent. The legislators declared that thereafter "no slave shall go armed with gun, sword, club or other weapon, or shall keep any such weapon, or shall hunt or range with a gun in the woods, upon any pretence whatsoever" unless his or her enslaver had a certificate from the county court to that effect. This law can be understood as a reaction to the 1739 Stono Rebellion in neighboring South Carolina, where sixty enslaved laborers, many of whom had firearms, killed more than twenty white colonists before the militia was able to put down their bid for freedom.[16] Nat Turner's uprising in Virginia, just over a hundred years after Stono, would have a similar impact. North Carolina's legislators responded by appropriating part of enslavers' authority, which the legislators believed would better protect the colony. The assembly sought to encourage the free colonists to actively police the enslaved population, which was important because North Carolina would not develop a formal patrol system until 1753.[17]

The 1741 law was not meant to interfere with enslaved people who were "hunting in the Woods on their Master's Lands with a Gun, to preserve his or her Stock, or to kill Game for his or her Family." The law sought instead to encourage enslavers to keep their armed laborers on their property and under their supervision, where the slaves would pose less of a threat to white people's interests than if they were permitted to freely move about. This supervision was an insurance system—enslaved workers who were thus regulated would pose less of a threat to neighboring landowners. Enslavers whose bondpeople were found on their neighbors' lands would have to pay the "taker-up" at least seven shillings and six pence, which was the same as the reward for capturing runaways.[18] This encouraged enslavers to follow the law, but it also attracted otherwise disinterested people to answer the "hue and cry" and risk personal injury to enforce the law. This oversight continued in a 1768 law, which restricted people from hunting deer on lands that belonged to the king or other landowners. Violators could be fined and have their guns confiscated; but the law was not intended to "bar or hinder an Overseer of a Slave or Slaves from hunting or killing a Deer with a Gun on his Employers Lands, or the waste Lands of the King."[19] The assembly continued to limit armed Black workers' mobility through the 1741 regulatory firearm law, but it thereafter made the local courts the arbiters on which enslaved people could be trusted with guns. In effect, the assembly sought to appropriate part of enslavers' mastery to maximize security for the colony's citizens.

The perceived problem of mobile and armed enslaved laborers raiding white people's property was difficult to resolve because enslavers were not always diligent in enforcing the laws, and in some instances they blatantly violated it. Even more importantly, many enslaved workers did as they wished regardless of the assembly's dictates or their enslavers' commands. Finally, consider that the law was difficult for the state to enforce, especially in the vast majority of North Carolina that did not maintain any regular police force. In 1753, the assembly determined that the existing laws had "proved ineffectual to restrain many Slaves in divers Parts . . . from going armed" and believed that this inadequate enforcement might very well "prove to be a dangerous Consequence."[20] The legislators took corrective action with a substantial and broad-reaching law that had several key points.

The 1753 law increased enslavers' accountability of their armed laborers in myriad ways. First, it declared that no county court could permit "any slave to carry a Gun and hunt in the Woods, unless the Master, Mistress, or Manager of such Slave, shall first enter into Bond, with sufficient security" for the enslaved worker's "good and honest Behavior." This bond would be paid to "any Person or Persons who shall be injured by such Slave."[21] It demonstrated the county courts' increasing involvement in enslaved people's gun use, specifically by scrutinizing the dynamic between enslavers and their workers. It underscored that the assembly recognized armed Black laborers' utility despite its concurrent attempts to criminalize their unsupervised gun use. The legislators sought a balance between this usefulness, specifically in agricultural work, and the potential dangers armed Black people embodied. In consequence, they allowed enslavers to arm a single laborer while they had crops in the ground, presumably without the bond, but this privilege would be rescinded after harvest.[22] Any enslaver or overseer of an offending worker would be fined twenty shillings, which would be paid to the person who discovered the trespass. Enslavers could dodge the fine if they could "by their own Oath, or other Proof" demonstrate that they had no knowledge that the enslaved person was armed.[23] This law threatened to punish inattentive enslavers where it hurt: their pocketbooks. This provided third parties in the neighborhood with peace of mind: If armed and unsupervised enslaved people committed depredations on their property, the county court would ensure that they were compensated.

Perhaps most importantly, this 1753 law also established the colony's first formal slave patrols—each county court was to appoint three freeholders as "Searchers" who combed through their districts' slave quarters and "other Places where Negroes resort" to find contraband weapons.[24] The appointees were exempt from paying taxes, working on the public roads, or serving as militiamen, jurors, and constables; but they were required to conduct at least four searches each year "when and where they found it necessary." The state encouraged the searchers' faithful service with both a stick and a carrot. On the one hand, searchers could be fined forty shillings if they failed in their sworn duties, which would be paid to the negligent searcher's successor. On the other hand, the assembly mandated that they could keep any contraband weapons that they uncovered.[25] While we often consider the patrols' primary duty as limiting enslaved people's unauthorized mobility, their origin in North Carolina was finding weapons. Each man took an oath that he would, "as searcher for guns, swords, and other weapons among the slaves in my district, faithfully, and as privately as I can, discharge the trust reposed in me, as the law directs, to the best of my power. So help me God."[26] The assembly saw enslaved workers' unsupervised weapons possession as a problem requiring preemptive action. In later years, the patrols expanded their scope—for instance, to include "any printed pamphlet or pamphlets of a seditious character"—but uncovering hidden firearms remained central to their work.[27]

While the searchers provided a valuable public service, they were also the physical embodiment of the state's intrusions upon mastery. This upset some enslavers, the wealthiest of whom were elites who could make life difficult for those who crossed them. In 1761, William Dry, Esq., a prominent planter, lodged a complaint against searcher David Smeeth, whom the court removed without even the courtesy of a formal hearing.[28] Similarly, during periods of heightened alarm, surveillance was increased; but the authorities were sometimes still cautious. After an insurrectionary scare, Perquimans County officials warned the militia officers to "take care that no disorders or excesses . . . be committed—no slave having a regular pass and against whom there is no charge is to be detained or molested and the searches are to be conducted as far as may be so as not to alarm the white people and with as little annoyance as possible to Blacks."[29] This was bigger than keeping the peace—the authorities were careful to avoid irritating enslavers by interfering with their property and productivity. These planters held sway, even in the colonial era. As Wood and Tise have argued, "Neither contemporaries nor modern historians have been much impressed by the scale and profitability of North Carolina's plantations," but nonetheless, the colony had "become a planter dominated place with all of the trappings of a slaver society" by the late eighteenth century. Further complicating the patrollers' duties were the Black people they harried, who could also create significant problems. They burned down patrollers' houses, outbuildings, and fodder stacks; injured, stole, or killed their horses and livestock; and sometimes even injured or killed the patrollers themselves.[30]

Enslaved people's mobility was a point of interest because those who traveled off their enslavers' lands encountered white people's property more frequently than those who did not. They therefore had greater opportunity to become nuisances to neighboring farms and the public.[31] Some armed workers could legally leave their enslavers' land—the local application of the law made allowance for it. Thomas J. Davis was granted permission to arm his enslaved man named Isaac, who was allowed to move between Davis's two New Hanover County plantations with a gun. It is not clear how far apart his Rock Hill and Catfish properties were, but they were not adjoining.[32] The court trusted Davis, and Davis trusted Isaac. Similarly, Chowan County's Elisha Copeland requested permission to arm Limbrick and expressed a great deal of trust in him. He wanted to "place in the hands of his negro man Limbrick a

Frederic B. Schell's 1863 sketch for *Frank Leslie's Illustrated Newspaper*. These patrollers were operating outside of New Orleans, Louisiana, but North Carolina's patrollers worked in a similar manner. Courtesy of the Library of Congress, Prints and Photographs Division.

Gun a quarter of a pound of Powder & a pound of shot for the use on his farm wherein said negro resides."[33] Copeland was not merely allowing Limbrick to use a firearm—he wanted him to keep a weapon and a stockpile of ammunition on his person, which would mean that this Black man could probably use the firearm at his own discretion. Others might have similarly supplied their enslaved workers, but some enslavers controlled the access to shot and powder. Davis and Copeland armed only those enslaved men whom they trusted to behave with "with propriety while in the exercise of this privilege" and not commit violent crimes.[34]

In accordance with this 1753 legislation, Chowan County enslavers Henderson Standin and James Sutton, in 1797 and again in 1806, cosigned a bond for the good behavior of a "certain Negroe called Harry," whom Standin enslaved. Their bond for 250 pounds sterling was typical for Chowan County in this period, and it permitted Harry to carry a firearm on Standin's property as long as he did "well & Truly Demean himself and do no Injury with his Said Gun to any Person or persons whatever."[35] This bond must be read in the context of the legislation from the 1740s and 1750s, and the stipulation that Harry "do no injury," which was formulaically repeated on virtually all the bonds from the late eighteenth and early nineteenth centuries, should be understood broadly.

The Chowan County court's concern was not just that Harry might physically injure other people but that he could potentially "do injury" to their property as well. This possibility was addressed by the express condition that Harry remain on Standin's land, where the chance that he could use the firearm to damage another person's property would be dramatically reduced. If both Standin and Henry followed the law and the bond's guidelines, then Harry would never encounter anyone else's property while he was armed.

The required bonds were oftentimes for considerable sums, and enslavers would have had to take them seriously. This financial liability pressured them to arm only those laborers whom they trusted to not commit violent crimes against other people's bodies or property. Consider that these bonds were often for $100 or $200, but they could reach as high as the $400 that New Hanover County's Frederick J. Swann and William B. Meares were jointly bound for in 1826 to arm Caesar, a man Swann enslaved, or the $500 that Northampton County's William B. Lockhart and John H. Patterson risked on Lockhart's slave Reuben in the late 1820s.[36] These amounts were enough to give pause even to North Carolina's wealthiest enslavers. These enslavers also needed to trust their bondpeople to arm them, as illustrated by Joseph Crecey of Perquimans County, who received permission for Joe to "keep a gun to use," suggesting that Joe not only labored with it, but probably kept it in his cabin as well.[37]

As the political unrest between Britain and her North American colonies grew increasingly tumultuous in the 1770s, both revolutionary and loyalist forces sought to arm enslaved workers for military purposes while simultaneously reducing the threats that they believed Black people embodied. Black North Carolinians pragmatically navigated through this tense situation and deployed their armed labor to achieve their own ends. The deteriorating political situation intensified the loyalists' and rebels' shared fears about Black violence, but these wartime concerns were essentially carryovers from the earlier colonial period. Officials on both sides of the conflict sought to control these perceived threats by regulating Black people's access to weapons. In 1773, the Colonial Assembly approved laws "for the better Regulation of the Town of New Bern," which declared that "whereas Sundry idle and disorderly Persons, as well as Slaves, and Children under Age, do make a Practice of firing Guns and Pistols within the said Town," the authorities would thereafter fine violators ten shillings per offense. The "Parent, Master, or Guardian" would be obligated to pay minors' fines, and enslavers could pay or allow the offender to be whipped. The act also "impowered and required" the town commissioners to appoint watchmen who would be paid out of the fines levied against offenders, which incentivized their diligence. The assembly intended for this law to remain in force for only three years.[38] The town of Charlotte, in Mecklenburg County, had a similar regulation. It noted that the townspeople engaged in the "frequent firing of Guns, Running Horse Races and playing at Long Bullets in the said Town" were dangerous, so thereafter, "no Person whatsoever shall shoot with a Gun except it be to kill Cattle or Hogs . . . within the Limits of the said Town." Violators could be fined twenty shillings.[39]

As colonial politics became increasingly divisive in the summer of 1774, North Carolina's revolutionaries usurped the royal government's authority and rapidly expanded it to cover, among other things, Black people's firearm use, which they framed as a threat to public safety. In an effort to head off this rebellious sentiment, Royal Governor Josiah Martin refused to call the assembly into session, which was a measured tactic to prevent the disloyal legislators from sending representatives to an upcoming pan-colonial congress. Martin failed; in August, the North Carolina revolutionaries held a Provincial Congress without his approval and sent delegates on to the first Continental Congress anyway. The unified Congress's continental association advised every county and municipality to elect a committee of safety to "observe the conduct" of its residents and to publish the trespasses of those believed to be "foes to the rights of British-America" so that they could be shunned. They also enforced the Continental and Provincial Congresses' dictates.[40] The committees were intended to coerce support for the Congress's boycott of British trade goods, but in North Carolina they soon assumed executive, judicial, and legislative authority to the point that their powers "soon became practically unlimited." Problematically, they thereafter decided which "acts and opinions" made a North Carolinian an "enemy of his country," declared suspects' guilt, and meted out punishments. The committees also raised money via fines and seized and sold imports that were contrary to the continental association's orders. They spent some of this money on firearms for the militia.[41]

This dearth of military stores, especially gunpowder, was a real problem for the rebels. In 1774, King George III banned its importation into the colonies, a ban built on earlier trade controls and the economic inefficiency of domestic production. These factors created a shortage in North Carolina, and some colonists feared "being left in a state totally deficient from the want of ammunition." The various committees of safety sought to stockpile powder, keep an account of how much was in their jurisdiction, and regulate its trade.[42] They were also in need of firearms. In mid-November 1775, Wilmington's Committee of Safety ordered a subcommittee to "go round the town, and examine the Arms that may be in each Family," and after allotting "one Gun for each white man that may be in the House," the others would be exchanged for receipts and given to the men in the state's First Regiment. A few months later, it returned to the people of Wilmington to "borrow from them such guns as they can spare" for the militia's use. Some other militiamen had to wait for earlier enlistees to be discharged in order to get a weapon.[43] The government also had a challenging time manufacturing new firearms. Finally, in January 1780, John Penn, Thomas Burke, and Allen Jones—delegates to the Continental Congress—wrote to Governor Richard Caswell that North Carolina "should have no fears" from a British military force, "if the Militia were completely armed."[44] Even if the delegates were overconfident in their militia's prowess, they understood how badly they needed arms.

Additionally, in the spring of 1775, some of North Carolina's local committees of safety set out to disarm their jurisdictions' Black populations as a precautionary measure. At a combined meeting of the Bladen, Brunswick, Duplin, and Wilmington–New Hanover Committees of Safety, the authorities "unanimously agreed" to appoint patrols in New Hanover County "to search for, and take from Negroes, all kinds of arms whatsoever." Further, these committees declared that the militia captain in the district where the weapons were found was to distribute them "to those of his company who may be in want of arms, and who are not able to purchase" any.[45] Through disarming their Black neighbors, the revolutionaries tried to eliminate the threat they saw in them and to simultaneously bolster their own defensive capabilities against the British Crown, a slave rebellion, or another domestic threats. This underscores how the committees did not see those free Black people whose arms they seized as potential militiamen. This was a shift, however, as Carolina's Fundamental Constitution of 1669 permitted free Black men to serve in the militia. It declared that "all Inhabitants and Freemen of Carolina, above Seventeen Years of Age and under sixty, shall be bound to bear Arms, and serve as Soldiers whenever the Grand Council shall find it necessary." And some did serve, at least as late as the 1750s.[46] The rebels sensed that they were in a precarious position. The Wilmington Committee of Safety wrote to revolutionary leader Samuel Johnston that their position was "truly alarming," as the royal governor was "collecting men, provisions, warlike stores of every kind, spiriting up the back counties, and perhaps the Slaves" and strengthening Fort Johnson.[47] These Wilmingtonians also kept a log of the town's military-aged men and a separate list of "all the free mulattoes and negroes in the said town."[48]

Pitt County's Committee of Safety worried about maintaining control over North Carolina's enslaved population during this tumultuous time, especially those who were armed or independently minded. It ordered that patrollers could "shoot one or any number of Negroes who are armed and doth not willingly surrender their arms, and that they have Discretionary Power, to shoot any Number of Negroes above four, who are off their Masters Plantations, and will not submit."[49] The following week, the chairman of the committee, Col. John Simpson, wrote to Craven County's chairman of safety to report that Beaufort County authorities had uncovered "an intended insurrection of the negroes against the whole people."[50] Rumors circulated that there were as many 250 rebelling enslaved people in the area, whom white men had pursued for a couple of days; "but none were taken nor seen tho' [*sic*] they were several times fired at." While these rumors were probably unfounded, the Pitt County Committee of Safety's chairman ended his letter with a postscript, "In disarming the negroes we found considerable ammunition," which was probably a reference to the authorities' preventive search for firearms among Black North Carolinians.[51] It is difficult to guess how much ammunition was actually confiscated from Black people, as those who reported on it might have lied. In the aftermath of Turner's rebellion, Harriet Jacobs noted that "low whites, who had no negroes of their own to scourge" entered Black people's homes and "scattered powder and shot among their clothes, and then sent other parties to find them, and bring them forward as proof that they were plotting insurrection." This planted evidence led to the whippings of adults and children "till the blood stood in puddles at their feet."[52]

The rebels' drive to disarm the Black population at the same time as their relationship with Britain was deteriorating reflects their long-standing cautious approach to armed people of color. Conspicuously, the Bladen, Brunswick, Duplin, and Wilmington–New Hanover Committees of Safety ordinances were not specifically geared toward the enslaved population but broadly targeted all the region's "Negroes." The revolutionaries were simply afraid that Black people's continued gun use presented too great a risk during the conflict with Britain. Ironically, the committees that decided on this disarmament were appointed by the Provincial Congress, some of the delegates for which might have been elected in part by free Black men, as Black male freeholders could vote from the early 1700s up until a constitutional change in 1835. This put North Carolina's free Black men into an exclusive group for a period—before 1820, the only states in which Black men could vote were Connecticut, Maine, Massachusetts, New Hampshire, New Jersey, New York, Pennsylvania, Rhode Island, and Vermont. These Black North Carolinian freeholders might have been enfranchised members of the colonial community, but that did not prevent some of North Carolina's Committees of Safety from disarming them in the pursuit of white men's political liberty.[53]

The assembly furthered the safety committees' efforts to restrict Black firearm use by increasing the frequency of searches, strengthening the penalties for negligent searchers, and improving the rewards for diligent searchers. These changes undergirded North Carolina's slave patrols into the antebellum period. After 1779, the forty-shilling fine for dereliction of duty ballooned upward to a costly 100 pounds sterling.[54] Further, the searchers' quarterly rounds were dramatically increased to a minimum of once per month. The assembly sought to attract quality men who would faithfully perform their duties through incentives; thereafter, the searchers would be paid "out of the county tax as the court shall think necessary." Additionally, during their tenure, searchers would continue to be excused from serving as constables, on public works, in the militia, or on juries. To further entice them, the law also exempted searchers from paying any "Provincial, County, or Parish Tax."[55] The searchers would no longer be permitted to keep any confiscated arms, as the 1753 law allowed, but they would thereafter be required to "make return on oath." These contraband weapons would then be "applied to the use of the county, or returned to the owner, as the court may direct."[56] Locally, counties would manage their patrollers as they deemed necessary; an 1802 law permitted "the several county courts" to set the "rules, regulations and restrictions" for the patrols within their jurisdictions, and they responded accordingly.[57] For example, in 1830, the Craven County Court commissioned Jordan Carrow and Zacheus Slade "to proceed immediately to seize all the fire arms which they may find in the possession of slaves and to retain the said fire arms to their own proper use." They were also authorized to "call upon the owners of said slaves for the fees allowed by law for the arrest of Runaway slaves" and to administer the whip as they saw fit.[58]

Back during the Revolutionary War, some North Carolinians worried that British authorities might turn enslaved men against the rebels' cause. In the summer of 1775, rumors swirled through North Carolina that Governor Martin "had formed a design of Arming the Negroes" to better defend the Crown's interests. It was alleged that he had promised that any of them who would "resort to the King's Standard" would thereby earn their freedom.[59] This rumor predated the actual proclamation by Virginia's royal governor John Murray, 4th Earl of Dunmore, in November 1775, which declared "all *indented* [sic] *servants, Negroes,* or others (appertaining to rebels)" free if they would join the British forces "for the purpose of reducing this colony to a *proper sense* of their duty, to his Majesty's crown and dignity." The Crown wanted allies, and Dunmore's Royal Ethiopian Regiment quickly attracted hundreds of Black men who wanted the chance to fight for their liberty.[60]

The rumors about Martin's plan were particularly alarming to North Caro-lina's revolutionaries because by that summer, the friction between the Crown and the colonies had already boiled over to armed conflict in the Northeast. The revolutionaries recognized that if there were any truth to the rumors about Martin and the fighting spread to their area, the results could be devastating. The royal governor avowed that he had "never conceived a thought" of giving any "encouragement to the negroes to revolt against their masters," but he provocatively added that such a move would be warranted only by "the actual and declared rebellion of the King's subjects, and the failure of all other means to maintain the King's Government." Regardless of how Martin understood his duties during that moment of crisis, this was a bridge too far for many of the local revolutionary leaders. They saw Martin's lukewarm defense as a threat "in plain English," and they blasted him as having openly "manifested himself an enemy to American liberty."[61]

The summer of 1775 also bore witness to additional ominous rumors. North Carolina rebels whispered that British officials had promised that any enslaved person who killed his or her rebel enslaver would be awarded with their plan-tation. This rumor was apparently intended to scare people into supporting the revolutionaries' safety associations and, ostensibly, their cause.[62] The ker-nel of truth in the matter was that British Gen. Thomas Gage had inquired about forming a Black regiment in Massachusetts, but he ultimately could not gain enough support for the project. Across the Atlantic, some "Gentlemen, Merchant, and Traders of the city of London" complained to King George III that the thought of "slaves incited to insurrection . . . filled the minds of your Majesty's faithful subjects with indignation and horror."[63] They were worried about these rumors, which could prove dangerous. A visitor to North Carolina remarked that the rebels who spread the story might end up paying dearly for it, as she believed that "the Negroes have got it amongst them and believe it to be true. Tis ten to one they may try the experiment, and in that case friends and foes [both white loyalists and rebels] will be all one."[64] Sometimes, the fear of uncontrolled Black violence trumped white people's political differences, even during this rapidly expanding revolution.

Civilians in North Carolina did eventually have to deal with British-armed Black men in their midst, Martin and Gage's rumors notwithstanding. Charles Cornwallis, 1st Marquess Cornwallis, used both Black and white foragers in North Carolina in the early months of 1781, much to the chagrin of the colony's rebellious white residents. By that summer, some civilians believed that Corn-wallis has as many as two thousand Black men under his command, though a few months later Gen. William Caswell estimated that the marquess was operating with a force of "400 British, 500 Tories, and if he can Arm them, 500 Negroes."[65] On paper, these Black auxiliaries served a less aggressive purpose than Dunmore's combat-ready Ethiopians, but this was not always the case in practice. Foraging parties were "often nothing more than plundering expeditions that resulted in the illegal seizure of civilian produce and livestock."[66]

While headquartered in Salisbury, Rowan County, in February, Cornwallis was forced to deal with civilian complaints that the countryside was in turmoil because of the "Negroes Stragling from the Line of March, plundr^g & Using Violence" against white people. The British general had to take this matter seriously, as he understood his goal to be to "Assist & Support those Loyalist's [*sic*] in North Carolina, who have ever been distinguish'd by their Fidelity to their King & their Attachment to Great Britain."[67] He could not afford to alienate the civilians in the area. Further, Cornwallis had his own concerns about some of his Black laborers. While in South Carolina, a few months before he marched into North Carolina, he had lamented to his superior, Sir Henry Clinton, that he had "a number of negroes who are very troublesome to us" but whom he had put to work driving cattle with the hope that this would occupy them from whatever irksome activities they were otherwise engaged in.[68]

Cornwallis could not afford to agitate the locals, but his very presence was detrimental to good order on their farms and plantations. During the spring of 1781, Jean Blair complained to her sister Hannah, who had married into the Iredell family, that all but two of her brother's slaves had fled and that another enslaver had lost twenty of his laborers over two nights. This flight might have been encouraged by the proximity of Cornwallis's army, and other enslavers were on alert.[69] Conversely, some enslaved workers actively prevented others from escaping. New Hanover County's Richard and Dolly, both of whom were enslaved by George Merrick, were able to earn their freedom in this way, along with freedom for Dolly's young son, Nathan. Their enslaver wrote to the legislature that they had "Uniformly Behaved with strict, and uncommon Fidelity" during the war and "were Greatly Instrumental in Preventing, Numbers of the slaves . . . from Deserting to the British Troops, when in the Neighboarhood of Cape Fear."[70] In some instances, freedom for some enslaved people came at others' expense.

Cornwallis tried to address the problem of "Stragling" Black folks by ordering that "no Negroe shall be Suffred to Carry Arms on any pretence." He added that his officers with Black laborers under their commands were to notify them that the provost marshal had orders to "Seize & punish on the Spot any Negroe foll^g the Army who may Offend against this regulation."[71] This measure suggests that prior to this order, some of Cornwallis's Black subordinates were armed. Further, Cornwallis's order appears to have been effective. By July, the British had moved to Suffolk, Virginia, but still had Black men operating close to Edenton, Chowan County, who reportedly had "no Arms but what they find in the houses they plunder." Some civilians in the area heard that Cornwallis's Black foragers had "applyed for arms" but that "they were told they had no occasion for any as they were not to go to any place where any number of Rebels were collected."[72] A man who spent time in Edenton that July explained that "every Body there was marching out to endeavor to surprise" the 600 Black men "who were sent out by L Cornwallis to plunder and get provisions."[73] These Black foragers recognized that they were vulnerable and less effective without weapons, but Cornwallis did not modify his orders.

Cornwallis's negative interactions with North Carolina's white civilians were not solely rooted in his Black auxiliaries, of course. He also received several "Shocking Complaints of the Excesses" committed by his white soldiers, who stole food and alcohol from civilians and torched several houses. Gregory Urwin argues that Cornwallis "strove constantly to restrain the predatory impulses of his soldiers" and even threatened his officers who were not trying hard enough to prevent it. Further, while Cornwallis did not address it directly in his orders, white civilians alleged that the British troops also sexually assaulted young women and girls near Hillsborough. Cornwallis ordered his brigade and corps commanders to rein in these disorderly soldiers because he feared that they would "Inevitably bring Disgrace & Ruin on his Majesty Service."[74] The threat that Cornwallis's Black workers and white soldiers posed rapidly disappeared after the British forces were bottled up at Yorktown, Virginia. Nonetheless, the tensions between safely harnessing people of color's armed labor and protecting white people's lives and property from unsupervised armed Black workers would continue to plague North Carolina in both civilian and military contexts from that moment until slavery's demise during the Civil War.

A few of the nearly 500 Black or multiracial North Carolinians who joined the rebels' revolutionary cause used their government-sanctioned armed military labor to carve a pathway toward freedom. W. Trevor Freeman calculates that at least nine of them were enslaved at some point. Ned Griffin, an enslaved Edgecombe County man, was purchased by William Kitchen, a white man, after Kitchen had been caught trying to desert from the army. Kitchen acquired Griffin specifically to take his place in the ranks, with the promise of freedom after his enlistment. When asked, the enslaver told the enlisting officer, his own former colonel, that Griffin was free. After Griffin enlisted, Kitchen tried to sell him, but the multiracial man and his allies intervened.[75] After the war, the assembly declared that as a result of his twelve months of "meritorious service" in a North Carolina unit, Griffin would "forever hereafter be in every respect declared to be a freeman; and he shall be, and he is hereby enfranchised and forever delivered and discharged from the yoke of slavery." The legislators explained that as Griffin, "did faithfully on his part perform the condition" agreed upon, it was only fair that he "should receive the reward promised" for his military service[76] Ned Griffin's musket and the latent violence within it secured him a liberty that white North Carolinians, despite their hyperbolic rhetoric about slavery under George III's administration, could not equally appreciate.

Some Black North Carolinians chose to distance themselves from both the British Empire and its rebelling colonists by disappearing into North Carolina's swamps and forests. A visitor to North Carolina in the 1780s remarked that the state's swamps were "perfectly safe" for "run-away Negroes," some of whom lived for as many as thirty years in hidden-away areas, "subsisting themselves in the swamp upon corn, hogs, and fowls, that they raised on some of the spots not perpetually under water."[77] This move did not completely protect these fugitives from the threats posed by either side in the conflict. In July of 1781, a man enslaved by William Bryan ran away "and joined himself with sundry other out lying slaves" in Craven County, who had "armed themselves with guns & committed several Feloneys and attempted sundry murders." A party was raised to stop these "outlying rebel slaves" and they killed Bryan's slave while trying to apprehend him. The assembly compensated Bryan with specie worth 100 pounds sterling. Marvin L. Michael Kay and Lorin Lee Cary explain that this "compensation system enabled the authorities and slave courts to implement the slave criminal justice system to its harsh, logical limits without fear of financially burdening slaveowners."[78]

During the Revolutionary Era, thousands of enslaved people were able to reach freedom as a result of either the period's popular liberal ideologies or their own flight, but as Ira Berlin explains, "slavery in the Upper South did not crack under the blows of revolutionary republicanism and evangelical egalitarianism" as it did in the Northern states.[79] North Carolina's slave system survived, despite a wave of manumissions and continued resistance from enslaved people. Enslavement was not the only continuation from the colonial era to the early national period, however. The unstable relationships between armed Black people and North Carolina's state and local authorities would continue well into the next century. The state's power structure and its enslavers would continue to see North Carolinians of color as a specific cause for concern, although they also continued to recognize that armed Black laborers could be put to many practical applications that were beneficial to white citizens.

During the War of 1812, the assembly extended its reach into its free Black residents' firearm use much as it had during the American Revolution, but with a much greater emphasis on harnessing Black people's armed labor for selective militia service. Nevertheless, many white North Carolinians remained as uncomfortable with armed Black men in a military context as they had been during the colonial period. North Carolina's 1800 militia laws ambiguously ordered the enrollment of "all freemen and indentured servants, citizens of this State or of the United States" who were between eighteen and forty-five years of age.[80] This broad inclusion was sometimes meet with opposition, however. In 1809, the militia's adjutant general asked that the assembly prevent Black men from enrolling because he believed that it "lessens the *respectability* of a military company to have men of colour in the ranks, and prevents many persons from mustering, who would otherwise do so." He believed that this undercut military efficiency. Despite his reservations, the adjutant general did not want to completely deprive the militia of Black men's labor. He argued that free men of color "ought to form Pioneer Corps, and be mustered separately, without arms."[81] The state decided to amend the militia laws in 1812 to prevent officers from enrolling free men of color in any capacity except as musicians. This exclusion was reversed in 1814 via another amendment, which declared that militia officers could again enroll free Black men if they were sure to "designate by proper columns the free persons of colour from the rest of the militia."[82] Black men's militia service was needed and welcome, though they were marked as different from the very moment they enrolled.

The assembly passed the 1814 act during the heightened pressures brought on by the War of 1812; but by 1823, the legislators again rejected Black men's armed militia service. The assembly banned them, with the repeated exception for musicians—Black men could serve only in an unarmed capacity.[83] The adjutant general's 1809 complaints about free men of color serving in the militia were not merely a concern about their broad participation in the war; rather, he also sought to preserve *armed* state service for white men and relegate Black men to auxiliary positions. Free Black quasi-citizens' participation in what North Carolinians considered to be a "civic duty," and perhaps also militiamen's prevalence in slave patrols, had ultimately made the idea of Black militiamen distasteful to many of the state's white residents.[84]

By the 1820s, enslaved Black men were no longer allowed to serve in the militia. Further, the legislators believed that enslaved men's attendance at militia musters was part of the larger problem of their proximity and potential access to firearms.[85] In 1831, the assembly passed a law to prevent enslaved people in fifteen eastern counties from going to militia musters or election grounds unless they were escorted by their enslaver or had his or her consent. The patrol in the district where the muster or election was held was duty bound to apprehend unauthorized workers and could give them fifteen lashes. Further, any white person at a muster or polling place could seize an offending enslaved person and bring him or her to a justice of the peace, where the enslaved person would "receive a whipping not exceeding thirty-nine lashes on his or her bare back" regardless of whether or not the patrol had already whipped them.[86] In the assembly's view, any ties between enslaved Black North Carolinians and the trappings of citizenship—here manifested via the participatory spectacle of nineteenth century elections and militia musters—were a potential problem that needed to be curbed via the threat of physical correction.

Incidentally, the North Carolina General Assembly's concerns about enslaved workers' familiarity with the militia mirrored some of the anxieties around free Black men's militia service and their firearm use in civilian applications. In January 1841, the legislators greatly curtailed free Black people's ability to use firearms and other weapons by requiring that they obtain an annual license from their county court before they could keep any "Shot-gun, Musket, Rifle, Pistol, Sword, Dagger, or Bowie-knife" or risk indictment for a misdemeanor.[87] This restrictive legislation was not unique; several other Southern states passed similar race-based firearms laws during the first half of the nineteenth century. The assembly used this 1841 law to regulate the process by which free men and women of color could be armed; but it also empowered the county courts to manage specifically which free Black people would be granted the privilege. This was much like the county courts' oversight of enslaved laborers' firearm use prior to 1832. Thereafter, free Black people's legal firearm use would be solely dependent on their white neighbors' good graces. Before January 1841, the only laws on free Black people's access to arms were the militia restrictions. After that point, however, Black applicants had to rely on white community members, business associates, and friends to support their requests for licenses and to vouch for their "good moral and peaceable character."[88] The license law was the last piece of legislation targeting Black North Carolinians' firearm use until the eve of the Civil War.

The state-mandated license provision marked a transitional period for free Black North Carolinians, who had enjoyed unregulated gun use for decades prior to the law's passage, but who were thereafter dependent on their white neighbors, who decided whether they, as free people of color, could bear arms. Per the new law, in the summer of 1841, a free man of color named "Free Willis" requested the Wayne County Court's permission to continue to "keep and use a Shot gun and Ammunition in his house as usual." Willis said that he had never been accused of any mischief and that he had even voluntarily turned his gun over to a white neighbor for safe keeping during a "Negro rising." A white farmer named Benajah Herring wrote a letter of support on Willis's behalf. He explained that he was confident in Willis, who lived "at one end of [Herring's] plantation," and that Willis's firearm use was beneficial to him. The white farmer explained to the court that "as he does me some benefit by destroying the Vermin around my fields I would rather he could retain his gun."[89] This benefit was indistinguishable from that which North Carolina enslavers gained from marshaling their bondpeople's armed labor.

Decades prior, in fact, Free Willis and Benajah Herring's relationship had been that of enslaver and enslaved. Eighteen years earlier, the Wayne County Court allowed Herring to emancipate Willis, who had "from his infancy" been "distinguished by his sobriety industry and faithfulness." This was not purely a gesture of kindness or a reward for "faithfulness." Willis paid the Herring family for his freedom.[90] His experiences with a firearm demonstrate how central white people's supervision was to this process—he was no longer the Herring family's property, but their continued oversight was a vital aspect of his firearm use. The 1840 US Federal Census lists Willis with the Herring surname, and he had lived in their neighborhood since gaining his freedom.[91] This was as high a level of white supervision over an armed free Black person that white North Carolinians could reasonably expect to have. Further, while "Free" Willis may have otherwise been able to acquire a gun, Benajah Herring's support—as both a former enslaver, current neighbor, and beneficiary of Willis's labor—undoubtedly helped his firearm application at the Wayne County Court.

The assembly and county courts' limitations on when and where an enslaver might arm his or her bondpeople were a fundamental aspect of North Carolina's slave law. Enslavers struggled to reduce the workers, who they claimed to be mere extensions of their wills, but they were forced to deal with more than enslaved people's resistance to this blatant dehumanization. The General Assembly also tempered mastery's highest aspiration as it struggled to find and maintain a balance between the perceived usefulness and dangers of Black people's firearm use. The assembly kept the onus on individual enslavers to remain vigilant; but the legislators increasingly saw themselves and the county courts as partners in this, and it passed laws to confine armed enslaved laborers to their enslavers' property, or to at least keep them under his or her direct control. It also empowered the county courts to ensure that these enslavers actually supervised their workers.

This relationship between the General Assembly and North Carolina's citizens was not unidirectional, however. When white people were dissatisfied with social and political matters, they voiced their concerns by petitioning their lawmakers and governors in Raleigh. The citizens' petitions about Black firearm use, which should be read as a series spanning several years, repeated the long-standing concerns about the threat that armed Black people sometimes posed to their white neighbors' property. Each individual petition represents a specific position on the firearms issue, and while it is difficult to discern how popular this viewpoint was at the time each petition was written, together the documents offer insight into some white men's views. These petitioners were particularly concerned that their property or that of other white citizens might be threatened by mobile and unsupervised people of color. Some white North Carolinians had been clamoring for decades that the assembly should strictly control Black people's firearm access. In the 1820s, white men petitioned their legislature that the threat of free and enslaved Black people's gun use warranted action. In 1828, thirty-five men in Craven County, fifteen of whom were then serving as jurors at the county court, petitioned the assembly about the "constant and growing practice of Persons of Colour hunting with dogs and guns whereby under the pretence of seeking game, they commit numberless depredations upon the farms by killing stock of every description."[92] Further, these white men argued that the "existing Laws, Prohibiting slaves from hunting as aforesaid, are evaded through the agency and assistance of free Persons of Colour," and that the laws should therefore be amended to restrict free Black North Carolinians as well. One should remember that some of those free Black men were voters. These Craven County petitioners framed themselves as representative voices for their community, noting that "great inconvenience and injury arise to them and others," because of the armed free people of color in their midst.[93]

These petitioners broadly indicted both free and enslaved Black people by omitting any mention of a condition of servitude for the "Persons of Color" who were allegedly killing white-owned livestock. Many white people suspected that free and enslaved people of color colluded with each other and that their relationships, which white citizens often framed as ill-intentioned, posed a threat to law and order. The petitioners believed that their free Black neighbors were encouraging and enabling enslaved workers to break the laws, which the white men implicitly believed that the workers would otherwise subserviently follow. They thought that these relationships between free and enslaved Black people ultimately fostered economic turmoil because they hunted white farmers' livestock. While it is difficult to ascertain how prevalent this was, it was not wholly unfounded. Free people of color, like Craven County's James Woods, were charged with killing their white neighbors' cattle. Finally, the petitioners believed that the assembly had to step in with stricter controls on free people of color and to pass any other law that "may seem [illegible] + Proper."[94]

Further, some white North Carolinians' complained that free people of color were providing enslaved laborers with illegal firearms. During the 1828–29 session of the General Assembly, the legislators tried to counter this threat by adding firearms into the state's official policy on trading with slaves. This was a response to the spirit of the 1828 Craven County petition, if not to the document itself. The new version of the law declared outright that no one could sell or trade "fire-arms, powder or shot, or lead" to any of them without their enslaver's permission.[95] White people who violated this law could be subjected to a $100 fine and the money would be paid to whomever reported the illegal sale. The perpetrator could also face up to three months' imprisonment and up to $50 in additional fines. Free Black North Carolinians who were convicted of selling firearms to enslaved people could be physically punished with up to thirty-nine lashes, as if they were enslaved themselves, but they would not be fined or sentenced to the county jail.[96] Further, during the winter of 1830–31, the legislature debated a bill that would have compelled "retailers of spiritous liquors by the small measure" in certain counties to take an oath and post a bond that they would not "sell spiritous liquors, powder, shot, lead or firearms to a slave."[97] The assembly did not pass the bill, but it highlights the concerns about enslaved people's access to firearms in this period.

Beyond this fear of the intraracial trade in guns, white North Carolinians were also worried that the enslaved workers who had been armed through the county's appropriate legal channels might also damage white people's property. In 1841, New Hanover residents William L. Ashe, James T. Miller, and Joshua G. Wright bound themselves to the court for $200 to ensure that Jack, whom Ashe enslaved, would not threaten other white property holders while he was armed. The document explicitly states that Jack "shall not abuse the use of the gun by unlawfully destructing the cattle and hogs of the neighborhood."[98] Black North Carolinians' appropriation of white property holders' goods did not rely solely on their firearm access; a hungry enslaved worker did not need a musket or a pistol to pillage a smokehouse, although he or she could, with a firearm, put up stronger resistance if discovered. Nevertheless, Ashe's bond and the citizens' petitions to curb Black people's firearm use explicitly connected armed Black people to the destruction of white-owned livestock.[99] This problem was heightened by the period's agricultural practices. Most farmers turned their livestock loose so that the animals could forage and graze on their own. This was both an effective cost-saving measure and a long-standing customary practice as open land was generally considered available for common use. This roaming livestock was easy pickings for anyone who had no misgivings about killing and eating their neighbors' property.

The bond provisions that threatened to punish enslavers for their workers' illegal behavior served an additional purpose beyond the crucial goal of bolstering their accountability. Such bonds also assuaged public concerns about the threat armed enslaved workers might pose when they left their enslavers' lands and ventured onto another citizens' property. Enslavers who had a financial investment in the process would likely be more inclined to arm only those laborers whom they trusted to not harm other people's bodies or property. Enslaved North Carolinians resisted in myriad ways, but the historical record is littered with newspaper reports, legislative petitions, and other documents in which white Southerners bewailed the desolation that slaves, runaways and maroons, and even free Black people were alleged to have wrought on white people's livestock. Again, mobility was a central concern here. Those armed enslaved laborers who traveled off their enslavers' land came into contact with the property of "white citizens and inhabitants" more frequently than those who did not, and they therefore had much greater opportunity to engage in behavior that would make them a public nuisance.[100]

The efforts to restrict enslaved people's ability to purchase guns and ammunition did not preserve white North Carolinians' peace of mind for very long. The assembly soon looked to more extreme measures when copies of David Walker's *Appeal in Four Articles* were reported to have been seen in North Carolina's port towns; Nat Turner made his bloody march across nearby Southampton County, Virginia; and rumors of a massive homegrown slave rebellion ripped through the Old North State itself, all within a short few years in the early 1830s. White North Carolinians responded quickly to these events, and their fears would have long-lasting ramifications on Black people's firearm use. The state legislators undertook measures to protect white citizens from the possibility of Black violence and soon after passed a complete ban on enslaved workers' firearm use.[101] No longer would the state trust individual enslavers to guarantee their chosen armed bondpeople's behavior, nor would it trust the local county courts to decide which local slaves could be trusted. The state government determined that allowing any Black person to carry arms would be too great of a risk to the public peace, as understood from white North Carolinians' perspectives.

David Walker was born to an enslaved father and free mother in Wilmington, but he was living in Boston, Massachusetts, in the fall of 1829 when he wrote his *Appeal in Four Articles*. In this piece, he criticized enslavers for their barbarous treatment of African-descended peoples, advocated that free and enslaved Black men offer manly resistance to the oppressive system of enslavement, and proclaimed that Black men had a God-given right to protect their families and communities. In August 1830, Wilmington's officials notified Governor John Owen that a "well-disposed" free Black man had alerted them that copies of Walker's *Appeal* had begun to appear in their port town. One enslaved tavern keeper, perhaps a man named James Cowan, was alleged to have had two hundred copies in his possession and to have been planning an insurrection. He and several other people, presumably Black people, were arrested. Wilmington's authorities began to suspect that the town's Black residents were plotting a revolt. Fayetteville's officials raised similar concerns about their own Black population.[102] In response, Owen advised local authorities to undertake "the most vigilant execution of your police laws and the laws of the state" and to keep watch for "agents" spreading the *Appeal*. For its own part, the assembly tried to restrict free Black people's movements and limit their interactions with the Black sailors who passed through the North Carolina's ports.[103] In Beaufort County, the town of Washington's officials disarmed the free people of color, increased the town's night watch, curtailed free Black people's ability to assemble, called out the militia, and requested additional arms from the state arsenal.[104] Craven County's grand jurors suggested that "a reward be offered by the Governor to any one who will furnish testimony sufficient to prosecute to conviction" anyone spreading either Walker's *Appeal* or William Lloyd Garrison's antislavery newspaper, *The Liberator*. Gates County's justices of the peace appointed four patrollers to "make diligent search for certain pamphlets written by a certain free man of colour of the town of Boston + if any such be found to take such person having them in their possession" and lock them in the county jail.[105]

This anxiety spread beyond Walker's *Appeal in Four Articles*. Joseph B. Hinton wrote to John Gray Blount about the public nervousness after Turner's rebellion. He related how in Hillsborough, in Orange County, an enslaved woman "in an ill-humor" told some white children that "she would soon be freed from all trouble of them" because "the negroes were to rise & kill all the white men—some of the handsomest of the white women would be spared for wives of the leaders." These comments caused great alarm, and Hillsborough's leadership scrambled to get weapons to prepare a defense.[106] Hinton wrote to Blount again, noting that "the cloud thickens: news from divers [*sic*] quarters, of an alarming character flows in upon us." He related reports of "extraordinary insubordination . . . among the blacks" and calls for arms in some places. He had also heard "that a fellow calling himself a preacher, was detected . . . at Chappel Hill inviting the negroes to meet him privately after night." University of North Carolina president Joseph Caldwell and some students "found it out, & went & found him inflaming the worst passions of human nature—& from his baggage he was suspected, & charged with having Walkers pamphlets." The stranger, "villain as he is with a white skin—& calling himself a preacher," managed to escape.[107]

Further, John Chavis, a Black Presbyterian minister in the area, was brought in for questioning and claimed that he was not aware of any insurrectionary plans; but, according to Hinton, "He said he knew enough to say, it was time the white people were looking about them & putting themselves in preparation for the event, for they would need all they could do, one of these days."[108] Finally, Hinton alleged that "an intelligent free man of Bladen County" was recruited to work with colonizationists, but he declined, saying that "he would not go & the people of Colour were fools to go—that if the United States would free the negroes & give them a territory for them to colonize within their limits—or in Canada—they would go there—if they would give them no freed territory—they must free the negroes & admit them to all the rights of Citizens & amalgamate with the whites without distinction—or the whites must take their certain doom."[109] Hinton went on to describe this as "very nearly the identical views & language of Walkers pamphlet." In his estimation, North Carolina had a parallel domestic threat that it could, hopefully, manage. He concluded, "We are on a mine, it would appear—the match, I hope will be snatched from the destructive hand."[110]

Only about a year later, Nat Turner's rebellion served as a brutal reminder of the latent but destructive violence that was coiled in the system of slavery. In August 1831, the literate enslaved preacher led an army of about seventy enslaved men across Southampton County, Virginia, in a bloody but ultimately unsuccessful bid for freedom. For Turner, "Christianity was a fighting faith, and prophets were not merely mystics but warriors." Turner's men managed to kill nearly sixty white men, women, and children, and white Virginians responded by killing over a hundred Black people, many during the orgy of violence that followed. These men "aimed to show Black people in Virginia and around the world that white Virginians were firmly and forever in charge."[111] The high numbers of white casualties and the proximity to North Carolina contributed to a panic that spread through some of its counties. Southampton County, Virginia, is adjacent to North Carolina's Northampton County and

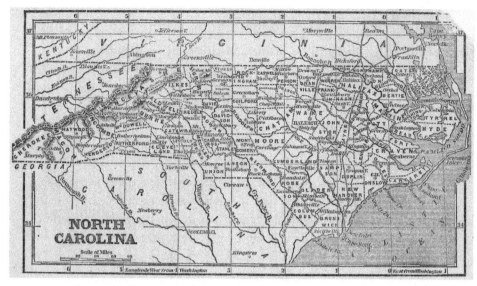

A map of North Carolina, depicting the 1849 county lines and some towns. Courtesy of the State Archives of North Carolina.

is also quite close to parts of Halifax, Hertford, and Gates Counties. Further, North Carolina militiamen rallied to aid the Virginians, and several Black North Carolinians were suspected of conspiracy. Many of them were taken into custody and some were killed.[112]

In mid-September 1831, while North Carolina reeled from Turner's revolt, word spread that a free biracial man named "Mr. Usher" had alerted white authorities of an extensive conspiracy among enslaved people in Sampson, Duplin, and New Hanover Counties. Distressing initial reports came in from typically reliable sources, like, for instance, a major general in the militia. The reports were terrifying: Rampaging Black people had sacked Wilmington— they slaughtered many white people, burned the town to the ground, and were then heading toward Fayetteville. Black people had massacred seventeen white families in Sampson and Duplin Counties and then razed the Sampson County courthouse. An army of 1,500 enslaved people had killed several white people in Sampson County and were marching toward Duplin County.[113] White people in these areas were terrified. In some neighborhoods, panicked white women and children, and certainly some men, took to hiding in swamps, not unlike runaway slaves. Others frantically crowded into neighbor's homes that they thought were more defensible than their own, steadying their nerves for battles that never came. Wilmington's officials declared martial law after hearing rumors that an army of 200 enslaved people was only two miles away.

New Bern's authorities requested and received support from a company of US artillerymen from nearby Fortress Monroe in Virginia, whom they enthusiastically welcomed.[114] Slavery was local, but maintaining the institution was also national.

This mixture of inflated reports and patently false stories traveled quickly and many white North Carolinians in the eastern portions of the state expected mobs of gun-toting Black people to suddenly appear, pillaging and killing their way through white communities. Most of them came to see that "no overt act of rebellion has taken place, and that the alarming reports now circulating through the country, about the burning of property and massacres of several white families, are entirely erroneous." Nonetheless, some white people worried that a real plot had been discovered in parts of Duplin, Sampson, Wayne, New Hanover, and Lenoir Counties.[115] Similarly, that September, many of the white people in the gold mining districts in Burke and Rutherford Counties believed that a literate enslaved preacher named Fed was fomenting a rebellion. The local authorities determined that there was no rebellion but nonetheless undertook security measures and appear to have jailed some white men for circulating "false reports of approaching bodies of negroes."[116]

In response to these real and imagined fears, the General Assembly zealously repealed the law that authorized the county courts to "grant certificates" for slaves to "carry guns in certain cases."[117] This response to Turner and the turmoil that swirled around his revolt echoed the state's response to the 1739 Stono Rebellion—white North Carolinians' collective anxiety led them to seek legislative solutions. Enslavers had previously been allowed to arm one of their bondpersons to hunt or eliminate agricultural pests, but after the 1831 rebellion, any enslaved worker caught with a gun would receive twenty lashes and their enslaver would be fined.[118] Further, in a typical response to rebellion, once the authorities regained control, they jailed dozens of suspected free and enslaved Black people—between forty and fifty of them in Sampson and Duplin Counties alone. Some were executed after trials of varying degrees of dubiousness and others were lynched by mobs who could not be bothered to go through the motions of a trial.[119]

White North Carolinians' fears were not wholly baseless and, in this state of mind, they "drew closer to one another . . . and tried to draw a firmer line between the races."[120] Nat Turner and the Sampson–Duplin–New Hanover scare caused many of them to question their local militia units' preparedness to suppress large slave rebellions. These doubts amplified their fears of armed Black people, and white citizens' efforts to more strictly control their Black neighbors' firearm use took on greater urgency. Many county and municipal officials and militia officers sent frantic appeals to Governor Montfort Stokes for weapons. Over an eight-week span, officers in both existing and newly formed militia companies inundated Stokes and Beverly Daniel, the adjutant general of the North Carolina Militia, with at least thirty-five appeals for guns from the state arsenals.[121] These officers worried that their units were ill-equipped to put down a slave rebellion.

This was not solely a problem for the militias. A few days after Christmas in 1830, Charles Pettigrew wrote to his father about an alleged plot by enslaved people in Hillsborough, and how his lack of firearms presented a problem. He explained that "two maid servants" told their mistresses that other enslaved people had planned to kill their enslavers and then "march directly to Hillsboro where they might have a [*sic*] plenty of arms and ammunition and kill all the people there and make a stand." Pettigrew added that, "the slaves at chapel hill all so[*sic*] were engaged in the plot" but they were found out.[122] Even though the plot was thwarted, Pettigrew related how armed patrols stayed out all night for several days as a precaution and had "taken away several of the negroes guns" as well. This shows the anxieties that at least some white civilians shared. Pettigrew recounted how if he had been caught unawares by the reports—he and the other people at the house he was at "would have had to fought with our hands" because "there was not a gun in the house," though they had since armed themselves as a precaution.[123]

Certainly, fear and anxiety could have drawn an overreaction, but the volume of these requests suggests that while great numbers of white North Carolinian men were familiar with firearms via hunting, patrolling, and drilling with the militia, they still worried that they did not have access to functional military-grade weaponry. In 1844, the Raleigh Guards complained to the governor that "the muskets now used by the Company are very common and inferior guns; they shoote ball with great inaccuracy and are not believed to be Safe should it be necessary to discharge them often in a short time." These weapons would be a liability in combat and the militiamen knew it. They hoped to rectify this via "better muskets" from the federal government's Fayetteville Arsenal.[124] William H. Bayne, the commander of the Fayetteville Rifleman, also requested new arms, as "the Rifles which we have now, I am informed, have been in this Arsenal near on quite *20 years*!" Bayne explained to Governor John Motely Morehead that he had showed one of these weapons to an officer at the Fayetteville Arsenal, who told him that they were "entirely out of use in [the] army."[125] While the militia units embodied the state's strength at the local level and were essential for organizing local defense efforts, many company commanders and even some regimental leaders doubted that their men would be able to counter a significant slave revolt without timely material aid from the state government.[126] This moment of crisis demonstrated that local leaders in many of North Carolina's communities understood that they were in a vulnerable position and needed the state government to shore up their militias with better weapons.

Despite these concerns, nearly a decade passed before the assembly required free people of color to apply for firearm licenses, and they would not face a total ban for twenty years after that. This was in part because some white citizens believed that the existing "Free Negro Code" served as a sufficient check on Black North Carolinians' behavior. Additionally, white men hoped that if they were able to successfully manage free people of color, then they could effectually foster an allyship against the state's enslaved workers.[127] The Old North State was not alone in these heightened concerns about free people of color's firearm use in Nat Turner's wake. Both Virginia and Georgia's legislatures banned their free Black residents from keeping firearms, and Maryland and Delaware enacted licensing provisions.[128] As Robert Cottrol points out, "The idea was to restrict the availability of arms to blacks, both slave and free, to the extent consistent with local conceptions of safety." North Carolina's post-Turner legislative repression of its free Black population was far less enthusiastic than in some other states, but Eugene Genovese's admonition against using the intensity of the written law as a reliable measure of lived conditions should be remembered: "If harsh laws did not mean equally harsh practice, neither did mild laws mean equally mild practice."[129] Free Black North Carolinians faced challenges.

White North Carolinians' sentiments on Black people's gun use cannot be understood solely through their fears of slave violence or through the assembly's laws. Their concerns about the antislavery movement's radical elements also informed their views on free Black people's firearm use. This was especially so after the early 1830s, when the American Anti-Slavery Society (AASS) supplanted the earlier efforts by the Quakers and the American Colonization Society, the latter of which the AASS dismissed as an "opiate to the consciousness" of people who might otherwise react more strongly against slavery.[130] In 1832, William Lloyd Garrison aggressively declared that the nation had a "sacred duty" to not only abolish slavery but also welcome people of color as "brethren and countrymen" and as constituent parts of a multiracial nation. Garrison and his associates argued that the institution was essentially a state of war that had to be ended before the nation could address its mounting sectional tensions.[131] Some of North Carolina's newspapers reported that Garrison's newspaper, *The Liberator*, was circulating "openly among the free blacks," and they believed that a thorough search would produce copies from among the enslaved population as well.[132]

Garrison's brand of reform was provocative, but he was far from the most aggressive of Northern abolitionists. John Brown agreed with Garrison that slavery was a state of war, but he took this position to its extreme conclusion. He maintained that violence was not only permissible in the fight, but that it was perhaps even indispensable to the institution's destruction. In later years, Frederick Douglass wrote about how Brown had once told him that "the practice of carrying arms would be a good one for the colored people to adopt, as it would give them a sense of their manhood. No people could have self-respect, or be respected, who would not fight for their freedom." This was not simply radical rhetoric for Brown; it was reflected in the way he lived the last several years of his life. Brown fought in Bleeding Kansas, rescued enslaved Missourians and safely guided them to Canada, and later launched an ill-fated attack on the federal armory at Harpers Ferry, Virginia, with plans to secure firearms for a slave uprising and a subsequent guerrilla war. John Anthony Copeland Jr. and Lewis Sheridan Leary—two men of color with North Carolina roots—took up arms and accompanied Brown into martyrdom at Harpers Ferry in 1859.[133]

White North Carolinians were frustrated with Garrison and Brown. The state's attorney general, Romulus Mitchell Saunders, was so incensed by *The Liberator* that he indicted both Garrison and his publisher, Isaac Knapp, in October 1831 for circulating "seditious publications." This crime was punishable by whipping and imprisonment for the first offense and death for the second, but the *Raleigh Register* speculated that Massachusetts's governor would probably not surrender the pair to North Carolina's authorities. Further, Brown's Harpers Ferry raid may have been the impetus behind an 1859 North Carolina bill that would have abolished the license provision and ended free people of color's legal gun access, but it did not pass.[134] Nonetheless, the assembly did offer an additional safeguard. It ordered the county courts to keep a record of those free Black people whose petitions for firearms had been rejected and declared that those individuals could not be granted a license on reapplication during the same court term unless a majority of the justices who initially rejected them gave consent. In February 1861, the pressures of sectional conflict finally pushed the General Assembly to ban free Black people's gun use altogether.[135]

White North Carolinians' fears of slave rebellions and aggressive abolitionism were exacerbated by their concerns about the relationship between free and enslaved people of color, and they demanded that their lawmakers act. Just a few years after Nat Turner and the fears of homegrown insurrections, some white Craven County residents echoed the pleas from their county's 1828 petition to restrict free Black people's gun use. On the October 31, 1835, they complained that many of the free people of color in their community had "evil and bad habits" and led "dissolute and immoral lives." These white petitioners feared that in the event of a revolt, their free Black neighbors "might be expected to join in with heart and hand" and aid the enslaved rebels. Their largest complaint, however, was rooted in their belief that armed free and enslaved Black folks were destroying white people's property and that this problem needed a legislative solution. The white men claimed that their county's free Black residents

> sustain themselves in a great measure by hunting or pretending to hunt, to the great nuisance of the good citizens of the State residing near them. From the the [*sic*] character which they set up as freemen, they claim license to roam about and acquire guns and ammunition; and so much have they used this privilege that many of them are the owners of many guns, by which they can, not only themselves commit depredations upon the property of the white citizens . . . but may furnish the means to others, as well free as slaves, to do likewise.[136]

The petitioners were willing to concede that Craven County's free Black residents needed firearms to feed themselves, but they also believed that Black people were a threat to white people's property, and they believed that free Black people were linked to the area's slaves in problematic ways. They also asked the legislature to impose safeguards against free people of color's "vagrant habits and roaming lives," which they saw as "a nuisance requiring correction." The white men explained to their government that

> the facility which the said free negroes . . . have to distribute guns . . . among the slaves for purpose of rebellion and insurrection, is dangerous and an evil demanding the consideration of the Legislature . . . especially in times like these, when many of the citizens of the Northern states are disseminating among our slaves the firebrands of insurrection. . . . Your petitioners will with due defference [*sic*] suggest that a law requiring every free negro . . . to obtain a license from the county court before he could have or use a gun or ammunition, which license he should only obtain upon satisfactory proof to said court of his good moral and peaceable character, and upon entering into bonds with good security for his good behavior and honest deportment, might perhaps remedy the evil.[137]

The specter of a partnership between Craven County's free and enslaved Black residents, replete with their "many guns" and indoctrinated with the abolitionists' "firebrands of destruction," was quite provocative. The 1828 petition demonstrated that some white men had deep concerns about their free and enslaved Black neighbors' firearm use and sought a state-level solution. Their need to protect themselves and their property superseded their Black neighbors' needs to provide for their families.

By 1840, white North Carolinians' criticisms of their free Black neighbors' firearm use had reached more extreme heights. Fifty-one men from Halifax County petitioned the assembly to "prohibit Free Negroes and and [sic] Mulatoes from carrying or using fire arms under any circumstances what ever."[138] They submitted the petition just weeks before the governing body passed the license law, and their concerns had a direct impact on the legislature's debates on the matter. The final law did not go as far as the Halifax petitioners wanted, but their request should be viewed alongside the earlier petitions calling for restrictions on free and enslaved Black people's gun use. When these documents are examined as parts of a cohesive series, they illustrate that generations of white people were concerned about the relationships between free and enslaved Black North Carolinians, their firearm use, and the damage they could potentially do to white people's property. As one can glean from these three petitions' related demands of the assembly, there were virtually no limitations on free people of color's firearm use during these years, except on their militia service; but nevertheless, some white people continued to worry about these masterless Black people.[139] The 1828 and 1835 petitions portray free people's firearm use as deviant from white people's standards and cast it as potentially destructive. These petitioners, and ostensibly many of their peers, did not trust the free people of color in their neighborhoods to meet the standards that white people set. These concerns were a continuation of many white people's long-standing perception that armed, unsupervised, and mobile Black people were a potential threat to white North Carolinians' lives and property.

This 1840 effort differed from the earlier Craven County petitions in that the Haligonians made no effort to justify the proposed disarmament of their Black neighbors. White people comprised only a third of Halifax County's total population.[140] Much like the earlier petitions, this effort loudly reiterated that even when white people were a demographic minority, they held the highest political and socioeconomic positions in both their local communities and the state. North Carolina's state legislators responded to the Craven and Halifax County petitioners' concerns. In January of 1841, mere weeks after the disgruntled men from Halifax County petitioned the government, the assembly passed a law that severely restricted free Black North Carolinians' ability to own, carry, or use firearms. This legislation was not unique, however. Several other enslaving states passed restrictive and racially specific weapons laws during the first half of the nineteenth century. North Carolina's iteration declared: "If any free Negro, Mulatto, or free Person of Colour, shall wear or carry about his or her person, or keep in his or her house, any Shot-gun, Musket, Rifle, Pistol, Sword, Dagger, of Bowie-knife, unless he or she shall have obtained a license therefore from the Court of Pleas and Quarter Sessions of his or her County, within one year preceding the wearing, keeping or carrying thereof, he or she shall be guilty of a misdemeanor, and may be indicted therefor."[141] This licensing procedure did not outright criminalize Black North Carolinians' firearm use, but it was a deliberate effort by the assembly to control the process through which free people of color could be armed. Some counties, like Craven County, went further and issued licenses that could be understood to limit the possessor's firearm use to his or her own lands.[142]

The next decade saw a continuation of these North Carolinians' concerns about armed people of color as the national debates around abolition intensified. Kellie Carter Jackson explains that during this era, during which the nation's political fiber would strain to its breaking point, many Black communities across the North and Midwest formed militia companies, some of which paraded through their towns while wearing smart uniforms and carrying firearms.[143] In North Carolina in 1851, thirty-nine Beaufort County residents chimed in with complaints that the ten-year-old licensing law had proved to be wholly ineffective in keeping firearms out of the hands of untrustworthy free Black people. They reportedly knew of many a free Black man who was able to "prove his character to be good altho he was the meanest villan in the whole county." Further, the petitioners suggested that some free Black people acquired licenses but then flouted the law and did not renew them. These petitioners believed that "owning guns also gives them the ~~power~~ opportunity which they make use of to kill a good many of our cattle and sheep And to corrupt the morals of our slave population by loaning them guns and hunting with them on the Sabbath." The initial word choice of "power," which they edited, is telling. Explaining that free people of color's firearms empowered them was probably too unsettling for these petitioners, even as they tried to push their legislature to action.[144] Even if some of these allegations were true, one should consider that in 1850, enslaved people made up roughly 38 percent of Beaufort County's population, but free people of color composed a paltry 6.5 percent.[145] This approach highlights how these Beaufort petitioners worried about the connections between their free and enslaved Black neighbors, even though the former were such a small portion of the community. The white citizens ended with a commentary on Black gun use generally, that "owning guns has the tendency to encourage their natural slothfull [*sic*] and idle habits."[146]

The Beaufort County men were not the only white North Carolinians who had little faith in the assembly's 1840 licensing law. In November 1856, ten Robeson County men petitioned the legislature to address this and a host of other issues. They wanted the assembly to prevent free people of color from carrying arms unless they were freeholders, "who could give bond with good security" for their good behavior. Further, the petitioners requested that the law keep armed Black freeholders confined to their own property, in an effort to protect white people's property. The Robeson County men wanted a range of additional restrictions on "free negroe or mulattoe": that they be barred from owning multiple dogs, prevented from filing suit in the county or superior courts, and forcibly hired out if they could not pay off their debts.[147]

WHEN THESE SEVERAL PETITIONS from white citizens to their elected representatives are considered together, they highlight how, for much of the first half of the nineteenth century, white North Carolinians worried about armed Black people and saw the state's regulatory efforts as insufficient. These petitioners pushed for additional measures, but their desire for more robust laws over Black North Carolinians was not unique to firearms alone. Consider that in 1842, Raleigh's town commissioners assigned a committee to investigate "the so frequent assembling of the slaves and free colored population" in the capital city. This committee reported back that "the laws in relation to our slave and free negro population, are considered by most of our best citizens as defective." The committee recommended that the commissioners look to the assembly for a solution.[148] White citizens grew increasingly wary of the potential for Black violence and in this mood of heightened vigilance, few preemptive measures taken in the name of public safety were thought to be excessive. The assembly reacted proactively to the threat of slave rebellion and the additional dangers that the abolition movement posed, but it was not exceptional in this regard. In fact, North Carolina's legislative responses were often less forceful than those of many other slaveholding states, but these restrictions nevertheless had a very real impact on the lives and labors of free and enslaved Black North Carolinians.

White North Carolinians believed that while armed Black people's labor could be useful, it was also potentially dangerous and needed to be regulated and supervised by white citizens. Some of these sentiments were fueled by the perception that free and enslaved Black people collaborated with each other at white property holders' expense, by the aggressive and sometimes militant antislavery sentiment that increasingly found its way into the South after 1830, and by enslaved people's resistance. The assembly's efforts to mediate these issues illustrate that while the state government initially trusted individual enslavers to police their own workers, the legislators increasingly came to believe that the county courts were better suited to regulating this contentious community concern. The legislators therefore entrusted each county court to oversee the armed free and enslaved Black people within its jurisdiction and the enslavers who wished to arm their workers, and this local focus made interpersonal relationships a vitally important part of this process. Finally, the state's development of racially specific firearm laws cannot be understood apart from white North Carolinians' persistent fears of Black violence against their bodies and property. White people were far more likely to lose their livestock than their lives—and this could be a real problem in some areas—but enough of them were killed or injured to make the threat of Black people's firearm violence a frightening possibility.

CHAPTER TWO

Enslaved People's Law-Breaking

Through the colonial and antebellum eras, North Carolina's General Assembly recognized that Black people's armed labor was useful both to themselves and to white citizens, and the state's legislators took steps to ensure that this labor was used safely. The assembly passed laws that permitted Black North Carolinians to carry firearms if they were supervised by white people or their county court. The state's efforts to supervise enslaved Black North Carolinians' gun use were insufficient, however. This arrangement rested on the premise that enslavers and other white people would oversee armed enslaved people's behavior and that the bondpeople themselves would adhere to the law. In their everyday lives, however, both Black and white North Carolinians took practical approaches to Black people's armed labor. They often looked to their own needs first, even when those needs violated the law. This dynamic created dramatic tensions across the Old North State.

Many Black North Carolinians disobeyed the state's firearm laws because, in many regards, their guns allowed them to live more comfortably. To circumvent the assembly's restrictions, they acquired their firearms from illegal sources. Enslaved people were both suppliers and consumers in an illegal weapons trade that flourished in some areas. While the state sought to maintain oversight of armed Black people, "one of the exacerbating factors in this illegal trade was the practical limit on the kind of oversight that masters could exercise."[1] Also, some white people took pragmatic approaches to their enslaved laborers and sidestepped the courts to arm their Black laborers for a wide variety of both legitimate and criminal endeavors. This could prove problematic for the armed enslaved people: They might be illegally armed by their enslavers, but the courts might nevertheless hold them accountable for the trespass and punish them accordingly.

Armed enslaved people's labor could be productive, but it threatened white people's lives and property. At times, this was a byproduct of the slave system: When their enslavers did not provide sufficient food, they took up arms and shot livestock in their neighborhoods. When the authorities harried them, they turned their weapons on their pursuers. Further, however, enslaved people's firearm violations ranged from illegal gun possession to well-coordinated murders. They robbed homes and smokehouses, and they sometimes shot the people who tried to stop them. Runaways and maroons also used their weapons to feed themselves, to defend their illegal camps, and to thwart the local authorities' efforts to capture them. Further, enslaved people's firearms enabled them to force dialogue with white people who opposed them. Their weapons gave them leverage that was otherwise difficult to come by. Essentially, while their actions violated the law, enslaved people used their firearms as a counterweight to white North Carolinians' oppressive and state-legitimated authority.

Enslaved people's armed labor on North Carolina farms was often vital to agricultural production. However, enslavers also channeled their bondpeople's armed labor into criminal undertakings. In 1777, to maintain "the peace and harmony of every neighbourhood," North Carolina's General Assembly passed a law requiring that every planter erect "a sufficient fence" around their cultivated fields. The law also shielded from liability individuals whose livestock destroyed any unfenced crops. It stated that farmers who did not fence their fields could not then "with guns, dogs, or otherwise unreasonably chase, worry, maim or kill" any of their neighbors' livestock that had damaged their crops. The legislators presciently added that these fenceless farmers could also not otherwise "cause the same to be done."[2] In early December 1791, John G. Scull, Esq., and a number of other farmers on the New Hanover side of the Cape Fear River complained to the assembly that their neighbors, who farmed alongside them but who lived across the river in Brunswick County, were not fencing-in their fields. Consequently, the petitioners' livestock had wandered in and trampled over or eaten the crops.

Scull's fenceless neighbors were in clear violation of the 1777 law, but these neighbors had escalated the situation when they gave their bondpeople "ammunition and fire arms" and instructed them "to distroy the Cattle + Hoggs" if the animals returned to the unfenced fields. Predictably, the petitioners' livestock returned to the easily accessible bounty of these fields, and the armed slaves proceeded to shoot them. Scull and his fellow petitioners lamented that these illegal, armed actions had nearly depleted their herds. The aggrieved New Hanover planters requested that the assembly "compel the owners of cultivated grounds to keep the same fenced" and that the legislators undertake some measure to prevent "Negroes" from committing "depredations with fire arms and other instruments of distruction to Cattle."[3] The petitioners seemed indifferent to the detail that these enslaved workers were killing these animals at their absentee enslavers' command.

The enslavers in Scull's neighborhood deployed their armed laborers to kill his livestock, just as they might also have used them to protect anything else with value or to hunt. Problematically, the commonness and broad scope of enslaved people's armed labor use made it convenient for some white people to blame Black people for their own violent crimes. Consider that in December 1824, a white man named Alexander Lammon was executed in Bladen County for what was, according to the *Carolina Observer*, "one of the most cold-blooded, deliberate, and atrocious murders" in recent memory. The previous August, Lammon had shot and killed a white boy named James McMillan while the youth was hunting raccoons late one night with his brother, Colin, and two "negro boys." Colin and the two Black companions, who were probably enslaved, were uninjured in the attack, and Colin became the prosecution's primary witness.[4] A minister read Lammon's last words from the hangman's scaffold, and he did not offer a mea culpa. The condemned man maintained his innocence and insisted that it had been one of his slaves who fatally shot and killed the young McMillan. He declared that he had recurring problems with nocturnal thefts from his watermelon patch and that he had suspected that the culprit was a local runaway, simply referred to as "McRee's Sam." Lammon stated that he had armed one of his enslaved workers and then instructed him to stand watch for whoever was stealing the watermelons "but not to use the Gun, except in his own defence." He insisted that the enslaved guard had returned late that night and confessed that he had shot James McMillan, ostensibly after mistaking him for the thieving Sam.[5]

Lammon painted a convincing story that highlighted how quotidian such armed labor would have been and how valuable enslaved workers might need to protect themselves. The evidence against him was too strong, however. Colin McMillan's testimony overwhelmingly pointed to Lammon as his brother's killer, and there was little that the convicted man could do to sway the jurors or public opinion. Nevertheless, the jury would not have found the notion of an enslaver arming a laborer as out of the ordinary. Lammon had hoped this would lend him a credible defense, Colin's testimony notwithstanding, and help him evade punishment at the expense of an innocent enslaved man who would likely have been punished if Lammon's story had stuck.

Enslavers could arm their bondpeople for destructive tasks—or simply blame them for their own misdeeds—but firearms provided Black people with a means to gain some autonomy. Armed and emboldened, they sometimes helped themselves to white farmers' property. Enslaved people ran away and made lives for themselves in North Carolina's swamps and forests, where they could be free from white people's interference. In these hidden spaces, Black outlaws lived off the land but also stole crops and hunted free-ranging livestock in nearby neighborhoods. White critics of Black people's firearm use often blamed this property damage on both free and enslaved Black folks, and

Harper's New Monthly Magazine's 1856 print of Osman, a fugitive in the Great
Dismal Swamp. Courtesy of the Schomburg Center for Research in Black
Culture, New York Public Library, Photographs and Prints Division.

they used it to bolster their arguments for more stringent firearm laws. This was not a wholly irrational concern; but one must consider, too, that some of the property loss was the work of maroons and others who were already living outside of the law and therefore disinclined to follow the assembly's dictates.

These runaways and maroons played a significant role in shaping white North Carolinians' impressions of Black people's mobility, their firearm use, and the threat that they sometimes posed to white people's property. Runaways and maroons were completely unsupervised, mobile, and often armed. Further, they did not always head for the relative safety of free states; many sought instead to carve out lives for themselves in the region's sparsely populated swamps, pocosins, and forests. They remained in North Carolina for myriad reasons, which included the difficulties of traveling out of the South and the fact that many of them had enslaved family members who remained in the area. As Judkin Browning noted, enslaved people "chose to escape slavery but could not completely discard all the positive relationships at home. What was the value of freedom if one had to abandon family, community, and all the social networks one had established?"[6] This behavior was common enough to be predictable; when an enslaved woman named Carry ran away, her enslaver believed that she could be found in New Bern "among her relations"; and Cot's enslaver suspected that he would head for his father's neighborhood and would "also be part of his time" near the plantation where his mother lived.[7] Family and kin could provide runaways with some food and supplies; but many fugitives lived off the land and helped themselves to the smokehouses, corncribs, and livestock in their neighborhoods.

This emphasis on *white* North Carolinians' property reflects the available archival sources. The petitioners from Craven and Halifax Counties who wanted to restrict Black people's firearm use on account of property concerns were all white men. They saw themselves as victims of both free and enslaved Black people's predations. This was an expression of white men's sociopolitical position in North Carolina, not necessarily an accurate reflection of reality. There is no reason to believe that free Black farmers did not also have problems with Black outlaws, despite the lack of direct textual evidence. After all, records clearly indicate that fugitives sometimes harassed other enslaved Black people. In 1828, the *Raleigh Register* noted that a group of runaways in New Hanover County were "committing thefts on an extensive scale, on several plantations ... killing many cattle and frequently robbing slaves, who were obliged to travel the road in that direction." The newspaper added that these victims ultimately got their revenge—they "informed against" the fugitives, and a posse was able to locate and capture several of them.[8]

White people believed that these maroons threatened local property and lives, and that public safety required that they be forcibly eliminated. Scores of newspaper reports demonstrated that these predations happened with enough frequency to cause significant problems in some areas, particularly in the eastern parts of the state. Many white men believed that it was incumbent upon their local communities to address this issue. For instance, on the day after Christmas in 1816, an Edenton newspaper sought to rally "old and young, rich and poor" white men from Chowan and Perquimans Counties for a three-day offensive into the nearby swamps that covered parts of both of their counties, "for the purpose of destroying the wild Vermin that infest them; and breaking up, if possible, the numerous camps of runaway Negroes, who outrage the peace and quiet of the neighborhood, and destroy the stock of the industrious Yeoman."[9] The newspaper editors and many white men recognized this as their shared responsibility.

In 1795, New Hanover's Henry Taylor complained to the General Assembly that "a number of outlying runaway negroes had collected themselves together and were continually committing depredations on the inhabitants of the counties of Brunswick and New Hanover, by killing and destroying their stock and robbing them."[10] Taylor noted that a white man "came upon them in their camp," and they shot and wounded him. This community of runaways also went after another white man named Lewis, who "had been active in taking runaways." Allegedly, they lured him out of his house in the middle of the night by calling out that they had caught a runaway. Lewis fell for this trick, and when he emerged from the house, "they first shot him and then beat him to death." Taylor and other Brunswick and New Hanover men set out to "put a stop to them by taking said negroes or breaking up their camps." The white men failed miserably. While on their campaign, Taylor was keeping watch with a man named Benjamin Howell in an area where they suspected the runaways would pass. Howell fell asleep, and when Taylor startled him awake, he panicked and fired, shooting Taylor through the shoulder, injuring him so badly that he was thereafter unable to work. This threatened his family's livelihood, and he applied to the assembly for relief, which he believed he was entitled to as he had been injured while trying to "suppress an Insurrection of Negroes." The legislators rejected his claim—reasoning that since he was wounded while working for the "immediate advantage of those Counties, in which those depredations were committed" he should look to Brunswick and New Hanover Counties for support.[11] As far as the General Assembly was concerned, Taylor's wounding was a local issue and should have a local solution.

In other instances, these local white volunteers proved to be brutally efficient at their work, as was demonstrated by a similar group effort in 1811 against a group of runaways who lived in Cabarrus's Pocosin, near Edenton. The party of white men stumbled onto the armed maroon camp, which was inhabited by two women and three men. They shot and killed two of the Black men, Arthur and Solomon. The third male runaway managed to escape, despite taking a bullet in the arm. But life as a fugitive was dangerous and often unforgiving, and a few weeks later, he accidentally drowned in the Chowan River while trying to steal fish from some shad nets. His injury might have played a role. It is unclear whether the two fugitive women were armed during the raid, but they were both taken into custody without injury.[12] Professionals also harried the runaways. Slavecatcher J. W. Hamlet and another man named Price were chasing runaways through a marshy part of Nash County and stumbled onto their camp. The white men tried to fire their pistols, either to frighten or harm the Black men, but to no avail—their powder had gotten damp. Undaunted, Hamlet used his "well trained pack of negro dogs" to pin them while Price ran "to the nearest habitation for a gun." The runaways were armed with scythe blades and could neither escape nor attack Hamlet because of his dogs. The *Tarborough Southerner* reported that when Price returned with the borrowed gun, "a regular melee took place, which resulted in the death of one dog and the maiming of a second—the serious if not fatal shooting of one negro through the head—one through the knee—and the, it is supposed, fatal cutting of the third." The Black men's makeshift bladed weapons were no match for their assailants' dogs and gun; but if the Black men had been carrying firearms instead of modified farm tools, this situation would have played out quite differently.[13]

The local authorities could also be harsh when they apprehended runaways and maroons, and the prospect of severe punishment or even execution encouraged some armed fugitives to violently resist instead of surrendering. The newspapers reported that when white men approached the maroon camp in Cabarrus's Pocosin, where Arthur and Solomon were killed, they and their third male companion had each "stood with his musket pointed watching for a favorable opportunity." The report gives no indication as to who fired the first shots of the fatal encounter, but the runaways got the worst of it. They had also been successful in their raiding. The camp allegedly contained "a vast deal of plunder . . . together with a great number of keys" the Black folks had taken from Edenton. The newspaper celebrated the community's efforts to capture the small band who had "nightly infested" the town and who were "encouraged, it is believed, by some of the dram shop gentry on the wharf, that are suffered to vend their articles at an unseasonable hour of the night, and on the Sabbath."[14]

Further, in 1788, a gang of outlaws near Wilmington who had the "audacity to carry fire-arms" and who were "continually committing depredations" on white people's property experienced the full brunt of the state's ire. One of the fugitives, a man "commonly known by the description of burnt mouth Peter," stole some poultry from a white man named Kenon. The angry farmer tracked Peter to another plantation and confronted him. Peter had a loaded musket and threatened to shoot Kenon, but the white man managed to wrestle the gun away. After a brief scuffle, Kenon and an apprentice overcame and captured the runaway. Peter's "infamous character" was reportedly well known, and he was convicted and executed. Aside from the robbery and what was likely an attempt to kill Kenon, the jury was moved to sentence Peter to death because he had fled from his enslaver several times prior, and also because he belonged to a notorious armed gang.[15] The authorities intended for his execution to dissuade others from resorting to a similarly armed and unsupervised lifestyle—as the 1715 slave code described it, he was "publickly [*sic*] executed to the Terror of other Slaves."[16] Local authorities sought to bring illegally armed and unsupervised Black people like "burnt mouth Peter" to account in order to deter potential future transgressors; but these outlaws' firearms allowed them to aggressively defend their rough-hewn and deeply valued independence. Maroons used their illegal weapons to feed themselves, but they also endangered the safety of those local white people who sought to regain control over them or kill them. Runaways who broke into houses or smokehouses and carried off their white neighbors' valuables could not be easily apprehended and corrected if they were armed. Their guns assisted them in remaining at liberty.

As a result of armed fugitives' defensive power, the county-level authorities could not always use force in response to the threat that they presented. The "scouring parties" and executions were part of a wider range of tactics that relied on local white men's support. Consider the experiences of an enslaved Craven County man named Tom. In the spring of 1829, he fled his enslaver, Church Chapman, and armed himself. He then roamed the countryside killing hogs and committing other crimes, much "to the terror of the citizens." Tom's unsupervised lifestyle threatened white property holders and stood as a glaring example of lawlessness in the county. Justices of the peace Charles J. Nelson and William S. Blackledge, both of whom were enslavers themselves, responded to Tom's "terror" by placing an announcement in the newspaper that commanded in the name of the state that he "surrender himself and return home to his owner."[17]

The justices appealed to three different stakeholders to halt Tom's destruction of white Craven County residents' property: the fugitive himself, the county's law enforcement officials, and then the county's white citizenry. First, they tried to persuade Tom to "surrender himself" of his own volition, which was the safest and least expensive option. Most importantly, it would have signaled Tom's acquiescence to the rule of law. Next, the justices called on Sheriff Elijah Clark, who embodied the county's coercive power, to "take with him such power of this County as he may think necessary" and apprehend Tom if he refused to surrender himself.[18] This was a public demonstration of the local authorities' resolve to preserve the peace. Craven County's officials would not stand idly by while Tom roamed the countryside, a nuisance to white property holders. Last, antebellum North Carolinians saw law enforcement as a communal concern. Blackledge and Nelson reminded the public that because Tom had been outlawed, anyone who crossed his path could "kill and destroy" the runaway "by such means as he, she or they, may think fit, without accusation or impeachment of any crime or offence."[19] This community effort was rooted in the "hue and cry" of English Common Law, which dictated that after a crime was committed, an effort should be made to "raise the neighborhood" to pursue the perpetrators "with horse and foot."[20] White North Carolinians took this seriously. The *Newbern Sentinel* printed a report on recent trials in August 1827, with the bold addition: "A vigilant police is essential to the execution of the laws. The execution of the laws is essential to good order, and good order is essential to our security. The wicked and disorderly must be opposed, and if not by the police, it will have to be done with our muskets. It is not expected that the violent and disorderly are to be exterminated, but they can be kept in check: and with the assistance of the *posse comitatis*, we are determined to do it."[21] The idea reiterated to white men was that they had a responsibility to help enforce the law in their community instead of leaving it to the flimsy local law enforcement apparatus. Further, it warned Tom that he would be putting his life on the line if he continued living in quasi-freedom. Fugitives' enslavers also appealed to the community for assistance. They sometimes called attention to the fugitive's potential destructiveness by going before the justices of the peace and swearing an oath that he or she had run away and was "committing depredations" in the neighborhood, threatening the peace.[22]

Through these actions, the Craven County justices of the peace marshaled the community to stop Tom. His plundering was problematic in and of itself, but Blackledge and Nelson believed that the situation would be remedied if Tom were to return to Chapman's authority. But if he refused to submit, the public good required that he be forcibly returned or killed. The justices' charge that the people in the neighborhood could kill Tom stands as a stark reminder that the county authorities saw him as a threat to their community. His fate is unknown. He may have successfully evaded the authorities. Sheriff Clark may have captured him and forcibly returned him to his enslaver. Tom may have also been killed while laying out, as some folks were. Further, he may have decided to return to Chapman's plantation on his own. What is clear, however, is that Tom's status as an armed runaway caused great consternation in his Craven County neighborhood, and the local authorities believed that the whole community needed to marshal its resources to prevent him from damaging its property.

White men did not always need their local authorities' encouragement to act against the unsupervised and armed enslaved laborers in their neighborhoods. They recognized that armed Black outlaws threatened white people's property and lives, but they also recognized that the white community's state-legitimized violence could eliminate these threats. In 1821, planter Durant Hatch wrote a letter to his friend Ebenezer Pettigrew to relate an encounter with some armed runaways who had been "lurking" on Hatch's plantation. They had been hiding out in the neighborhood and killing his hogs for about a year. Hatch, who enslaved about sixty people himself, was out hunting on his land when he stumbled onto a camp where three armed fugitives were living. He immediately tried to take control of the situation, and as he later explained to Pettigrew via letter, he demanded that the armed squatters "Drop their Guns or I would kill one on the Spot." The Black men quickly took cover behind the trees and explained to Hatch that "we cannot Drop our guns but if you will not Kill us we will lower their mussels & come to you if you will give your word you will not kill nor try to take us." Hatch agreed and two of the fugitives, whom the planter recognized as men Pettigrew enslaved, approached him. He recognized that this was a tense truce, as the Black men kept their firearms "in good order to defend them selves."[23]

These Black men's firearms created a situation wherein the planter had to engage them in discussion rather than force his will on them. Hatch tried to convince the pair to return to Pettigrew, but only one of the men would even speak to him. That young man, who was only about twenty years old, "Bitterly refused" Hatch's entreaties and declared that he would rather die as a fugitive than return to slavery. He informed Hatch that even if Pettigrew, his enslaver, were also present and "had as good a gun as yours appear to be & I had nothing to Defend myself I wou'd not be Taken alive by you." Fortunately for this young runaway and his comrades, he *did* have something to defend himself with. He resisted Hatch's efforts even after the planter tried to convince him that his illegal lifestyle would get him killed. The young man did not need Hatch's lecture about the dangers of marronage, however. He had already been shot at in an earlier encounter with another white person.[24] Hatch realized that he could not convince the three Black men to return to their enslavers' authority, so he ordered them to leave his lands by the end of the day. This was a ploy, however. He explained to Pettigrew that he wanted to rush home "and get some of my Friends & take them before they left their Camp," but by the time he returned with reinforcements, the men were already gone.[25]

It is not difficult to imagine that if the three fugitives had been unarmed or if Hatch had been out hunting with a party of white men, this encounter would have ended very differently. Hatch offered to mediate the runaways' return to their enslavers, but he clearly had no intention of allowing them to continue living armed and unsupervised, especially not on his land. White North Carolinians understood that fugitives posed a threat to white people's property and lives, but armed Black outlaws were also an affront to the peace because they rejected the white power structure's monopoly on violence.[26] The fugitives' guns created space for a dialogue with Hatch, and this ultimately allowed them to escape. Consider that when a posse of white men raided a camp of maroons who had been "committing thefts on an extensive scale" in 1828, the white men caught four of the outlaws. Three of them were shot and wounded during the attack. The runaways were unarmed at the time because other members of their camp had taken their shared firearms off on some other business.[27] Those fugitives might have been able to force a different outcome if they had been armed when the posse arrived.

Antebellum Southern morality played a significant role in how white people understood fugitives. Many Christians of the period believed that violations of the law were similar to moral sin, in that any morally upright person could lapse into crime just as easily as one might slip into sin; but in either case, the fallen could be accepted back into the fold if he or she repented.[28] In this socioreligious framework, both moral sinners and people who broke the law had to acknowledge their wayward acts and atone, at which point the transgressor could reconnect with the church and the local community. According to this worldview, these maroons were essentially living in an unrepentant state because their crimes could not be completed until they remorsefully returned to their enslavers' service and authority. North Carolinians who ascribed to this religious doctrine would have seen these unapologetic armed Black outlaws' firearm use as a sign of their continued bad behavior that required correction.

Firearm use and violations of the gun law were subjective. Unregulated Black firearm use could be a substantial problem for many white North Carolinians, and sometimes also for Black folks, but this was not always the case. In an audacious incident in the spring of 1824, six armed runaways attacked two slave traders named Whitfield and Tomkins in Hertford County as the white men neared the Chowan River with their coffle. The armed Black men emerged from the woods "presenting and snapping their guns" and forcefully demanding that the traders surrender the captives in their possession. The white men had set out from Elizabeth City with eleven enslaved people, had taken on six others at the Gates County jail, and were headed back to their home state of Georgia. Dubiously, the newspaper reported that the traders were unarmed and therefore "compelled to fly for their lives, leaving their negroes, wagon, and baggage, in the possession of the robbers." The *Star, and North Carolina State Gazette* reported that the armed Black bandits could convince only two people in the coffle to join them, whom they then unshackled and provided with weapons before fleeing the scene together.[29] One of the "robbers," an enslaved man named Jim, had a brother in Whitfield and Tomkins's coffle, whom they rescued. Jim's brother had been banished from the Old North State for a horrific murder he had committed a few months prior.[30]

Firearms were more than instruments of physical violence, of course. They could also be used to intimidate people, and these bold Black men in Hertford County used them in just that manner: "presenting and snapping" their weapons. They could have shot and killed Tomkins and Whitfield but instead just used the weapons to frighten and threaten them. In another example of armed threats, in 1812, an enslaved man named Elias got into an argument with his enslaver, Dixon Bogg, about Elias's family, probably because Bogg planned to sell him. Bogg explained that Elias came to his house one night and "was very impertinant to me, took by f[hole in the page . . . probably "force"] a double barrelled gun from me, and went off," though he added that the weapon was unloaded. Emanuell, another man Bogg enslaved, spoke with Elias and later told the authorities that Elias and Bogg "had fallen out . . . that he had taken the Gun from his Master" and that he was "willing to die + would die." They moved to another location where Elias "cleaned the Gun + loaded both barrels with powder + shot" before telling Emanuell to "go to Master + tell him that I will die his property." His armed position offered a threat to anyone who might try to capture or sell him, and while he could have tried to kill Boggs, Elias instead ran off, never to be seen again.[31]

Beyond intimidation, firearms could also convey messages by injuring another person's animals. In the autumn of 1817, Easter Lytle, a free woman of color, complained to the court that during the previous spring, someone shot and "severely wounded" a mare that belonged to her and her daughter Nancy. The following week, someone shot and killed her dog. Easter believed that Francis Lytle Jr., a "young man of Colour," had "wickedly and willfully committed" both shootings. The jurors charged Francis, whom they framed as "a person of a wanton + mischievous disposition + disposed to break the public peace," with shooting Easter's dog but did not comment on the horse.[32] While the nature of Francis's problem with Easter and the precise nature of their relationship are not clear, Francis sent a message via this violence against her animals.

Firearms were also used to threaten people directly, of course. In the 1824 incident with the slave traders, it seems far more plausible that the armed Black men took Whitfield and Tomkins by surprise, and the outnumbered and outgunned white men decided to surrender their captives rather than risk their lives in a shootout. Further, consider that while the raiders were perhaps able to convince only two of the newly liberated people to join them, an alternative explanation might be that they had refused to accept the others. They were not on a humanitarian mission, after all. Raids like this were extremely rare, but this one showcased how firearms could level the playing field for some enslaved Black people. It would have been a much more difficult and probably a much bloodier affair for the outlaws to have attempted their raid without their firearms, especially if Whitfield and Tomkins were armed, which was likely the case. Even the editors of the *Star, and North Carolina State Gazette* were skeptical—they cushioned their report that Whitfield and Tomkins were "unarmed" with "as we are informed." Willis was described as "a fine athletic fellow, full six feet three inches high"—the two traders were just as likely armed but frightened into inaction.[33] Also consider that the coverage of such an audacious raid reiterated to many white North Carolinians that while armed and unsupervised enslaved laborers threatened white people's property and could revolt, they also presented the specter of dangerously unpredictable violence and disorder.

The raid on the Hertford County coffle was not the first time that some of these particular armed outlaws had engaged in well-organized violence. Jim and Jack were also part of a group that killed planter Elisha Cross in neighboring Gates County in January 1824. Jack, Jim, and another fugitive named Elisha were caught stealing people's meat and the authorities locked them up in the county jail. Soon after, however, they "broke out and armed themselves" and the court declared them outlaws.[34] Reportedly, "no one was more active" than Cross in pursuing the Black men, who had been engaged in local theft for about two years. Cross's efforts against them "had so excited their resentment" that they threatened to kill him at the first opportunity. Further, at some point Cross spotted Jim trying to steal bacon and personally tried to stop him. He was unable to capture the runaway but shot him in the thigh. It is unclear, but this was likely after Elisha, Jack, and Jim had been outlawed. Cross's injuring of Jim further stoked the fugitives' simmering animosity toward him.[35]

The Black men had their opportunity for revenge on the night of January 23, 1824, several months after they had been outlawed, as Cross walked home from an auction with some of his neighbors. Armed as they were, the outlaws set an ambush that foreshadowed how they would later attack the slave traders' coffle. Cross left his friends and turned alone onto the path leading to his house. The conspirators waylaid him when he was only 400 yards from the relative safety of his house.[36] Jim shot the planter with a shotgun—the load of a ball and goose shot hit him in the lower back and hip—and then cut his throat. Some newspapers reported that he was shot twice—once in the lower back with a large ball and goose shot and then again in the chest with another ball—and attributed this description to the coroner's report.[37] The most dramatic newspaper accounts reported that, beyond the shooting, the attackers had expressed their contempt for Cross by mutilating him. His wife, and perhaps some of their seven children, discovered him and found that "one of his thumbs was also nearly cut off" and that he had "diverse stabs and cuts on many other parts of his body." Further, "his throat [was] cut nearly from ear to ear, and his mouth cut on both sides as far as the jaw bones would suffer the knife to penetrate." The murder was so horrendous that local tavern owner and enslaver Henry Gilliam offered a $600 reward for anyone who would capture the killers, dead or alive.[38]

The fugitives involved in Cross's murder were narrowly captured in Petersburg, Virginia, the following June, while trying to escape. Jim, Jack, and two other men named Sam and Willis (who may have been Jim's brother) identified themselves as free men of color and tried to book passage on a ship headed for Richmond, where they hoped to pass as free and secure work. The vessel's captain was suspicious of them—perhaps they were nervous or stood out too much—and after he checked their papers, he knew that something was amiss. He allowed them to board, but once they were below deck, he locked them in and summoned law enforcement. When the authorities took the Black men into custody, they were still heavily armed, "one with a very large gun, the barrel of which had been broken in two, about half way; it was loaded with shot, slugs, old buttons, &c.—Another had a pistol, and a third a most dangerous knife, evidently intended for the purposes of a dirk, having been ground to a very sharp point."[39] This sawed-off shotgun was an unconventional but formidable weapon—the modification rendered it useless for hunting but highly destructive against people at close range. When the authorities interrogated them, Jack told them that Jim had murdered Elisha Cross. Jim was executed on November 12, 1824, for "first shooting . . . and then barbarously mangling" the planter with a knife. He reportedly confessed at the gallows.[40]

Enslaved people acquired illegal weapons for many reasons, including to harm themselves. Slavery required a great deal of violence to maintain the fiction that people could be property; and within the system, enslaved workers hurt their enslavers' pockets when they intentionally injured themselves. This self-harm was sometimes far more poignant than resistance, however. Enslavement took a heavy toll, despite the support that communities and families were sometimes able to provide, and people responded to it in numerous ways. Some chose to take their own lives. This self-harm had an impact on other people, often tragically. Sampson, an enslaved Randolph County man, took his own life in 1833. He propped up a rifle between two rocks, used a stick to manipulate the trigger, and shot himself in the head. Sampson was one of eleven people that John H. Armistead enslaved—and his violent death probably had a pronounced impact on this small community.[41] In 1849, an enslaved Fayetteville man named Sam tried to shoot both his wife and mother-in-law, the latter of whom he injured, though both women survived. After this frightful domestic violence, he then put the muzzle against his head, "pushed the trigger with his toe, and killed himself instantly."[42] It is not always clear why enslaved people like Sampson and Sam made these decisions, and the details of their lives are lost to the historical record. Nonetheless, their illegal guns were a deadly and effective means to this end, much as they remain to the present day.

Enslaved workers' criminal firearm use was often a point of conflict between Black and white North Carolinians. The enslavers' society was structured to keep Black people in subordinate positions, and if they stepped outside of the expected boundaries, the state and white citizens often saw them as a threat. This perception increased the chances that any interaction might become violent. Still, the antebellum social landscape was complicated, and despite these tensions, Black and white North Carolinians sometimes cooperated in criminal endeavors. For instance, one late summer night in 1814, four men—a free man of color, an enslaved Black man, and two white men—"inhumanly murdered" Col. John Clayton in Tyrrell County.[43] The attackers shot Clayton from the cover of a cornfield outside of his house. One of the white men fired the ball and eight large pieces of shot that tore into the victim's chest but all four of the attackers were armed. Clayton had previously served in the General Assembly, but at the time of his murder, he was serving the local community as a "respectable and vigilent Magistrate." Some locals believed that his "inflexible discharge" of his duties in that office had made him "obnoxious to a lawless set of beings . . . in his neighborhood" and provoked them to commit the "horrid murder."[44]

Many white North Carolinians would have been particularly disturbed by this episode because it highlighted the inadequacies in the assembly and county court's efforts to regulate armed Black people. Aside from the problem of the interracial cooperation in this episode of armed lawlessness, this quartet had channeled their violence to kill a representative of the state and local government who was attempting to enforce the law. The assembly's laws were supposed to protect white citizens from Black violence and, to some extent, to maintain racial separation between these two demographic groups. Although they were probably not conscious of it themselves, this "lawless set of beings" engaged in violence that both shattered that arrangement and struck a blow at the personal embodiment of the law's power in their neighborhood.

The men who killed Clayton were probably a gang of outlaws, who may have been bound together in ways beyond the joint execution of their crimes. Other white men hired enslaved people with the clear goal of engaging in criminality. This collaborative lawbreaking required a very high degree of trust between the parties involved. Nonetheless, some white people's predisposition to fear armed Black men could mask other white people's involvement in violent gun crimes. Consider the murder of storekeeper Henry Culpepper in 1823. The white Camden County man was killed at his home on the Great Dismal Swamp Canal, the victim of an interstate criminal plot that partly relied on Black men's armed labor. Culpepper's assailants made two attempts, the first of which occurred on June 26, 1823. The newspapers reported that "several negroes" knocked on his door and then fired a shot through it when they heard him approaching it from the inside. The bullet passed harmlessly through the door, but Culpepper dropped loudly to his floor as if he had been hit. The attackers fired twice more through the closed door and then fled. Fortunately for Culpepper, neither he nor any of his five dependents was injured during the shooting.[45]

The danger had not passed, however. Culpepper was assaulted again about two months later. Just before daylight he was "called upon by a negro man, who had slept in the house that night, to furnish some liquor." Culpepper left the house to get his boarder a drink from his store, but two gunshots blasted out of the darkness and cut him down before he got there. More than a dozen pieces of lead hit a post behind which he happened to be passing, but seven others found their mark. The shots inflicted massive damage to Culpepper's thigh, and despite a physician's efforts to treat him, he died after four days of "much suffering."[46] The boarder who asked for the drink made himself scarce immediately after the shooting, and the newspapers reported that he was "strongly suspected of being connected" with the killers.[47]

The newspapers suggested that Henry Culpepper had been targeted by a group of Black men who lived in the Great Dismal Swamp—presumably local runaways. This broad natural expanse covered parts of Currituck, Camden, Pasquotank, Perquimans, Chowan, and Gates Counties, and many maroons lived within it. The truth was not nearly as black and white, however. At the time of the shooting, the Culpepper family was involved in a land dispute with a white man named Willoughby Foreman, who lived across the nearby state line in Norfolk County, Virginia.[48] Foreman was a problem on the North Carolina side of the border, and he intimidated Camden County's authorities by being "continually under Arms so that no officer" would confront him or his associates. Whenever Foreman thought the North Carolina authorities had steeled their nerves to move against him, he would "fly back" to Virginia. He was probably the person who shot and killed Culpepper, but he had also paid two enslaved Black men to try before he took the matter into his own hands.[49]

An individual who was familiar with the murder, and whom Foreman had threatened, wrote a letter to North Carolina Governor Gabriel Holmes to recount the conspiracy behind Culpepper's death. Foreman had apparently organized seven white men to help him secure the disputed tract of land "by the force of arms," and he had promised each of them a share of the property in return. This source declared that Foreman had gathered his men at his house "with arms and ammunition" and told them how he had "struck Henry Culpepper with a stick + thrown him Down and flogged him well and tuck his gun away from him." One of Foreman's accomplices proposed that the group should swear to never betray each other and then shoot Culpepper, but Foreman presented a more cautious plan. He told his accomplices that he would pay $50 to have Culpepper killed. Foreman had kept Culpepper's firearm after he had beaten him up and stolen it, and one night he gave the weapon "to a nigro" to kill the disarmed storekeeper. This resulted in the initial, failed murder attempt, during which Culpepper was apparently nearly killed with his own gun.[50] Foreman recovered Culpepper's firearm from the unsuccessful Black shooter and reloaded it with both balls and buckshot. He then gave it to Tony Wordins, a Black man who was enslaved by Jessy Moris. The unnamed informant told Governor Holmes that Foreman had paid both Wordins and another enslaved man, Willoughby Corpy, to kill Culpepper. Corpy might have been the shooter in the first attack, or he might have participated in the successful second attempt. When suspicions about the Culpepper murder turned to Foreman, he deflected them by saying "it was not him But he new very well who it was." Nonetheless, the grand jury charged Foreman with the murder and his white accomplices with aiding and abetting him. It made no mention of Foreman's Black associates, despite the letter to Governor Holmes, which alleged that he had paid and armed two of them to kill Henry Culpepper.[51]

The newspapers' focus on the Black men in the attacks on Culpepper highlights white North Carolinians' suspicions and fears of armed Black people. This was heightened by the storekeeper's proximity to the Great Dismal Swamp. Some historians estimate that there were hundreds of Black fugitives living in the swamp at some point.[52] There were enough armed Black men in those otherwise uninhabited spaces for the newspapers' readers to believe that Culpepper could have been attacked by some of them. Additionally, Foreman saw these Black men's armed labor as personally useful, even if for illegal purposes. He both provided the firearm and paid them for their labor. At least one of Foreman's armed Black accomplices was enslaved by another person, even though Foreman enslaved more than thirty people himself whom he might have thus employed.[53] Foreman likely had a social or business relationship with Wordins and Corpy. Perhaps they had even conspired together on previous crimes. Whatever the nature of their relationship, Forman trusted these Black men enough to include them in his conspiracy to kill Henry Culpepper and to arm them.

In 1822, the year before Culpepper's murder, the General Assembly had passed a law to "encourage the apprehension of runaway slaves in the Great Dismal Swamp." The legislators admitted, however, that it was "dangerous and difficult" to capture these people who were committing depredations "to the great injury of the citizens of the neighboring counties."[54] This law specifically targeted those who had been hiding out in the swamp for longer than three months. It relied on community-based law enforcement and incentivized white men in the neighborhood to take up the task; any captured fugitives' enslavers were required to pay the capturers a reward equivalent to one-quarter of the enslaved person's assessed value. This law was repealed in December 1823, but the swamp continued to provide a home for many fugitives.[55] Under these worrying circumstances, Culpepper's murder would have stoked white North Carolinians' concerns about armed Black strangers in those swamp-adjacent neighborhoods, even though it was plotted by another white man.

Enslaved workers who carried arms without permission could be unsettling to other Black people, too. Luke, a man whose enslaver sold him from Wilmington down to Georgia, escaped and made his way back to North Carolina within two months. He snuck into his former enslaver's home, where another laborer watched him steal a firearm and ammunition before fleeing. Their enslaver raised a search party when he discovered what had happened, but to no avail. Several months later, however, another enslaved person who had himself been lying out, returned to the enslaver and explained that Luke was in the area but heavily armed with a rifle, two pistols, and a sword. Luke, however, was finally done in by his hunger. He had gone to another plantation to find food, and an enslaved woman fed him; but when he fell asleep, she alerted her enslaver. The white man called two neighbors to assist him, and grabbing their rifles, they went after Luke. It is not clear if this enslaved woman knew him beforehand, but Luke's presence worried her. As Tony Kaye has noted of enslaved folks in Mississippi, those who reported strangers were often thinking about "the dangers to their own family," either through their enslaver's ire or the strangers' potential for "theft, intimidation, and force." The three white men surrounded Luke and demanded his surrender, but he called back that "he would not; and if they tried to take him, he would kill one of them; for if he gave up, he knew they would kill him, and he was determined to sell his life as dearly as he could." Using their numerical advantage, they outmaneuvered Luke and fatally shot him in the head.[56]

Many of North Carolina's fugitives carried firearms and, like Luke, they sometimes used deadly resistance to maintain their precarious independence, which made tracking them a dangerous endeavor for everyone involved. The armed enslaved people were more likely to get killed in the process, but so too were the white men who chose to pursue them. The slave hunters had to be willing to risk their lives, and at times they lost that wager. In 1824, three white men on a Bladen County slave patrol went out to "put an end to a negro carousal" when they came across three fugitives. A fight broke out when the patrollers confronted the Black men and tried to take them into custody. One of the patrolmen seized a fugitive named Jack, which prompted the runaway to draw a large knife to defend himself. The two men fought hand-to-hand, and Jack cut the patrolman before the white man wrested the knife away. As their fight continued, Jack was mortally wounded with his own knife. One of Jack's comrades, however, then shot and killed the patroller, and the two surviving Black men escaped.[57]

Also, consider that in the summer of 1856, a group of white citizens sought to clear the descriptively named "Big Swamp" between Robeson and Bladen Counties of the many "runaways of bad and daring character" who made their homes in it. The band of maroons had been killing "all kinds of stock" and some white people believed that they were "dangerous to all persons" in the area. The white men also did not know which enslavers claimed many of these laborers, which suggests that some of the men were not originally from the neighborhood. When the patrol arrived, the maroons were unimpressed, however, and gave the white men a warm reception. They opened fire and grievously wounded David Lewis, one of the Bladen County men. After shooting Lewis, the Black men then taunted the disoriented patrol, "cursing + swearing and telling them to come on they were ready for them again." The patrollers had no desire to continue their expedition after this resolute demonstration of force. They beat a hasty retreat, though they were "anxious and willing to *catch*, or *kill*, these negroes." The injured man died the next day, and his father and several others pleaded with the governor to offer "a sufficient reward" to "induce persons to spend their time in hunting said negroes."[58] The white men still saw these maroons as a problem, but they were afraid that they could not resolve it on their own. They turned instead to the power of the state for help.

These potential dangers, though sporadic in occurrence, fostered anxiety among white North Carolinians who, during the late antebellum era, also worried that the armed fugitives in their neighborhoods had been both equipped and encouraged by meddling abolitionists. In 1851, the *Fayetteville Observer* printed R. F. Murphy's letter to the editor that addressed the national repercussions of "the great question now agitating the North and the South, viz: slavery." Murphy represented J. Buchanan, a former Wake County resident who had since relocated to Mississippi but who maintained property in both states. Through his letter, Murphy related his efforts to recover two of the men Buchanan had enslaved in North Carolina. He explained that he had hired a slave catcher named Bryan from Moore County and that they picked up the runaways' trail with the aid of his "four powerful bloodhounds." The Black men were still laid out in the neighborhood, and the well-trained dogs overtook them after a "hard run of several miles." The runaways were armed, and one of them fired a load of buckshot at Bryan but missed, and the slave hunters took them into custody.[59]

Murphy framed this endeavor in the context of an abolitionist threat. Murphy explained that once the enslaved workers were captured, they confessed that they had been aided by white reformers and "supplied with arms, wherewith to defend themselves." He declared that the identities of these white supporters were known, and that "the punishment they are deserving of" would soon be meted out. Murphy's avowal that "those pretended philanthropists— the abolitionists"—had armed the men Buchanan enslaved helped to fuel white North Carolinians' anxieties about meddling antislavery advocates and unsupervised Black firearm use in their neighborhoods.[60] Armed fugitives

An 1879 version of C. H. Reed's engraving "A Bold Stroke for Freedom," which appeared in William Still's book *The Underground Railroad* (Philadelphia: Porter and Coats, 1872). Courtesy of the Library of Congress, Prints and Photographs Division.

were a constant problem, but those runaways who had been supplied by abolitionists (or were perceived to have been) were even more alarming. This politicization of their quest for freedom was even more salient after Turner's rebellion and the increasingly radical abolitionism in the decades after 1830.

In the spring of 1859, a "party of gentlemen" pursuing an armed maroon through Halifax County also had a violent confrontation with the man they were chasing, who—as the newspaper explained—"had been outlawed and defied the world." The fugitive was one of the fifty people enslaved by John Reeves Jones Daniel—a wealthy planter, lawyer, and former six-term US congressman—who had been laid out for an astounding two or three years before this party confronted him.[61] The outlaw defiantly killed one of his pursuers' dogs. One of the white men, John H. Ponton, Esq., rode ahead of the other slave hunters to cut the fugitive off and then found himself face to face with the defiant Black man. The fugitive's shotgun reportedly misfired three times before Ponton shot and killed him.[62] In these incidents, fugitives used their firearms to resist capture, with varying degrees of success. Sometimes the chase turned deadly for the white pursuers, but in others, the runaways themselves paid the ultimate price. The fact that both parties could be carrying weapons raised the stakes and made both running away and slave hunting dangerous endeavors. The heightened risk of violence notwithstanding, armed runaways' firearms also provided them with an effective means to resist pursuing slave catchers. These armed fugitives might have threatened white people's property, but they also posed a very serious threat to anyone who might try to force them back into enslavement.

The potential for armed violence did not emanate solely from armed fugitives—at times it came from bondmen who remained within their enslavers' households and ostensibly under their control. The county courts scrutinized which enslavers could arm specific workers, but this layer of oversight could not prevent enslaved people from accessing firearms on their own. Many enslavers, and other people in the antebellum era for that matter, did not secure their firearms under lock and key, and enslaved laborers could sometimes access these without much difficulty. Also, some enslavers were at ease with their own vetted bondpeople's access to firearms. Before they could feel safe in their households and neighborhoods where some of them were outnumbered by enslaved laborers, they had to believe that their control over their workers or the slaves' faithfulness was a sufficient safeguard against violence. As a result of these sentiments, firearms were more readily available in North Carolina households than might be immediately apparent. Nonetheless, situations like these could have grave consequences for both Black and white people.

At about nine o'clock in the evening one Wednesday in May 1850, Samuel R. Potter, Esq., and his family were startled by a loud sound in their Wilmington mansion. The wealthy planter had gone to bed early, but after the commotion, he heard the voice of a woman he had enslaved scold, "Who has put cannon crackers in the room to disturb the white people?" But then she cried out, "My Lord some one has kill'd my child!" at which point he rushed to investigate. He found Annette, a young enslaved woman, "lying dead upon the floor, a large charge of buckshot having passed into her brain." Her mother, whom he had heard complaining about what she thought was a festive noisemaker, and her brother had been the first to arrive at the horrific scene.[63] Annette's killer had already fled the house, but Potter could see that his own shotgun was the murder weapon—he noticed that it was not in its usual place. The circumstances implicated a man named Dick, who was enslaved by Joshua G. Wright, Esq., and he was taken into custody and examined by the magistrates.[64] After a three-day investigation, the court acknowledged that "many suspicious facts were proven" but that there was insufficient evidence to bring Dick to trial, so he was released. Wright nevertheless "sent his slave off," which spoke volumes about his confidence in Dick's innocence, and the *Fayetteville Observer* applauded Wright's decision to do so.[65]

While important for Annette and her community, the relevance of whether Dick was guilty of this brutal murder is of little consequence to the larger discussion of firearm security and availability. Potter did not believe that his household's safety required him to keep his gun or ammunition locked away. He simply stored his firearm in the corner of an upstairs room. The planter trusted his Black and white dependents, but his insecure storage of the loaded shotgun allowed an outsider to access it and turn it against his household. Also, while Wright probably could not have anticipated Dick's murderous actions, he had been supportive of supervised firearm use for enslaved laborers several years prior to Annette's murder. In 1841, he and James T. Miller signed William L. Ashe's bond to arm a man Ashe enslaved.[66] It is unclear whether any of Potter's bondpeople were licensed to use a firearm, but the casual manner in which he stored his gun illustrates why the assembly wanted the county courts to manage enslavers' arming of their workers. The lawmakers believed that maintaining the public peace required far more strenuous oversight than many enslavers were willing or able to provide.

Thomas Jenkins's household in Raleigh offers another example of the problems that arose from white people's indifferent gun storage. Ellen, a young woman whom Jenkins enslaved, was alleged to have shot and killed the young white woman Virginia Frost, who was visiting his household in the fall of 1855. Seventeen-year-old Frost's father was one of Jenkins's coworkers on the Petersburg and Weldon Railroad.[67] At the time of the shooting, she was alone in the backyard, and Ellen was scouring floors in the house's back rooms while the Jenkins family and the rest of their guests were in the front. The white people suspected that Ellen shot the visitor for "reproving her for insolent language." After the shooting, Ellen climbed over the back fence and tried to escape into Raleigh's streets; but she was soon captured.[68] She explained to the jury of inquest that she was "going out of the house with the gun" and tripped over a dog that caused her to accidentally discharge the weapon. In another statement, Ellen noted that she had tripped over a piece of wood while carrying the firearm.[69]

The *Fayetteville Observer* reported that the "medical men in attendance" examined the massive damage done to the victim and determined that the weapon had been only about a foot away from Frost's head when it was fired. The instantly fatal shot had taken off "nearly the whole of the back part of the head" with so much force that Frost's "brains lay strewn all over that part of the yard."[70] Wake County's Superior Court ultimately decided not to prosecute Ellen—the grand jury rejected the indictment a few weeks after the shooting. The newspapers speculated that it "must have appeared that the shooting was accidental."[71] The court's decision was not, in and of itself, unusual. In the antebellum era both free and enslaved Black people were sometimes acquitted or had charges dropped—even for violent crimes against white citizens—if the evidence was lacking or if the court perceived them to have greater social credit than the white plaintiff.[72] Dick, for example, benefited from the former after he killed Annette. The newspapers offered no reason as to why Ellen might have been carrying the firearm out of the house without her enslaver's supervision or consent. This silence suggests that both Jenkins and the newspapers' readers would not have found her carrying the gun to be a problem and that Jenkins did not keep it locked up. Ellen's story about the accidental discharge was accepted by the assembled jury of inquest as another one of the "dreadful accidents resulting from the careless use of fire-arms, which so often cut short human life and carry distress into the bosom of families," and that some people believed were all too common.[73]

In January 1841, on John Harget's Craven County plantation, an enslaved man named Joe "went to the House + got the gun" and then went out to shoot crows. He then reloaded the weapon and left it "in David's House." He told Alfred, another enslaved man, that "there is only a load of small shot in the gun, not to be afraid of shooting her," and then left. A few minutes later, Rigdon Lewis and David Manly, two of Harget's laborers were horseplaying with the gun in the kitchen outbuilding, when it accidentally discharged into the left side of Lewis's face. John Harget told Caleb Bell, the coroner, that "one of the Boys was hired—the other bound," but the coroner did not record Rigdon Lewis's racial identity in his report, nor did he record David Manly's for that matter. This was typical when dealing with *white* people; nonetheless, other records clearly mark Lewis as "a free boy of colour." He appeared with his two brothers and sister—Jim, Amos, and Abby—in the apprenticeship records after their father's death. The court ordered that the four youths "be provided with suitable masters or mistresses" and their next of kin be notified.[74] Rigdon Lewis's siblings were not in the room when he was killed, but they were probably within earshot. His violent death was an accident but would have nonetheless been deeply traumatic for his siblings: Their father had been *murdered* by John Moseley, another free Black man, less than two years prior, which had led to their shared apprenticeships.[75]

Alfred and an enslaved woman named Abeline, who was cooking, were in the kitchen when Rigdon Lewis was killed. Alfred explained that his back had been turned to Lewis and Manly, but that he "looked over his shoulder, saw them playing with a gun." He "cautioned them not to" but then heard it go off and turned to see Lewis drop to the ground.[76] He went over and "stretched him out," probably an effort to render aid. Abeline reported that she heard Lewis tell Manly, apparently in jest, "I will shoot you," before they playfully grappled over the firearm. Manly "got hold of the gun and after playing with [it] a short time the gun fired." Joe recalled Manly exclaiming, "Lord have mercy," because, as Joe told the investigators, they "did not know the gun would fire." As far as Harget knew, "the boys were on terms of friendship—& always had been." He explained to the coroner that it was his gun, but that he "always left it there for the purpose of plantation uses." It was stored where these subordinate laborers had access.[77]

Joe might have been the shotgun's primary user, and perhaps he felt some ownership over it, even though the coroner described Harget as "the owner of the gun." In the coroner's notes of his interview, the enslaved man referred to the weapon in the feminine. He explained that he "reloaded her, and left her," and that he told Alfred to "not be afraid of shooting her." In contrast, Alfred, Abeline, and Harget simply referenced the tool as "a gun" or "the gun," or "it."[78] Joe was far more familiar with it. While this is speculative, Joe was clearly comfortable with permitting others to use the shotgun, but he understood it in different terms than they did. This accidental shooting, which claimed Lewis's life, stemmed from Harget's comfort with the subordinate laborers on his farm—enslaved, hired, and apprenticed—having access to the firearm. Harget trusted Joe, who did not have nefarious intentions, and he did not feel the need to secure the weapon from the other people he enslaved.

These incidents where Black people gained access to a firearm through white people's lackadaisical storage stemmed from enslavers' trust in their laborers' judgment; but it also meant that Black people could potentially acquire a firearm without much trouble if they wanted, regardless of their intentions. Of course, there were other venues through which a person could acquire firearms. Some Black North Carolinians came across firearms during their work, like the theater attendant who was suspected of stealing a "small pocket Pistol, with a brass lock, brass barrel, and mounted with silver" from a patron during a performance.[79] White people also lost their weapons, like F. W. Potter, who misplaced his Colt revolver in December of 1864 and offered a $50 reward for its return.[80] Further, enslaved North Carolinians could also access firearms through illegal markets, from merchants who disregarded the law, or from more casual personal connections. These options further problematized the county courts' mostly enslaver-and-enslaved centered regulation of Black people's firearm use. Those workers who could bypass their enslavers had broader and more discrete access to weaponry, although their illegal gun use made them vulnerable to an array of outcomes.

Interracial illegal commerce extended far beyond firearms, but the weapons stand out from the various agricultural products, liquor, stolen goods, or other items that were commonly traded because of the extensive rhetoric and legislative action centered on firearms' destructive potential. While some of the Black and white people who sold illegal weapons to enslaved workers did so purely for financial gain, these merchants were not all blind opportunists. The parties to these sales were sometimes well acquainted with each other, and that familiarity could inculcate a sense of trust despite the General Assembly, the county courts, or individual white citizens' views on the matter.[81] Finally, many white North Carolinians were infuriated by the fact that maroons and other Black people could acquire weapons from these illegal Black and white dealers, weapons that enabled Black people to more efficiently appropriate property owners' goods if they felt so inclined.

However white people felt about illegal arms dealers on a day-to-day basis, these trade-related crises could trigger public contempt and sometimes even violence directed toward the sellers. Many white citizens saw the control of Black people's access to firearms as a crucial line of defense for public safety. In February 1844, a fourteen- or fifteen-year-old enslaved youth named Charles shot and killed his brother, "a slave of great value" who earned his enslaver some $250 per year. The *Raleigh Register* reported that during the investigation into the murder, the Wilmington authorities discovered that "a number of small black boys about town had pistols in their possession, which they have been in the habit of sporting with, firing at marks, &c, in retired places."[82] The "small black boys" admitted that they purchased their pistols from "certain men in the town" who clearly had no scruples about selling to enslaved Wilmingtonians. While white people tried to emasculate Black men of all ages by calling them "boy," it was not unheard of for youths under ten years of age to use firearms without adult supervision. These pistol-toting Black sportsmen might very well have been children.[83]

These challenges continued into the Civil War. A few months into the conflict, New Bern's *Daily Progress* printed the aggressively titled article, "Niggers and Pistols," after an armed burglary attempt. In it, the editors demanded, "Where did the negro get his pistol? Where do other negroes get pistols and other weapons? . . . We have heard mysterious whisperings for some time past and we know that many have their suspicions concerning certain individuals." While they did not have any concrete evidence themselves, the editors challenged the public to be on guard as "this was no time for slaves to be permitted to have weapons, nor should any white person be permitted to remain in a Southern community who would furnish them with weapons."[84] The rumors highlight how some people ignored the firearm laws, despite enslaved workers' gun use having been legislated out of existence thirty years prior and free Black people having been disarmed a few months prior to the attempted burglary.[85] Further, the *Progress*'s fixation on pistols instead of on firearms generally suggested that this was about pistols' limited practical use for labor.

Many Black people used shotguns, which were multipurpose weapons. Enslavers who applied to the county courts to arm their workers explicitly framed that gun use as *labor*. Free Black people who applied for firearm licenses also presented their gun use in this manner. For example, Stephen Evans's application stated explicitly that he wanted it for "Hunting . . . for the purpose of killing Game."[86] Others carried pistols, and North Carolinians in this era understood full well that different firearms had different uses. Whether a person carried a pistol for offense or defense, it was portable, concealable, and useful against people. Thus armed youths were seen as a particular problem: When a white child accidentally shot a playmate, one newspaper admonished the public that "any boy seen with a loaded pistol, if not reprimanded by his parents, ought to be taken up and severely flogged, and have his pistol taken from him."[87] The state also recognized that pistols were different from shotguns. Early in 1851, the assembly passed a revenue act to replenish the state's coffers through an array of taxes.[88] State representative Kenneth Rayner of Hertford County made a motion to remove the weapons from the bill but could not gain support. He did successfully add a clause, however, that the tax would be only on those "pistols in use."[89] The final version added an annual 1 percent ad valorem tax on an exhaustive list of purchases, luxury consumer goods, vices, a variety of performers and entertainers, tolls and ferries, and some professional annual incomes of over $500. It also taxed "all pistols (except such as shall be used exclusively for mustering, and also those kept in shops and stores for sale)" and all bowie knives. Dirks and sword canes were taxed at half of a percent. Rayner's clause specified that the tax applied only to those weapons "as are used, worn, or carried about the person of the owner."[90]

These armed Black youths in Wilmington might have had the means to purchase their own weapons. Enslaved workers who were able to hire out their own time, steal, borrow, or otherwise accumulate a little bit of cash could probably afford to buy a firearm. They needed only a willing supplier.[91] The *Raleigh Register*'s editors declared that public sentiment ran against these black-market merchants and disparagingly labeled them as "violators of the law, and disturbers of the peace." The *Register* also reported that "one of the largest public meetings . . . that we ever witnessed" was convened on short notice to discuss the illegal firearms trade and to make plans to "visit justice upon the offenders."[92] The newspaper funneled the locals citizens' outrage at Charles's troubling crime, but the town's recreationally armed youths certainly could not have been a very well-kept secret, especially if they habitually fired their pistols within or near town. For many white Wilmingtonians, these "small black boys'" sporting gun use was a theoretical problem only and did not warrant direct action until the moment of crisis brought on by Charles's fratricide.

The uproar over the "certain men" in Wilmington who sold guns to enslaved workers does not appear to have turned violent, despite the threat to "visit justice" on the arms dealers; but some white people sometimes forcefully responded to these transgressions. One February evening in 1858, William D. Davenport, "a highly respected and wealthy citizen" of Washington County, was shot and killed at his home, and suspicions fell on three of the men he enslaved: Gansey, "Yellow George," and Aaron. The trio apparently "had obtained a gun for that purpose of[f] a young man in the neighborhood," who was white. The authorities took that "young man," William Goodman, and the three enslaved men into custody.[93] The Black men were believed to have shot Davenport to prevent him from testifying against Gansey's father, who was also named Gansey and who was on trial for murdering a white man some twenty-five years prior. The elder Gansey had long been suspected, but insufficient evidence prevented the state from prosecuting him until he was overheard talking about the crime around 1856 and incriminated himself.[94]

Davenport's murder generated a great deal of outrage in Washington County. The authorities locked the three enslaved men and their white associate in the county jail, but the situation was volatile. Hundreds of white men descended on the building and would have lynched all four of the prisoners if the authorities had not prevented them from doing so.[95] Many of the details surrounding Davenport's killing are unclear. Goodman was probably an eighteen-year-old laborer, but it is unclear how well he knew the three enslaved men or whether he had sold or loaned them the weapon. It is also unclear whether he knew that Davenport's life was at risk, or whether that knowledge would have influenced his decision to provide the men with the gun. But once Goodman provided the enslaved men with the firearm, his initial intentions no longer mattered. Gansey was eventually executed, as was his father for his decades old crime; but "Yellow George," Aaron, and William Goodman appear to have been acquitted.[96]

The General Assembly and local courts had a vested interest in preventing these illegal firearm sales that circumvented the official processes for enslaved people's firearm possession. Some white North Carolinians believed that they needed to control enslaved folks' access to firearms to reduce Black people's destructive potential. These men who sold weapons to enslaved laborers were operating contrary to the General Assembly's laws and contrary to public safety, as framed by the white power structure; yet they were an integral part of some Black North Carolinians' unauthorized firearm use. It is difficult to find more than a glimpse of these dealers in the historical records, but a few of them can be identified, and some of their motivations are discernible. Many of the white people who sold firearms to enslaved workers did so casually, like William Goodman. They did not manage extensive trade networks or sell large numbers of firearms. They were simply providing weapons to Black people whom they knew. Consider that in the autumn of 1854, a fourteen-year-old white boy named Angus Campbell was indicted by the Richmond County Superior Court for selling a firearm to an enslaved man named Will. Campbell does not immediately evoke the image of a well-connected and unprincipled member of the "dram shop gentry," about which antebellum newspapers so often complained. He and Will were certainly acquainted, however, as Angus's mother, Isabella Campbell, was Will's enslaver.[97]

Further, consider German immigrant Charles Hamburg, who catered to a diverse clientele in his Wilmington store. He maintained enduring trade relationships with some of the area's enslaved laborers. Dianah Bohnstedt, who regularly shopped at his store, swore to the New Hanover County Court that one Saturday night in 1854, she watched Hamburg sell a pistol and a half-pound of shot to Ned Quince, who was enslaved by Parker Quince.[98] The white woman swore that she overheard Ned tell the shopkeeper that he wanted to buy a pistol, to which Hamburg replied, "I can sell you one," before placing a weapon on the counter. The enslaved man examined the pistol, determined that it was to his liking, and told Hamburg that he would take it. Hamburg poured Ned a quantity of gunpowder and shot as well. Bohnstedt admitted that she did not actually see Ned pay for these items, but she watched as he put the illegal items into his pocket and left the store.[99] Ned purchased the pistol and ammunition for himself, but shopkeepers sometimes also sold enslaved people ammunition on their enslavers' behalf. For instance, Mary Doxey came to John Gray's Currituck County store herself at times, but she also sent her son and a man named Beasley, who was likely enslaved, to make purchases for her.[100] Beasley put two pounds of shot and a half-pound of powder, valued at thirty-nine cents, on Doxey's account. Mary Doxey also sent Beasley to get a gallon of whiskey.[101] Both she and Gray trusted Beasley to make these purchases.

Angus Campbell and Charles Hamburg's firearm sales were probably motivated by similar factors. Campbell and Will's familiarity with each other certainly played a role in their trade. Will's intentions with the weapon are unclear in the records, but the white teenager trusted him enough to provide it. By contrast, Hamburg was involved in several other illegal transactions with enslaved people in his neighborhood. He also sold them liquor, and he bought rice from Ned and from at least one of Parker Quince's other slaves. Whether he was unaware of the laws or simply did not care, Hamburg made no effort to be secretive. Dianah Bohnstedt witnessed several of these illegal transactions. Ned and Hamburg's frequent trades probably explain why Bohnstedt did not see him pay for the pistol. The two men had a comfortable relationship and probably did not require immediate payment. On at least one other occasion, Ned sent a quantity of rice to Hamburg and came to see him and collect payment a few days later. Hamburg was certainly engaged in more illegal commerce than Bohnstedt witnessed, and his familiarity with his Black customers undoubtedly played a role in these sales as well.[102]

Additionally, some white people provided known fugitives with firearms. Whether rooted in amicability or in economic opportunism, this trade undermined the rule of law at nearly its most extreme extent. Runaways were inherently unsupervised and were often thought to be a menace to white people's property. Still, some white North Carolinians' financial decisions trumped the law's broad condemnation of armed and unsupervised enslaved workers. Consider the unnamed poor white man who traded a firearm to a runaway named William Kinnegay in exchange for a pig, which Kinnegay had stolen. The resourceful fugitive explained that there were "a great many cattle and swine" who were left to feed unattended and that "the poor people about, frequently kill them, and the owners seem not to be aware of it, or do not care for it." This was not an isolated transaction; Kinnegay later gave his trade partner a cowhide that he also had stolen, in exchange for a measure of gunpowder and some shot. These two marginalized men trusted each other enough to leave their trade items in a predetermined place and thereby avoided meeting in person, which made their illegal commerce difficult for outsiders to detect. Kinnegay explained to an interviewer that he "saw him but rarely."[103] Their arrangement seems to have been a relatively equal and mutually beneficial trade partnership. While enslaved Black people and poor white folks sometimes sustained an "interracial subculture," this should not overshadow the potential frictions between these groups. Economic competition between low-income white North Carolinians and their Black neighbors sometimes led to racial animosity as well.[104]

Both Charles Hamburg's and William Kinnegay's white business partners traded firearms to enslaved laborers, but many white North Carolinians were more concerned about the trade itself than the substance of these transactions. Some of them worried that *any* trade with enslaved people was a threat to their discipline. They were so opposed to white people selling or buying items from enslaved people that they petitioned for a law that would punish any offenders "not only with fine and imprisonment; but, by one or more whippings on the bare back at the whipping post."[105] This proposed punishment was about far more than physical pain. The lash was generally associated with slavery, and while white people in certain situations were occasionally whipped, they saw it as a particularly degrading corrective measure. This sentiment was true even in the maritime industry, where flogging was a common punishment for all sailors.[106] These petitioners' advocacy for punishment by public whipping shows the disdain with which some white North Carolinians viewed this commerce. In their view these exchanges with enslaved workers were illegal and also potentially dangerous.

Despite these criticisms, a few white people also provided weapons to enslaved people with the hope that the Black folks would engage in insurrection, though some were wrongly accused. In 1845, an enslaved Davidson County man allegedly wrote a letter to other men about a planned insurrection. He listed two white men—William Taylor, a landless farmer, and Eli Penry, a struggling merchant—as his accomplices. His letter outlined plans to shoot every man who would not join the revolt and noted that the conspirators would seize "all the powder and shot in sailsbury and all the guns and mony there too." The enslaved writer alleged that Taylor had agreed to serve as a captain in the insurrection and that Penry would sell the conspirators "all his powder and shot for haf the mony" that other vendors charged. This plot was very likely a hoax, but as historian Charles Bolton points out, "Even if the letter is a fraud, it still shows that the involvement of white men, including poor whites, in black uprisings was considered an ever-present possibility."[107] David Blount offers a more credible example, though the white men who visited his plantation were outsiders—the Civil War brought the United States Army to the neighborhood. These soldiers were unsuccessful in their efforts to arm some of the men on the Beaufort County plantation where Blount was also enslaved.[108]

Many white North Carolinians were willing to illegally sell firearms to enslaved Black buyers for a variety of reasons, regardless of the law or the potential for interracial violence inherent in these sales. For their part, enslaved North Carolinians were not merely passive consumers in these unlawful firearm transactions; rather, they sometimes played a central role in acquiring the weapons and distributing them to other enslaved people. This business could be profitable, but those thus engaged risked incurring the wrath of the assembly and local courts, their enslavers, and a public that often took law-enforcing violence into its own hands. The state was most frustrated when these weapons were stolen from its militia stockpiles, as those government firearms presented both real and symbolic threats to North Carolina's entrenched, race-based power structure.

In 1816, the Chowan County grand jury issued a presentment against two enslaved men—Dick and Pompey—for providing weapons and ammunition to fugitives in and around Edenton. The court reprimanded another enslaved man, listed as "negro Jack," for similar actions. Presumably, the jurors had heard rumors about these men's illegal activities and acted. As Sally Hadden explains, grand juries weighed the evidence that prosecutors presented and determined whether it was strong enough to progress to trial. Further, grand juries sometimes sought to effect change—their presentments "indicated faults, failings, and violations of both social norms and legal rules" that they hoped the community would address. Hadden further explains that presentments were sometimes communally inspired—the grand jury received "complaints from their own members, from judges, from constables, and even from private individuals."[109] The Chowan County grand jury indicted Jack's enslaver, Michael Wilder, for allowing him to live alone in Edenton where the business savvy man was a "frequent purchaser of powder" for the area's fugitives. Wilder enslaved about five people between 1810 and 1820, and the jurors saw his poor management of them as a threat to stability. They believed that Jack, "a great scoundrel," would not have been involved in this trade if Wilder had exercised better mastery; proper supervision was the central tenet of the state's slave law. The court also stated that Jack had received "plunder" from local fugitives, probably as payment for the gunpowder. Through this trade, Jack had enabled and profited from runaways' depredations, much to the annoyance of white Chowan County residents.[110]

These enslaved people attempting to procure gunpowder were alarming to many white North Carolinians. In 1812, just a few short years before the Chowan County authorities unraveled this illegal arms trade, the Rowan County Court charged two enslaved men, Jacob and Antony, with "attempting to prucuring powder &c and raising a body of Negroes for killing the white People."[111] As they plotted during the early months of the War of 1812, Antony asked another enslaved man whether he supported the British or the Americans, though it is unclear how the man answered. Ultimately, Jacob and Antony were undone by some of the people they tried to recruit. An enslaved man named Bob testified that Antony told him to "procure all the powder he could in order to kill white people" and that Jacob asked him to "get as Much the powder he could" and bring it to their meeting, where the ringleaders would reveal the plan's details to the others. Antony seemed to see this plot as connected to the war. He allegedly explained to an enslaved man named Vincent that "the war was coming on & then they would have choice of the white girls for wives."[112] The illegal arms trade predated Antony and Jacob's plotting, however; the trade was as old as the United States itself. Even during the tumultuous Revolutionary War, when gunpowder was a precious commodity in North Carolina, some Black folks, like "a negro called Nicholas" in Wilmington, had it and were selling it.[113]

Regarding the 1816 indictments, the court charged Dick with "purchasing or attempting to purchase" gunpowder and lead for the Black outlaws who lived in and around Edenton. He was a middleman—he received stolen goods from them, which he then sold and traded to buy them ammunition and other supplies. The presentment suggested that Dick had been caught red-handed in an illegal transaction, and one of the witnesses against him was listed as "Negro Jack." The record is not clear, but this appears to have been the Jack whom Michael Wilder enslaved—and who was probably engaged in business with Dick.[114] The final presentment was against Pompey for stealing five or six "United States Muskets." The federal government supplied each state with an annual allotment of weapons for the militia, per an 1808 law, and Pompey had stolen several of these, which probably belonged to a Chowan County militia unit and were stored in the county courthouse or jail.

This storage was not as secure as it might initially have appeared. Years after Jack's theft, the grand jury in Beaufort County reported that the jail's first floor had four rooms "for the use of Prisoners + One is used for the Safe Keeping of Muskets + Bayonets belonging to the State." While the prisoners and weapons were under lock and key, the county authorities did not always secure them as well as they might have.[115] Some jails, like that in Craven County, had severe structural issues. Additionally, after inspecting their jail, New Hanover County's grand jurors complained that "the keys of the jail have some-times been kept by coloured persons" and recommended that "the keys shall never pass into the hands of coloured persons, or slaves, under any pretext whatever."[116]

Black and white North Carolinians stole firearms much as they did other types of property, and these could end up in the hands of a host of people. The state arms were not the only target of thieves, of course—consider E. B. Bryan, whose Wilmington store was broken into one Saturday night in May 1832 by persons unknown. The thieves took two shotguns, a "very large" rifle, nine pistols (which included four "large pistols," a double-barreled pistol, a "small brass barrel percussion," and three "small iron pistols"), and also a flute.[117] Nevertheless, Pompey's theft of some of Chowan County's militia weapons was significant because of both their quantity and their source. He traded these state-owned military firearms—which were strong metaphors of the state government's coercive power—to some of the area's runaways. This was a dramatic shift in that power, both symbolically and literally.

Pompey, Dick, and Jack's trade networks with other enslaved people around Edenton provided them with a reliable customer base, but it also increased their vulnerability to the state's law enforcement apparatus. If the Edenton authorities could apprehend one of these firearm vendors' enslaved patrons or fellow traders, then the authorities could coerce that person into turning against the rest of the network, thereby putting them all at risk. The state granted pardons to conspirators who cooperated, as was the case for Dennis, an enslaved man who was discovered to be involved in a "Daring and horrid plot" in Perquimans County. He was "promised his pardon on condition of Disclosing all he knew of the business."[118] At least some of Pompey's stolen militia muskets were later recovered when the authorities caught Jack in possession of them. After his arrest, Jack, became Chowan County's witness against both Pompey and Dick.[119] His testimony against these enslaved Black businessmen highlights how precarious their weapons trade really was.

Illegal firearms dealers like Pompey, Jack, and Dick ensured that many Black people who were barred by North Carolina law or by their enslavers from accessing firearms, shot, or gunpowder could nonetheless obtain these goods . . . for the right price. These three men were certainly not the only group engaged in this business. Anyone looking to sell firearms or ammunition could have found willing customers in North Carolina's larger towns or its rural areas. In 1855, New Bern's Intendant of Police, John D. Whitford, petitioned Governor Thomas Bragg "by request of a number of our citizens" for a more secure arsenal for the town's state-issued arms. He claimed that "Muskets swrds [*sic*] and Pistols (the property of the state) are scattered over the town and county, and frequently found in the possession of both slaves and free negroes and in [*sic*] the person and in the camp of runaways."[120] Whitford was not the only person worried about this. New Bern's officials were concerned that their weapons were inadequately stored and "it would be very easy for our enemies to obtain them and use them against us" during a rebellion.[121] Some unauthorized persons, whom Whitford identified as free and enslaved people of color, had gained access to the militia's firearms, much as Pompey had done forty years earlier in Edenton. This put North Carolina in a dangerously ironic predicament—as Whitford noted, "the people and property of this section of the State are put in jeopardy from the fact that [the militia firearms] fall into the hands of negroes and lawless white persons." He further told the governor about an enslaved man who had been killed a few years prior and who inexplicably had had a state-owned pistol in his possession.[122]

R. W. Haywood, the adjutant general of the North Carolina Militia, had a different opinion on how enslaved people acquired militia weapons, but he did not dispute that these firearms ended up in these Black men's hands. In 1855, he argued that these guns had not been stolen from the arsenal but that they had been issued to volunteer militia companies whose officers did not ensure that they were returned when the units disbanded.[123] Haywood saw careless local officers and their irresponsible militiamen as the issue, not the county's storage and security. This was not a new complaint—in 1819, one of Haywood's predecessors grumbled that "more than half of the public arms have either been lost or destroyed, by the negligence of the officers or soldiers in whose hands they were confided."[124] Whitford and Haywood disagreed over who was at fault, but both saw that state-owned militia weapons were problematically ending up in the hands of unauthorized Black North Carolinians. White citizens' worries about their safety were considered at the highest levels of state government. In 1855, Governor Bragg reported the deplorable condition of the state's arsenals to the assembly and urged action. He warned the legislators that in the present condition of the storage facilities, "the arms are scattered about, frequently falling into the hands of slaves, free negroes, and dissipated white people."[125] Many white North Carolinians wanted far greater supervision of the slave population, but even if the legislature completely banned their gun access, it would never be a perfect solution because of the wide range of Black and white actors who stood to benefit from the clandestine firearms market.

The counties' inadequate storage of the state's firearms left them vulnerable to theft, but they were also threatened by the elements. In 1856, New Bernians created a committee to assess "the safety of our town in case of servile insurrection." They were alarmed by what they found and wrote to Governor Thomas Bragg to explain, "Our public arms are in a most deplorable condition; being stored away in an old Ware-House."[126] Another official from the town, also in mid-1850s, feared that the public arms would be "totally destroyed" without a better storage system. He explained that the firearms had been "much neglected" and "thereby greatly injured and many of the small arms ruined."[127] In theory, better preserved firearms would aid New Bern's militiamen in putting down any insurrectionary effort on the part of the county's enslaved residents.

One did not have to secretly steal arms from decrepit state storehouses, however; strong-armed force could secure a range of items, guns included. In

1791, Sampson, a man enslaved by John Houseman, confessed that at the end of October he had acquired a gun by force. He "met Stephen Kinsey on the public high way," and the white man, seeing an unsupervised enslaved man who had probably been reported as a runaway, tried to tie Sampson up. Sampson knocked Kinsey down and then took his gun before making his escape. A "short time after," he stole "some molasses, some Powder + shot," and a few other items from Levi Sanders's house, and he stole a beehive from another white household. He had the firearm and other stolen items in his possession when he was captured a few weeks later. The Jones County justices of the peace sentenced him to be "hang'd by the neck untill he is dead."[128] Similarly, Cumberland County's Stephen joined another enslaved man in "roaming at large committing depredations on the commonwealth," including robbery. While in Granville County in 1814, they "beat, stabbed, & robbed" Thomas Thomason "of a Shot Gun, of superior quality."[129] During the Revolutionary War, individuals could get their hands on the state's arms via sale, which the assembly had approved for the "considerable number of Fire Arms . . . entirely unfit for public use or service," some of which were described as "broken Guns . . . rendered useless."[130] While the legislature designated these arms as unfit for service, they were still functional enough to be sold, and some people bought them. Some of these weapons probably ended up in the hands of "slaves, free negroes, and dissipated white people."[131]

In addition to theft and purchase, enslaved workers also gave each other firearms for protection, much to the chagrin of their enslavers. In 1858, Gen. William A. Blount of Beaufort County wrote a letter to another enslaver, E. Stanly, to inform him that, "your Boy Clarence has committed . . . offences" connected to David, a man whom Blount enslaved. David had given Clarence "at different times large sums of spices stolen from me." Further, Clarence had "harbored, fed + concealed" David for weeks, knowing full well that he was a runaway. To make matters worse, Clarence had also given David a "six barrel, revolver (pistol) and ammunition + advised him to use it to prevent his being taken; and told him if he found he could not succeed, fully protect himself to throw the pistol away for if found upon him it would ruin him." Blount continued his complaints to Stanly, noting that "my Boy fearing the Pistol he had was not sufficient Clarence lent him another new single barrell pistol, he was thus dressly armed on going back from his visit to Chocowinity he returned the new pistol."[132] Blount wrote that Clarence had concealed David because he planned on "shipping him to New York," though it is not clear if this was a plan for a dramatic Henry "Box" Brown escape or simply a plan to travel by ship. Allegedly, Clarence had "advised him to this course + aided him to carry it out."[133]

Blount worked with E. Stanly's nephew, attorney Jonathan A. Stanly, who served as his representative, and others to resolve this matter. The parties "agreed that legal proceedings should be stopped on condition that Clarence rec'd 39 lashes, a lawful whipping publically" and be confined in jail until he could be sent to Alabama. For his part, David was "sold to a speculator to be sold out of N.C." as was another runaway who had also been involved with Clarence and David's plan. Other enslaved people in the area were "concerned in different degrees + have been or will be properly delt with." Blount was satisfied that his examination of the witnesses proved David's and Clarence's guilt.[134] While he was confident in his ability to interrogate the witnesses, he struggled to understand his bondman. He lamented to Stanly in closing, that "David was born + raised my property has been waiting on me + sleeping in my bed room for 8 or 10 years, he is about 20 years old, my confidence in him was very great + he was raised like a white Boy—I found in the sequel that he was a great rascal."[135] William Blount was surprised to learn that David's yearning for freedom, reinforced by his pistols, was greater than his ties to his enslaver.

ONCE FREE AND ENSLAVED people of color were armed, whether they had the court's permission or not, there was no guarantee that they would use their firearms for what white North Carolinians and the assembly considered to be constructive ends. This was not the exclusive result of workers who defied their enslavers' authority, as enslavers claimed complete control over their laborers, and some used them for illegal purposes. This could create challenges. During the late 1850s, Bladen County's John T. Councill armed two of the men he enslaved, Ned and Hannibal, and set them to work guarding his country store.[136] All three of them landed in legal trouble, as the General Assembly had banned enslaved Black people's firearm use nearly three decades prior to this incident. A justice of the peace had Hannibal and Ned whipped for the offense and Councill was fined. He would appeal the decision, but the two enslaved men—who might have been whipped before the appeal—were drawn into this drama by Councill's decision-making.[137]

Finally, while Hannibal, Ned, and the enslaved New Hanover County men who killed John Scull's livestock were all operating under their respective enslavers' orders, they were nonetheless employed in labor that was harmful to white people's property and personal safety. Many white citizens felt as though the threat of armed Black people hung over the Slave South like the Sword of Damocles, regardless of the assembly's efforts to create safeguards. The fact of the matter was that the law could never fully protect white North Carolinians or their property both because the oppressed workers resisted the debilitating laws and because some enslavers took individualistic approaches to using their armed workers, despite the disapproval of their peers or the courts. The Old North State's communities broadly favored laws that mandated supervision for armed enslaved workers, but these laws worked only when enslavers were committed to them. Their noncompliance with the law complicated the county court's regulation of Black people's firearm use, and further, when enslavers selfishly or recklessly deployed their laborers firearm use, they had the potential to threaten the peace.

Enslaved North Carolinians' firearm use was a common occurrence in the eighteenth and nineteenth centuries, as enslaved people took up arms for a range of reasons—both within and outside the law's bounds—as they sought to make meaningful lives on their own terms. Guns were accessible through a variety of formal and casual venues, but many Black North Carolinians' experience with firearms were categorized as criminal because this use violated the law, even when it came at enslavers' commands. Nevertheless, this gun use could be lifechanging for them. The law could never be wholly effective because so many people stood to benefit from ignoring it. For so many Black and white people alike, firearm use was a way to get things done, and they chose their own productivity and lives over the state's dictates.

CHAPTER THREE

Armed Labor

From the colonial era to the Civil War, North Carolina's General Assembly recognized that armed Black laborers were very useful to the state's citizens, and to create safeguards, it regulated the process by which enslavers could use their workers' armed labor. The assembly's increasing regulation of armed Black people led to a complete ban on enslaved workers' gun use in 1831 and county court oversight of free Black people's gun use in 1840. Two decades later, the legislature completely eliminated free Black people's legal gun access.[1] These measures impacted Black North Carolinians' personal lives and restricted how freely they or others could use their armed labor. Firearms held a great deal of symbolic and cultural power in the antebellum South, but on a very basic level, firearms were simply tools that could bolster laborers' effectiveness and efficiency. North Carolinians, both male and female, Black and white, used firearms for work both within and outside of their households and both within and outside of the law's confines.

Enslavers in North Carolina used their workers to hunt for both their own tables as well as for the enslaved communities' needs. Many white people saw enslaved workers' purpose as unflinchingly providing labor and consequently, they harnessed this subordinate yet potentially destructive labor for their own purposes. Both free and enslaved Black laborers provided an armed security presence that countered the threats that both wildlife and other people posed to agricultural fields and other valuable possessions. African-descended people's armed labor offered important benefits for others, but more importantly, it was advantageous to themselves, their families, and their communities. Black people physically protected themselves and others. Free and enslaved Black North Carolinians' armed labor allowed them to improve their lives and gave them another venue through which they offered social, familial, and economic resistance to a racist and overbearing enslavers' society.

North Carolina was a very rural landscape well into the middle of the nineteenth century. As such, wildlife could pose a threat to farmers' livestock and crops. In 1785, the General Assembly empowered the courts of Bladen, Brunswick, Burke, Carteret, Caswell, Davidson, Duplin, Hyde, Lincoln, Mecklenburg, Moore, New Hanover, Onslow, Randolph, Rockingham, Rowan, Rutherford, Sampson, Surry, Tyrrell, Wake, and Wilkes Counties to levy taxes to raise money for bounties on "Wolves, Wildcats, Panthers, Bears, Crows, and Squirrels."[2] Beyond these bounties, the legislature required every head of household or their overseer in select counties to "kill or cause to be killed in every year, seven crows or squirrels" or be fined four pence for each deficiency. Crows, squirrels, and wildcats were agricultural nuisances, but larger animals could injure or kill livestock or people. The *North Carolina Christian Advocate* noted that "persons were sometimes attacked by bears[,] wolves, &c."[3] North Carolinians availed themselves of bounties on these animals, too. For example, between 1762 and 1786, Granville County residents killed about 121 wolves and about 91 wildcats.[4] This problem persisted into the nineteenth century. In 1841, the legislature passed a law "to encourage the destruction of Wolves in Haywood County." People in the western parts of the state also shot and killed panthers. These large cats were still spotted, shot, and killed in the east. Bears were also a persistent threat to free-ranging hogs.[5]

The Colonial Assembly recognized that Bute, Carteret, Granville, Mecklenburg, Rowan, and Tryon Counties were "infested with Wolves, and other Vermin, to the great Prejudice of the Inhabitants," and in response, it offered bounties of seven shillings and sixpence for the scalps of wolves and panthers. Importantly, the legislators recognized that Black and Indigenous laborers engaged in this work, and they framed the law to include that "if any Slave or Indian" killed "any vermin . . . the Master or Owner of such slave or Indian" could claim the reward.[6] Some bounty receipts indicate that the applicant was not the person who killed the animal. Others passively note that the predators "were killed." Few of the receipts directly credit an enslaved person, but there were certainly enslaved people who performed this labor. The justices who approved these bounties were not generally interested in the details if the nuisance animal had been destroyed.

Like their counterparts across the South, North Carolina enslavers used their armed laborers in several capacities. This broad application reflected the popular views that the General Assembly's guidelines offered safeguards to prevent armed labor from spiraling into armed rebellion when the guidelines were coupled with local supervision by responsible white people. These labor arrangements were often useful for enslavers, as workers thus equipped could complete tasks that would otherwise have been far more difficult. For example, New Hanover County's John F. Burgwin petitioned his county court for permission to arm "a negro man slave by the name of Marcus," who would then be permitted to carry a gun and hunt on Burgwin's lands. Other enslavers used hunters to secure a great deal of their plantation's meat from the wild, which could spare them from needing to butcher livestock.[7] Marcus's armed labor would have greatly reduced Burgwin's expenses in this regard. Enslaved hunters used a range of tools when they could not get firearms, but a gun increased the variety of game they could easily kill. This was important for those slaveholders who had preferences for specific wild species, and it was necessity for some, depending upon the local variety of wildlife.[8] Some enslavers wanted to arm several of their workers and received the state's blessings to do so. For instance, in 1741, Edward Moseley, Esq., armed four of the people he enslaved. Sally Hadden suggests that Moseley's prominent social and political standing in the colony might have played a role in this. In the early 1730s he served as the speaker of the assembly's lower house, and by 1741 he had become a member of the Governor's Council; a mere three years later he was appointed Baron of the Exchequer. Further, the court might also have found Moseley's request to be reasonable—he owned thousands of acres of land, and having several armed workers would have been quite useful to him for a range of labor applications.[9]

Burgwin's 1805 petition to the New Hanover County Court specified that Marcus's armed labor would be directed toward hunting, but other enslavers sought and received much broader discretion on how they might employ their armed workers. Guns were incredibly versatile tools in agricultural settings, and armed Black laborers also killed agricultural pests that threatened their enslavers' fields. They shot predators for bounties, but this problem was bigger than wolves and wildcats.[10] Free people of color's armed labor was also useful and desirable on North Carolina's farms. A white farmer in Wayne County, Benajah Herring, asked his county court to allow a free Black man to keep a firearm after the assembly passed the restrictive license law in 1841, because, as Herring explained, "he does me some benefit by destroying the Vermin around my fields I would rather he could retain his gun."[11] "Free Willis" lived adjacent to Herring and subsisted on the animals he shot in the white farmer's agricultural fields that would otherwise have ravaged his crops. The white farmer supported Willis's license application, at least in part because of the personal benefits he gained from this armed labor.[12]

North Carolina enslavers armed their workers not only to protect their standing crops from hungry rodents or birds but also to protect their agricultural holdings from roaming domestic livestock and encroaching neighbors. This labor was particularly useful because livestock was customarily left unpenned in the antebellum era so the animals could graze and therefore not require feed. Armed labor was further useful because plundering maroons and runaways presented a considerable problem in parts of North Carolina where there were sizable tracts of undeveloped wilderness and where the outlaws could hide and construct lives for themselves. Maroons and runaways raided nearby plantations and were a persistent problem from the colonial era through to the end of the Civil War. These raiders were so busy in some eastern counties—helping themselves to agricultural fields, crop stores, livestock, and smokehouses—that during the 1820s, the General Assembly was forced to "encourage" citizens' efforts to forcibly eject them from their hiding places in the Great Dismal Swamp.[13] North Carolina enslavers' thus set their workers to a variety of projects, including defending their valuable crops and livestock, which had been produced by enslaved hands in the first place.

Bladen County's Alexander Lammon demonstrated how commonplace this armed defensive labor was when he was tried for the murder of a young white man in the mid-1820s. Lammon swore that he had armed an enslaved man to protect his watermelon patch from a thieving runaway and that it was, in fact, this watchman who had shot and killed the victim.[14] While Lammon concocted this story to cover his own role in a cold-blooded murder, his defense rested upon the premise that it was perfectly reasonable for him to use an armed enslaved worker—a man who was prepared to use deadly force—to guard his fields from thieving runaways. He proclaimed his innocence with his final words from the scaffold, and his story serves as a testament to the pervasiveness and unexceptional nature of enslaved people's armed agricultural labor. Further, it highlights how the Bladen County jurors recognized that those runaways who raided farmer's fields at night were dangerous—implicitly carrying firearms—and that anyone guarding property from them would need to be similarly outfitted, even if the defenders were enslaved workers. Just five years prior, in nearby Brunswick County, John Swann and Jonathan Waddell bound themselves for fifty pounds sterling to ensure that Lothario, a man Swann enslaved and whom he allowed to "carry a gun for the purpose of hunting and protecting his plantation," would not abuse his "privilege or liberty by trespassing upon and destroying the property of his neighbors or any other person."[15] Lothario's armed labor had several applications, including "protecting" his enslaver's land. It is not clear if Swann intended for Lothario to defend his property from wildlife or from human intruders, but he saw a firearm as the proper tool for the job.

North Carolina was rural and heavily agricultural, but there were other ways to make a living, and enslavers also used armed Black laborers to protect these financial interests. In the late 1850s, Bladen County's John T. Councill illegally provided firearms to two men whom he enslaved, Hannibal and Ned, so that they could protect his rural store at night. One of the men slept in a room adjacent to the storeroom, and the other slept in a house about a hundred yards away. Councill had Hannibal and Ned keep their guns in their respective dwellings so that they could quickly access them in the case of an emergency.[16] Unfortunately for them, someone reported the two Black men to the authorities, and a justice of the peace ordered them to receive twenty lashes each and then be locked in jail. Less painfully, Councill was fined a total of ten dollars for his laborers' transgressions, although he himself had initiated their carrying of the firearms.[17] The enslaver disagreed with the justice's actions and appealed, albeit unsuccessfully, to the Bladen County Court.

Undeterred, Councill sought relief from his county's superior court, and while the state solicitor tried to have the case dismissed, the higher court decided in his favor. The superior court declared that Hannibal and Ned had not violated the law because they were armed and laboring on Councill's orders and not "willfully, and of their own head."[18] The superior court's ruling rested on a creative interpretation of the 1831 firearm law, arguing that it limited enslaved people's access to firearms but not their enslavers' ability to use their armed labor. Not to be outdone, Bladen County successfully appealed the superior court's decision to the Supreme Court of North Carolina, which took a very strict interpretation of the 1831 law. It declared that the ban on arming enslaved laborers was "expressed in the strongest and broadest terms, and rendered emphatical by the concluding words, '*upon any pretense* whatsoever' and the policy of the provision is so obvious as to require no observations." North Carolina's highest court thus declared in no uncertain terms that Ned and Hannibal could not carry firearms of their own volition or on their enslaver's orders. Councill might have needed armed guards to protect the goods in his store, but after the ruling, he would have to find alternative solutions, like hiring free laborers or arming Ned and Hannibal with farming implements. The supreme court added that Councill had been unfairly fined but that the two enslaved men had broken the law and therefore the magistrate's decision to have them whipped was appropriate.[19]

By the eve of the Civil War, the courts rested more heavily on the letter of the law than on individual enslavers' decision-making. The Supreme Court's decision to uphold Ned and Hannibal's punishment was a departure from Justice Thomas Ruffin's ruling in *State v. John Mann* (1830), which declared that an enslaver's power should never be usurped by the state because that action could undermine the slave system.[20] Enslavers like Councill struggled against the assembly's dictates on the legal uses of their bondpeople's armed labor. They wanted to arm their enslaved workers in personally profitable ways, but this could be directly opposed by the state and local authorities, thereby creating conflict. The North Carolina Supreme Court settled the issue in *State v. Hannibal and Ned*, declaring that enslavers could not legally arm their enslaved workers "for any purpose."[21] Hannibal and Ned's shared experience demonstrated how unstable enslaved Black workers' firearm use could be for both Black and white people and the state. The two men followed Councill's instructions to protect his property, but the North Carolina Supreme Court determined that their backs should bear the marks of the state's displeasure at their enslaver's decision to arm them.[22]

Further, in a justice system that rested heavily upon local prerogatives, enslavers like Councill could sometimes use their workers' armed labor contrary to the General Assembly's laws without facing any legal consequences. The notion of what constituted a crime was contextual, and sometimes only enslaved people faced the repercussions of this dynamic, not their enslavers. This was complicated after the assembly completely banned enslaved people's firearm use in response to Nat Turner's violent freedom struggle in neighboring Virginia. Nevertheless, enslavers stood to benefit from arming Black laborers, and as a result, some of them would continue to use them, even when it transgressed social and legal boundaries. Additionally, in 1844, Hillsborough, Orange County, enslaver Alex Mebane described the runaway Harry as a "good gun-smith" and offered a reward of twenty dollars for his capture.[23] While Harry was not necessarily *using* firearms on a regular basis, he had access to them, was knowledgeable about their function, and talented in their repair. This skillset would have been invaluable to Mebane before Harry's escape as well as afterward, if the Black man were able to rebuild a life elsewhere; his skills would provide him a way to make a living.

John T. Councill and Alex Mebane made choices to flout the spirit of the law, if not its direct letter, but they were not alone. Other enslavers similarly sidestepped the General Assembly's dictates when it benefited them. During the Civil War, Beaufort County's William Tripp left home to serve with a coastal artillery battery. He entrusted Roden, a man whom he enslaved, to oversee the operations of his plantation in his absence. Tripp was not unique in deploying Black management: Tyrrell County's William S. Pettigrew left control of his two plantations to enslaved overseers, two men named Moses and Henry. As Robert Starobin's work illustrates, Pettigrew "permitted them to make all of the day-to-day decisions on the farms." The primary distinction between Pettigrew and Tripp is that, unlike Roden, Moses and Henry did not have access to guns, though they were set apart from Pettigrew's other slaves because they did have "most of the symbols of authority—whips and high boots and greatcoats."[24] This met North Carolina's legal standard at the time. Tripp valued Roden's armed labor and chose to violate the law to use him, even when he could not directly supervise the Black man. Nevertheless,

Roden faithfully managed the plantation's daily operations during his enslaver's absences. Tripp relied on Roden's decision-making and armed labor to protect the farm from thieving Black and white people in the neighborhood, much as he himself did during the antebellum era.[25] Despite Roden's increased responsibilities, his experiences as an armed laborer were like Free Willis's hired work. Both Black men—one free and the other enslaved, albeit in an extraordinary situation—enjoyed a modicum of personal freedom and other benefits on account of their armed labor, but their work supported white men's social and economic endeavors.

Many enslavers illegally armed their bondpeople to put them to work on a variety of otherwise legitimate tasks. For instance, both John Councill and William Tripp wanted enslaved laborers to guard their property, a task which was legal. These enslavers broke the law only when they decided to arm their bondmen to better accomplish these tasks. Their actions, however, stand in stark contrast with those white people who took a broad view of armed Black laborers' applicability and who therefore chose to put armed Black laborers to work on far more destructive, criminal endeavors. Despite antebellum Southerners' concerns about unchecked Black violence, some enslavers pushed the utility of armed laborers to the extreme. Recall for instance John G. Scull's agricultural dispute with his neighbors over his roaming livestock in New Hanover County. Scull's absentee neighbors armed their enslaved workers to shoot his cattle and hogs when the animals trampled the neighbors' standing crops, which they had not fenced in as the law required.[26] These neighbors illegally deployed their armed laborers, as the enclosure law specifically prohibited farmers who did not fence their fields from making any effort to "unreasonably chase, worry, main or kill" roaming livestock that damaged their crops or from allowing their laborers to do so.[27] Further, consider Virginian Willoughby Foreman's hiring of two enslaved men to kill Camden County shopkeeper Henry Culpepper over a land dispute in 1823. Foreman had no qualms about providing them with a loaded shotgun specifically for this task.[28] These examples of blatant crimes highlight the broad utility of Black people's armed labor and the dubious intentions with which some white North Carolinians approached it. Black laborers sometimes broke the law, but so too did so many of their enslavers.

White people found armed Black laborers to be useful for both legal and illegal work, but Black North Carolinians' also used firearms for work that benefited themselves and their broader communities. Remember that Free Willis's armed labor provided his white neighbor with a service, but it also allowed Willis to hunt for his own subsistence. Further, some enslaved people could direct their armed labor in a similar fashion and thereby bypass enslavers with tight purse strings and keep protein on their tables. This armed labor provided crucial support for some enslaved families and communities, and it allowed some workers to address what was a very real problem on some of the Old North State's plantations. Harriet Jacobs noted that in the mid-1830s, on the Chowan County plantation where she was raised, each of the enslaved men received a weekly allowance of only three pounds of meat, about eight quarts of corn, and "perhaps" a dozen herring. She added that women received a similar allotment but with only a pound and a half of meat, and that all the children under the age of twelve received half of the women's allotment. Jacobs was fortunate that when she was a child her free grandmother was able to provide her with additional food and a "scanty wardrobe." Reverend Thomas H. Jones was not as lucky. He noted that he and the others in the enslaved community on a New Hanover County plantation were given only a peck of corn per week, which they made into a "coarse bread," and that they were "compelled to steal" any additional food.[29]

Enslaved people's armed labor would have been invaluable under circumstances such as these, and Jacobs's and Jones's experiences were not unique. The Manumission Society of North Carolina reported in 1826 that enslaved laborers in the eastern parts of the state lived under conditions that were "wretched beyond description. Impoverished by the mismanagement which we have already attempted to describe, the master, unable to supply his own grandeur and maintain his slaves, puts the unfortunate wretches upon short allowances, scarcely sufficient for their sustenance, so that a great part go half naked and half starved much of the time. . . . Generally, throughout the State, the African is an abused, monstrously outraged creature."[30] Additionally, some North Carolina enslavers withheld even these meager provisions from bond-people whom they believed were no longer productive. Jacobs noted that at a ration distribution one week, "a very old slave" who had faithfully served three successive generations of their enslaver's family "hobbled up to get his bit of meat," and their mistress frankly told him that "he was too old to have any allowance." She firmly believed that "when niggers were too old to work, they ought to be fed on grass."[31] In their mistress's estimation, this elderly man was no longer worth the food needed to keep his aging body alive, despite his previous decades of labor. Jacobs does not elaborate on this incident; but consider that even if their enslavers only occasionally denied this aged man his food allotment, he would have had to rely upon his community's support to survive.

Other North Carolina enslavers were more attentive to the dietary needs of the people they held captive. Catawba County's W. L. Bost was much more fortunately situated than the enslaved community in which Jacobs's lived. He recalled that "Ole Massa always see that we get plenty to eat. O' course it was no fancy rashions. Jes corn bread, milk, fat meat, and 'lasses." Bost explained that he was very grateful for this routine food, because "the Lord knows that was lots more than other pore niggers got. Some of them had such bad masters."[32] Nevertheless, the people on plantations like the one W. L. Bost grew up on could have used firearms—if they could gain access to any—to reclaim some of their labor from their enslavers. They could also have added variety to the otherwise repetitive and mundane rations that they received. This could have had a notable impact on their lives.

Tightfisted enslavers who deliberately underfed their bondmen were a problem not merely on North Carolina's farms and plantations but in urban spaces as well. Lunsford Lane noted that he provided much of his family's needs himself. He had purchased his own freedom, and while his wife, Martha, remained enslaved by Benjamin Smith in Raleigh, he worked to alleviate the terrible conditions she labored under. Lane recalled that Smith, a merchant and leader in the Methodist Church, "withheld from her and her children, the needful food and clothing, while he exacted from them to the uttermost all the labor they were able to perform." Smith begrudgingly provided Lane's family with what "amounted to less than a meal a day, and that of the coarser kind."[33] Lane was fortunate in that he had a profitable skill. His father had taught him an appealing way to prepare tobacco, and Lane also crafted specialty pipes with which to smoke it. He kept up a lucrative business and even counted several members of the General Assembly among his patrons. Through these ties, Lane became well known "in many parts of the State, as a tobacconist" and earned an impressive income for himself.[34] He could afford to purchase the additional food and clothing that his family needed. But Lane was quite exceptional in this regard. Most enslaved North Carolinians would have needed to take more direct action to acquire supplemental food, whether with or without a white person's consent. Alex Woods's father, Major, hunted with a firearm on their enslaver's plantation in Orange County. The elder Woods "was a good hunter an' he brought a lot o' game to de plantation." Alex proudly remembered his father's hunting prowess and recounted that Major "killed deer and turkey. All had plenty o' rabbits, possums, coons, an' squirrels" to eat.[35] The game that Major killed was cooked in the plantation's "great house" and then divided among the enslaved community and perhaps the white Woods family as well. The elder Woods was hunting with his enslaver's expressed permission, but this did not lessen his labor's impact on the community of enslaved people at the Woods plantation.

Alfred Rudolph Waud's 1871 drawing "A Snipe Shooter." Armed Black
hunters were a fixture in eighteenth- and nineteenth-century North Carolina.
Courtesy of the Historic New Orleans Collection, 1965.90.61.

The food that Major acquired for his fellow laborers was also important to
him for a more personal reason. It allowed him to assume the "patriarchal man-
tle of provider," and it thereby affirmed his manhood, which both his enslaver
and the broader institution of slavery had otherwise deeply circumscribed.
The Woods's enslaver had sold Major's first wife away from the plantation. It
is not clear where she was sold to, but she seems to have been removed from
the area, perhaps making Major part of one of the over 300,000 interstate sales

in the United States that separated a nuclear family.[36] Their enslaver saw Major Woods's hunting as another means to extract productive labor from him. This hunting saved the enslaver money but was worth far more than that to Major and the Black people in his community.

Other enslavers were less amenable to their laborers going hunting, which meant that enslaved people would sometimes take the initiative to provide for their communities regardless of their enslavers' feelings on the issue. Wake County's George Rogers told a Works Progress Administration interviewer that the enslaved folks on the plantation he grew up on went out to shoot "squirrels, turkeys, an' wild game" without bothering to get their enslaver's explicit permission to do so. They waited for him to leave the plantation and then some of them "stole de guns" and "went to de woods huntin'" for game and, it seems, camaraderie. They had an easier time borrowing these firearms than many other enslaved people would have had—Rogers remembered that their enslaver "would come back drunk" at times and "would not know, an' he did not care nuther, about we huntin' game."[37] His point about his drunken enslaver not caring about their unsupervised access to his guns might not have been completely true. After all, Rogers admitted that his peers were discreet about their hunting excursions and that the enslaver did not know what they were up to.

The chronology in Rogers's interview is difficult to follow, but these secretive hunting trips appear to have taken place during the Civil War, which further complicates this illicit firearm use. The white citizens in the neighborhood might certainly have cared about this situation—armed slaves and lenient enslavers could be a source of consternation. Consider Maggie Mials's experience in Johnston County, where she was enslaved by Tom Demaye. She remembered that he "allowed his slaves to visit, have prayer meetings, hunt, fish, an' sing and have a good time when de work was done." Unsurprisingly, these privileges drew scorn from some of the white people in the area. Some of the neighbors derisively referred to the people that Demaye enslaved as "Old Man Demayes damn free niggers."[38] Mials did not indicate whether they carried firearms on their hunting trips—with or without Demaye's permission—but his lax attitude and their white neighbors' vitriol are suggestive of this.

Enslavers used free and enslaved Black North Carolinians' armed labor for the benefit of individual white people and their families. At times, they broke the law to do so. Some towns also recognized this utility and employed gun-toting free Black men for some menial public labor projects. Consider that in 1828, Constable Frederick Moore hired Claiborne Wiggins, a "colored man," to assist him in keeping Raleigh's dog population under control.[39] Their job was very straightforward—find the unlicensed dogs that roamed the streets of the state's capital and shoot them. This brutal animal control was initially permitted under an 1817 state law, as the assembly believed that "the number of dogs kept in the towns . . . as well by slaves as by free persons, have so increased as to render them a nuisance, and greatly increase the danger of the dreadful malady Hydrophobia." In addition to spreading rabies, the dogs attacked and killed livestock in both incorporated towns and rural communities. This legislature therefore empowered the town commissioners to impose an annual tax on dogs and to either sue dog owners who did not pay it or to see to the animals' "distruction as they may think fit."[40] The racial component of the 1817 law should not be overlooked: Some white North Carolinians' believed that in some areas, three-fourths of these dogs were thought to be owned "by the negroes." One newspaper derisively remarked that "very few . . . are of any value."[41]

Wiggins's employment was useful despite its ghastliness, particularly considering the perceived threat the dogs posed to other animals and public health, but it paled in comparison to the militia's practical and symbolic importance, which Black men were excluded from. Militia duty was enshrined as a constitutive element of antebellum white men's exclusionary masculine identity. They built the state's government for themselves, and relegated Black North Carolinians to a secondary position, where their legitimate uses of violence came under white people's supervision. Many white North Carolinians were averse to undertaking this gruesome and dirty work that Wiggins was hired to do; the *Newbern Sentinel* commented that hunting down and killing stray dogs was "a duty that few like to undertake." Some white men did so, nonetheless. A "tall, muscular, well formed" constable, James A. McCain, apparently used a club to dispatch the dogs whose owners had not paid the taxes on them. Black men were not alone in this work, but the white men who did could also choose to undertake honorable armed labor.[42]

Wiggins's work was completely subordinate to Raleigh's constable and disagreeable to many people with better employment options, but like so much menial labor, it was also unremarkable in its context and appeared in the newspapers only because of an unfortunate accidental shooting. While on the job, Wiggins fired at an unlicensed dog but missed. His shot ricocheted off a post and then struck a white woman in a nearby yard whom Wiggins did not see when he fired. The injured bystander's wounds were not life threatening, but they nonetheless presented a "distressing appearance."[43] Claiborne Wiggins's armed public labor was not otherwise noteworthy to white North Carolinians. While he was able to feed his family through this labor, he was in many regards simply one of many Black people whose marketable skills with a firearm provided a service. Other free Black folks applied for firearm licenses after the 1841 law was passed, explaining that they were farmers. Stephen Evans, a "Free Man of Couler" in Wayne County, applied for "the privilege of 'Hunting with a Gun for the purpose of killing Game.'"[44] These petitions centered the free person of color's labor in their pursuit of legal firearm access.

Firearms were staples in rural spaces and in agricultural work but appeared often enough in towns and urban spaces to be unremarkable. Cooley Wiggins's firearm use was probably impacted by the accident. While he does not appear to have faced any punishment for it, the "distressing appearance" of the white woman's wound was probably traumatic for them both, although in different ways.[45] Firearm use brought many advantages to the field of labor, but people could get injured. Further, the weapons could also be hazardous to Black laborers' safety and well-being. First, while the nineteenth century witnessed advancements in firearm technology, weapons were often dangerously unreliable, particularly those that were aged, worn-out, or not well cared for. Further, much like in the present day, even with the most reliable firearms, people accidentally shot themselves or others. Sometimes this happened when they played with weapons. More people should have followed the timeless adage, "guns though *known* to be empty, should never be pointed where they would do harm if loaded."[46]

Like free Black people, enslaved laborers who worked with or around firearms sometimes accidentally shot others or were themselves injured or killed in accidents. These mishaps could result in horrific injuries or deaths, which should be understood as a part of the violence that was endemic to nineteenth-century Southern life but perhaps most poignantly felt under enslavement. Much like in the present day, many of these accidental shootings were born of carelessness. In 1825, Capt. William Richmond, a white man in Wake County, borrowed a firearm from a neighbor so that he could kill a cow. He momentarily set it down to attend to his daughter. While he was thus occupied, a "black boy who was residing in the family" picked it up and fired it, probably in sport, but fatally shot Richmond's son, Thomas, in the head. The *Raleigh Register* used the incident as a teaching moment, declaring that it "should serve as a serious caution to those who are in the daily habit of handling fire arms, and as a warning to those who use them to see they are properly put away and taken care of."[47]

Two years earlier, Eliza, an enslaved Lenoir County woman, shot her husband in the back of his head, killing him instantly. William Gaston, who enslaved the pair, sought to have her trial moved to an adjacent county because her husband was "much esteemed" by the neighborhood and, further, Eliza was "almost as much disliked."[48] He worried Eliza could not get a fair trial at home. Gaston wrote to his daughter, Susan, just a few weeks after the trial and explained that Eliza was acquitted, as "it appeared pretty evident that the dreadful act" was accidental. She had "picked up a gun not knowing it to be charged and as she entered the door of her house, ignorant that any person was there, it was fired in her hands." As the muzzle flashed, she saw her husband "fall senseless to the ground." Gaston did not comment on why Eliza had the firearm, who owned it, or why she was bringing it into her house, but his matter-of-fact approach in relating the story suggests that none of this struck him as surprising.[49] In another accident, Bob, a "young and valuable" enslaved man, was killed while helping an overseer clean a firearm. William Bray was "sitting down with his children and the negro around him" and after replacing the flint, he accidentally fired it, "discharging the contents of the gun in the groin of the slave, and burning the face slightly of one of the children." Bob lingered for about a week, likely in excruciating pain, before succumbing to his injuries. The newspaper editors used his death to rhetorically ask the public, "When will people learn prudence in the handling of fire arms"?[50]

While these accidental shootings and lax firearm storage were not unique to enslaved workers, they were a hazardous aspect of the labor that they were forced to do. The latent violence in lackadaisically stored firearms should be considered in broader discussions about the dangerous conditions that some enslaved people worked under. In the spring of 1859, three enslaved boys between eight and ten years of age came across a loaded firearm that had been "carelessly left on the piazza" at Samuel Rogers's Martin County farm. They began playing with it and it went off, either by accident or because they did not know it was loaded and had pulled the trigger in sport. The shot injured and "seriously wounded" two of the children.[51] The records are unclear, but their small bodies probably did not recover from the trauma of the gunshot wounds—the census the next year lists only one boy in that age group among the nineteen people that Rogers enslaved.[52] These losses would have been devastating for this small Black community.

Similarly, the *Newbern Spectator, and Literary Journal* reported how a "coloured boy" was playing with a firearm loaded only with wadding and "deliberately, though we believe sportively, shot his companion." The force of the charge made this load fatal, although without a ball, it might have seemed harmless to one unaccustomed to regular firearm use. Perhaps encouraged by that fatal accident, "A CITIZEN" wrote a letter to the editor, which the *Spectator, and Literary Journal* printed in the very next column of the same issue, wherein they asked three questions to the town commissioners, noting that "the whole town is interested in the subjects of inquiry." The first two questions were about how the city did not light the streetlamps in the winter (presumably not early enough) and how the city streets were impassible in rainy weather. The third question implored, "Is there no town regulation, or cannot there be one enacted, to prevent boys from carrying guns?" Tellingly, the writer was not sure about the firearm regulations, which suggests that this was not a primary concern until the accidental shooting death of an enslaved worker. The writer related, as further evidence, how "a white boy and a negro" were trying to shoot a duck when, similarly to Cooley Wiggins's mishap, they accidentally shot a Black woman who was working in her enslaver's yard.[53]

This woman, whose name did not appear in the records, was one of many enslaved people whose labor put them in harm's way, even when they were not using firearms themselves. Late one November evening in 1858, Dinah, an enslaved teenager, went to J. V. Jordan's drugstore in New Bern to get medicine, presumably for her enslaver, Nancy Lawrence. A fifteen-year-old white boy, Elisha Cuthbert, and a few of his peers, were in the shop and handling a rifle when it "went off accidentally." The ball struck Dinah at the rear base of her skull, "terribly fracturing" her jaw and exiting at her chin. Cuthbert cried, "great god what shall I do" and ran for a doctor, but Dinah died shortly after help arrived. One of the medical professionals who examined Dinah, Alexander Taylor, believed the ball "Severed or cut the Interal Jugular vein and Caroted Artery."[54] The coroner confirmed that the shooting was accidental, and the newspapers raised yet "another warning against the careless use of fire-arms."[55] Similarly, in the spring of 1859, James L. Murphy went out to shoot birds in his yard and, running low on ammunition, he sent a "valuable house girl" to retrieve powder and shot for him. Later, as she returned the leftover ammunition to the house, Murphy slipped, fumbled the weapon, and accidentally "discharged the entire load in the girl's head, literally cutting the entire top of her head off and scattering it in fragments upon the floor and surrounding objects." A jury of inquest confirmed that the shooting was an accident.[56] Again, this unnamed young woman's violent, untimely, and graphic death would have been hard felt in her community. There were probably several other enslaved workers—her family, friends, and kin—who bore witness to the carnage that Murphy's carelessness created.

A firearm could also be dangerous for the individual who was handling it, which for enslaved people could result when working under an enslaver's orders. It is also often difficult to determine whether an enslaved person was working for their enslaver or for themselves; for instance, someone who could hunt benefited from the process, but it could also have spared their enslaver the cost of purchasing meat. In 1841, Lewis, a twelve-year-old enslaved by a Mr. Ratcliffe in Wilmington, found an old rifle, the barrel of which was partially obstructed by lead that had melted and then resolidified. Lewis tried to use a flame to melt it and clear the barrel but probably did not realize that the rifle was loaded. The gun went off into his face—the load entered above his eye and exited through the back of his head—and he died a few painful hours later.[57] It is unclear if Lewis was attempting to clean the rifle for himself, for an adult relative, or for Ratcliffe. Alternatively, enslaved people might experience a dangerous malfunction while using a firearm. In 1844, an enslaved Alamance County man named Jesse was out hunting, perhaps for sport, to feed himself or others, or under his enslaver's orders. He took aim at a squirrel but when he fired, the gun's breech pin came "flying out" of the back and "lodged in his head." The bit of broken metal killed Jesse instantly; though his aim was true, and he killed the squirrel despite his own fatal accident.[58]

Finally, armed free and enslaved Black people sometimes lost their own lives in ways that were not clearly accidental. Consider that in November 1857, a Washington County man who was identified only through his enslaver, Allen Grist, Esq., was killed "by the discharge of a gun in his own hands." Similarly, the Brunswick County coroner held an inquest over an enslaved man named Alexander, who was found dead in the woods. The coroner believed him to have died "by the accidental firing of a gun in his own hands."[59] While it cannot be definitively traced through the records, these men's firearm use was likely a part of their labor, whether for themselves and their families or their enslavers. Further, we cannot know what either of these men's intentions were, and while the authorities believed the deaths were accidents, other men and women have similarly taken their own lives. These are just a small sample of those accidental shootings that involved enslaved and free people of color, but the antebellum newspapers were also littered with abundant examples of white North Carolinians who accidentally shot and injured or killed themselves, their friends, their children, and even fellow members of slave patrols.[60]

The assembly and many white citizens believed that African-descended people's armed labor was different from and subordinate to white men's idealized form of armed labor, which was rooted in their gendered defense of their social and political communities. The assembly removed free Black North Carolinian men from the militia by 1823, officially disenfranchised them in 1835, and thereby denied them the full citizenship that white men claimed for themselves.[61] This constructed inequality into the armed work of each group, inequality that was manifested on North Carolina's farms and in the menial armed labor Black men performed in the public sector. Returning to the example of Free Willis, both he and Herring benefited from his hunting vermin, but Willis was the subordinate providing the labor in their transactional relationship. Further, the free Black man understood that his firearm use was possible only at white people's pleasure—whatever independence he gained from it was an illusion, waiting for a crisis to give it the lie. Even before the General Assembly passed the firearm licensing law, Willis voluntarily surrendered his firearm to another white neighbor during a "Negro rising." The white man held onto the weapon until the situation subsided.[62] Free Willis's gun allowed him to feed himself and perhaps helped him to maintain a white benefactor, but it did not mitigate his position as a racial subordinate in an enslavers' society whose labor reinforced his white employer's position. Willis understood that he needed to maintain a particular positionality in the community to keep himself armed and thereby keep his belly full.

George Rogers's fellow slaves took their enslaver's firearms and hunted game to provide for their community, but North Carolina enslavers also harnessed their Black subordinates' armed labor for their own sport hunting excursions, and on these trips, the white hunters maintained a racially stratified and hierarchical division of labor. Hunting was one of Southern men's quintessential gendered performances. This was especially true for those who fashioned themselves as men of leisure. In their lives, hunting was not labor but sport, a venue through which they might display their manly skills. They were financially comfortable and unmotivated by concerns of subsistence—some of them even gave their quarry away to less fortunate members of their community, which both affirmed and publicly displayed their own elite status.[63] Both Black and white men of means focused on these sporting and social aspect of hunting. This performance of independence and manhood was probably of even greater importance to the free Black men who chose to embrace it than it was for white men of similar socioeconomic standing because the General Assembly's laws and local social customs harshly circumscribed their ability to live their lives with few limitations, as white men did.[64] This was wholly dissimilar from the "entirely uneducated, poverty-stricken vagabonds" who lived in North Carolina's turpentine forests and, as Frederick Law Olmsted described, raised "a little corn, and possibly a few roods of potatoes, cowpeas, and coleworts . . . own a few swine . . . and pretty certainly, also, a rifle and dogs; and the men, ostensibly, occupy most of their time in hunting."[65] Olmsted painted an extreme picture of these poor white North Carolinians, but the reality of this situation was that both Black and white people in lower socioeconomic positions hunted out of necessity, even if this labor secondarily provided socialization or amusement.

Hunting trips offer insight into how many white men understood Black people's firearm-related labor as separate from, and ultimately subordinate to, their own. Historian Nicolas Proctor's work demonstrates that white hunters brought subordinates along on hunting trips to bolster their own manhood and to serve as witnesses of their prowess and skill, which they understood as inseparably masculine and white.[66] This gendered performance required an audience, of course. In January 1833, a white hunter who boldly styled himself "Natty Bumppo" after James Fenimore Cooper's "hunter, or scout," recounted a hunting trip in Brunswick County for the readership of *American Turf Register and Sporting Magazine*. This trip was arranged to celebrate "the recollections of that glorious day which shed such bright and unfading lustre upon the American arms at New Orleans," and in the account, masculine military and hunting prowess were intentionally combined in both the battle and the figure of Bumppo. This hunting party consisted of "five gentlemen and a youth" in the celebratory group, but the writer very briefly admitted that there was at least one other person present: a "servant" who looked after the white men's horses when they mounted their stands.[67] This person was likely enslaved. Alonza Hodge, a Wake County farmer, held his own far more casual hunting trips, but he similarly used subordinate Black labor on them. The squirrel hunter would bring along his young son and a similarly aged child whom his wealthy father-in-law enslaved. Hodge would shoot the squirrels but then watch in amusement as the two boys raced each other to retrieve his quarry.[68]

Upper class white women sometimes accompanied social hunting parties, albeit generally only when they were young and unmarried. These young women were still "poised on the brink of womanhood" and served a mostly social function—they did not pose a threat to the otherwise masculine enterprise.[69] Similarly, the Black auxiliaries who attended their enslavers on hunts were there as outsiders. They were present to perform labor. They managed their parties' horses and dogs, prepared refreshments for the hunters, carried equipment, and retrieved the hunters' kills. They undoubtedly massaged the white hunters' egos as well. These white women and Black men may have served different roles, but they were all merely accessories to the white hunters' manliness. Many enslavers had no qualms about deploying their bondpeople's armed labor in supporting roles on hunting trips or taking individuals target shooting, because they were able to downplay those Black men's actions. Those workers were not acting on their own accord, but much like the laborers who accompanied hunting trips, they were present merely as extensions of their enslavers' wills.[70] These hunters' Black laborers demonstrated their enslavers' wealth and manliness and provided labor and perhaps company; but whether they enjoyed themselves was beside the point.

In the antebellum period, labor was often performed along heavily gendered lines. There was some flexibility in this for those people who lived under challenging economic conditions or outside of the dominant social constructions. White male hunters expected white women to be casual subordinates on hunts; but women from economically struggling families made far more practical decisions about what types of labor they performed. Further, the assembly recognized that women of color labored differently than many white women did, and it therefore explicitly framed the 1840 firearm licensing law to apply to both men and women of color. This was a deliberate move by the legislators; one should note that the other laws passed during this session did not use such gender inclusive language.[71] The assembly included Black women in the license law because the lawmakers believed that Black women's armed labor was common enough to need white people's supervision. Women of color's quotidian armed labor is difficult to track through the historical record, but examples abound of their using weapons in crimes, which landed them in courtrooms and their stories in North Carolina's newspapers. There is no reason to believe that they did not use their armed labor to feed their families. Indeed, consider that enslavers put their Black men and women to work on many of the same physical tasks and did not generally shield enslaved women from tough agricultural labor. Also, free women of color likely labored similarly to their enslaved counterparts, and their socially marginalized status relegated them to a place outside of the dominant society's gender expectations. Certainly, women of color found employment in some skilled trades like spinning, weaving, and dressmaking; but many of them also performed a range of labors on their families' farms.

Further, many common and poor white women performed arduous physical labor, including tasks that elites would have considered outside of the bounds of respectable womanhood. In fact, their poverty "violated norms of white femininity" and bordered on racial transgression.[72] As Deborah Gray White explains, "Black women often worked with black men at tasks considered by most white Americans to be either too difficult or inappropriate for females. All women worked hard, but when white women consistently did field labor it was considered temporary, irregular, or extraordinary, putting them on a par with slaves."[73] In his deeply racist antislavery writing, Hinton Rowan Helper acknowledged white women's labor and refuted the proslavery argument that white people could not bear the South's challenging climate. He roared, "Too hot in the South for white men! It is not too hot for white women. Time and again, in different counties in North Carolina, have we seen the poor white wife of the poor white husband, following him in the harvest-field from morning till night, binding up the grain as it fell from his cradle."[74] Even some white women whose households enslaved a few people did farm work, although elites often ignored this because it problematized the racial hierarchy that they painstakingly constructed and defended. Helper argued that abolition would bring industry to the state and allow white women to find "far more profitable and congenial" employment. He believed that hard agricultural labor degraded them, and he wanted "to see no more plowing, or hoeing, or raking, or grain-binding" by these "poor toiling white women."[75] North Carolina's women made practical decisions about their labor.

Women of color did not shy away from pragmatically using their armed labor to the benefit of themselves and their communities. Black women recognized their ability to labor as arduously as men did, but this did not conflict with the ways that they understood their womanhood. During a speech she gave in 1851, Sojourner Truth criticized many white people's views of women generally, and of Black women particularly, as inferior to men. She emphatically called to the audience, "Look at me! Look at my arm! I have plowed, and planted, and gathered into barns, and no man could head me—and ar'n't I a woman? I could work as much and eat as much as a man (when I could get it), and bear de lash as well—and ar'n't I a woman?"[76] In her bold claim for equality, Truth argued that her gender did not preclude her—and more importantly, nor did it protect her—from performing the same arduous labors that her male counterparts undertook. North Carolina's legislators recognized this same equal labor potential in the 1841 firearm licensing law, though they drew a detrimental conclusion.

Neither Sojourner Truth's grueling work experiences nor her ability to withstand them diminished her womanhood because she understood her identity differently than her white contemporaries did. Even though they were not enslaved themselves, free Black women's social positions were devalued because they lived in a society that saw enslavement as Black people's default condition. As such, many African-descended women pragmatically embraced a separate female culture in which armed labor was unremarkable. Some Southerners understood armed labor to be a masculine domain, but this does not mean that women who worked in this manner were necessarily performing masculine roles.[77] Women of color's constructed culture included labor that many considered to be manly. They hauled logs, drove plows, dug ditches, cleared roads, and even constructed railroads. This work led some women, like Wake County's Plaz Williams, to remember working "like a man" while they were enslaved. As one historian points out, every member of enslaved Black households was "expected to contribute to the household economy."[78] This was no

John G. Darby's woodcut of Harriet Tubman, which appeared as the frontispiece to her biography. Tubman carried firearms in her abolition work and during her service with the United States Army during the Civil War. While the records are scant, Black women in North Carolina and elsewhere also carried and used arms in various capacities. Courtesy of the National Portrait Gallery, Smithsonian Institution.

less true for free people of color. If these Black women and their families were living in rural North Carolina, they might have engaged in subsistence hunting. This was especially likely for those women who headed their own households or who lived in one wherein the male head did not hunt.

Enslavers deployed armed Black workers for a variety of jobs, but both free and enslaved people of color used armed defensive labor for their own purposes, deploying a "heroic masculinity" to protect themselves and others.[79] When they turned their armed labor into defensive force, they were sometimes able to put their oppressors on dangerous ground. In 1860, runaways were living somewhere in Julia Chapman's Craven County neighborhood. Her son John, who also had his own household and family in the area, decided to find and break up their camp. For backup, he called on his sixteen-year-old brother and a twenty-three-year-old white "farm laborer," both of whom lived in Julia's household.[80] The three men managed to find the camp, but "before they could learn anything, or make any examination," one of the Black men fatally shot John Chapman in the chest. The two younger white men managed to escape.[81] Local white people believed that the shooter was Ben Soon, a man who had fled Pitt County's William Grimes "several years" prior. Chapman was well-liked, and his neighbors offered a $400 reward for Soon's capture; but he evaded them. The advertisements for help to "catch the murderer" continued through at least August 1862, almost two full years after the shooting.[82] Soon's armed defense drove back this move against his family's home and cost John Chapman his life, but enslaved workers were sometimes placed in these dangerous situations as well. In 1781, a man enslaved by William Bryan was killed while aiding in the "suppressing of Rebel Slaves."[83] The records are silent on his name, but one wonders how he felt about this task. Fugitives sometimes created problems for enslaved people, and this enslaved man had limited opportunity to resist Bryan's orders, which ultimately put him in the rebels' crosshairs.

Armed labor was useful, and it was occasionally coupled with people of color's skillsets to develop performances. While there were limited opportunities in this field, some people of color in were able to market their firearm use, among other skills, as a spectacle. During the summer of 1864, Henry Armand London, a student at the University of North Carolina, paid two dollars to see what he described in his diary as "the greatest wonder of the world a Quadroon who shaves, writes, loads and fires a pistol, shoots a bow + arrows, &c." London was clearly impressed—he added that this man of color was "truly a wonder."[84] This diary entry is more insightful than it appears at first glance. London enjoyed this man's performance, but the shaving, writing,

An advertisement in the *Daily Progress* for the novelty act that Henry Armand London saw in July 1864. The University of North Carolina student described the talented performer as a "Quadroon" in his diary. Courtesy of Newspapers.com.

and weapons use are not particularly interesting actions by themselves. What the young scholar failed to record in his diary, however, is that this performer was born without arms. Curiously, the advertisements in the Wilmington and Raleigh newspapers, which fit London's description, did not mention the performer's race but offered up a range of activities that he performed with his feet.[85] This omission of a person's racial identity was typically an indication that the individual in question was white—racial "others" were generally marked as such in the newspapers, legislative and court records, and militia rolls.

As for this performer, the *Daily Progress* explained that he was "poor and has no hands to work for his living, but is willing to work in the only way he is capable-by exhibiting himself and endeavoring to please the public." This allegedly multiracial man turned his armed labor into a novelty act, intended to be displayed to a broad audience of people looking for a break from the exhausting war. The conveners offered half-priced admission for "soldiers and soldiers' wives" and for "servants and children."[86] How London determined this man's racial identity is unclear. He might have guessed—an effort to ascribe racial meaning to the performer's perceptible physical traits. Of course, he might have been incorrect—the newspapers offer no corroboration of London's interpretation. In either case, however, this performer's racial identity impacted the young man as much as his physical state, if not more so. Whether intentionally or subconsciously, London understood this entertainer as a qua-droon who could "load and shoot a pistol," among other things, but not as a person who had been born without arms, which was the point of this novelty act.[87]

AFRICAN-DESCENDED NORTH CAROLINIANS used their armed labor to benefit themselves and others. From the colonial era through to Nat Turner's rebellion, both the General Assembly and individual white citizens agreed that Black people's armed labor potential was far too important to allow their com-plete disarmament. Despite firearms' racially charged social and cultural value, the legislature created a series of laws to allow white people to safely use this labor. Even after the state's post-Turner reversal, many white citizens continued to harness enslaved Black people's gun use in ways that benefited themselves, regardless of the state law to the contrary. Through this labor dynamic, white North Carolinians understood Black people's armed labor as subordinate to their own. On an individual basis, they decided which of their laborers they trusted to handle firearms, much in the same way that they might choose who might undertake a range of other jobs. For instance, not every enslaved person on a plantation would be trusted to drive a prized team of oxen, travel to a dis-tant market with goods to sell, or live separately without their enslaver's direct supervision. White people's commitment to using this labor, even when it broke the law, speaks to armed Black laborers' remarkable utility in the South.

This labor, however, was performed not only for white people. Black North Carolinians used firearms for their own benefit, and this was far more import-ant than the ways in which white people sought to make use of them. Black people also sometimes labored with little regard for the state legislators or white citizens' demands on their gun use. Many free people of color lived in rural areas and relied on game to feed their families. As farmers, they also used their weapons to protect their livestock and manage the vermin in their fields. For those who were enslaved, their firearms allowed them to supplement their often-meager food allotments. Armed, they were better able to protect their communities from the constant encroachment of enslavers and other outsid-ers. This armed labor allowed some of North Carolina's free and enslaved Black residents to carve out more independent and fulfilling lives for themselves and their communities in the face of oppression.

CHAPTER FOUR

The Free Black Community

While North Carolina's free people of color were able to make comfortable lives for themselves and a few free Black families managed to acquire considerable wealth, which sometimes included slave property, most of them lived under tenuous socioeconomic conditions. As late as 1860, around 75 percent of free people of color were "farmers, common laborers, ditchers, and wood-choppers," or similarly employed. On average, they earned a paltry thirty-four dollars each year. North Carolina's laws and social customs locked its free Black residents into a highly restrictive intermediary position that lay between the severe constraints placed on enslaved workers and the bountiful liberties that white male citizens possessed. About 70 percent of the free people of color were multiracial.[1] These challenging conditions led one historian in the 1920s to declare that "the most pathetic figure" in the state before the Civil War "was the free negro. Hedged about with social and legal restrictions, he ever remained an anomaly in the social and political life of the State."[2] This point was exaggerated and lacked nuance—free people of color played a minor but active role in politics prior to 1835 and continued to foster political discussions afterward—but they were heavily constrained by the potent combination of state law and white citizens' prejudice.

Free Black North Carolinians were discouraged from keeping social relationships with either white people or enslaved Black people. They often disregarded the state laws on the latter, but in doing so, they were not displaying any "inclinations to criminality. They were merely struggling to find an outlet for their pent-up emotions and natural sociability."[3] Nevertheless, many white citizens worried about these ties, particularly as the free Black population continued to grow. In addition to the natural increase in numbers of free Black people, in the early nineteenth century, the assembly permitted manumission as a reward for "meritorious service," a softening of the colonial era's more stringent policies. The vague term was often left undefined, even in the case of a child.[4] The free Black population grew more rapidly than both the white and enslaved populations until the 1850s, despite an 1830 law requiring enslavers to post $1,000 bonds for their freed workers' good behavior and a mandate that freedpeople leave the state. In this context, some white tradesmen began to worry about competition for jobs.[5] These anxieties help to explain why many white people wanted the activities of their free Black neighbors restricted, including their gun use. North Carolina was not alone in this racial gun control—several other slave states passed similar laws, and most did so earlier. North Carolina's 1841 law was part of a larger code that marked free Black people as a subordinate class. As John Hope Franklin wrote, the "mantle of suspicion was always around them" and consequently, their freedom was precarious.[6]

White people's opinions on Black North Carolinians' firearm use mattered because of the local application of the firearm laws. White men's support for Black firearm license applicants was an important part of this regulatory process, and some people of color even challenged their county's application of the gun law. For instance, in 1841, a Craven County patrol came across Benjamin Morgan and his son George as both mixed-race men were carrying firearms without the required licenses. The patrollers seized the Morgans's guns on the spot, as they would have done to enslaved people. Some white neighbors stepped forward to support the Morgans and petitioned the county court on their behalf. William Simmons, John Harris, John Ferrand, Obid Palmer, Burton Carmon, and James M. Beasley protested that the Morgans's guns were "taken away by Patrols arguably to an Act of the General Assembly." The six white men testified that they had known the Morgans for fifteen years and that while the father and son hunted "with Dog and Gun," neither had ever "done any Injury to any person for and by reson [*sic*] of their having been privileged to hunt." The white petitioners therefore requested that the county court return the Morgans's weapons and permit them to carry them in the future.[7] Further, the petitioners questioned whether this seizure was warranted in the first place. They wrote that the Morgans's guns were taken "arguably" in accordance with the law. The father and son had both broken the law, but their sympathetic white neighbors did not see them as threats to white people's lives or property. Finally, while this support benefited the Morgans, it also recalled the supervision placed over armed enslaved workers. The Black men remained vetted and approved by the courts and the white community.

White advocates were also instrumental in Black people's successful applications for licenses. The mandated licenses mitigated the interference of patrollers and other white people, but acquiring a firearms license was not a foregone conclusion. Some applicants were unsuccessful because they could not rally the support of credible white associates. Some of those people of color who did not have white advocates probably avoided this process entirely and might have simply chosen to carry their firearms illegally. White sponsors vouched for their Black associates, and their support indicated that the Black petitioners were established and trustworthy members of the community. This was vital in an era where many white people were antagonistic toward the free Black population, some to an extreme degree. A writer to the *Western Democrat* believed that free Black people should be sold into slavery, which would "be equivalent to bringing an equal number of able-bodied men from abroad." Beyond strengthening the state's workforce and its economy, the writer believed that this would help free Black people, noting, "I know the degraded and unhappy condition of free negroes, and I am fully persuaded that reducing them to slavery would be the very best thing that could befall them."[8]

These white advocates who appear in the records were exclusively male, and some of them were men of considerable standing in their communities. As Laura Edwards explains, white men's testimony "supposedly captured and conveyed truth precisely because they were independent, not subject to the pressure of superiors, landlords, or employers, and therefore free to think and speak for themselves."[9] It would have been difficult for a person of color or a white woman to meet these criteria. Further, white men's support for Black gun users could extend over several years. Benjamin Morgan relied on a few white men's ongoing support on multiple occasions over about a decade. He first appeared in the records after he and his son had their weapons seized by a patrol in 1841; but in 1850, the Craven County grand jury issued a presentment against him for carrying a firearm without a license. In June of that year, he signed a $100 recognizance bond to ensure that he would answer the indictment and was matched by a cosigner named Obid Palmer. Palmer had stepped forward nearly a decade earlier as a supporter on the 1841 petition to have the Morgans's firearms returned from the patrol.[10]

Despite examples of white North Carolinians' support for free people of color's firearm use, before the 1841 license law, large segments of the white population called for limitations on free Black people's firearm use, and some advocated for a complete ban. In December 1828, some white men in Craven County complained to the legislature about the "constant and growing practice of Persons of Colour hunting with dogs and guns," which they saw as a threat to white property owners.[11] North Carolina's free people of color had even less political influence after they were disenfranchised in 1835, so white citizens were instrumental in both the maintenance and restriction of free Black people's gun use. Already in 1835, several white Craven County residents petitioned the assembly to pass a law that would require every free person of color to "obtain a license from the county court before he could have or use a gun or ammunition, which license he should only obtain upon satisfactory proof to said court of his good moral and peaceable character, and upon entering into bonds with good security for his good behavior and honest deportment." They also worried that their free Black neighbors might cast their lot with the enslaved community in the event of an uprising. A similar petition from Halifax County in 1840, weeks before the state licensing law was passed, sought to keep free Black people from "carrying or using fire arms under any circumstances whatever."[12]

Some white North Carolinians continued to agitate over free Black people's gun use, even after the law was passed. In 1851, Beaufort County representative William H. Tripp introduced a petition from thirty-nine men in his district who believed that the license law was ineffective. They argued that a free Black man could "prove his character to be good" and get licensed, "altho he was the meanest villan in the whole county." Further, they stated that guns gave their free Black neighbors the "opportunity which they make use of to kill a good many of our cattle and sheep And to corrupt the morals of our slave population by loaning them guns and hunting with them on the Sabbath."[13] In solidarity with his constituents, Tripp introduced a bill to "prevent free persons of color from owning or carrying fire arms," though the assembly's Committee on Propositions and Grievances did not share this sentiment.[14] If passed, this would have effectively disarmed all the state's African-descended residents, as enslaved people were already banned from using firearms. Ironically, Tripp would later violate the spirit of the petition during the Civil War, when he armed a man he enslaved. Ultimately, during the tense Secession Winter, North Carolina banned free people of color from carrying or keeping any weapons and also removed the license provision. Violators who persisted in possessing arms would thereafter be fined "not less than fifty dollars."[15]

These petitions must be understood within their social context. While firearms stand out because of their usefulness and symbolic value, the license law was part of a larger trend of racially motivated restrictions on the lives of free people of color. White citizens encouraged their elected representatives to pass a wide range of measures that targeted the people of color living in their communities, not just laws about firearms. A petition from December 1850 argued for a tax on "negro mechanics" to discourage them from competing with white workmen.[16] Other white North Carolinians argued that the state's free Black residents should be exiled to colonies in Liberia, to "the Abolition and Free Soil States," or to US territories in "the far West."[17] Nonetheless, free Black North Carolinians had practical uses for their firearms. They were predominately agricultural people, and many lived in rural areas, which played a role in their license applications. Randolph County's William Calvin explained that he needed a gun "to shoot hawks, crows, +c." His petition would have resonated with many other free Black farmers—both species of birds were agricultural nuisances, alongside the foxes, skunks, and other wildlife that preyed upon their poultry and livestock or damaged their crops.[18] Additionally, many North Carolinians, both Black and white, hunted for their food. Firearms were practically useful, and it is unsurprising that many free people of color requested firearm licenses from their county courts and that those without licenses were brought before the courts for violating the state's gun laws.

Navigating the legal system in order to access a weapon could be difficult. In addition to relying on their families to do so, Black North Carolinians, like Benjamin Morgan, also turned to white neighbors, business associates, and friends for aid. These interracial connections were undoubtedly important sources of support, but white men's useful influence did not negate the role that Black people played. An individual's reputation-based credit was also vitally important to the process. As Laura Edwards explains, credit functioned similarly to honor but was more applicable to marginalized individuals like free people of color who, due to legal and social constraints, were unable to deploy or defend honor in the same ways as white men. Within their communities, Black men "could acquire credibility, negating elements of their subordinate status through their own actions and others' assessment of them." They had to meet their white neighbors' set expectations and could then bolster their social cachet and potentially gain privileges.[19] Families could marshal important financial resources, but they also extended social credit. This credit was less impactful at the county court than the support white men offered, but licenses partly rested on how white people perceived the Black applicant's family. Free people of color could sometimes transform their families' credit into financial and judicial support from the white men in their neighborhoods.

Individuals used their family's credit to strengthen their own credentials. In February 1842, five members of the Walden family petitioned the Randolph County Court for licenses on the condition that the "Worshipful Court" satisfactorily determined that they were "of good moral character." Sixty-eight-year-old William Walden and four of his sons—forty-year-old William D., forty-two-year-old Anderson, thirty-five-year-old John C., and fourteen-year-old Stanford B.—submitted a joint petition in which they described themselves as "mulattos, or free persons of color."[20] This collaborative effort stands out because each of the Walden men was old enough to have petitioned the court on his own accord, as every other applicant seems to have done, and Stanford was the only one of the brothers who still lived in their father's household.[21] This petition was not wholly proactive. In the fall of 1841, one of the William Waldens was charged with habitually "keeping, using and

Many Black people used their firearms for farm labor, like this man who is shooting crows. Collection of the Image of the Black in Western Art Research Project and Photo Archive, W. E. B. Du Bois Institute for African and African American Research, Harvard University. Image courtesy of Lisa Schiller Fine Art, New York.

carrying about with him, firearms." The following February, Anderson was also indicted for carrying a rifle during the previous September "to the evil example of all other free negroes, Mulattoes and free persons of color."[22] Further, the two Waldens were among the first free Black people in the county to be thus charged. Their collaborative approach allowed the sons to rely on their father's social credit to reinforce their own places within the community. This paternal connection was most important for the youngest son, but all of them benefited. William Walden Sr. had lived in the neighborhood for a few decades and had accumulated many personal and business relationships over that period.[23] His four sons probably did not have similar community connections. Their father was a farmer, and the Walden sons continued the practice. Many of the social and business connections they did have probably came through the years they spent working in their father's fields.

William Walden Sr.'s social credit manifested itself in the broad community support for the combined Walden petition. His good standing was evidenced by the assistance that William Macon; William Brown; John R. Brown; John D. Brown, Esq.; John Rainse; Levi B. Branson; William Brady; John Brady; Matthias Bray; Thomas Macon; Thomas C. Moffitt, P M; Brazil H. Hix;

James Gilliland; Jerh. S. Bray; Henry Dorsett; and Tidance Lane offered on the Waldens' behalf. Fourteen of these sixteen white men lived in Randolph County, and the other two were in neighboring Chatham County.[24] The white men wrote a letter to the court, certifying that they were "well acquainted with [the Waldens], that they are free persons, And that the said William Walden Sen has lived in our neighbourhood at least thirty years, + has raised his family in the same + that so far as our Knowledge Extends Neither . . . William Walden Sen nor any of his family has Ever been charged with the least immoral conduct Whatever. And they have always bourn an honest Character obtaining their support by the cultivation of their own Lands."[25] These white men believed that the Waldens were trustworthy and hardworking farmers who had not previously posed a threat with their firearms and would not do so in the future. While this was an exercise in benevolence, it was also a statement of confidence. If the armed Walden family created a dangerous situation in Randolph County, then the signatories' own lives and property would have been at risk.[26]

The Walden sons likely could not have drawn such support on their own merits. Some of the signatories were noteworthy. John D. Brown was a justice of the peace, a probate judge, and a judge on the court of chancery; Lane and Macon served as justices of the peace, and Moffitt was a member of the clergy.[27] Their father's decades of social and business ties were instrumental. He knew these white men. In 1839, he and John Rainse had jointly signed a promissory note for almost $100, probably after borrowing money together. In the fall of 1841, before the application, Walden Sr. was charged with carrying a rifle without a license and John D. Brown signed for fifty dollars on the free Black man's recognizance bond. Henry Dorsett was the justice of the peace who acknowledged receipt of Walden and Brown's bond.[28] After the Walden patriarch's death in 1842, Thomas Macon became the administrator of his estate, and he settled Walden and Rains's debts with another deceased man, whose estate was managed by another of Walden's license petition signatories, John R. Brown.[29] The other signatories proved challenging to connect directly to Walden Sr., though these connections likely exist, but many of them can be linked to each other.[30] The Walden patriarch might have known each of them, or perhaps he relied on his connections with some of them to draw the others in. Ultimately, however, how he was related to them is less important than his ability to marshal their support for his family. The Walden sons drew on this long-standing community network to define themselves as upstanding members of their community whom the court should allow to carry firearms.

In addition to this support from white neighbors, the free Black community played a major role in its own license acquisitions and in the protection of its members' gun use. Aid from the Black community was at least as important as that provided by white people, and perhaps even more so. In the present day, many Americans do not consider family relationships an integral part of an individual's gun use, outside of older relatives teaching youths to shoot or hunt, or someone passing down an heirloom firearm. This *was* the case for free African-descended North Carolinians, however. The 1841 license law identified free people of color as a group that the state needed to police, but it also inadvertently connected their firearm use to their families and communities. This reliance on the broader community dramatically set their firearm use apart from white citizens' ties to their own weapons. The government in Raleigh and the county courts dictated the process by which free people of color could use firearms, but Black North Carolinians did not passively accept the assembly's mandates. They exerted their own wills on this matter as well.

In addition to the applications for firearm licenses, Black North Carolinians oftentimes relied on their family members and on Black friends and associates for help when they were brought into court for violating the law. This was no small matter for the often cash-strapped free Black households. During the December 1849 term of the Craven County Court, thirty-seven-year-old Wright Pettifer was indicted for carrying a firearm without a license, and his mother, Rose, matched the $100 that he put up for his own recognizance. Sixty-nine-year-old Rose and her eighty-year-old husband lived on a farm in Wright's neighborhood.[31] Additionally, in 1851, fifty-one-year-old Thomas Fenner was indicted for violating the license law. John Fenner, likely Thomas's older brother, was co-bound for his court appearance. This pair of Fenners were men of modest means and they lived on adjacent plots in a neighborhood that contained other free Black Fenner households.[32]

People of color sometimes found themselves in firearm-related legal trouble alongside family members. Benjamin and George Morgan provide one example; but consider that John, William, and James Godette were also all indicted for unlicensed gun possession during the Craven County Court's June 1851 term. Their precise relationship is difficult to determine from the records, but they are connected through their unique surname, spatial proximity, and support for each other through these legal troubles. John matched the fifty dollars that William was bound for on his own recognizance. Nineteen-year-old William was a laborer living in George Godette Jr.'s household. John, also nineteen, was a blacksmith living with and probably working for a mixed-race blacksmith

TABLE 4.1 White Craven County Residents Connected to the Pettifer and
Moore Families' Indictments and Trials (1849–1850)

Charge Initiator or Witness	*Indicted Free Persons of Color*	
Arthur Gaskins	Wright Pettifer	
	Frank Pettifer	
James G. Gaskins	Wright Pettifer	
Joseph Gaskins	Wright Pettifer	
Arthur Ipock	Rose Pettifer	
Edward Ipock	Wright Pettifer	
	Frank Pettifer	
	Israel Pettifer	
John P. Ipock	Rose Pettifer	
Daniel Simmons	Frank Pettifer	
James Harrington	John Moore	Baker Moore
	Nathan Moore	Banon Moore
	Stephen Moore	Alfred Moore
James Toler, Jr.	John Moore	Baker Moore
	Nathan Moore	Banon Moore
	Stephen Moore	Alfred Moore

in the county seat of New Bern.[33] Seventy-one-year-old James was a farmer
with fifty dollars' worth of property, and he signed a fifty-dollar recognizance
bond for himself, which John matched, as he had also done for William.[34]

This family support meant that those free people of color who broke the
law, for whatever reason, were taking a collective financial risk. Black and white
friends and colleagues also signed recognizance bonds, but the potential ramifications for family members could be big. Bonds sometimes amounted to a
few hundred dollars, and most free Black families had modest resources. Black
families were not the only sources of legal and financial support, but when individuals made the decision to carry firearms without licenses, they were drawn
into the legal system where their family's financial resources were in jeopardy.
Indicted free Black persons often had at least one family member or friend as
a cosigner. Bonds like these threatened many free Black households' resources
and some members' freedom.[35] In September 1858, twenty-five-year-old farmer

Jacob Fenner was indicted and bound for $100, though he only had some fifty dollars in real estate. Thomas Fenner stood with Jacob and was bound for the same amount. The census indicates that he did not have any property, but his wife, Penelope, owned land worth twenty-five dollars.[36] Beyond the risk of the bonds, convicted persons faced fines and court costs, which could be much more substantial. For instance, the Craven County Court fined John Godette only one dollar, and Farnifold Moore six dollars, but it also ordered that each of them pay the court costs. It is not clear what the total costs were in their cases, but they might have had to pay anywhere between the $9.20 that George Bragg faced to the $21.15 leveled against Thomas Fenner for court costs.[37]

A guilty plea would not necessarily evade heavy costs, though the expense would likely be reduced by a speedy resolution. Ben Banton and Jesse Mitchell were indicted separately in Craven County, and each pleaded guilty in 1850. They were each fined twenty two dollars and costs. Banton, a thirty-year-old farmer, and Mitchell, a fifty-year-old laborer, were both heads of households, but neither owned any real estate. Those who could not afford these mounting costs could find their freedom at stake. Craven County's Joseph Banton could not afford the twenty two dollar fine plus costs after his own license violation, and the court ordered that he "be hired out" until the sum was paid.[38] Any free people of color who were convicted of breaking the firearm law and who were unable to pay the fines could be hired out for up to five years. The impact would be magnified if two members of the same household were out hunting or sport shooting together and then indicted and convicted. The family would then face double these costs. This could have a significant impact on the involved families' economic situations as well as on the individuals' freedom. Laura Edwards notes that the "fines, imprisonment, and court costs" associated with trials could drive families into poverty. Warren Milteer adds that in some cases, high fines might have been a tactic by the court to ensure that the defendant would be unable to pay and would then be hired out.[39] In this sense, illegal firearm use risked a family's financial standing.

Free Black people who violated the firearm laws often relied on their family members for assistance, but they also turned to friends and associates in the free Black community. During 1854's December term, Craven County issued a presentment against George Bragg, a sixteen-year-old biracial boy, who broke the 1841 license law.[40] It is not clear why Bragg had a weapon, but he may have been hunting or sport shooting with a twenty-year-old mixed-race laborer, George Gatlin.[41] In some instances, free Black people turned to their relatives' professional networks for support. Bragg, who lived with his father, John, a mixed-race tailor who owned a very respectable $350 in real estate in 1850 and who put up a $100 recognizance bond to ensure that he would answer the indictment. He was joined on the bond by a twenty-nine-year-old biracial tailor named Charles Stanly.[42] Stanly's recently deceased father, John Carruthers Stanly, a free "dark-skinned mulatto," was a respected barber, landlord, and enslaver who had blood ties to one of North Carolina's elite political families and who had been, before some reversals in his later years, one of the wealthiest men in Craven County. Charles Stanly's connection to the Bragg family extended beyond his shared profession with George's father—two years prior, he had married George's older sister and fellow tailor, Sarah Bragg.[43] Stanly might have been a friend of George's before becoming his kinsman, but John, the Bragg patriarch, might have been his initial connection to the family. The elder Bragg might have employed Stanly at some point, though the extant apprenticeship bonds are silent on this. Finally, Stanly's support was probably worth far more than the $100 he offered on his brother-in-law's bond. The Stanly family's name likely lent George Bragg some social credit.

The armed teenager plead guilty in March 1855 and was himself bound for $100 to appear for sentencing. A thirty-six-year-old propertyless white tailor named Lewis Phelps joined this bond for $100.[44] These three tailors—John Bragg, Charles Stanly, and Lewis Phelps—comprised George Bragg's web of legal support. He did not have an occupation listed on the 1850 census, but while two of his sisters and two of his brothers took up their father's trade, George would eventually become a butcher. Nevertheless, he relied on his father's social-professional network for support through his legal trouble.[45] As Catherine W. Bishir notes, free Black tradesmen's business endeavors provided them with "opportunities to form relationships with a wide range of community members, including both fellow people of color and influential whites, and to establish reputations for high-quality work and solid character."[46] Free Black North Carolinians' labor created interpersonal networks that they relied on during times of distress, and as one can see in Bragg's case, their families could rely on these networks as well. Further, Stanly's and Phelps's assistance demonstrated their confidence in Bragg's character, or at least that of his family. The former's race and the latter's low socioeconomic status would have limited their effectiveness as court petitioners, but these men nevertheless offered George Bragg what support they could.

While free Black families supported members who legally or illegally carried guns, families could also be a liability. Family ties could bring undue pressure from others. Consider that Craven County indicted at least twenty-five free Black county residents for gun license violations between 1849 and 1851, and in this flurry of enforcement, several free Black families had multiple members indicted for carrying firearms without licenses at nearly the same time.[47] This surge was part of a statewide crackdown—a wave of anti–free Black sentiment that swept through North Carolina in the late 1840s and early 1850s in response to the steadily increasing free Black population.[48] Consider that the first major issue that Governor David Settle Reid addressed during his 1851 inaugural speech was the "misguided fanaticism of Abolitionists at [sic] the North" who threatened "the overthrow of the Constitution and a dissolution of the Union"; but he also briefly raised questions about the state's Black residents. He noted that it was "well worthy of consideration whether our police regulations in relation to slaves and free persons of color are sufficient."[49] Despite local points of interracial cooperation, this was a hostile environment for Black North Carolinians.

In this context, the county authorities sometimes charged multiple members of the same family with violating the license law. Sometimes, two relatives were probably out hunting or sport shooting together and then reported together. For instance, Daniel and William Keese were both indicted on September 1, 1849, for carrying weapons without licenses. They were likely kin—William was a twenty-eight-year-old Black laborer who lived near a forty-five-year-old Black farmer named Allen Keese, in whose household fourteen-year-old Daniel lived. William may have been the younger Keese's uncle, or an older brother. Fortunately for them, the grand jury did not find sufficient evidence to send them to trial.[50] Further, consider Tyrrell County's Abner and Edmund Hill. Abner, a sixty-seven-year-old multiracial farmer, and his twenty-three-year-old shingle-maker son were both indicted in June 1858 for carrying shotguns without licenses. Dempsey Brey, a mariner; Ludford Cahoon, a well-to-do farmer; and Franklin Phelps, a farmer and enslaver who likely lived nearby, witnessed both men's violations. This was not the elder Hill's first gun related legal problem—he had been charged in the fall of 1850 as well for "carrying fire armes and having the same in his house."[51] This second charge, this time in the company of his son, suggests that they were hunting or sport shooting together when the three witnesses came across them and notified the authorities. Finally, in 1858, Craven County indicted fifty-three-year-old Thomas Fender and thirty-five-year-old Jacob Fender for gun violations. The Fenders—also listed as "Fenner"—were almost certainly related.[52] Jacob, a propertyless day laborer, and Thomas, a cooper with $150 in personal and real estate, each bound themselves for $100 on Thomas's recognizance bond and also put up $100 on Jacob's bond.[53] Free people of color were legally restricted from maintaining social or economic relationships with enslaved workers and were also discouraged from close relationships with white citizens. Consequently, those who lived

TABLE 4.2 Craven County's Black Firearm Licensees, 1850–1854, per the County Court's List

Name	Occupation	Age (1850)	Race on census	Issued 1850	Issued 1851	Issued 1852	Issued 1853	Issued 1854	Indicted (Term)[1]
Ben. Banton	Farmer	30	Black	Sep		Sep	Sep	Sep	Dec 1850
Richard Brown	Farmer	66	Mulatto	X		Jun	Jun	Jun	
Ezekiel Chance	Laborer	20	Black	X		Jun	Jun	Jun	
Loftin Chance	Farmer	57	Black			Jun	Jun	Jun	
Rufus Chance	Laborer	18	Black			Dec	Dec	Dec	
William Cully[2]	Farmer	50	Black			Jun	Jun		Sep 1847
Kelso Davis[3]						Dec	Dec	Dec	
John Fenner	None listed	55	Black				Mar		
Thomas Fenner	None listed	50	Black				Mar		Jun 1851
Sylvester Gaskins							Mar		
James Godette	Farmer	70	Black		Sep	Sep	Sep		Jun 1851
John Godette	Laborer	28	Mulatto		Sep	Sep	Sep		Jun 1851
William Godette	Laborer	18	Black		Sep	Sep			Jun 1851
Elijah George	Boatman	35	Black				Mar		
Theophilus George	None listed	13	Black			Jun			Sep 1847

Name	Occupation	Age	Race					
George Lewis	Boatman	33	Black			Jun		
Willis Lewis	Farmer	65	Black	X		Mar	Jun	
Stanly Moore[4]	Laborer	37	Black				Sep	
Benjamin Morgan	None listed	69	Mulatto	X				Jun 1850
Richard Morris[5]	Farmer/Laborer	71/35	Black/Black	X		Jun		Sep 1847
Frank Pettifer	Laborer	30	Black	X			Sep	Dec 1849
Israel Pettifer	Farmer	25	Black	X	Sep	Sep	Sep	Dec 1849
Wright Pettifer	Farmer	38	Black	X	Sep	Sep	Sep	Dec 1849
George Robeson	Farmer	50	Black			Sep		
Jacob Wiggins	Farmer	33	Black				Jun	Jun 1850
John A. Wiggins						Sep	Jun	
Jonathan Archibald Wiggins[6]	Farmer	64	Black	X	Sep		Sep	

[1] The initial indictments are taken from Craven County State Docket, Court of Pleas and Quarter Sessions, 1847–1859, Craven County Records, NCDAH.

[2] William Cully had a teenaged son with the same name, but the license was likely his.

[3] The men with italicized names could not be traced via the census.

[4] Stanley Moore lived in neighboring Beaufort County at the time the 1850 census was taken. See "Stanley Moore" [Blounts Creek District, Beaufort County, North Carolina], 1850 US Federal Census database, population schedule, p. 414, Ancestry.com.

[5] There are two Richard Morrisses in the records, presumably father and son, as the younger is listed as Richard Morris Jr. See "Richd Morris" [Craven County, North Carolina], 1850 US Federal Census database, population schedule, p 312A, image 186, Ancestry.com; and "Richd Morris Jr" [Craven County, North Carolina], 1850 US Federal Census database, population schedule, p. 315A, image 192, Ancestry.com.

[6] It appears that the census taker phonetically recorded John Archibald Wiggins as "John R. Wiggins." "John R. Wiggins" [Craven County, North Carolina], 1850 US Federal Census database, population schedule, p. 378A, image 320, Ancestry.com.

in rural areas were more reliant on their kin for social interactions than most white people and certainly more so than enslaved laborers. When they went hunting, they probably did so with relatives.

Some of these family-based incidents were more complicated than the Keeses' situation. During Wright, Rose, Frank, and Israel Pettifer's legal trouble, they were mostly harangued by a few members of two white families in their neighborhood. This common thread suggests some prior conflict between the two extended families. Arthur Gaskins and Edward Ipock initiated Wright Pettifer's case and were also witnesses, along with James G. Gaskins and Joseph Gaskins. Arthur Ipock and John P. Ipock initiated Rose Pettifer's case and were witnesses against her. Edward Ipock and Daniel Simmons were the complainants against Frank Pettifer. The court called them and Arthur Gaskins as witnesses. Edward Ipock initiated the indictment against Israel Pettifer and was also the only witness summoned against him.[54] The Ipock and Gaskins complainants all lived in the Pettifers' neighborhood or had kin who did. The household of a sixty-four-year-old white man named Lazarus Ipock was listed in the 1850 census documents between Rose Pettifer's household and Wright Pettifer's household. Farmer James G. Gaskins was listed as living on the other side of Rose's home. Joseph Gaskins, who also farmed, lived farther away but was listed near Arthur Gaskins and in a part of Craven County where their surname was quite common. Frank and Israel Pettifer were listed as living next to each other, and Arthur Ipock lived in their neighborhood.[55]

Family and community are complicated constructions, particularly when explored through the often-fractured lens of history. The relationships between members of the Ipock and Pettifer families were no exception; but in 1849, a few months before the Pettifer weapons charges, Wright Pettifer and a woman named Elizabeth Ipock were indicted for "fornication & Adultery" during the court's September term. They had a child out of wedlock and never married.[56] In 1850, Wright Pettifer lived near both Richard and Rose Pettifer and Lazarus Ipock's homes. Twenty-five-year-old Elizabeth Ipock and her two-year-old biracial daughter, Emeline, were living with Peggy Dove, a fifty-six-year-old Black woman.[57] Ipock's relationship with Dove is unclear, but Elizabeth was likely a boarder. To further complicate this, a decade later, Wright and Elizabeth's daughter, listed as fourteen-year-old "Emaline *Petiford*" on the census, lived with her father, who was then a farmer with $1,000 worth of property, and an eight-year-old boy named Henry Pettifer. The census-taker listed all three of them as Black people. It is not clear where Elizabeth Ipock was at that point. This bureaucratic process highlighted one of the ways that race was constructed—the biracial Emeline had, in the eyes of the state, become a Black child by virtue of her moving from the multiracial household of her white mother to that of her Black father. Linking Wright and Elizabeth's relationship and the broader Pettiford weapons charges, the charges against the parents lists two witnesses, "Ed" Ipock and Daniel Simmons, both of whom were also involved in the firearm cases.[58]

The Pettifers were not the only family to experience this interfamily drama, but some others had clearer and long-standing ties to their detractors. Craven County indicted John, Nathan, and Stephen Moore for unlicensed gun possession in 1849 and summoned both James Harrington and James Toler Jr. as witnesses in each of the cases. Further, Toler and Harrington had initiated all three of those Moores' indictments as well as the charges against Alfred, Baker, and Banton Moore.[59] This raises questions about the relationships between these two white men and the Moore family. In the mid-1830s, several of the Tolers took on four orphaned Moore children as apprentices in the cooper trade, three of whom would later be among the six Moores who faced gun license indictments. James Toler Jr. apprenticed John Moore in 1836, when he was fourteen years old. That same year, James Toler Sr. apprenticed ten-year-old Nathan.[60] These family ties continued the following year, when Charles Toler apprenticed both Alfred and Joel Moore, who were fourteen and twelve years old, respectively.[61]

Further, sixty-eight-year-old James Toler Sr. and William Toler, likely his son and James Toler Jr.'s brother, lived near one of a few different free Black Craven County residents named John Moore. Stephen Moore and thirty-four-year-old farmer James Harrington also lived nearby.[62] The location of these individuals' households—estimated from their positions on the census—suggests that the families were acquainted. It was no coincidence that James Toler Jr. and James Harrington were involved with each of the Moore indictments. This view of how these family groups were related is not to offer definitive causes for the indictments; rather, it highlights that these people were not strangers to each other. They knew each other, intimately in some instances. The records do not clearly connect the family relationships to the indictments, but they suggest that the patterns in these indictments were rooted in highly localized relationships. Whether these white family groups specifically targeted the Pettifers and Moores or whether they merely happened to witness them hunting in a group and believed that they had a responsibility to notify the authorities, they took an active role in pushing the county authorities to enforce the law against them. Further, only a small percentage of Craven County's free

Black people were licensed, which, recognizing guns' importance as tools, suggests that many others managed to evade criminal charges. This makes the multiple indictments within singular family groups even more conspicuous.

White citizens sometimes used free Black people's armed labor for tasks that were of questionable legality, much as they did with enslaved workers. In 1848, a Perquimans County's Ephraim Lane was indicted for violating the license law, and the state's supreme court upheld his right to do so because he carried the gun under his employer's direction. A white man named Barker hired Lane to make shingles in Pasquotank County and had him transport supplies to their worksite, including a pistol. Someone saw Lane with the gun and reported him to the authorities. The Perquimans County Superior Court found Lane not guilty, and although the prosecution appealed the decision, the state's highest court upheld the verdict. Justice Frederic Nash declared from the highest bench that Lane carried the pistol to fulfill a contract that he made "in good faith" and that his job was not a ruse to evade the law.[63] Further, Nash maintained that the 1841 law was intended to prevent free Black people from threatening "the peace of the community and the safety of individuals" but that it was never intended to be a total ban, or there would have been no need for a license provision. The justice continued that "degraded as are these individuals . . . among them are many, worthy of all confidence, and into whose hands these weapons can be safely trusted, either for their own protection or for the protection of the property of others confided to them." This affirmed that free Black people had legitimate reasons to be armed for themselves or their employers. The court decided that Lane only carried the pistol for his employer and had "no title to the instrument or right to use it" and had no "purpose or intent so to do."[64] In the eyes of the court, Lane was essentially an extension of his employer's will. Enslaved workers were controlled by their enslavers, but free people of color like Ephraim Lane were managed by their employers, local communities, and the state. Despite this similarity, the courts showed Lane more grace than had been shown Hannibal and Ned, whom the court punished after their enslaver armed them.[65]

White citizens subjectively embraced what they understood to be utilitarian Black firearm use, but many free people of color used their weapons as they themselves wished, not as the law dictated. The legal system put Black North Carolinians at a disadvantage because, as Laura Edwards explains, it was "founded and built on inequality, fully equipped to discipline those on the margins, who were also unable to use it in their own right."[66] Because the system was arrayed against them, many people of color chose to operate outside of it. Free Black people's firearms were multipurpose tools that they used for both productive and destructive purposes, although the difference between these was often a matter of perspective. John Hope Franklin explained that free Black North Carolinians' "criminality" and "general backwardness" were the result of the "contempt, disdain, and reprehension" that their white neighbors heaped upon them.[67] They broke the law because the laws confined them into a secondary class, but those trespasses put them into conflict with the legal system. Franklin was writing more generally about crime and social conditions, but his observations can be specifically applied to free Black people's firearm use.

None of the extant court records explicitly lists the licenses' associated costs, but fees accompanied most county services. The cost could have discouraged some free Black people from applying. After 1832, free Black peddlers were required to have a license, which cost them eighty cents each year.[68] In the mid-1850s, court clerks were paid seventy-five cents for marriage licenses, sixty cents for guardianship bonds, eighty cents for bonds of administration, and sixty-five cents for any indenture or apprenticeship bonds that they issued. The applicants undoubtedly bore these administrative costs themselves.[69] The firearm license fees were likely left to the discretion of the individual counties, and this might explain why some free Black residents decided not to apply for one. Land values in the middle of the nineteenth century were such that "it was quite possible" for someone with real estate holdings worth $100 "to have an adequate amount for farming purposes." Further, "with a few hundred dollars he could erect a house that would be about as modern as the age could provide."[70] Consider, however, that many free Black North Carolinians did not reach this threshold; their statewide per capita wealth was only about thirty four dollars in 1860.[71] Fees could influence a person's decision to apply for a license or risk the penalties.

Some Black North Carolinians rejected the notion that the assembly even had the right to regulate their gun use and therefore refused to submit to the law. Elijah Newsome argued that he was a citizen and the 1841 license law was a revocation of his previously enjoyed rights. He chose to continue using his firearm as he had before the restrictive legislation passed.[72] Newsome and many other free people of color had hunted and otherwise used their guns for several decades before 1841. Their refusal to acquire licenses thereafter was an act of resistance consistent with the disregard that some free Black people had for the assembly's regulation of their commerce, their voting, and their sexual and social relationships with both enslaved workers and white citizens. Those who deigned to follow all the state's restrictions on their class would find themselves neatly confined to an isolated and depressed caste.

Noncompliance with the firearm law was common. Richard Rohrs points out that in Wilmington, New Hanover County, licenses were "routinely granted," and some men, like William Kellogg, "annually received permission" to keep a gun.[73] An examination of Craven County licensees during first half of the 1850s shows that only a small percentage of the free Black residents even bothered to apply. In 1850 there were 1,538 free Black people in the county, and 392 of them were males between the ages of fifteen and sixty-nine. Between 1850 and 1854, less than 2 percent of the free Black men in this age range were granted firearm licenses (see table 4.2).[74] This list is not exhaustive, but it provides a glimpse into some free Black Craven County residents' decision-making. The highest number of licenses during this period was granted in 1852, and those recipients constituted only about 3.3 percent of the group of fifteen to sixty-nine-year-old men. This low percentage cannot accurately reflect the number of free Black firearm users, because about 56 percent of those within this age range lived in the rural parts of the county.[75] Many of them did farm work and would have relied on their guns more than their peers who lived in town. In fact, all the licensees who can be traced through the census lived outside of New Bern. Further, the free people of color who applied for licenses did so inconsistently. They might choose to apply in one year but not the next, and then reapply again. Many other people of color chose to disregard the law entirely. Despite this rural dynamic, firearms were useful for more than farm labor or hunting. Consider Rowan County's Mack Rankin or Perquimans County's Blake Robbins, both of whom were charged with carrying pistols.[76]

North Carolina's license requirement was about oversight, much like the requirement that enslavers monitor their armed laborers. This was not the only similarity between free and enslaved Black North Carolinians' firearm use, however. Consider that Craven County issued licenses with the expectation that the free Black licensee would remain on his or her own land while armed. This strongly inferred that the state saw this gun use as an outlet for labor. In 1850, Craven County's Richard Brown was permitted to "keep a bird gun in his house and to use it on his own land."[77] The court believed that, thus limited, Brown would be less likely to threaten white people's lives or property. This echoed the restrictions on armed enslaved laborers in earlier legislation and was also a pronounced difference from white North Carolinians' unregulated gun use. In 1859, Jonathan Harriss, who had a license, was indicted by the Craven County Court for violating the law after he hunted with a group of white men on someone else's property. The authorities declared that his license permitted him only to "keep about his person and carry on his own lands, a shot gun" but that it did not cover him once he left his property.[78] Harriss successfully appealed the decision, arguing that Craven County had no right to thus limit his license. The county successfully challenged the superior court's decision at the state's highest bench, which decided that if the county courts had the power to grant licenses that covered the entire county, then it followed that they could "grant the less, provided the applicant be willing to accept it."[79]

Further, the court argued that the restrictive licenses did not stray from the original spirit of the law, but that "in many cases, the county court might think it a very prudent precaution to limit the carrying of arms to the lands of the free negro, and we cannot discover any thing, either in the language or spirit of the act to prevent the restriction from being imposed." To close, the court noted that these licenses would nevertheless "oftentimes operate in favor of the free negroes, who may thus be enabled to keep a gun, &c., for killing game on their own land, or for protecting their own premises, when they could not obtain a license extending to them greater privileges."[80] While these limited licenses were not issued by every county, they highlight some of the pitfalls of this process as well as how free Black families used their firearms. A limitation like this would have prevented them from legally hunting with friends and severely constrained their ability to hunt with family members, unless they all resided on the same tract of land. In this court's opinion, free people of color should be happy with the restricted license because the state might have legislated an outright ban. Instead, they were relegated to their own lands, where they would be less of a hazard to white property owners and less able to provide enslaved laborers with weapons.

The limited licenses would have been detrimental to those free people of color who either did not own any land or who possessed land that offered few hunting opportunities. Under those conditions, they would have been limited to protecting their homes and crops, and such a license would not have "operate[d] in favor" of free people of color, as the state's highest court suggested. White people had no such handicap on their firearm use, and they hunted on one another's properties with enough regularity that a few of them tried to block trespassers.[81] Some multiracial North Carolinians simply rejected the state's oversight of their firearm use. The state's free people of color were not a phenotypically monolithic group, of course, but because the enslavers' society was founded on a racist Eurocentric hierarchy, they placed people with varying degrees of African descent into the same broad category, regardless of how they may have self-identified. This categorization was important because it marked who could access the trappings of citizenship—including unregulated firearm use—and who could not. The construction of racial difference also rested on the public's perception of "external marks" which allowed some multiracial families to influence how others perceived them.[82]

The nebulousness of racial constructions means that the firearm laws could never be wholly effective. North Carolina's courts prosecuted some cases that hinged on the firearm bearer's racial identity. The defendants in these cases contested the local courts' framing of family lineage and racial identity or challenged how the court defined its racial categories. Race is a social construct, but one that held an incredible amount of power historically and continues to do so. As such, the state sought to construct and enforce the boundary of race and the privileges tied to whiteness. Three of these court cases made their way before the North Carolina Supreme Court: *State v. Whitmel Dempsey* in 1849, *State v. William Chavers* in 1857, and *State v. Asa Jacobs* in 1859. When these cases are examined alongside 1844's *State v. Elijah Newsome*, they demonstrate how some free people of color outright rejected the racial identity that the county and state courts ascribed onto their bodies. They were not challenging the license law; rather, they were trying to shape the public perception of their racial identity to maintain their firearm rights.

Bertie County's Whitmel Dempsey was brought before the court for carrying a gun without a license, and during his trial, the court tried to determine whether he was a free man of color or a white man with some Black ancestry.[83] Though discomforting to modern sensibilities, state law framed blackness as a stain that remained within a bloodline until it could be diluted through the admixture of white blood, a process which would be completed in the fifth generation, after four generations of partnering with white people.[84] During the trial a witness testified that he had known an old man who had since died but who told him that Dempsey's paternal great-grandfather, Joseph Dempsey, had been "a coal-black negro." Whitmel objected to this testimony, but the court admitted it as evidence. The defendant maintained that his great-grandfather was "a reddish copper-colored man, with curly red hair and blue eyes." Whitmel Dempsey stated that Joseph's *father*, his own great-great-grandfather, was Black but that Joseph's mother was a white woman. His biracial great-grandfather Joseph Dempsey married a white woman, as did that couple's son, William. William and his wife had a son named Whitmel, who also married a white woman and thereby sired the defendant, who carried on his father's name.[85] The Dempsey family's multiracial history is interesting because during both the colonial and antebellum eras, the state dissuaded interracial marriage first through financial penalties and then by banning them outright.[86]

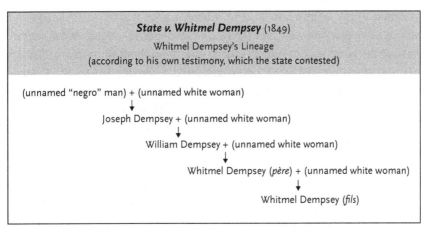

State v. Whitmel Dempsey (1849)

Whitmel Dempsey's Lineage
(according to his own testimony, which the state contested)

(unnamed "negro" man) + (unnamed white woman)
↓
Joseph Dempsey + (unnamed white woman)
↓
William Dempsey + (unnamed white woman)
↓
Whitmel Dempsey (*père*) + (unnamed white woman)
↓
Whitmel Dempsey (*fils*)

Whitmel Dempsey's lineage according to his own testimony, which the state contested.

Dempsey's counsel boldly argued that the court should instruct the jury that although Joseph Dempsey's father (the defendant's great-great-grandfather) "was a negro, the defendant nevertheless, was not a free person of color" under state law. The state's highest court rejected this argument, however, and instead told the jury that if Joseph were "of half negro blood" then Whitmel would be in the fourth generation from "negro ancestors" and therefore a free person of color by the law.[87] Dempsey's gun access hinged on whether his great-great-grandfather was "a negro" or a biracial man. The state supreme court's chief justice explained that Whitmel Dempsey had himself described his heritage in a manner that indicated he was within the four generations of "negro blood" and was therefore subject to the license law, despite his majority European heritage. The judgment stood.[88] Per the law, if Joseph's father had been biracial, then the defendant would have had access to the privileges of whiteness. Dempsey presented himself to the court as a white man and may have understood himself as such. Unless he had decided to take up hunting when he was about sixty years old, Dempsey, and many other free people of color in the 1840s, had probably been using a firearm for several decades before the license law passed. If Dempsey's own description of his lineage was correct, and had the court accepted it as so, then his father's heritage was only about 12 percent African. This fractionalizing had legal meaning and consequences in the mid-nineteenth century courtroom. When the assembly passed the firearm law, Dempsey did not believe that state's consent was necessary for *his* firearm use.

A decade after Dempsey's trial, the North Carolina Supreme Court decided *State v. Chavers*, another case that revolved around a free man of color's violation of the license law. Warren Milteer argues that *State v. Chavers* and similar cases that followed *State v. Newsome* evidenced a tactical shift from harnessing the language of rights to raising questions about the state's definition of racial identities. William Chavers appeared before the Brunswick County Superior Court on a license violation, and the court tried to determine his racial identity because Chavers disagreed that he fit the legal definition of a "free negro."[89] During the trial, a witness described Chavers's father as "a man of dark color and had kinky hair; that he was a shade darker than the defendant himself, and his hair was about as much kinked."[90] Another witness testified that when Chavers was traveling on a steamship that charged white passengers one dollar but "colored persons" fifty cents, he identified himself as the latter. The witness explained that Chavers paid a dollar for both himself and his brother, and had told an attendant that he heard the fare was half price for people of color.[91] These testimonies were damaging to Chavers's case, but his counsel still insisted on his whiteness. His ambiguous features allowed him to pass back and forth across the color line, and he chose the identity that most benefited him at a given moment. Those opportunities were few and far between for people of color, but not nonexistent, as the Chavers brothers' steamship travel illustrated. He took what advantages he could from the racist society he lived in, including the right to unregulated firearm use.

Chavers's lawyer called on the jurors to visually inspect him, and to determine his racial background for themselves. This physical reading of one's body was a common practice in antebellum courtrooms.[92] Superior Court Justice Samuel J. Person charged the jury that anyone whose heritage included at least one-sixteenth part of "negro blood" was a person of color and that only through a "purification" of that blood could they "become free white persons by law." Person further declared that "no person in the fifth generation from a negro ancestor becomes a free white person, unless one ancestor in each generation was a white person; that is to say, unless there shall be such a purification of negro blood by the admixture of white blood as will reduce the quantity below the one-sixteenth part; and unless there is such purification it makes no difference how many generations you should have to go back to find a pure negro ancestor; even though it should be a hundred, still the person is a free negro."[93] In Person's view, an individual remained a free person of color unless the African ancestry was washed out by whiteness at the tune of one full white ancestor per generation into the fifth generation. The Brunswick Superior Court ruled that Chavers was indeed a "free negro," but he appealed the decision, arguing that the court had insufficient evidence and that the judge's instructions to the jury for determining racial status were misleading.[94] Upon review, the Supreme Court of North Carolina announced that the indictment against Chavers as a "free person of color" could apply to "persons colored by Indian blood, or persons descended from negro ancestors beyond the fourth degree" and not just a "free negro" as the 1841 law originally intended. The court therefore decided that the indictment could not be sustained, and judgment was arrested.[95] Chavers's firearm rights were preserved—but on a technicality; the Supreme Court had not agreed that he was a white man or entitled to unchecked firearm access; rather, the court had decided that the state's prosecution was too sloppy to be sustained.

In 1859, Asa Jacobs was charged with illegal gun possession. He admitted that he was a multiracial man but argued that he had enough white ancestry to avoid the burdens that the state placed on free person of color.[96] During his trial, Jacobs objected to the state's request that the jurors be allowed to inspect his physical characteristics so they "might see that he was within the prohibited degree [of African ancestry]." The state argued that an examination would not violate his rights, since he was already required to be present for the trial where "the jury must necessarily see him." The Brunswick Superior Court overruled Jacobs's objections. After a physical examination, the jury found him to be a person of color. Jacobs appealed the decision and its framing of his identity.[97] The Supreme Court of North Carolina's primary consideration was whether he could be compelled by the lower court to exhibit himself before the jury, for them "to decide upon his *status* as a free negro." The highest court cited *State v. Chavers*—Justice Matthias Manly declared that although Chavers had the right to present himself to the jury of his own volition, Jacobs could not be compelled to do so, as the court could not force him to present evidence against himself. Jacobs preserved his unchecked firearm use by preventing the court from closely scrutinizing his phenotypic traits.[98]

Dempsey, Chavers, and Jacobs broke the firearm laws and responded to the state's prosecution by pushing back against its framing of their racial identities. Pragmatically, they did not comment on the law itself. In 1844, Elijah Newsome, however, deployed a different tactic. He boldly claimed the *right* to bear arms as a citizen. This approach challenged the very validity of the license law. The North Carolina Supreme Court heard Newsome's case on appeal from the Cumberland County Superior Court. Newsome had been convicted of unlicensed possession of a shotgun "to the evil example of all others . . . and against the peace and dignity of the State." Newsome appealed on the grounds that the license law was unconstitutional and that the state could not thus limit his *rights*. Consider that Newsome was born around 1780 and had probably been using his firearms as he pleased for more than fifty years. He might have served in the militia alongside his white neighbors before 1823, when the state banned Black men's participation. He might even have voted and participated in Election Day festivities prior to 1835, when the new state constitution stripped him of that as well.[99] Under these conditions, Newsome may have seen himself on equal footing with his white neighbors, at least in some regards.

Newsome had reason to hope that the court might agree with him. In 1833's *State v. Edmund, a Slave,* Justice Joseph John Daniel declared that a free man of color could "hold lands and personal property including slaves" and added that he was a "citizen" under the state's laws despite not having "the same full and complete political privileges and immunities with which the constitution and laws have clothed a white man." Justice Daniel painted a picture of inequality, but his decision also highlights that the trappings of citizenship were open for judicial interpretation, and it speaks volumes about free people of color's tenuous position.[100] The North Carolina Supreme Court rejected Newsome's gun rights framework. Echoing portions of Daniel's earlier argument, Justice John Lancaster Bailey declared in Newsome's case that "from the earlier period of our history, free people of color have been among us, as a separate and distinct class, requiring, from necessity, in many cases, separate and distinct legislation." The court declared that the 1841 law was a legitimate use of the state's police power because it did not strip free Black people of the right to carry arms, it only placed the right under the "control" of the county courts.[101] Despite his protest, Newsome would need its expressed consent to arm himself.

In 1844, well over a decade before Roger Taney's aggressive denial of Black people's citizenship and the rejection of their rights at the national level, North Carolina's Supreme Court decided in *State v. Newsome* that free people of color were "a separate and distinct class" that needed "separate and distinct legislation."[102] Taney's opinion that Dred Scott was "a slave, and certainly incapable of suing in the character of a citizen" represented the court's ruling, but it was not unanimous. Justice Benjamin Curtis dissented, relying in part on North Carolina's history and arguing that one needed only to look at Black people's positions in the states at the time the Constitution was ratified. Curtis pointed out that "there can be no doubt" that they were citizens, as "all free native-born inhabitants of the States of New Hampshire, Massachusetts, New York, New Jersey, and North Carolina, though descended from African slaves, were not only citizens of those States, but such of them as had the other necessary qualifications possessed the franchise of electors, on equal terms with other citizens."[103] Further, Curtis leaned on the North Carolina Supreme Court's 1838 case, *State v. William Manuel,* where Justice William Gaston's argued that "slaves, manumitted here, became freemen, and therefore, if born within North

Carolina, are citizens of North Carolina, and all free persons born within the State are born citizens of the State."[104]

Some white men agreed with the framing of Black citizenship in both Gaston's *State v. Manuel* decision and Newsome's posturing, even though they might not have contested the law. In May of 1841, just a few months after the legislature passed the license law, Edgecombe County's Basdill Thomas relied on three white associates to support his application.[105] In it, these white men did not deny that Thomas was "a free person of Collar" but they referred to him as "a Citizen of District no 7 of the 1 regiment of the EdgComb Militia." The white men explained that "as the said Thomas Craves the privilege to geather with his assigners of being empowered with the authority of carrying or using a shot gun or musket in his neighbor hood or about his domestical afares." Further, the three white supporters again reiterated that Thomas was "a peaceable + quiet citizen and stands fare as an honest man and as an unblemished a character as any man in the neighbourhood having been a citizen of the neighbour hood for the Last Four or Five years." This reiteration of Thomas's citizenship stood in contrast with the applications of others, like Wayne County's Hilary Coor, whose advocates could "recommend" him "as deserving the benefit" of the license but did not claim his citizenship. Basdill Thomas and his white associates' bold efforts were ultimately to no avail—the Edgecombe County court rejected his license application.[106]

The most salient aspect of *State v. Newsome* (1844) was the North Carolina Supreme Court's declaration that the state's free Black residents were not full citizens. In addition to justifying the racially specific firearm law as necessary to deal with the "separate and distinct class" of free Black people, the court declared that "the act of 1840 is one of police regulation" and that it did not destroy their right to carry firearms. Instead, the court argued that the firearm law allowed the county court to "say, in the exercise of a sound discretion, who, of this class of persons, shall have a right to the licence, or whether any shall." The court maintained that free Black people were "not to be considered as citizens, in the largest sense of the term, or, if they are, they occupy such a position in society, as justifies the legislature in adopting a course of policy in its acts peculiar to them—so that they do not violate those great principles of justice, which lie at the foundation of all laws." Unassailable firearm use may have been a right of North Carolina's citizens, but the highest court was ambivalent on Newsome's claim to that citizenship and subjected him to a separate "course of policy."[107]

These several court cases highlight how the state's interpretation of phenotypic difference, and the consequent construction of race, could have major impacts on the ways that some African-descended North Carolinians accessed and used firearms or contested the laws that stood in their way. These arguments over race-based gun rights highlight that some free people of color could be acknowledged as such and, if their family's history demonstrated the "appropriate" racial composition, still be full members of the body politic and use their firearms without interference. North Carolina's racially tailored laws occasionally floundered on the terrain of firearm use because race was nebulous at the margins. Still, the state managed to relegate most free people of color, even those who were predominately of European heritage, into a class of noncitizenship, where their county courts claimed oversight of their firearm use. This remained the case until February of 1861, when the General Assembly reversed policy and passed legislation to ban free people of color's firearm use altogether.

IN THE MIDDLE OF THE NINETEENTH CENTURY, North Carolina subjected its free Black residents to a range of restrictions that reflected many white citizens' views that free people of color were a "perfect Nuisance, to civilized Society" and that were intended to safeguard white citizens and their property from their Black neighbors.[108] By the winter of 1840–41, the assembly was concerned about a growing free Black population and nervous about this population's connections to enslaved laborers, so it mandated county-level oversight of free Black people's firearm use. Similar to the state's earlier restrictions on enslaved laborers, this license requirement rested on the premise that armed people of color needed white supervision. Free Black people sometimes broke this law and ended up in court. Some of them ignored the law because they could not amass the requisite white support or fees and others because they lived under a system that prioritized local application of the law and their neighbors would have to be concerned enough about their firearms to alert the authorities. Despite the state's aggression, people of color's individual's firearm use rested on the faith, advocacy, and economic backing of their Black and white friends, neighbors, associates, and family. Many white North Carolinians were supportive of their free Black associates, neighbors, and friends' firearm use, although they may have felt differently about strangers.

Finally, some people of color with diverse racial heritages resisted this law by claiming the privileges of whiteness or constitutional protections. The state's decision in *State v. Chavers* was important. Milteer argues that it "displayed the illogic and intellectual limitations encoded in some of the state's discriminatory legislation. Over the generations, lawmakers had failed to develop a consistent racial vocabulary to use in discriminatory legislation."

In the aftermath, the state was pushed to define free people of color.[109] Free Black people themselves resisted by disregarding the firearm law. John Hope Franklin best explains many free Black people's legal transgressions: The laws that targeted them were "of little avail" because "the free Negro's social and economic difficulties were so great that crime was often merely the reaction to his dilemmas."[110] The state's laws and many of their white neighbors' social customs limited free people of color's opportunities, but they responded pragmatically.

CHAPTER FIVE

The Civil War

The US Civil War had a profound impact on free and enslaved Black people's lives and labors across the South, including those in North Carolina. Their firearm use offers new perspectives on the conflict. In the turmoil of the secession crisis, some white people began arming themselves. In January 1861, Hillsborough's Hal Jones explained to his cousin Cadwallader Jones that while North Carolina was "very slow in moving, when she does move, she will do so to some purpose." He noted that Orange County was "being armed very fast" and that a local merchant sold "a great many improved rifled-muskets, the country people are buying all that he brings."[1] The military and related labors took people—Black and white, free and enslaved, male and female—away from their daily routines and sent them to coastal forts or military camps across the state and region. Many white North Carolinians worried that this depletion of white male strength on the home front would embolden enslaved people and compromise public safety. In 1861, Emily Jenkins wrote a letter to Governor Henry Clark expressing just such a concern. She was afraid that "the negroes wile Kile ale we women and children if they take ale the men away."[2] In contrast, however, some enslavers who served in the military relied on their enslaved workers' armed labor even more during deployments. They even trusted some enslaved people to defend white people's lives and property. This use of armed Black laborers was a continuation of antebellum practices, but it was more useful and increasingly dangerous during the war.

As the conflict became a war of attrition and casualties steadily mounted, the Confederate government grappled with how it might utilize armed Black men on the battlefield. Most white North Carolinians opposed their national government arming enslaved men for military service because they saw Black soldiers as an unwelcome shift in the limited and local use of armed Black labor to which they had grown accustomed. Further, some enslavers resisted their state and national governments' appropriation of their slaves during the later years of the war because they simply did not want to lose their enslaved people's labor.[3] Enslaver Calvin Cowles was relieved that his bondmen were not called into the war effort. He explained to a neighbor, "20 slaves + all our Free negroes are ordered to Wilmington—the allotment has been made + does'nt touch me—I escape." Many enslavers saw this impressment as antithetical to their national allegiance, which was rooted in a "desire to protect their property."[4] Cowles did not want his enslaved workers impressed for construction efforts, but many Confederates resisted armed Black military labor through the war. This distinguished the Confederates' war from the nineteenth-century Latin American wars of independence, wherein both the royalists and nationalists recruited and armed African-descended men under their respective banners. White North Carolinians wanted to continue with locally mediated regulation of free and enslaved Black people's firearm practices. This supervision was at the core of the wartime debates over the best uses of Black people's armed labor in domestic and military contexts.

As the political turmoil escalated, North Carolina sought greater safeguards to protect itself and its citizens from violence emanating from within or outside of its borders. This included an intensification of the restrictions on free and enslaved Black North Carolinians, which meant exercising greater control of their firearm use. In February 1861, just a few months before North Carolina left the Union, the assembly repealed the license provision of its 1841 firearm law, effectively ending free Black people's gun access. Those who violated the 1841 law could be fined "not less than fifty dollars," a steep price when one considers that their meager average income. Enslaved people had been legally barred from carrying firearms since 1832, so when the state seceded in May 1861, the entire enslaved Black population was already disarmed, although as noted in earlier chapters, local communities and individual enslavers did not always enforce the law.[5] Additionally, in May 1861, the assembly strengthened the provisions for overseeing enslaved laborers. The legislators empowered any three justices of the peace within a county to appoint patrollers in their district if they thought it necessary. Previously, the convened county court had been responsible for appointing patrols under the previous guidelines, but empowering the justices would speed up the process.[6] The lawmakers also defined treason against the state of North Carolina: Any person who waged war against the state or assisted others to do so could be sentenced to death. Anyone who knew of a treasonous plot and did not report it could be fined and jailed. Finally, any free people who encouraged or assisted enslaved laborers to rebel could also be executed.[7] Anxieties ran high at both the state and local level.

In this tumultuous period, many counties and towns undertook measures to ensure their white residents' safety. In September 1861, Hillsborough, in Orange County, passed an ordinance to prevent any "white person, free negro, or free mulatto" from firing guns within the town's limits. A free person who did so could be fined up to two dollars, and an enslaved person would get between

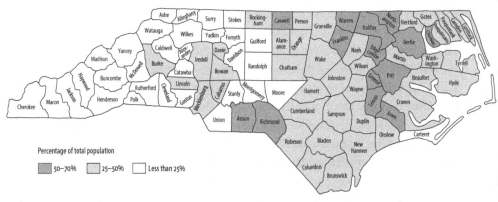

North Carolina's 1860 slave population by county.

ten and twenty lashes on their bare back.[8] Per state law, Hillsborough's free and enslaved people of color were not supposed to be armed at all, but this ordinance suggests that the restrictive laws had been only casually enforced prior to the war. A month earlier, after an armed Black man in New Bern tried to rob a house, a newspaper demanded, "Where did the negro get his pistol? Where do other negroes get pistols and other weapons? Is everything as it should be in this department of trade in Newbern?" The editor noted that "certain individuals" were under suspicion and warned the townspeople to be alert, as "this was no time for slaves to be permitted to have weapons, nor should any white person be permitted to remain in a Southern community who would furnish them with weapons." This trafficking in weapons did not disrupt the town in peacetime, but it evidently had a different impact as the war unfolded. As the *Daily Progress* put it, they were "not afraid of the slaves" but worried about "those sneaking whites who corrupt them."[9] North Carolinians also formed vigilance committees to keep watch over individuals whom they deemed to be suspicious, much like the coercive Committees on Public Safety had done during the Revolutionary War. From the Civil War's outset, some newspapers warned the home front against complacency and declared that "every good citizen should consider himself a committeeman."[10]

The committees focused their attention on their districts' residents who were unemployed or suspected of "tampering with" or trading with enslaved people and those who expressed "treasonable sentiments," circulated incendiary documents, or had otherwise violated the area's "peace and security."[11] These organizations sought to protect their communities from domestic threats and to coerce support for the war. As a part of that process, they dragged some of their Black neighbors before the justice system. For instance, in September

1862, the Lenoir County Court paid R. W. Moore for "delivering" nine free Black people to the vigilance committee in the county's Mosely Hall district.[12] Also in 1864, a group of white men set out to conduct an "investigation of the conduct of the negroes of the neighborhood" during a raid by United States troops. The group called on Dr. George W. Burwell to "bring any Negroes or evidence" that he thought might be useful for the "trial."[13] The nature of these Black people's trespasses are unclear, but the state and local governments had scrutinized them during prior periods of unrest and continued to do so as wartime conditions exacerbated white people's worries about public safety.

White North Carolinians worried not only about their Black neighbors but also about any white people who might encourage Black people to violence. Accordingly, they were suspicious of outsiders' interference during this period. In December 1860, a sixteen-year-old white boy named Solon Larkins and two others—T. M. Chatterton and a young man with the surname Taylor—were arrested for "criminal correspondence with abolitionists in New York." Larkins, who came from a "highly respectable Family," and the others wrote a letter to "the President of the Abolition Society" wherein they requested weapons and $200 in cash to plan an interracial insurrection in North Carolina.[14] Larkins lied to William H. Anthon, a lawyer and the treasurer (not the president) of a New York antislavery society, that he had "100 Negros 40 Whites and 40 Free Negros redy to march out into action." Additionally, the teenager stated that he had stockpiled forty muskets, forty broadswords, and some axes for the rebellion.[15] The specter of intraracial insurrection also came from enslaved Black North Carolinians. In 1862, authorities in Perquimans County questioned several enslaved individuals who testified about a conspiracy in which some of their peers planned "to massacre the whites without any Distinction of age or Sex." The would-be rebels expected other enslaved people to join them as they marched through the area, but they also thought that "a number of poor people," including white folks, would, too.[16]

Larkins's scheme quickly unraveled when Anthon did not send money or weapons but instead, after consulting with Horace Greeley, alerted North Carolina's governor, John Willis Ellis. The abolitionist explained to Ellis that anyone who thought he would support inciting enslaved folks to "murder and rebellion" was "very much mistaken" and misunderstood the "aims and objects of the Republican Party." When the authorities confronted Larkins, the whole ordeal was found to be a "farce and humbug." Taylor and Chatterton were released, but Larkins confessed that he had written the letter. He pleaded that he had only done so "to make mony out of the Abolitionists." The ploy was a foolish plan to raise money to start up a printing office.[17] Larkins was released because the judge "found no authority under the Statute for binding him over," but the *Daily Herald*'s editors blasted this decision, as they believed that Larkins "ought to be made to feel the consequences of his conduct" because he was "too intelligent and too old" for his actions to be a "boyish freak."[18] A Raleigh newspaper went even further and chastised the state's response. It argued that "while all persons should be vigilant in times like the present, reports of insurrections ought to be well sifted by the authorities before they are made public."[19] Tensions were high enough without the false alarms.

Whatever Larkins intended to accomplish with his letter to Anthon, the specter of a multiracial army—composed of enslaved, free Black, and white North Carolinians and supported by white Northerners—was enough to raise some white people's anxieties. An internal threat like that which Larkins's ruse suggested paired dangerously with the real and imagined external threats posed by both the incoming Lincoln administration and aggressive Northern abolitionism. Solon Larkins's revolt was never real, but he still became a popular reference for a few weeks. In an article about "sensation mongers," a newspaper noted that "*Solon*, unfortunately for the peace of the country, is not the only *Larkins* in the South."[20] White Southerners' feelings of vulnerability were not only rooted in incendiary political rhetoric and abolitionist literature; some of them also feared that Northerners could distribute firearms to enslaved workers, much like Larkins's letter had suggested. This stress would have roused concerns like those about the inadequately stored militia weapons during the antebellum period—white citizens worried that these hypothetical Northern-sponsored weapons could end up in the hands of runaways or other unsupervised Black people, just as so many of those militia weapons had in earlier years.

White North Carolinians had been concerned about outside interference and improperly supervised armed Black people since the colonial era. From early in the war, thousands of Union soldiers entered eastern portions of the state and increased the opportunity for outsiders to reach the enslaved population, where they could offer ideas or at least help the workers realize their own plans. David Blount grew up enslaved on Maj. William A. Blount Jr.'s Beaufort County plantation, in a sizable community of about sixty other enslaved laborers. He remembered that one day, when he was about fifteen years old, a group of white men came up the river and landed on the Major's place. They approached the workers in the fields, and David Blount recalled that "dey says dat our masters ain't treatin' us right" and that "we orter be paid fer our wuck, an' dat we hadn't ort ter hab passes ter go anywhar."[21] He noted that the strangers told them that they "ort ter be allowed ter tote guns if we wants 'em" and warned them that "sometime our marsters was gwine ter kill us all." The teenager left the conversation because he did not like the subject matter, but he later learned "dat dese men gib de niggers some guns . . . an' promised ter bring 'em some more de nex' week." Blount reported these clandestine weapons to the Major, who laughed and told him that the others were "headed for trouble" before asking Blount to keep him apprised.[22]

As promised, the strangers returned with more firearms. The plantation's newly armed workers then planned to meet secretly in the Major's pack house to discuss a collective course of action. Blount, however, reported them to the Major and, on his orders, nailed the pack house's shutters shut before the meeting and hid in the loft to wait for the conspirators. Blount watched the armed people enter and eavesdropped as they plotted to "ter go up ter de big house an' kill de whole fambly" with their new weapons. These guns, along with the encouragement of the white strangers, held the potential to dramatically alter the power dynamics on Major Blount's plantation.[23] Blount escaped the pack house via a small loft window and immediately alerted his enslaver. He, the Major, and one of the Major's sons ran to the pack house and locked the door as "quick as lightnin.'" Once they had secured the armed conspirators inside, the Major threatened to burn the pack house down on top of them if they did not toss their firearms out through the loft window. Thus trapped and with no viable options, they complied. David Blount made sure each of the guns was accounted for and then carried them up to the Major's house.

Blount was pleased with his role in suppressing this armed conspiracy. He noted that afterward, "We keeps dem niggers shet up fer about a week on short rations; an' at de end of dat time dem niggers am kyored for good." Thereafter, the Major hired two additional overseers and put stricter rules in place. When he left home for his Confederate military service, he took Blount with him "fer his pusonal servant an' body guard" and left "de rest of dem niggers in de fiel's ter wuck like de dickens."[24] David Blount's interview did not divulge how many enslaved people were involved with the conspiracy, but his recollections still demonstrate that during the war, some laborers needed only the opportunity and maybe material aid to try to break their bonds. This was certainly not lost on Major Blount or his white neighbors. Incidents like these, even if infrequent, exacerbated their safety concerns. Further, while Blount did not identify the arms-bearing strangers, his interviewer's notes include the words, "Slaves make pact with Yankees," suggesting that part of their unrecorded conversation led her to believe that the visitors were United States soldiers or sailors. Federal forces occupied parts of North Carolina's coast in March 1862 and used the state's river systems to launch incursions farther inland. The Pamlico River ran to Blount's neighborhood. At times, the Union troops assisted runaways, some of whom then directed the federals toward plantations, which the troops then plundered.[25] William Tripp lamented living on the river—one could look out onto it from his house's windows—as Union troops often traveled by water because the transportation was easy and they could take advantage of their gunboats' firepower.[26] He and Major Blount lived near each other in Beaufort County.

The threats to North Carolina property holders were real. In February 1863, Currituck County's Joseph B. Morgan wrote to his son, Patrick, a cadet at the Virginia Military Institute, and lamented that "the enemy occasionally makes raids upon us & plunder & destroy our property." The United States soldiers "plundered several citizens, taking horses, carts, [tear]groes, salt & c."[27] These actions continued, much to the chagrin of the white North Carolinians in the area, sometimes coming at the pace of once a week.[28] Lee Barfield, a cavalry-man from Georgia who served in North Carolina, wrote home from camp near Winton, Hertford County, and explained that "the Gun Boats came up again today and fired on us but as usual hurt no body. I think their object in coming up the river so often is to steal Negroes. They carry off some every time they come—There are some disloyal persons called "Buffaloes" who assist the Negroes in getting away—The Yankees—give the Buffaloes $30. for every negro man they bring to them."[29] Some of the US gunboats picked up fugitives, but others turned them away, leaving many of those would-be self-liberated people to return to their enslavers. In another of his letters home, Barfield added that the "sorry, low down" Buffaloes would "generally rob & Plunder like the Tories did in the Revolution. They are certainly the worst men in the world."[30] Arming the enslaved population in this chaos was a frightening prospect to many white North Carolinians in the area.

The unwelcome visitors on Major Blount's plantation failed to stoke an insurrection, but other white outsiders had greater success. White North Carolinians were concerned that these outsiders would not only agitate enslaved workers but also recruit free people of color as allies. During the summer of 1862, the *Carolina Observer* reported that United States soldiers induced nearly a hundred enslaved workers and "a party of free negroes" to flee Pasquotank County and hide in the Great Dismal Swamp. Though instigated by the Yankees, this sizable group was allegedly led by a wealthy free Black "dictator," who had between $4,000 and $5,000 in property. North Carolina authorities broke up the Black renegades' camp and were able to capture about fifty of them as well as seize "a considerable quantity of ammunition." The next night, three local patrollers ran into another thirty of the armed group, who were reportedly "led by white men; supposed to be Yankees" and who opened fire on the patrol. The newspaper reported that two of the fugitives were killed in the fight and another was wounded and then captured. One of the patrollers was also killed.[31] The editors might have taken some creative liberties with the story, but regardless, this account highlights that this armed band of free and enslaved Black folks and Union soldiers were operating similarly to the maroons and fugitives who had threatened white people's livestock and safety since the colonial era. The *Carolina Observer*'s readership would have recognized the same themes of unsupervised, armed, and menacing Black people. Further, the state's free Black population and abolition-minded Northerners had long been suspected of negatively influencing enslaved people. The exigencies of war aside, many white North Carolinians would have seen this armed band of free and enslaved people of color and white abolitionists as the realization of an antebellum nightmare.

Despite the formation of vigilance committees and civilians' and the state government's concerns about armed Black people, some white people thought that stronger wartime firearm policies were unnecessary. Instead, they sought to maintain the localized control of earlier decades for free and enslaved Black people. In September 1861, fifteen justices of the peace in Hertford County petitioned the assembly for a "modification" of the restrictive law passed seven months earlier "whereby free persons of color are wholly prohibited from keeping or having shot guns irrespective of their character and good conduct." In a strong example of legal localism, the justices wanted to preserve their free Black neighbors' firearm access. They argued that their local court remained a competent judge on the matter, as it had been since 1841 for free people of color, and from 1741 to 1832 for the county's enslaved residents, and that the state should continue empowering local communities to manage their Black neighbors' gun use. The justices specifically referenced shotguns, recognizing that Hertford County's free Black residents needed weapons to hunt and perform farm labor. The petitioners further argued that the licensing provision could have a positive impact on the overall community. If those free Black people who proved they could be "safely entrusted with the privilege" were allowed to keep arms, it could induce them "to maintain a good character and deport themselves properly."[32] In the petitioners' view, this could avoid antagonizing them during this crisis, when their support was needed. The Hertford County men did not see an increased threat in their free Black neighbors and believed that they had enough local support for their petition.

Armed Black people labored in several capacities throughout the first half of the nineteenth century and some continued to do so during the Civil War.

Many people in the Confederacy believed that the "Twenty Negro Law," which exempted from military service "one person as agent, owner or overseer, on each plantation of twenty negroes" was necessary to keep enough white men at home to ensure that enslaved laborers' maintained their production.[33] Nevertheless, some workers continued laboring without their enslavers' coercive presence, including those who were armed. Black people with guns protected some farms and plantations from outsiders. Consider that this armed labor, which rested on prewar precedents, benefited the farms' white and Black residents and also threatened to put Black laborers into conflict with both Black and white outsiders. Armed labor also provided some enslaved men with the opportunity for greater independence. Consider Roden, a roughly forty-one-year-old man who managed his enslaver's farm while he was deployed. Capt. William Tripp led B Company of the 40th North Carolina Regiment. He served in the coastal forts defending Wilmington, one of the most important ports in the heavily blockaded Confederacy, particularly during the latter half of the war. In January 1864, Union Maj. Gen. Ulysses S. Grant noted that Wilmington and its port were of "more value to the enemy than all the balance of their sea coast."[34] Tripp was rarely able to return home, as the vital forts were under constant threat of assault and provided crucial cover for blockade runners; and as the senior captain in his regiment, he assumed his colonel's duties during the commander's absences.[35]

Tripp managed his Beaufort County farm via letters home to his wife, Araminta, who was thirteen years his junior. The Tripps' letters highlight the complexity of Black people's armed labor during the chaos of the war. Through the duration of his wartime service, William encouraged his Araminta to "try and be as courageous as possible" because "the government of the family" depended on her. He relied on Roden's mind and body, however, for the plantation's daily operations. William asked his wife to "tell Roden from me to take care of all my property and it will be well with him"; and he encouraged, "You my dear wife must try and take care of yourself and our dear little ones until I get home again."[36] Sally McMillen explains that many single women managed their farms and plantations in the antebellum era and others took over their husbands' duties when the men left to serve. Some women even protected their family's property from invading Union troops. Tripp's letter reflects that Araminta had her hands full with her quotidian domestic labor, which was even more difficult during the war. The Tripp children were also quite young—in 1860, Josephus was seven, Lavenia was five, Benjamin was three, and Rebecca was only a year old. The Tripps would have another child, Thomas, the following year.[37] In this context, Tripp's trust in Roden was significant. The farmer held $3,500 in real estate and another $15,000 in personal property, which made him one of the wealthiest men in Beaufort County. This high degree of trust is also manifested in the broad instructions that Tripp sent for Roden. He told Araminta, "I think you can rely a great deal on Roden's judgment at least I do"; and he also instructed her to "tell Roden to do what he thinks best" or have him "do the best of his judgment in all things," and "to continue to do the best he can."[38] William relied on Roden's labor and decision-making to protect the Tripp family and their farm and to ensure that it continued to produce. After all, during times of both war and peace, the plantation's residents, both Black and white, had to eat, and the taxes had to be paid.

Tripp's concerns about his property's safety were not unfounded; unwelcomed outsiders had been committing "depredations" on North Carolina plantations and farms throughout the antebellum period, and this problem worsened during the war. Armed enslaved laborers could deter those thieves who sought easy targets, or they could actively stop those who were more determined. In late December 1862 Araminta wrote her husband that enslaved people from the neighborhood had committed "outrages" on their farm. He lamented that he was powerless to "prevent or avenge" these actions from so far away.[39] This feeling of ineffectiveness would have been familiar to many Confederate soldiers whose farms were raided by enslaved people during the war, but that was only part of the issue. Union "strolling parties" and hungry Confederates posed additional threats when they were in the area. In addition, free people of color and white civilians also stole food and supplies from their neighbors. Hunger is a unifying force, and they sometimes collaborated: Reportedly, Confederate deserters and runaway slaves banded together to raid plantations and army depots in the western parts of the state. The United States blockade, coupled with the state's inadequate intrastate infrastructure, created and exacerbated supply shortages. This in turn drove prices up and pushed the prices of many commodities—when they were available in the first place— even further beyond the reach of North Carolina's struggling families.[40] These shortages of necessities were heightened by the Confederate army's needs. The soldiers had to eat, even if that meant civilians, particularly enslaved ones, would have to do with less. In January 1864, Stephen Dodson Ramseur, a Confederate officer from Lincoln County, explained to his brother that, "the Army must be fed even if people at home must go without it." He encouraged their father to plant "all sorts of vegetables in the greatest abundance" and suggested that another relative limit "the negroes to ⅛ to ¼ lb. of meat, when they have vegetables." Ramseur believed that "our whole people should do this & send the surplus to the army." He believed that the men in his brigade were "willing to whip Yankeedom" when fed ¼ to ½ lb. of meat instead of the ⅛ to ¼ that they were issued.[41] The enslaved laborers would bear the brunt of the shortages. Wartime pillaging put them at risk.

Further, the Union soldiers in the area seized from some homes or plantations "everything of value that was movable" and committed other depredations, sometimes aided by local "tories."[42] When federal troops occupied Warrenton, Warren County, in 1862, they allegedly proceeded to "steal whatever they can lay their hands upon in the shape of corn, bacon, silver, &c." They also came to "eat, without invitation, at every house they choose to call in at, and when called upon to pay have it charged to 'Uncle Sam.'"[43] Even if exaggerated, these anecdotes point to the shortages that civilians faced. William Tripp recognized that Roden's armed labor could potentially mitigate this. In the fall of 1862, he asked Araminta to have Roden "keep a sharp look out for the ons that are taking my things and tell me when I get back home again and they will pay for it."[44] This "sharp look out" was the first step, but Tripp had faith in Roden to do far more. In early 1863, he told Araminta that he lost sleep "thinking about those cursed negroes coming down to steal all that others by honest labor has made I wish Roden had of had my gun loaded with big shot and killed one or two they would not have disturbed you again in a hurry."[45] In closing, William asked his wife to "tell Roden to hide the gun in his house and when the thieves come use her to the best of his judgment and fear not."[46] Tripp's letter is torn and the rest of his commentary is lost, but his instructions suggest that Roden was familiar with this shotgun and that his enslaver believed he could rely on Roden's armed labor to preserve his property. Black people's labor on the Southern home front was complicated. Scholars show that even in the early stages of the war, many Black people had clear goals and loyalties and "ultimately became indispensable instruments" of United States success. They fled and deprived the Confederacy of their labor and transferred it to the federal war effort. Black people performed work or enlisted in the army or navy. Abe, a man whom William Tripp enslaved, was among the many who liberated themselves. His flight was a blow to Tripp's wealth and his farm's productivity.[47]

Further, consider that the enslaved people who raided the Tripp plantation were not strangers to the white family or to Roden and the enslaved community. When Araminta told her husband about the plundering, he surmised that "it no doubt was negroes from our neighborhood with some of your fathers" who were responsible, and Tripp continued, he wanted Roden to "keep a sharp look out." He suspected that Roden would recognize the culprits.[48] This area was not just a census district—it was a neighborhood. Many people in it knew Tripp's farm and the people who lived there. He had used the people his mother enslaved on his own land. He also hired local free people of color, like Israel Moore and George Moore, employing as many as nine of them at a time.[49] Some of the free people of color had long-term labor commitments with Tripp—he paid Harman Blango forty dollars to hire his son Henry for a year—and Tripp hired white neighbors as well. Further, Roden was probably related to the local Moore families—he took their surname in freedom.[50] The people on Tripp's plantation knew these people. Also, some of Tripp's enslaved laborers moved through the neighborhood. Roden and others worked at Tripp's mother's house, which could be reached on foot.[51] Araminta's parents, Noah and Rebecka Guilford, lived in the town of Washington, which was close enough for the Tripps to visit them in the evening after dinner.[52] Tripp occasionally took his workers to religious services, noting in August 1858 that he had taken "myself and most of my family white and black at South Creek to the Camp Meeting." That year, they stayed overnight on Saturday and Sunday night, where the Black laborers were likely able to meet, socialize with, and share services with other Black people, perhaps some of whom were family and friends. When attending May Day celebrations in 1858, the Tripps brought along Roden and Harriet, his partner, whom the family also enslaved.[53] Finally, Roden was trusted to travel through the area without supervision. He sometimes took Tripp's canoe into town to sell chickens or produce. Sometimes he traveled alone and at other times with another enslaved man, like Moses. Araminta also sent him alone to her father's plantation on errands.[54]

Tripp could not know who was raiding his farm, but he knew that many of the people of color in the area were connected via kinship or community. After all, he had indirectly facilitated many of the interactions that the people he enslaved had with others in the area. Further, the Black community in Beaufort County could not be neatly divided between free and enslaved. In 1861, the county court charged Sam, an enslaved man, with "living in illegal connection" with Bettie Collins, a free woman of color. Augustus Blango, a free man of color who used the alias Augustus Moore, was charged with "Beding and Cohabitating with Negro Slave woman[,] slave name not known[,] the property William M. MaCabe." The enslaver was one of the witnesses against Blango. Additionally, Shade Moore was drawn into the court system for "selling Liquor + gambling in his house," which he shared with two enslaved men, Horace and Bill, who had different enslavers. Tripp's turning to Roden on this matter demonstrates his faith in his laborer to act against other Black people whom he knew—as Tripp wrote to Araminta in 1862, "I have confidence in him and believe he will do right."[55] Roden's armed labor for the Tripp family does not negate the many the ways in which enslaved Southerners eroded the Confederate home front by running away, enlisting in the Union army, or otherwise resisting claims on their labor. It does, however, highlight how intricate Black and white Southerners' labor and social relationships were at the local level, even during the war.[56]

While unclear in the records, Roden and Tripp might have spent several years together, which might help to explain this high degree of trust. Further, Roden might have been seen as dependable enough to at least occasionally hire out his own time for wages, another marker of this trust.[57] Tripp did not share this experience with all his workers—Roden chose to help; but Abe chose to liberate himself when the opportunity presented itself. Stephanie McCurry and others have stressed Southerners' concerns that the people they enslaved might take advantage of the tumult of war to run away or revolt and how the Confederates were consequently prepared "to wage war on two fronts."[58] Other scholars have noted that the "old antebellum fears of slave insurrections, fueled by memories of Santo Domingo, Nat Turner, and John Brown" had created an "intense negrophobia." Court clerk James Rumley, writing from occupied Beaufort, Carteret County, expressed similar concerns. In March 1863, Rumley ominously declared that "visions of armed and infuriated bands of these black traitors, like imps of darkness, rise before us and darken the future."[59] Though the raging Civil War heightened these fears, white people's wartime anxieties about armed Black people in North Carolina's towns were a continuation of long-enduring antebellum concerns.

At the same time, many enslaved workers preferred to "bide their time, lacking confidence in Union motives or anticipating reversals that could turn deadly."[60] People made pragmatic decisions, which could look very different. Roden had a family on the Tripp plantation. William's and Araminta's letters made several references to Roden's son, who was named after him—the Tripps referred to him as "little Roden" or "Roden Jr." The full nature of their relationship is difficult to uncover. Additionally, Roden was partnered with Harriet, another person the Tripps enslaved.[61] Harriet may have been Little Roden's mother, though this is admittedly speculative. They might have influenced Roden's decision to remain laboring on the Tripp farm instead of fleeing to the Union lines, as Abe did. Both Roden men were of military age, and Tripp recognized this possibility. He warned Araminta to "tell Homer & the two Rodens to keep their eyes open as [Union Gen. Benjamin] Butler is going to try to get all in his lines in the service Tell them to run away before doing it as they have seen no trouble to what they will see if they do get them in the [Union] army." Tripp also said that the federals might take the Black men away from their homes, writing to Araminta that "the negroes that have gone to them are complaining bitterly of their treatment a great many from Washington and Newbern have been carried to Virginia to build fortifycations."[62] Georgia's Lee Barfield served in Tripp's home county, and he similarly wrote home that, "an old Negro" came to the United States lines in the area, "but they treated him so badly that he preferred slavery to such freedom."[63]

Additionally, some enslaved people who fled headed for the Confederate lines. Freedom was complicated, and there were different ways to pursue it or navigate it once acquired. In February 1865, Charlotte's William Treloar offered a $500 reward for the capture and return of Bill, a man he enslaved. The twenty-two-year-old, who had stolen $250 worth of gold when he absconded, was believed to have "went off with some soldiers going to the army near Petersburg." Bill had previously labored for a Confederate officer in the army, perhaps his previous enslaver, and might have developed a preference for the opportunities available in the military camps.[64] The young man saw some better opportunity for himself with the Confederate army than he did with Treloar. Perhaps he could make money hiring himself to these soldiers, or perhaps he knew other laborers in the camp, or perhaps he wanted to get to the front to better make an escape across the lines. Roden's armed labor on Tripp's farm was likely rooted in a similarly pragmatic approach to his circumstances.

In May of 1863, William warned Araminta to be on alert. He explained, "I expect nothing less than that the Yankees & negroes are to strip you of all your poultry and stock of every kind," but by August, he recognized that the threat was evolving. He sent Roden instructions to "keep a sharp look out for our things as I expect there will be a good deal of stealing this fall and it will be laid to the Yankees no doubt when other people done it." William predicted that "some of those free negroes will come around to kill beef and in fact steal all they can lay hands on also some of those mean low lifed white folks outback of us will be just as bad." He also suspected that a "tory and . . . black hearted vilian"—a white person from the area—had led Union troops to his farm where they committed "depredations" and "thievish acts."[65] Threats to the Tripp farm came from all corners—free and enslaved Black folks, soldiers, and "low lifed" white people. William did not explicitly order Roden to shoot these free Black and white neighbors, as he had wished for with the enslaved trespassers the previous January, but his intentions are unclear. He expected Roden to keep an eye out for pillagers and had already suggested that he might use a gun to protect Tripp's property.[66] The enslaver trusted Roden a great deal, but an illegally armed enslaved man during the war would have troubled many of his white neighbors. Tripp knew how some of them felt about armed Black people; back in 1851, when he represented them in the General Assembly, he presented a petition on behalf of his constituents who wanted to prevent free Black people from carrying firearms.[67] Further, consider how Tripp might have felt if his own farm were visited by armed raiders—the danger was real. In 1864, about twenty miles from New Bern, two Black men broke into Alfred Reel's house, when only his thirty-year-old sister and an enslaved worker were at the house. The two men "took all the valuables, including money, that they could obtain and then murdered Miss Reel." Alfred Reel returned home during the robbery and the men shot him dead in the yard.[68]

Tripp relied on Roden at home, but many free and enslaved Black people worked in military camps, both voluntarily and coerced. Tripp himself brought men he had enslaved, Mars and Louis, to camp with him.[69] Their labor precipitated the Confederate debate on using Black soldiers. Many enslaved workers, like David Blount or Tempie Herndon Durham's brother, Sim, accompanied their enslavers to the front, where they prepared meals, cleaned, took care of the horses and weapons, washed clothes, and did other chores. Both officers and enlisted men from the enslaving class had relied on this labor in their civilian lives and saw it as indispensable during their wartime service as well. As he settled into the soldier's life, eighteen-year-old William Calder wrote his mother, "There is one thing that I want and must have, a servant. It is absolutely necessary to have one to cook and wash especially the latter. If Bob comes back he must procure a negro in some way. It is not necessary that he should be free it is easy to hire one. Owners generally make no objection to their coming in the army. They are really safer there than at home. There is very little chance for them to get out of the lines. . . . I cannot be comfortable without one."[70]

Chatham County's Tempie Herndon Durham, who grew up enslaved, remembered that when her enslaver's son left home for the army, he took her brother, Sim, "to look after his hoss an' everything." Some of the Black men in military camps had little real choice in the matter, though they could sometimes exert pressure by threatening to run off. Other enslaved men wanted to go, like Bill, who ran away from William Treloar, but camp life could be brutal. Edgecombe County's William Dorsey Pender noted that while he commanded the Sixth North Carolina Infantry Regiment, some of the enslaved camp laborers were "allowed to die without any care on the part of those who are responsible for their well being."[71]

Free Black North Carolinians were also swallowed by the insatiable war machine, as officials often found it "impossible to get a sufficient number of hands" for salt production, coal mining, the maritime trades, or the construction of fortifications.[72] Like enslaved camp workers, some of these free Black

Tempie Herndon Durham, photographed in the 1930s when she was 103 years old. Courtesy of the Federal Writers' Project, United States Work Projects Administration (USWPA), Library of Congress, Manuscript Division.

men sought out work that directly supported the Confederate military. Some of them might have hired themselves out to Confederate troops, or at least white officers believed that they would. We should not assume free Black men to be inherently opposed to this fledgling nation, despite its infamous "cornerstone"—as Warren Milteer's work highlights—their relationship to the state was complicated and their "legal position . . . generally remained closer to that of whites than to that of slaves."[73] While it is generally difficult to trace many free Black people's motivations through the historical record, their actions might have been a calculated tactic within clearly defined power relationships. Further, free men of color connected with their broader communities in complicated ways—as Milteer describes, they were "a diverse population with various opinions about slavery, secession, and simply how to survive," and they "responded in a variety of ways to the major changes in their society." They were contributing, though not equal, members of communities that were in crisis in 1861. Many free Black men had carved out space for themselves and were not keen on risking that by siding with outsiders, especially early in the war when the United States' expressed goals were limited and its prospects for success were unclear. Nevertheless, this should not overshadow that some free Black men were unmistakably coerced into service.

In October 1861, the *Weekly Raleigh Register* reported that a white man had been "murdered by a free negro" in Wilkes County. The incident occurred when several white men in Wilkesboro, at least some of whom were Confederate soldiers, attempted to "press a free negro by the name of Fletcher" into the service as their servant. There was a legal mechanism to do this, as a few weeks prior, Adj. Gen. J. G. Martin ordered that every company raised in the state was "allowed four servants, for which they receive rations." He stated, "Free negroes can be taken with their consent, but not without it, except on the order in writing of the Chairman of the County Court, or of three Justices of the County."[74] The Wilkes County men were probably not acting in an official capacity, but they might have been inspired by Martin's orders. In any event, Fletcher did not want to go, so he resisted. This policy on seizing nonconsenting free Black men predated the Confederate Conscription Act by about six months, which further emphasized the antebellum court's view that Black men's citizenship was in doubt and that they could be treated differently than white citizens. Fletcher fled, but the white men gave chase and caught him. He then drew his pistol and shot one of them, a man named Carrender, who was instantly killed. His compatriots seized Fletcher and had him locked up. The free Black man sat in the county jail at Wilkesboro for two days until "an excited crowd" took him from the jail and "hung him until he was dead."[75]

It is not clear how widespread this kind of coercion was, but many soldiers wanted servants. Stephen Ramseur Dodson wrote to his brother in April 1864 and asked, "Is it possible for you to get a good free Negro to wait on me? Can you not scare one into it by the conscription? As a teamster or on fortifications they will have a hard fare & hard work & $4 pr month. As my Svr't. they will live as I do, have little to do, & get clothing food & $15 or $20 pr month."[76] Fletcher's pursuers believed that free Black people could be compelled to work for the state or for private citizens. The lynch mob that ultimately murdered him reinforced this belief; but if Fletcher had instead faced a judge, the court would likely have considered the state supreme court's decision on *State v. Lawrence Davis*. In this decision, Justice C. J. Pearson pronounced that free

Black people were "not deprived, absolutely, of the right of self-defense." They would be "required to allege and prove that it became necessary" to strike a white man to prevent "great bodily harm or grievous oppression." He explained that "while on the principle of self-protection, the paramount rights of the white population are secured, the rights of this inferior race are made to give place, as far, but not farther, than is necessary for that purpose." *State v. Davis* offers an interesting precedent, especially as Fletcher's assailants did not have Wilkes County's permission to seize him. In *State v. Davis*, Lawrence Davis struck a constable who came to serve notice for him to show cause on a civil matter. The constable then, according to Justice Pearson, sought to arrest and bind Davis "without any authority whatever," which the Supreme Court decided was "gross oppression" and a "high handed and lawless" action. Davis was within his "natural right of self-defense" to strike this white man under these circumstances.[77]

Other Black men who worked for Confederate soldiers did so willingly. Some of them gained practical martial skills, and they sometimes later turned these skills against the Confederacy. Craven County's William Henry Singleton, who was enslaved by John Handcock Nelson, recorded that during the rising secession crisis, his enslaver permitted him to work as a servant for a young white man named Samuel Hymans. Hymans, who was Nelson's nephew, had recently returned home from his studies at the United States Military Academy and, in anticipation of the war, had organized a company of soldiers who would later join the First North Carolina Cavalry.[78] While he worked for Hymans, Singleton learned to drill the white recruits himself and was sometimes entrusted to do so when Hymans was otherwise occupied. One wonders how the white North Carolinians who practiced their maneuvers under the Black man's watchful eyes felt about the arrangement. Singleton later fled to the Union lines where, then a free man, he served as a scout. He also found an outlet for the skills that Hymans had taught him; he raised and drilled a regiment of Black men in New Bern for the United States Army. Perhaps anticipating that some of his readers might question his earlier decision to help train Confederate soldiers, Singleton explained, "I was so anxious to go with Hymans . . . because I wanted to learn how to drill."[79] He does not explain why this skill was initially attractive to him, but whatever his motivations, Singleton used his experiences with the Confederate service to bolster the United States war effort in North Carolina.

Southerners praised the service of Black people whose armed labor bolstered the Confederacy. These reports are difficult to corroborate, but they show that some white North Carolinians narrowly framed the military labor of "trusted" armed Black people in a manner that rested on prewar under-standings. The *Fayetteville Observer* reprinted a story in which an enslaved man named William was out foraging for the Confederates when he came across a straggling Union soldier. The northerner immediately claimed William as a prisoner and while the Black man considered pouncing on his captor, disarm-ing him, and then killing him with his own bayonet, he instead decided on a ruse. William feigned joy at being found and then tricked the Union soldier into following him . . . right back to the rebels' camp. They celebrated William when he returned with his prisoner. The regimental commander extended "high commendations" and William's enslaver, another Confederate officer, re-warded him with "a fine pistol."[80] This award must be seen in context: William could have carried it on future foraging trips, and it demonstrated the faith that his enslaver and the other Confederates in their camp had in him. He may have needed it—the United States' Black auxiliaries certainly did. Vincent Colyer, the US superintendent of the poor in North Carolina, wrote how Union offi-cers gave passes to some Black men within the lines so they could both visit local family and gather intelligence. In one instance, Colyer gave three of them a revolver when they requested a "weapon to defend themselves." This was not just for show. One of the Black men was found while visiting his wife. Local white people recognized him as "a negro whom the Yankees had armed and sent up as a spy." The rebels shot and captured him. Other formerly enslaved scouts used their pistols to fight their way through Confederates to get back to the Union camp.[81]

William was trusted and proven in his Confederate enslaver's eyes. His pistol could be a useful defensive tool when he foraged. While in limited num-bers, some armed enslaved workers engaged Union troops in combat. Virgin-ia's John Parker was being forced to labor near Richmond when he was sent to fight in the First Battle of Bull Run with several other enslaved men. They were assigned to an artillery battery and served, albeit unwillingly; he explained that the Confederate officers would have shot the coerced Black artillerymen if they tried to flee.[82] In North Carolina, Frank McGhee's enslaver enlisted in the Granville Rangers and brought him along as his servant. A newspa-per interviewed him in the late 1930s, and the ninety-six-year-old "vividly" remembered "fighting with his master at Fort Fisher, Seven Pines, Charles-ton, and Appomattax." He also added that he was "plumb overcome wid joy" upon emancipation, and the interviewer asked him how this squared with his fighting in the Confederate service. The elderly Black man explained that "his master was a good man, and that his duty as a good slave was to follow the 'old marse.'"[83] Milteer related how Orange County's Samuel Chavers, a biracial man who passed at white, enlisted in and saw combat with the Twenty-Eight North Carolina Infantry Regiment. He was captured and then exchanged in a prisoner swap, but was later discharged for being "partly of negro descent." Despite this reversal, the committed Chavers managed to reenlist with the Twenty-Eighth and later died while in service.[84]

The North Carolina newspapers published stories that also blurred the line between Black men's military labor and white men's military service. In August of 1861, the *Semi-Weekly Standard* told the story of "a negro boy" who discovered a federal soldier resting against a tree with his rifle. Unlike William, this enslaved man was not connected to the Confederate army. Nevertheless, he saw an opportunity and took full advantage of it. The young Black man "slipped up" to the solitary Yankee "and seized the gun." He then used the rifle and its fixed bayonet to capture the Northerner, whom he marched over to nearby Confederate troops. The newspaper matter-of-factly alleged that "many cases" had been reported wherein enslaved men captured Union soldiers.[85] The rifle that this Black man used was not even his own. These stories could be celebrated by North Carolina rebels because they continued the antebellum expectations that armed labor could be undertaken by those *individual* Black men of good character, as subjectively assessed by white people. Even though the Black man in the *Semi-Weekly Standard*'s article was unsupervised and not connected to the Confederate army, he immediately went to the proper authorities after arming himself and capturing the dozing United States soldier. In the eyes of many white North Carolinians, this was the proper course of action. These capture stories in the *Semi-Weekly Standard* and the *Fayetteville Observer* shared a few themes. Although the press praised the Black men's armed labor, their actions were not officially sanctioned but were allegedly born of their loyalty to the Confederate nation, or in William's case, at least, his loyalty to the white soldiers in its ranks. Additionally, both newspaper reports were written during the first fourteen months of the conflict and rest on both happenstance and individual Union soldiers' bumbling incompetence. In that regard, these were as much a comment about North Carolinians' perception that "Lincoln's hirelings" were inept, unmanly, and could be easily defeated as they were a comment about Black men's service for the Confederacy.[86] Even unarmed Black men, whose manhood white Confederates did not see as equal to their own and alongside of whom they generally did not care to fight (with notable exceptions), could outwit and capture the incompetent Yankees.

Despite these stories about Black men who loyally provided armed labor for the Confederacy, many white Southerners held a clear aversion to enlisting Black soldiers. North Carolinians were no exception. The Confederate government refused to arm Southern Black men on any significant scale because of its white supremacist notions about what their nation was and who was fit to defend it as well as their concerns that Black freedom would be the ultimate cost for that service. Historian Gary Gallagher and others have argued that this latter point does not indicate lukewarm support for the idea of a Confederate nation. While ruminating on the idea, Catherine Ann Devereux Edmondston, who lived on a Halifax County plantation with nearly ninety enslaved people during the war, observed that "slaveholders on principle, & those who hope one day to become slaveholders . . . will not tacitly yeild their property & their hope & allow a degraded race to be placed at one stroke on a level with them." Despite her aversion to the idea of Black soldiers, Edmondston went on to proclaim that it was her "faith in the country" that sustained her through the long and difficult war years.[87] Her vision of a Confederate nation did not include the loss of enslaved property or Black and white men serving alongside each other for that nation's survival.

Historian Joseph P. Reidy argues that the Confederacy hesitated to use Black soldiers because of its persistence in holding onto long-standing traditions. Jefferson Davis and the Confederate Congress marshaled the South's white citizens to arms to fight the nation's battles, but they used free and enslaved Black people to produce goods and provide physical labor, much as they had done before the war. Reidy notes that this racially divided labor arrangement supported both "the political ideology and the material requirements" of the Confederate cause, which can be broadly understood as white supremacy and a reliance on the labor of exploited Black workers.[88] To go one step further: The Confederacy's general resistance to arming significant numbers of its large enslaved population stands out as a hemispheric anomaly. Free and enslaved people of color served in most colonial militias and revolutionary armies throughout the Americas. This was particularly the case in the Spanish and Portuguese colonies, but the French, Dutch, and British engaged in similar practices, albeit to a lesser degree. For over three centuries, the European imperial powers used both free and enslaved men of color's armed labor to subjugate Indigenous populations, protect European colonists and property from pirates or maroons, and wage war against their imperial rivals. Enslaved and free men of color fought under both the royalist and republican banners in the Latin American and US wars for independence.[89] The Confederate nation was remarkable in its resistance to this long-standing trend, which had already been proven to be effective on a hemispheric scale. As earlier sections of this book have presented, North Carolinians had their own historical precedents in the colonial and early republican eras that they could have drawn on; but the weight of antebellum regulations and pressures of the slaveholders' war was too great to overcome.

The federal government had a different approach. While there were a few earlier efforts and many who initially dismissed the idea, by January 1863, the United States army began to officially recruit and arm Black men. As a direct result, the Confederate debate intensified.[90] The Union military's use of Black soldiers and sailors flew in the face of North Carolina's antebellum practices of locally vetted and trusted individual Black men carrying arms, and consequently, the white men who opposed the practice could frame it as a stain upon white Union soldiers' manhood and an indication of their military ineptitude. Further, in an effort to dissuade Southern Black men's interest in the United States army, some Confederates characterized military enlistment as an assured violent death for the Black men themselves: William Tripp thought enslaved men should stay with their enslavers because those who enlisted with the Union troops were certain to be "killed up."[91] Ultimately, however, the Confederate Congress began to consider arming men of color in a desperate effort to save their struggling nation, despite broad opposition from North Carolina's congressional representatives.

Some white North Carolinians were staunchly opposed to the "utterly inadmissible" idea of enlisting Black men as soldiers but continued to push for using Black laborers in unarmed military capacities, even through the last months of the war. Advocates pointed out that there were thousands of Confederate soldiers employed in auxiliary positions, perhaps one for every ten soldiers who served in a combat role, and they argued that the army should "have negroes for these employments, but not in the ranks." They noted that white soldiers would thereby be relieved from support or fatigue duty and could raise the Confederates' combat strength without compromising the racial integrity of their army. In theory, this would make more Black laborers available but would prevent any adverse effects on unit cohesion and morale. The *Fayetteville Observer* used this point to take a jab at the Lincoln administration's deployment of Black troops and exclaimed, "To the Yankees let the *honor* belong exclusively, of making negroes fight their battles."[92] In North Carolina, white men would retain the honor of fighting for their nation's survival.

Union forces began recruiting Black North Carolinians in New Bern in February 1863, and in Beaufort in May of that year, much to the chagrin of these towns' white residents, who saw this as a threat to white women and white people's property. Even some of the Unionists and federal military officers in the area were wary. John A. Hedrick thought that "if the white men will not fight" the United States should "make a draft on the contrabands,"

Enslaved North Carolinians, emboldened by the Emancipation Proclamation and finding opportunities to liberate themselves, head to New Bern, Craven County. *Harper's Weekly*, February 21, 1863. Courtesy of the Library of Congress, Prints and Photographs Division.

but he noted that most of the army and navy officers were "bitterly opposed to arming the negroes." He added that he thought that "some of them, at least, will make good fighting material. I do not believe that they are all cowards."[93] Hedrick could offer only a lukewarm endorsement, but others were more enthusiastic, if only on account of circumstances. As Confederates attacked the United States forces at Washington, in Beaufort County, on a foggy September morning in 1862, the outnumbered federals ordered "every able-bodied negro" to the lines, most of whom were North Carolina contrabands. W. P. Derby, who served in the Twenty-Seventh Massachusetts Regiment of Volunteer Infantry, recalled, "This was our first experience with armed negroes, and it was wonderful how quietly it was submitted to by many who had loudly declared, 'they would never fight side of a nigger!' Whitworth shots, exploding shells, and bullet tz-z-zps, were wonderfully persuasive arguments on such a question."[94] They successfully drove off the Confederates. By the war's end, over five thousand Black North Carolinians had enlisted in the federal service.[95] Further, Edward Wild, a twice-wounded brigadier general from an abolitionist family in Massachusetts, lead his "African Brigade" on operations in the area. Some of Wild's men came from Northern towns, but others were North

Carolinians. As Barton Myers explains, since some of them were locals, "there was an added dimension to Wild's upending of the racial order. Not only was he putting black men over white by giving black men the power to confiscate white men's property and fight them on the battlefield, but he was also placing former slaves or black employees in a position of power vis-à-vis their former owners or employers."[96] This "power to confiscate" and to fight emanated from the federal government but it was applied through these Black men's rifles.

As early as the summer of 1862, white residents worried that the Black sailors who entered North Carolina's Union controlled ports were armed. This added another layer of tension to the United States' occupation.[97] This was even more dramatic when the federals began arming Black soldiers. Lee Barfield, a Georgia cavalryman serving in North Carolina, wrote home in December 1863, that a "Regt. of Negro troops & 500 Cavalry" were "committing great depredations in the region of Elizabeth City & Hartford," in Pasquotank and Perquimans Counties, respectively. He added, "the Negroes are the most brutal invaders our country ever had to contend with. There is nothing too base for them to commit. Their insults to ladies are almost unequaled."[98] The *Fayetteville Observer* covered the Black soldiers in the occupation force at Elizabeth City, Chowan County. The editors stated that they threatened the standing social order and that the Northerners "not only permit this but encourage it." They lamented that "the treatment to which the white people of that unfortunate town are subjected to is heartrending. The negroes compel white women of delicacy and refinement to cook and wash for them." The *Observer* alleged that these Black troops demanded food from white residents and engaged in "the most loathsome ribaldry" by putting white women into sexually charged situations. It reported that one of the Black soldiers flipped a white woman's clothes "up over her back and shoulders whilst [his comrades] sent up loud peals of laughter!"[99] The accuracy of these reports was less important than the impact they had on the home front. For white North Carolinians, they symbolized an abhorrent shift from the antebellum order.

Armed Black United States soldiers sometimes posed an even more sexually provocative threat to white North Carolinians' constructed hierarchy. Union chaplain Henry McNeal Turner related that when his regiment, the First United States Colored Troops, approached the town of Smithfield, in Johnston County, they discovered that the nearest bridge had been burned down. The men stripped naked, held their clothes aloft with their fixed bayonets, and waded across the river. When they emerged, they entered the town and the white women of Smithfield "watched with the utmost intensity." Turner reports that they "thronged the windows, porticos and yards, in the

finest attire imaginable" to see the spectacle. Historian David Blight described
Turner's depiction of this scene as capturing "a memory that haunted the white
South for generations to come: naked Black men with muskets, striding out
of a river into a town's streets with an audience of white women." Jim Cullen
argued that at that moment, the Black soldiers had "attained mastery over
their bodies which they use for their own purposes, a mastery that compels
white southerners to observe it in action."[100] The scenes like those offered
by the *Fayetteville Observer* and Henry McNeal Turner inflamed some white
Southerners' racist anxieties about armed Black men in powerful positions that
would have been inconceivable in the antebellum era. Even if the newspaper's
editors exaggerated the occupying Black troops' behavior toward Elizabeth
City's white women, the underlying concerns about victorious armed Black
men's interactions with conquered white women would have still resonated
deeply with its white readers. Reports like these offered very little reassurance
to those Confederates who contemplated arming enslaved men for their own
war effort.

The Union army made much better use of Black people's armed labor than
the Confederacy. Nonetheless, when the federal government decided to open
its ranks to them, there was no guarantee that Black Southerners would flock to
recruiting offices with an eagerness to fight for the Union's preservation. Black
North Carolinians pragmatically looked to their own community's needs, and
the Union army had to work to convince many of them that aiding the United
States would be beneficial. When the federals began recruiting among eastern
North Carolina's Black population, community leader Abraham Galloway met
with Union official Edward Kinsley to discuss the details of any potential military service. Galloway held the power in these discussions; the white Northerner was blindfolded and led to the meeting's location, and when his covering
was removed, he found himself sitting in an attic and surrounded by armed
people of color. Reportedly, Galloway negotiated the terms under which the
local Black men would be willing to enlist while pointing a pistol at Kinsley's
head.[101] Black men did not immediately trust the United States government,
nor were they instantly and unconditionally willing to offer their armed labor
and their lives for the Union's cause. To them, Kinsley was merely another
player in the wartime drama that was unfolding across the state. These Black
men's firearm use was a key factor in their ability to maintain their agency.
Their illegally possessed firearms helped them to leverage the terms under
which they would offer their legal armed labor to the United States Army. They
could deploy or withhold this labor at will. As Galloway taught Kinsley, these
Black North Carolinians were armed, organized, and going to have a voice in

their community's future. As David Cecelski explains, Galloway represented a Black community that would shoulder rifles for the United States if the federal government would make the war "a crusade for black liberation." However, if Lincoln simply planned to exploit their armed labor to preserve the Union, then he would be hard pressed to secure the support of Black recruits in New Bern. Kinsley could not coerce labor from them, as the Confederate government had sought to do, but would instead have to provide equal pay, support their families, educate their children, and assure them that the Confederates would not be able to exact revenge on them if they were captured.[102]

The Old North State's newspapers were quite critical of the Union army's use of armed Black North Carolinians in its ranks. In an effort to suppress the United States' recruiting efforts, they portrayed the federals as forcing Black men into the service and carelessly using them with little regard for their lives. The newspapers suggested that Black people would be foolish to enlist with the Yankees, who would quickly usher them off to horrifically violent deaths on the battlefield. In the spring of 1864, the *Fayetteville Observer* covered the Battle of Olustee, during which Black regiments were engaged, one of which had been raised in New Bern. The editors declared that, "if anything could exceed the yankee inhumanity to the negroes, as displayed through this war in separating husbands from wives, and both from their helpless children . . . it is this thrusting of the negroes in the front in battle, to save their own cowardly carcasses from Confederate bullets."[103] The *Observer* maintained that the Union officers had no qualms about using Black men as cannon fodder and smugly reported that the Black North Carolinians had been "slaughtered without mercy, as was right." The *Fayetteville Observer* printed a letter from a Lake City, Florida, resident who explained that "there were but few black prisoners taken; but the ground is covered with them—have heard it stated as high as 800 It is having a good effect upon the blacks. They all understand they were put in front and made to fight."[104] The writer believed that the Black soldiers had received their just rewards for both serving with Union generals who did not care for them and for bearing arms against their racial superiors and native region. The newspaper obliquely suggested that Black men should keep out of the fighting, but in this it ignored the thousands of free and enslaved people of color who had been and were still being coerced into the Confederate war effort.

William Tripp warned the people he enslaved about the dangers of running off to the United States army. This was in some regard a tactic to preserve his own labor force, but he also had strong opinions about Black men fighting for the United States. He wrote Araminta about an earlier conversation that he had had with Roden, wherein he told him that those who sided with the Northerners in the hope that "Lincons proclamation" would free them would "get the worst of it." Alternatively, according to Tripp, those who stayed with their enslavers would "keep out of the scrape and fare well and be free equally as soon and besides keep up their good character." Tripp was biased—even if enslaved workers remained at home, they would not necessarily be kept "out of the scrape" because, as another Confederate soldier commented about his service in Kinston, they were "pressing into service all the horses they can get and Some Negroes and Waggons and teams."[105] Further, Tripp himself took two of the men that he enslaved to camp, as did other enslavers.[106] The artillery officer meant that Black people's labor should be used only in a manner that reflected familiar antebellum patterns—subservient work that bolstered their enslavers' interests. Challenges to that arrangement were unacceptable.

William Tripp continued, offering commentary on the dangers that awaited those enslaved people who fled to the United States forces. He told Araminta that Union Gen. David Hunter had conscripted "all the negroes able to bear arms" and had ordered the officers under his command to "kill all of them that attempt to run on the day of the battle." Other enslavers tried similar tactics. Some told their laborers that if they ran off to Fortress Monroe they would "either [be] sold to Cubans or have their hands cut off."[107] Despite his self-interested counsel, some of Tripp's enslaved workers did flee. He tried to persuade those who remained that the Yankees would coerce them into the military, which he reiterated would prove fatal. William instructed Araminta to:

> give my best respects to all Mother's negroes that remain faithful and give my verry[sic] best respects to all my folks that are at home Tell them to remain at home it makes no difference what others may tell them of Yankee freedom and they will see in the end that they have done wisely Out of all those that have gone to the Yankees but few will die a natural death. Poor fools they are not satisfied to let well enough alone but must go they know not where nor what for They will rue it in tears and blood.[108]

Tripp's praise of these enslaved people's faithfulness and good character resounded with the antebellum conditions under which Black people could be armed. His "folks" who remained at home had proven themselves and could be trusted, especially Roden, who protected Tripp's farm and thereby helped to sustain the status quo. While the war presented new potential opportunities for Roden, these were mitigated in Tripp's eyes by the labor relationship between them.

William Tripp was not only bothered by the loss of his fleeing bondmen's labor; he was also enraged at the thought of self-liberated Black men clad in Union blue and carrying federal rifles as they met their former enslavers in battle. After hearing that the United States had raised a regiment of Black men in New Bern in February 1863, Tripp passionately wrote to Araminta, "I am willing to take my company and clear them out for my share of the war. We can whip them I am certain When you hear of our army meeting negroes in fight you will hear of no quarter given and also hear of a great death among negroes."[109] While some of Tripp's words may be attributed to wartime bravado, he understood these Black troops to be fundamentally different from the white soldiers and sailors with whom he had already traded artillery fire. He was not alone in this sentiment. When Confederate troops under Brig. Gen. Robert F. Hoke and Brig. Gen. Matt Ransom, both native North Carolinians, recaptured Plymouth, Washington County in April 1864, they gave no quarter to the Black soldiers they captured. Sgt. Samuel Johnson, a Black man who fought in the Second US Colored Cavalry, later testified that "all the negroes found in blue uniform or with any outward marks of a Union soldier upon him was killed—I saw some taken into the woods and hung—Others I saw stripped of all their clothing . . . and then they were shot—Still others were killed by having their brains beaten out . . . All were not killed the day of the capture . . . the following morning . . . the remainder of the black soldiers were killed."[110] The white men's anger continued after the shooting had stopped. It also extended to the dead. William Biggs, a Confederate soldier who was stationed near Plymouth in the weeks after the battle, wrote to his sister that he was "occasionally relieved from the monotony by the sight of dead Yankee or negros. which no one Seems to care about taking the trouble to put into the ground." Judging from Union recruiting successes among people of color in the eastern parts of the state, many Black North Carolinians thought quite differently about the prospect of "colored folks soldiers in blue clothes."[111] These Black men made a powerful statement about their manhood and their commitment to dismantling the institution of slavery, and it was not lost on people from their own communities or on the Confederates.

Tripp and many other white North Carolinians in the Confederate army, enslavers or not, had been steeped in white supremacy their entire lives. They could not brook the idea of Black men rejecting subservience and meeting them on the battlefield, where bullets and bayonets had no respect for racial hierarchy. This disdain was not limited to white soldiers. John Washington Graham, the son of William A. Graham, served in the Fifty-Sixth North Carolina Infantry Regiment and faced the Second US Colored Cavalry Regiment in nearby Suffolk, Virginia, before the fighting at Plymouth. He later explained to his father, "As we went through the town, the ladies that were left there were standing at their doors, some waving handkerchiefs, some crying, some praying, and others calling to us to 'kill the negroes.' (Our Brigade did not need this to make them give 'no quarter,' as it is understood amongst us that we take no negro prisoners)."[112]

While the stressors of war exacerbated racial animosity and violence on the battlefield, gun violence against the enslaved was one of slavery's long-standing features. It continued during the war as the institution was threatened by individuals' flights for freedom and the United States' military and political tactics. Fanny Cannady was only around six years old at the end of the Civil War, but her biggest memory of the conflict was "how Marse Jordan shot Leonard Allen, one of his slaves." Though she was nearly eighty years old at the time of her interview, she added "I ain't never forgot dat." Her enslaver's sons were Confederate soldiers, one of them was "struttin' 'roun' de yard" in his uniform while on furlough, which prompted Leonard to comment, "Look at dat God damn sojer. He fightin' to keep us niggahs from bein' free." Jordan asked Allen what he was muttering about and, undaunted, the Black man repeated it verbatim. Furious, Jordan ordered another laborer, Cannady's father, to bring him a shotgun. Sally Jordan, the enslaver's wife, protested and tried to stop her husband from killing Leonard, but the angry white man "reached over an' slapped Mis' Sally down, den picked up de gun an' shot er hole in Leonard's ches' big as yo' fis.'" Cannady was traumatized by the scene—she was so scared she ran and hid in the stable but recalled that "even wid my eyes shut I could see Leonard layin' on the groun'" with a hole in his chest and face still fixed in a defiant sneer.[113] Much changed during the war, but enslavers continued to keep a tight, violent grip.

As the war dragged on, casualties rose to nearly unbearable heights, desertions increased, recruitment decreased, and economic problems mounted on the home front. Consequently, the Confederate authorities had to consider radical means to reinforce their dwindling army. Southern hopes for a negotiated peace evaporated in November 1864, with Lincoln's successful reelection over Gen. George B. McClellan and the Northern Democrats. Even before the situation had progressed that far, some Confederates had proposed using the South's multitudinous Black laborers for combat duty. In early January 1864, Maj. Gen. Patrick Cleburne had outlined the potential benefits of mobilizing Black soldiers for the Confederacy, and he pointed to the true cost of such a project, which was also one of its biggest obstacles. Speaking of the enslaved Black men living within the Confederacy, the Irish-born Arkansan declared: "If we arm and train him and make him fight for the country in her hour of dire distress, every consideration of principle and policy demand that we should set him and his whole race who side with us free. It is a first principle with mankind that he who offers his life in defense of the State should receive from her in return his freedom and his happiness."[114] Cleburne believed that freedom was prerequisite for enslaved men's reliability on the battlefield. Further, he believed that one of these men, when fighting for his freedom, would "tempt dangers and difficulties not exceeded by the bravest soldier in the field." Further, he thought that "the hope of freedom is, perhaps, the only moral incentive that can be applied to him in his present condition."[115] In Cleburne's estimation, the promise of freedom would convert Black laborers into a very capable fighting force and perhaps help secure Confederate nationhood.

This was a sharp departure from the antebellum standards that white North Carolinians, and many other Southerners, had come to expect. Cleburne recognized that the North could also offer freedom to induce Black men's enlistment; but he understood that the South could be in a position to offer a better inducement. It could "give the negro not only his own freedom, but that of his wife and child, and can secure it to him in his old home." This was a bold idea, and Cleburne recognized that to achieve it, the Confederate government would have to "immediately make his marriage and parental relations sacred in the eyes of the law." These steps were unattractive to many white Southerners, as they would have radically changed their society; but the Arkansan saw them as indispensable to guaranteeing the loyalty of hundreds of thousands of enslaved men who would be "a thousand fold more dangerous" once organized, armed, and trained for combat.[116]

Some white people worried that Cleburne's proposal to free the Black soldiers and respect their families could bring about a broader program of emancipation. This would have been an alarming and unprecedented development. While some armed bondmen had relied on their "meritorious service" during the Revolutionary War to secure their freedom, the Southern legislatures had never created an official policy to this effect. In North Carolina, the process of service-based emancipation was primarily determined in the courts. Confederate President Jefferson Davis recognized that Cleburne's plan was a political liability, and he ordered that it be suppressed. He cited the document's potential to create "discouragement, distraction, and dissension" both in the ranks and among the civilian population. Cleburne was not oblivious to the plan's potential challenges. He was concerned that there was "a danger that this concession to common sense may come too late" because of popular opposition and his belief that the Black men would need extensive training before they were combat ready.[117]

These arguments spilled over into North Carolina's state-level politics. The debates in the 1864 gubernatorial campaign primed white people to resist anything resembling racial equality, including using armed Black men in defense of their state and nation. Incumbent Zebulon Vance staved off challenger William Woods Holden's peace platform in large part because he successfully stoked white North Carolinians' fears of racial equality and then linked those fears to the war effort. Holden, a newspaper editor from Orange County, had supported Vance politically earlier in the war, but the peace movement gained traction after the Confederacy's military reversals at Gettysburg and Vicksburg in the summer of 1863. Holden became an active participant and eventually won the nomination for the governor's race. During the campaign, Vance declared that the peace platform would quickly guide the state "into the arms of Lincoln" and abolitionism. He further argued that a separate peace would not even get North Carolina out of the war and that, to the contrary, it would mean that the state's white men could be conscripted into Lincoln's army "to fight alongside of his Negro troops in exterminating the white men, women, and children of the South." While speculative, this presented a bleak future and helped propel Vance to a landslide victory. North Carolina remained committed to the war through late 1864, partly because its white residents' "need to preserve slavery and white supremacy outweighed wartime material hardships."[118]

Some white North Carolinians' opposition to enlisting enslaved men was fueled by their worries about labor. In early 1865, the state's representatives in Richmond voiced concerns that losing control of their bondmen's labor to the national government could weaken the institution. White North Carolinians resented the state's reach onto their farms, where many of them had already lost laborers to conscription for construction details or to flight to the expanding Union lines. Nonetheless, the war effort needed a labor force, and the Confederate Congress sought to find it though a bill to "provide for the employment of free negroes and slaves to work upon fortifications and perform other labor connected with the defences of the country." During the debates at this crucial phase of the war, North Carolina's representatives were extremely critical of the plans to use the Confederacy's bondpeople for the vaguely defined "other labor."[119] This was not a new development, however. Several weeks earlier, in December 1864, Daniel G. Fowle, while serving in the state legislature, raised the question of whether Jefferson Davis and the national government had the authority to conscript enslaved people. Fowle believed that the Confederate constitution established that "no law impairing the right of property in negro slaves shall be passed." Therefore, as he understood it, the Confederate

Congress had no power "to interfere in any degree with slave property" but would have to "leave it entirely to the control of the States."[120]

At the national level, when a South Carolina congressman moved to strike out the stipulation in the bill that the army could use no more than 30,000 enslaved Southerners in the regions east of the Mississippi River and another 10,000 west of the river, William N. H. Smith from North Carolina's First Congressional District expressed serious concerns. He warned that without a clearly defined limit, "the whole slave population would be in the hands of the military authorities." He would be disappointed. The house was divided but ultimately removed the numerical limitation by a vote of 46 to 28.[121] Congress trusted Jeff Davis to responsibly appropriate Black laborers without a defined limit. Fifth District congressman Josiah Turner Jr. understood the bill as a potential move toward abolition, which left him concerned about Davis's "soundness" for office. He roared that "the country had been too long and too often deluded and deceived by Presidential plans," which he believed had been largely unsuccessful. Additionally, Turner feared that the plan could potentially put armed Black men into the army, which he believed the public would not support; and he therefore encouraged his colleagues to "stamp upon it the indelible stigma of public abhorrence."[122]

James T. Leach, who represented the state's Third District, also "feared that if this bill passed the negroes . . . would be employed as soldiers." He was "unalterably opposed" to such a course of action and argued that it might very well be the "death knell" of the Confederacy. Even worse, he drew upon the ever-present specter of Haiti and suggested that the bill might even "make a San Domingo of our land." The memories of Haiti's victorious Black armies and the Black nation that they had forged, both despite massive resistance from white people, were still powerfully evocative some sixty years after the fact. Leach also shared Josiah Turner's belief that the Davis administration should allow the individual states to decide how enslaved laborers should be used. He protested that there was already "too much of brass button and bayonet rule" and that, as bureaucrats plagued the land "as thick as locusts in Egypt," North Carolina's residents would appreciate less interference from Richmond.[123] In Leach's mind, this notion of arming Black men for the Confederate military was a potential threat to the state. The eighth district's James G. Ramsay echoed much of his colleagues' sentiments. He also believed that the bill's vague labor provision needed clarification, and he offered a solution via an amendment to "relieve the matter of all doubt" and ensure that the enslaved laborers in the Confederate states "shall not be armed or used as soldiers." Ramsay's motion failed, however.[124]

James M. Leach from North Carolina's Seventh Congressional District unsuccessfully proposed a similar amendment, but it was tabled on the motion of one of his Alabamian colleagues. Leach and the rest of the frustrated North Carolina delegation were voicing concerns that many of their constituents had held for decades prior to the war—though to no avail on the national level as the Confederacy struggled to survive.[125] The state's senators also struggled on this issue in their chamber. Senator William A. Graham opposed the "bill to conscribe negroes in the army" particularly after the House passed it; and the Senate postponed it indefinitely. He wrote to a colleague that he had "argued it at length as unconstitutional according to the Dred Scott decision as well as inexpedient and dangerous." However, in Graham's view, the bill was still a threat. He worried that "there may be attempts to revive this fatal measure." Jefferson Davis's administration, Gen. Robert E. Lee, and Secretary of State Judah Benjamin were all working to that end.[126] The prospect of the national government appropriating enslavers' and their county courts' power to regulate Black people's armed labor was too much for them to bear, even in a war for their independence.

Back in Raleigh, the General Assembly shared the congressional delegation's vehement opposition to the Confederate government's attempt to harness Black people's armed labor for the military. The state legislators understood this effort as an abrogation of the antebellum practices that they thought had kept the state and its racial hierarchy relatively safe. They wanted the state legislature to retain control over how the national government deployed enslaved North Carolinians' labor. Most of the legislators were enslavers themselves and therefore had a personal stake in how the Confederate military used their labor.[127] On February 3, 1865, the assembly passed a resolution "Against the Policy of Arming the Slaves" that asserted that any such decision was a state prerogative. The resolution was a direct response to Jefferson Davis's comments from the previous autumn that armed Black men could be used in dire circumstances and to the Confederate Congress's debate on a bill for that purpose.[128] The resolution declared that it was firmly "against the arming of slaves by the Confederate government, in any emergency that can possibly arise" but that it would nevertheless "consent to their being taken and used as laborers in the public service, upon just compensation being made."[129] Further, the legislators argued that the national government lacked the constitutional authority to undertake any such course of action "without the consent of the States being first freely given." The assembly's resolution explicitly maintained that North Carolina was not inherently opposed to the central government using Black men's military labor, but it was committed to state control over the decision to use *armed* Black laborers. This resolution reflected the persistent antebellum view that local populations were best suited to decide which Black people should be armed and to supervise them.[130]

The Confederate Congress ultimately passed the "Negro Soldier Bill" over the opposition of eight of North Carolina's nine representatives.[131] North Carolina politicians' broad opposition to arming enslaved men was not lost on some Northern newspapermen, who ridiculed the state as giving up the fight. The *New York Times* contrasted it with Virginia, whose legislature was "almost unanimously in favor of arming."[132] The editors concluded that North Carolina was "not anxious to see the depleted ranks of the rebel army filled up at all." While the state had fewer enslaved laborers than Virginia, the *Times* suggested that the assembly "apparently fails to see the necessity of continuing the fight, and, therefore, ignores, in a logical way, the other necessity—of arming the negroes."[133] By March of 1865, many white North Carolinians were exhausted and not interested in further prolonging the war but, the *Times* made no effort to understand why they resisted sending their bondpeople to defend their faltering nation.

Despite the passage of the "Negro Soldier Bill," many North Carolinians remained critical of the decision to use armed Black men's military labor. The state's congressmen knew that Union soldiers, both white and Black, were operating within the state and were probably aware that white North Carolinians were so enraged by this that some of them preferred to kill the Black men rather than take them prisoner.[134] Senator Graham, a weathered veteran of North Carolina politics, believed that neither his state's citizens nor its government should acquiesce to what he saw as an infringement on the state's power. He helped to indefinitely table the first version of the bill. North Carolina's other senator, William T. Dortch, was reportedly in favor of the measure, but he missed the vote on account of a family illness. After the second bill passed, Graham lamented that, "the bill to arm slaves has become law. It professes to take them only with the consent of their masters; and in the event of failure in this, to call on the State authorities to furnish. I trust no master in North-Carolina will volunteer or consent to begin this process of abolition, as I feel very confident the General Assembly will not."[135] He understood that if enslaved men were expected to reliably serve in the military they would probably need to be freed, but he believed that most white North Carolinians would oppose any such project.

Senator Graham's assessment of white North Carolinians' sentiment on the issue was accurate. Even as United States soldiers occupied the eastern portions of the state, and William Tecumseh Sherman marched on toward

Raleigh with an army that included Black soldiers, and the "Negro Soldier Bill" had already become law, many white North Carolinians remained reluctant to use Black men's armed labor in this unpalatable shift from earlier practices. They had strong convictions about the ties between "manhood, military service, citizenship, and suffrage," and these beliefs "proved a powerful ground of opposition to the arming of slave men in the C.S.A." Defending the nation was part of how they conceived of their own citizenship, and the prospect of anything approaching equality with Black men was profoundly upsetting.[136] A North Carolina soldier named Daniel Boyd wrote to his father to express his displeasure after he heard about the "Negro Soldier Bill." He complained, "i hear that they ar puting negras in the army it wont do to put them with the white men for they wont stand it. We are nie enough on a equality with them now."[137] Boyd's sentiments were similar to those of Confederate Gen. Howell Cobb, one of the loudest critics of the plan to field Black soldiers. During the congressional debate on the issue Cobb railed that

> the proposition to make soldiers of our slaves in the most pernicious idea that has been suggested since the war began . . . My first hour of despondency will be the one in which that policy shall be adopted. You cannot make soldiers of slaves, nor slaves of soldiers. The moment you resort to negro soldiers your white soldiers will be lost to you . . . Use all the negroes you can get, for all the purposes for which you need them, but don't arm them. The day you make soldiers of them is beginning of the end of the revolution. If slaves make good soldiers our whole theory of slavery is wrong—but they won't make good soldiers. As a class they are wanting in every qualification of a soldier.[138]

Robert Toombs was even more direct—in June 1865, the *Daily North Carolina Times* printed a letter he had written the preceding March in which he called the idea of arming Black soldiers for the Confederacy "a piece of imbecile stupidity, as well as treachery to the cause." White North Carolinians like Boyd were vehemently opposed to using armed Black laborers in combat roles because they believed there were fundamental differences between Black and white men, particularly regarding their ability to live up to society's ideals of manhood. As a result of this outlook, they also refused to tolerate any manly posturing from Black men, a mindset that was also manifested in how some Confederate soldiers brutally murdered some of the Black Union soldiers that they captured.[139]

This was not lost on Black North Carolinians themselves. Even if the state had armed its enslaved population for military service, there would be no way to guarantee their loyalty. In March 1865, Sherman's armies captured Fayette-ville, and his aide-de-camp, Maj. George Nichols, spent some time conversing with some of the city's Black residents. He found that many enslaved men "generally understood" that "the Rebel Government intend to put them in the army to fight against the 'Yankees.'"[140] According to Nichols, an older woman of color explained that her sons-in-law's enslaver promised them freedom if they would "go into the army voluntarily," but she insisted that the two men would "never would fire a gun against the Federals." One of the men added that, "I would not fight for the man who is my master and my father at the same time. If they had forced me into the army, I would have shot the officer they put over me the first time I got a chance." Further, the older woman explained to Nichols that, Fayetteville's Black residents knew that the Confederates would "never put muskets in the slaves' hands if they were not afeared that their cause was gone up. They are going to be whipped; they are whipped now." Further, she added that even if the Confederates freed the Black men who fought for them, that would not be extended to their families.[141] This was not an attractive arrangement.

Other North Carolinians expressed similar concerns about this tense inter-section of race, citizenship, and manhood. The *Fayetteville Observer*'s editors proclaimed in October 1864, that "every manly feeling, every *un*-yankee feel-ing, revolts against the idea of being indebted to slaves for our defence, and against thrusting them forward to fight our battles and lose their lives to save ours."[142] If enslaved men helped to secure Confederate nationhood through their feats of arms, their manhood would be undeniable. This is what scared Daniel Boyd. In the end, the Confederacy paid a cost for its initial opposition to Black men's armed military labor, which slowly turned into begrudging ac-ceptance. The Lincoln administration's approval of Black soldiers deprived the Confederates of these men's armed and unarmed labor, and at the same time, it turned them into a destructive force that helped to smash the Confederacy. This is a critical point when one considers that many free Black Northerners enlisted in the United States Army and Navy, but most Black military men were Southerners. Five thousand of them hailed from North Carolina.[143]

THE CIVIL WAR BROUGHT extensive changes to the social and political fabric of North Carolina as a state, to the South as a region, and to the United States as a fractured and then reconstructed nation. Nevertheless, the Old North State's assembly, national congressmen, and many white people maintained their belief that unsupervised armed Black men were a threat, while armed Black laborers could nevertheless be useful in the right context: namely, on the home front in supervised roles. Enslaved Black men's armed labor was vital to the maintenance of North Carolina's plantations prior to secession, but became even more important when so many white men marched off to battle. During the last months of the war, the state struggled with the Confederate government over the appropriate application of armed Black labor. This pitted the state's local traditions of Black people's firearm use against the collective needs of the Confederate nation. Those national goals were not always preeminent concerns for North Carolinians. Some of them fought to secure independence, some fought to secure the social and economic system of enslavement, others fought to preserve the constructed dominance of the white race, and still others fought simply to keep Union soldiers out of their backyards.[144] In February 1865, Jones County's Joseph F. Maides wrote his mother that some of the men in his company had deserted when they heard that Congress was considering enlisting Black men. There were other factors contributing to the mounting desertions in the early months of 1865, but the twenty-six-year-old was quite candid. He explained to his mother, "I did not volunteer my services to fight for a free negroes country but to fight for a free white mans country & I do not think I love my country well enough to fight with black soldiers." Maides did not speak for all his comrades, but he worried about the cost of harnessing Black men's armed labor in military applications. If they fought and helped win Confederate independence, they would have a stake in the nation, which would then become, per the young Jones County man, a "free negroes country." This dramatic departure from the white supremacist society that he was fighting to preserve was a bridge too far for him. In Joseph Maides's estimation, even the military defeat and political death of the Confederate nation were preferable.[145]

Firearms, Race, and the Steady March of Time

In the aftermath of the Civil War, North Carolina and the other former rebel states were in a challenging position. Slavery was abolished, and the end of the war brought sweeping social and economic changes. Horace James, who had served as the Twenty-Fifth Massachusetts Regiment's chaplain before becoming Superintendent for Negro Affairs in North Carolina, saw an opportunity for national improvement. He declared that "the 'Union as it was' is not what I want to see restored. Let us rather have it purified and perfected, coming out holier and freer from this dreadful ordeal, sanctified by the baptism of blood."[1] Many white North Carolinians were wholly unprepared for the changes that this revolutionary period threatened, and they openly opposed what they called "military despotism and negro supremacy."[2] Despite the sweeping changes, some long-standing antebellum concerns persisted. Firearms were an important part of the Southern sociocultural landscape and, as Carole Emberton points out, "slaves came to freedom with some degree of personal knowledge of the practical and political benefits of having a gun, having used one himself, or if not, having been threatened with one or seen one used on other human beings."[3] Black North Carolinians continued to rely on firearms as they had before emancipation, and their white neighbors continued to worry about Black people's access to these tools, a long-standing concern that was heightened by the challenges that Reconstruction brought.[4]

In 1866, the General Assembly did not grant equality to the state's Black population but instead noted that they were thereafter "entitled to the same privileges and subject to the same burthen and disabilities as by the laws of the State were conferred on, or were attached to, free persons of color, prior to the ordinance of emancipation, except as may be changed by law." As stated, in North Carolina, free people of color were not equal to white citizens, and this change elevated formerly enslaved North Carolinians only to that flimsy standard. The assembly also repealed the 1861 law that stripped free Black people of the right to access arms by eliminating the license provision.[5] Thereafter, the licensing provision became the standard for the state's residents of color. Even after emancipation, the assembly continued to regulate Black people's firearm use by empowering local courts to manage their legal access. This was difficult, as many people had acquired weapons in the conflict. For instance,

Hattie Rogers remembered that in the war's immediate aftermath, some federal soldiers gave her mother's husband a firearm and instructed him to shoot anyone that harassed their family.[6]

In the autumn of 1865, more than a hundred Black men from around North Carolina gathered in Raleigh for the state's Freedmen's Convention. They had a singular purpose—calling for "equal rights before the law." The convention president, New Bern's, John Good, declared, "There has never been and never will be a more important assembly than this now convened here."[7] Not all North Carolinians supported the convention's call for equality, and the opposition often turned violent, as the convention attendees discussed. William W. Coleman, a prominent white lawyer in Cabarrus County worried that "unfortunately the prejudice is too strong against you (I fear) to expect justice from the State." While several attendees spoke positively of race relations, Richmond County's Calvin MacCray noted that the Black people in his county "are most shamefully treated by the whites," who took their money and guns "under the pretext that it is an order issued for them to take these things away." He added that freedpeople were "most cruelly whipped" on the plantations.[8] Convention attendees from Montgomery and Burke Counties added that people of color in their neighborhoods had been shot, and Thomas Hawkins of the latter added that "the whites entertain a feeling of prejudice and animosity against the blacks."[9]

In January 1866, Hertford County's John Bizzell, James Manly, Andrew Reynolds, Miles Weaver, Richard Weaver, and Briant Manly—"faithfull and regler Soilders of the US"—were discharged from the Fourteenth US Colored Heavy Artillery. Afterward, the six Black men "had the privledge" of purchasing themselves "shot guns to take home with us to use on our farms." They intended to perform agricultural labor with these, and perhaps also defend their households. Other discharged Black men bought pistols—as Scott Giltner's work illustrates. Across the South, Black people "made firearms both a powerful symbol and an immediate priority of liberation," which was "not lost on white observers," many of whom struggled to adjust to the postwar period's new realities. A white militia officer named Joshua Garrett, along with his troops, "formed in a line of Battle," stopped the Black veterans, and demanded that they surrender their firearms. Garrett declared that he "had orders to take guns from all persons of color by orders from the War department." The men peaceably surrendered their new shotguns but later that night, yet another squad of armed white militiamen came to Bizzell's house and seized his ammunition. He wrote the Bureau of Refugees, Freedmen, and Abandoned Lands on behalf of the group of veterans, seeking to avoid "any further privilege being taken" and to have their weapons returned or paid for.[10]

It is not clear whether Bizzell and his fellow veterans ever reached a satisfactory resolution with the federal government's help. The federal presence on the postwar landscape, embodied in institutions like the Freedmen's Bureau, raised the ire of some white citizens. William A. Graham grumbled that the Bureau was "to be fastened upon us for some time: and if so, there can be but little security to the white men in any asserted rights. Thefts are of daily and nightly occurrence in this vicinity, and negroes with arms are traversing the country under pretence of hunting but really for stealing."[11] In Graham's view, the federal presence emboldened Black plunderers, who were targeting white citizens' property. This echoed concerns about outsiders fomenting unrest among the state's Black population and fears of armed but unsupervised Black people creating problems for white citizens. This criticism extended to organizations, too. Rumors about the Equal Rights League of Wilmington prompted William Cutler, its president, to publicly refute the "unjust suspicions and anxious fear" that his organization sought to use violence or insurrection to "the repeal of all laws and parts of laws, state and national, that make distinctions on account of color." They were, however, pursuing "all the social and political rights of white citizens."[12] New Hanover County's James B. McPherson shared Graham's concerns about property. In the summer of 1868, he complained to his wife, Susan, that "Old Ned," a black neighbor, "shot one of my mules and killed him almost instantly. Really it is hard to tell what is going to become of us." Ned fired a load of squirrel shot into the mule's heart, though he apparently intended only to injure the mule. McPherson declared that "the infernal negroes will not work + make any thing, but seem determined to destroy every thing we have!"[13] Black and white North Carolinians struggled to make sense of their new social and political orders, but some white people's antebellum anxieties about armed Black people persisted.

In May 1866, the *Newbern Daily Times* continued this theme of emboldened armed violence by Black people in its report on an attempted robbery. "Four ruffian negroes" who carried "regular army muskets and revolvers" were alleged to have "made two regular charges upon the house, advancing and firing under regular commands, in regular military style."[14] The two white men inside reportedly fended off the attack, but the *Times* offered a solution to prevent this incident from being repeated. In the newspaper's hyperbolic framing, this was not as a solitary criminal act, but a clear sign that armed Black people posed a threat to civilization itself. The newspaper suggested that the white community should, "disarm the negroes, and thus save the country from devastation and ruin, and furnish security for human life." Predicting that some readers might question the propriety of disarming *free* Black people, who ostensibly had rights, the *Times* added, "But you say, they are free men, and cannot be restrained from the enjoyment of freedom. We answer, so is a lion or a tiger free; but if he dare intrude himself upon the quiet walks of civilization he'll very soon find his freedom come to an end. Free, indeed! Must a man or a brute, because he is free, be equipt and licensed to go through the country and kill and rob his fellows? Away with such foolishness!"[15] From this viewpoint, these Black men who carried "regular army muskets and revolvers," which did not have the same practical uses as shotguns, were predators who had been equipped and trained by the federal government in tactics that they then turned onto the prostrate postwar South. White manhood could drive them off, but these armed Black men were a problem that needed to be addressed.

Implicitly, the *Newbern Daily Times* suggested that the entire race needed to be policed, or else society would suffer. This echoed the North Carolina Supreme Court's 1844 opinion in *State v. Elijah Newsome*. According to Justice Bailey, free people of color were "a separate and distinct class," and the legislature was justified in "adopting a course of policy in its acts peculiar to them." The *Newbern Daily Times*'s evening edition added that the "lot of hyenas, or savages . . . armed with deadly weapons" was a problem that "all thoughtful, honest people" would recognize.[16] Writing from the still smoldering ruins of the long-standing system of racial slavery, these newspaper editors proceeded to argue that well-armed Black men were operating with even more freedom than white men could. They added, "Let these scoundrels be disarmed as white men would have to be, if they were to act as they do. If freedom in America has come to be a right to go around robbing and killing, then, away with such freedom, we say. Give us despotism or any thing else, rather than such freedom as this."[17] While the state must enforce the law and protect the citizenry, this push to "disarm the negroes, and thus save the country" was about much more than one particular armed robbery. It was about a revolutionary change in Black North Carolinians' antebellum status, a change that was partly reflected in their relationship to firearms.

According to the *Newbern Daily Times*'s argument, North Carolina's Black population should be disarmed because some Black people were alleged to be committing dramatic violent crimes. Some of these concerns were "falsehoods, manufactured out of whole cloth, with not one grain of truth in them," but others were rooted in actual crimes that individual armed Black people engaged in.[18] These concerned white people were deeply steeped in generations-long expectations of Black people's deference and submission to white authority. Black North Carolinians resisted this restrictive framework in the colonial and antebellum eras and continued to do so after the war. Some found more comfortable lives on the margins of society and separated themselves, much like so many maroons did before emancipation. Similarly, they also raided the farms in their neighborhoods. One such group living in Onslow and Carteret Counties might have had as many as one hundred of fifty people in it, who were reportedly "armed with every conceivable weapon of death."[19]

Of course, Black men were not the only ones engaged in armed crime in the years after the Civil War, or in any other period for that matter. During the months following the Confederate defeat, there was a "swarm of soldiers" leaving their broken army, who were "left straggling through the country to pry upon the people." These men would "roam about in small squads of three, five, or six, steal horses if they are lucky enough to find them," and then, if they could avoid the United States soldiers in the area, they would "rob houses with impunity." In April 1865, two Bladen County men "in violation of the laws and customs of war" beat Matthew P. Sykes to death, because he had "acted as a guide for a portion of the forces of the United States."[20] White North Carolinians continued to threaten, assault, or kill each other as they had always done, but Black people's similar actions were far more likely to upset white people who were already anxious about the massive changes that emancipation wrought on the South. White people had lost the control they enjoyed during the antebellum era, though that control had never been without its challenges. Even white people who recognized that diverse actors engaged in this postwar violence persisted in maintaining a racialized understanding of it. The *Raleigh Sentinel* declared, "Horse stealing and robbing has become the order of the day, or at least of common occurrence," and added that unless something could be done to "put an end to these depredations committed by debased and degraded white men, and lazy loafing negroes, living in this country will become very dangerous. One can scarcely sleep at night now, for fear of being called up and shot, or robbed, or burned up in his house by these villains."[21]

This editorial highlighted the anxieties stemming from threats to property and domestic tranquility but blamed the problem in part on "lazy loafing negroes" who, prior to emancipation, would have been kept occupied by their enslavers. They exercised their freedom by spending their time as they wished instead of as obedient producers of white North Carolinians' wealth. Many of those white people simply wrote off Black people's control over their own time and labor as "loaferism." Whatever the *Raleigh Sentinel*'s editors' feelings on the matter, neither the federal intervention in the postwar South nor Black people's base nature could explain the "degraded white men" who were engaged in violent crimes during this period. The editors continued, "While the South, the negro and the whole country remains cursed with the Freedman's Bureau, I fear that the condition of things will not be improved. The negro looks upon the Bureau as a license and perfect protection for him to commit all kinds of depredations."[22] The war facilitated changes that exacerbated antebellum concerns.

The *Raleigh Sentinel*'s editor noted that "some degraded white men" used Black criminality as a cover "to commit depredations on the negroes' credit."[23] One night in January 1866, three white men armed with revolvers raided a house of "provisions, clothing, furniture and bedding, completely," and the victim believed them to be "white men with their faces and hands blacked." In November of that year, a "number of white men, blacked to pass off as negroes" added another layer to these theatrics by donning US Army uniforms before trying to rob a white family's home in Holly Springs, Wake County.[24] This behavior persisted through the turn of the century. In 1870, robbers in Robeson County attacked tobacco merchants en route to the South Carolina markets. They raided the merchants' camp at night and stole their guns and then robbed them the next day. The "crowd of men with blacked faces" took the merchants' watches, money, and some of the tobacco. In the spring of 1868, a white man with a blacked face "committed an assault and battery" on William Howard, a Black man who suffered from "fits of insanity." A small group of "white men blacked" shot and wounded a former Robeson County sheriff and robbed his house. "Three blacked men" attacked a peddler and took his cash and "a fine double-case patent lever silver watch." At late as 1898, a pair of "white men with blacked faces" robbed Vance Rhodes's home in Rutherfordton while he was away. They beat up his wife and stole a "considerable amount of gold coin."[25]

As the newspaper commentary suggests, some of these masquerading white criminals were unsuccessful in passing themselves off as Black men, sometimes because they inadvertently "left marks of blacking" on things they touched at the scenes of their crimes or on their victims.[26] Others undoubtedly successfully perpetrated crimes that were ultimately blamed on Black North Carolinians, some of whom likely suffered punishments. These white men were "not willing to content themselves" with their crimes "but anxious to cast the vile stigma on the colored men" in their neighborhoods.[27] Some of these black-faced robbers appeared ambiguous enough to create doubt in their victims' minds. One robber, who was shot and wounded for his efforts, was described as "a rough looking man who was either a negro, or white man blacked." Further, when a white man in Jones County was murdered, probably by "white men with their faced blacked," the initial "confusion" over the matter ensured that some newspapers immediately reported that the killing was "the work of negroes" and proceeded to "make a general onslaught upon all colored people as murderers, thieves, &c." The editors who challenged this falsehood framed the initial reporting as political, and charged that these were "Democratic lies, made up and circulated to injure the Union cause."[28] Of course, those engaged in plundering did not always segregate themselves or their victims. In April of 1866, "twelve or fifteen mounted men of both colors" raided the Lenoir County home of William R. Loftin, a white man, probably to steal his horses. During the raid, they shot him in the arm and shot a Black man—likely one of Loftin's workers—in the face. Loftin or some of his Black workers managed to shoot back and wounded some of the attackers. These interracial bandits then attacked the home of Dr. S. A. Bartleson, a white dentist, and shot him "several times" before burning down his house and some outbuildings.[29]

As part of the US Congress's Reconstruction plan, North Carolina and the rest of the short-lived Confederacy had to convene constitutional conventions at which Black men would be eligible as delegates, the Fourteenth Amendment would be ratified, and new state constitutions would be written that enfranchised Black men.[30] Some of North Carolina's white people opposed this process and some declared that if the 1868 constitution were ratified, the state would become "a second Hayti" and the white population would have to flee. Racial animus ran high in some corners of the state. Newspapers railed, "White men, arouse! Save your State from the horrors of negro rule. Poll your full strength. Make a last desperate effort to maintain the supremacy of your race," least the Old North State "become a negro paradise."[31] Wilmington's *Morning Star* warned that unless the "bogus constitution" was thwarted, white men would be taxed out of their property, "thrown into negro militia companies under negro officers," their children would be "forced into the same school with negroes," and courts would assign white children to Black guardians.[32] Karen Zipf argues that this conservative push was unattractive to many white North Carolinians "in a society rent by war, emancipation, and poverty," who worried about the stability of their own positions and were suspicious of the conservatives' disregard for propertyless white men.[33]

The 1868 constitution frightened many white people, and while it was not as radical as they feared, it did solidify Black men's place as viable armed auxiliaries of the state. In this dramatic reversal of the antebellum standard, the delegates declared that "all able bodied male citizens of the State of North-Carolina, between the ages of twenty-one and forty years, who are citizens of the United States, shall be liable to duty in the Militia."[34] Further, suffrage and the ability to hold political office were extended to "every male person" who was born in the United States or naturalized, who was twenty-one years of age, and who had not been otherwise disqualified.[35] Race would no longer be a factor in determining which armed labors North Carolinians could undertake, and Black men—and their families by extension—would thereafter be a part of the state's political community. This could be dangerous, however. During the 1868 elections, by which point the Ku Klux Klan and similar terrorist organizations were operating in the state, some Black people picked up their weapons to protect their hard-won rights. Members of the Union League armed themselves when they went to register to vote. The sheriff in Rutherford County provided weapons to some of the local Black men so that they might serve as guards in reserve of his white force. In New Hanover County, the local Black population organized, took up arms, and patrolled Wilmington's streets in the days before the election to ensure that the conservatives did not interfere.[36] The *Daily Journal* complained that while the Second Military District's Headquarters had "strictly prohibited" people from "carrying deadly weapons," some Black Wilmingtonians were nonetheless "constantly" armed. The editors noted that after a meeting in mid-April, several Black men "amused themselves and annoyed the citizens by firing several shots and yelling at the top of their lungs," which frightened the local white population. The editors hyperbolically asked their readers, "Why is it that these negroes should be permitted to go armed, while white men, by the strict demands of the law, are rendered completely defenceless."[37] Of course, many Black North Carolinians had very good reason to be armed in the postwar years.

W. L. Bost recounted to an interviewer that the Klansmen "were terrible dangerous . . . them was bad times, them was bad times. I know folks think the books tell the truth, but they shore don't. Us pore niggers had to take it all."[38] A farmer and seasonal railroad worker in Chatham County named Essic Harris was targeted by the Klan. He lived and worked on the land of a white man named Ned Finch and "had a gun in his possession, which he used for hunting purposes sometimes." The Klansmen came to his house one night near Christmas and took his shotgun, powder, and shot. They did not injure him, his wife, or their six children, but they also took four other freedmen's firearms and sexually assaulted a black woman in the neighborhood. Harris bought another shotgun and was ready when the Klansmen returned a few weeks later. They terrorists shot up his house, but while Harris was wounded several times, his wife, children, and a nephew emerged unscathed. The attackers tried to enter after their fusillade, assuming that the Harrises were dead, but when they broke open the door, Essic Harris unloaded on them. His gun was loaded with "very small shot," which the Black father and husband probably used to hunt small game for his family. It was not lethal, but it served its defensive purpose. He wounded two Klansmen—one of whom lost an eye—and forced the group to beat a hasty retreat.[39] Most others were not able to muster such resistance, and the Klan's violence was brutal. Further, while many men had firearms, not everyone did. The Klan's disarming campaigns exacerbated this situation. J. B. Eaves, a white Republican in Rutherford County, explained that the Black men in his community had "some old rifles, some muskets, and some pistols" but that he had never seen more than five or six of them carrying guns.[40]

The Ku Klux Klan harassed, beat, raped, and murdered Black people in a counterrevolutionary backlash that was aimed at maintaining the antebellum era's social, political, and economic frameworks. As Hannah Rosen explains, this violence had clear political goals. Through their terror, they "invented and communicated a fantasy post–Civil War world wherein white men's power approximated that before the war, thereby erasing military defeat and reclaiming the political privileges of whiteness bestowed by the system of slavery even on nonslaveholding white men." Further, the Klansmen did not limit their vitriol to newly emancipated people; they also lashed out at Black people who had been free before the war and at other white people with whom they disagreed. They whipped Cleveland County's Jonas Watts, a man of color who had been born free, in retaliation for his having voted. His political engagement was an affront to the Klansmen's vision of what North Carolina was supposed to be. They seized his firearm, which the assailants themselves described as "a damned good piece," after asking if Watts had it "to shoot Ku-Klux." His denial was not enough to save him from the whipping. It is not clear if his wife and their four young children were present at the time, but this ordeal would have terrified them.[41]

Black North Carolinians used their guns both to counter outside threats and to commit violent acts within their communities. This was true before emancipation, and it continued in the postwar years. In 1868, the *Wilmington Journal* reported that six armed Black men—"one with a drawn sword, and five with guns"—approached the wealthy white farmer George Johnson's home to see "Frank and John," two Black laborers. John was away from the property, but the armed men wanted to take Frank away with them, as these two men had "voluntarily abandoned" the Union League. It is unclear why Frank and John did so, but Frank was understandably reluctant to go with the armed men. When his employer drew a pistol to prevent his being taken, the group of Black men opened fire. Johnson and one of his assailants were wounded in the ensuing shootout. The newspaper decried that the only two magistrates in the area were Union League men, "appointed by 'Gov.' Holden" and that this was "the legitimate outcropping of Radical rule in North Carolina."[42] This linking of armed Black violence with outside agitators—in this instance, the Union League and the Republican governor—was rooted in antebellum concerns.

Many white North Carolinians, and some Black ones, too, viewed at least some armed Black men as a threat to the standing order.[43]

North Carolina's statewide politics would swing to favor the Democratic Party, but as H. Leon Prather explains, in 1894, a Fusion Party defeated them, ending their decades' long control. The Fusionists consisted of Black and white Republicans and thousands of white Populists who were disgruntled with "plummeting agricultural prices, high railroad freight fees, and the laissez-faire economic approach of the Democratic Party."[44] The Democrats' electoral chances faded against this Fusion majority, and they launched a white supremacy campaign to seize political power in 1898. The conservative press reported inflated and fabricated stories about uncouth, violent, and antagonistic Black citizens, some of whom were alleged to be carrying firearms, which encouraged white people to arm themselves.[45] A month before the election, one newspaper alleged that a "negro mob" had threatened the white residents of Ashpole, Robeson County. The issue began when the registrar rejected a Black man's effort to register to vote after the deadline had passed and escalated to Black and white men grabbing their guns and skirmishing in the streets. Some Black citizens allegedly threatened "that the 'damned Democrats ought to be killed and that the negroes were going to rule this country.' The leaders advised them to shoot all the white men they could and not go home to get justice but to kill the white men and run."[46] The veracity of this report is less important than the newspaper's broader plan in running it. This story was followed by an enthusiastic advertisement for Reverend T. H. Leavitt's upcoming address on "White Supremacy," which would encourage white people to unite to "on the great question of Anglo-Saxon civilization." This was the preacher's effort to win over the Populists. The next printed item told readers to "meet at the polling places promptly" on Saturday to "examine the registration books closely and challenge all persons not entitled to vote." This newspaper's presented specter of armed Black men in Ashpole gunning down "all the white men they could" cannot be separated from the editors' goals of promoting white supremacy and political control through terror.[47]

Inspired by South Carolina Senator "Pitchfork Ben" Tillman's speech at a rally in Fayetteville, Cumberland County, white men flocked to the Redshirts and other paramilitary groups. At a parade in Wilmington, one of their captains reported that he had thirty-two well-armed men under his command, who had "18 rifles, 10 shotguns and some 20 pistols"; the captain further stated, "My men can be depended upon. . . . If the worst must come we are ready to do our duty."[48] Black Wilmingtonians struggled to keep pace with this arms race. They may have purchased a few weapons from a white clerk, who was later banished from town by the terrorists. The *Semi-Weekly Landmark* reported that Black Wilmingtonians were "trying to buy firearms in large quantities" from vendors as far away as Greensboro, Guilford County, and the state of New Jersey. Worried about their intentions, the merchant in Greensboro inquired with white associates in Wilmington, who reported that the requests came from some Black people in town who "wanted the guns to arm negroes with on election day." The editor blasted, "It seems that the negroes of Wilmington and perhaps other places in eastern North Carolina are determined to retain control of affairs if it takes Winchester 38 calibre sixteen shooters to do it." The Black community was turned away from the sale and left with whatever weapons were already on hand.[49]

Reports like these were printed to stoke white fears and to ready white citizens for the election and any political violence needed to carry it—it is not difficult to understand why Black citizens were looking for additional firearms. In the days before the election, "the atmosphere of Wilmington became charged with passions that a mere spark could ignite."[50] As was all too often the case in that last quarter of the nineteenth century, political violence subverted democracy. Ultimately, perhaps as many as 500 white men who were armed to the teeth with repeating rifles, shotguns, pistols, and even two rapid-fire guns, intimidated most of the Black voters and their Fusionist compatriots away from the polls. They also stuffed ballot boxes, harassed poll workers, and otherwise made a mockery of the democratic process.[51] In the days following, militiamen and civilians burned and murdered their way through Brooklyn, Wilmington's Black neighborhood, driving over 1,000 terrified Black people into hiding out in the woods outside of town. The mobs might have killed as many as 250 Black Wilmingtonians, but reports varied wildly and the murderers may have dumped an unknown number of bodies into the Cape Fear River, so an accurate count is impossible. The Black citizens fought back as best they could and inflicted a few casualties on their assailants. In the aftermath, the terrorists exiled some of the surviving Black and white political leaders— many survivors packed up and left—and forced the town's aldermen to resign, replacing them with Democrats.[52] The massacre was a coup and swept aside the election's results.

THE UNITED STATES WILL NEVER fully exorcise slavery's ghost until it comes to terms with its past and fully contextualizes its present. The institution's echoes reverberate in the present in several ways, including in some white people's efforts to manage Black public actions. Plenty of Americans from a variety of racial and ethnic backgrounds engage in this kind of "policing," but the dynamic is inextricable from its antebellum precedents of supervision and control. Many of these aggressions are not physically violent and because of our technological advancements, there is a wide array of these instances wherein a white observer calls the police on Black people—or other persons of color—for doing quotidian things like barbecuing, using hotel or public swimming pools, painting progressive messages on their own property, selling water, birdwatching, or taking naps that are captured on video.[53] Black citizens carrying or using firearms are a significant part of this continued surveillance, though it does not dominate the aforementioned incidents. These contemporary acts of policing were not a part of this project's genesis—it began in a seminar with Bill Blair at Penn State in 2009, when I came across an 1831 legislative petition from white Delawareans who wanted to disarm their state's free and enslaved Black people.[54] Nonetheless, the tense and often tragic interactions between the state and Black citizens who were armed, or who were believed to be armed, were a significant part of the sociopolitical backdrop to much of my work on this book. These shootings are part of a longer history, but as a licensed gun owner who used to routinely carry a concealed weapon, this past and my present—my life and my scholarship—collided with jarring force.

The policing of armed Black citizens, whether by civilians or law enforcement, echoes some antebellum dynamics. Several studies suggest how racial biases often inform individual's perceptions of others. This research highlights how many white people see Black children as less innocent and older than their white peers and Black adults as larger and stronger, combative and threatening, all of which can ultimately lead to deadly violence. As one study shows, "black victims are unarmed twice as often as white men in shootings by law enforcement."[55] While the precise reason for a shooting is often difficult to definitively ascribe, the tragic deaths of John Crawford III; Philando Castile, Jemel Roberson, and Emantic Bradford Jr. present a theme that recalls the early nineteenth century. In 2014, Crawford was killed by police while carrying an air rifle around in a Walmart near Dayton, Ohio; he had picked up the air rifle from a shelf in the store. Ohio was an open carry state at the time, meaning a person of legal age—eighteen for long guns and twenty-one for handguns—could openly carry a legally owned weapon in most public spaces. There were a few exceptions to this, including places with signage to the contrary, courthouses, airports, schools, and police stations.[56] Nonetheless, Ronald Ritchie, another customer, called 911 and reported that twenty-two-year-old Crawford had loaded a rifle and was pointing it at people—including two children. A responding officer fatally shot Crawford shortly after arriving. No criminal charges were filed against Ritchie, who "felt bad" but insisted that he would "probably do the same thing" in a similar situation as he was trying only to protect the other shoppers.[57]

In July 2016, Philando Castile was shot and killed by a member of the St. Anthony, Minnesota, Police Department during what was described as a "routine" traffic stop. Since he had been pulled over about fifty times in thirteen years, this sort of "routine" is a problem.[58] Castile informed the officer that he had a legal firearm in his car, and as he reached for his identification, the officer shot and killed him in front of his family.[59] He death was made even more galling because of the fetishistic place the Second Amendment holds at present—politicians campaign on defending gun rights from their political opponents, run campaign adds where they make political props of their own personal firearms and even display their weapons on their family Christmas cards.[60] In November, 2018, Jemel Roberson, a twenty-six-year-old security guard at an Illinois bar, who aspired to become a police officer, stopped a man suspected of shooting people in the bar and pinned him down. He used a pistol, which he was licensed to carry, to detain the suspect until the police arrived. A responding officer immediately opened fire on Roberson, fatally shooting him four times in the back and side. The state insisted that Roberson could not be identified as security and that he ignored police commands to drop his pistol, but witnesses insist that Roberson's clothes identified him as a security guard and that they told the responding officers that he was security. While no charges were filed against the officer who killed Roberson, the state settled with his family for more than $7 million.[61]

In the same month Roberson was killed, a police officer in Hoover, Alabama, who was working as mall security at the time, shot and killed twenty-one-year-old Emantic Bradford Jr. after mistaking him for a mall shooter. The son of a former corrections officer, Bradford was legally armed and trying to help other shoppers escape from the actual shooter—acting as the proverbial "good guy with a gun"—when the officer assumed he was the shooter and killed him.[62] In his coverage of Bradford's death, the *Daily Show*'s host, Trevor Noah, offered thoughts on these legally armed Black men who were perceived as threats. He wondered aloud, perhaps "the Second Amendment is not intended for black people. It's an uncomfortable thing to say but it's the truth. Like, people will be like, 'the right to bear arms.' Yes, the right to bear arms if you're not a black man. If you're a black man, you have no business bearing arms at all." Noah also brought Roberson's death into the segment as an example. He concluded with, "It's some bullshit but it's true—the second amendment was not made for black folks."[63] His pronouncement was provocative, but it reflects centuries-old themes. Carol Anderson makes a similar argument in *The Second*, noting that "from enslaved to post–Civil Rights Black Americans, the application of the Second Amendment, in whatever traditional interpretation, was not applicable." She argues that Black people's legal status in the United States "did not change the way the Second Amendment worked against their rights."[64] The state and white civilians scrutinize Black men and women's innocuous actions, which repeatedly leads to confrontations wherein the Black person gets shot and killed.

These challenges to Black people's safe firearm possession stand in contrast with how other armed citizens exercise their rights. In September 2020, Justin McFarlin—who is a Black combat veteran and a National Rifle Association–certified pistol instructor—reflected that armed white protestors, like those who went to the Michigan State Capitol to demand an end to COVID-19 pandemic stay-at-home orders, were demonstrating a "privilege as white people to open carry guns wherever they want and the ability to implicitly, and sometimes explicitly, threaten violence if they don't get their way."[65] Kyle Rittenhouse exemplifies a different sort of privilege. He shot and killed Joseph Rosenbaum and Anthony Huber, and wounded Gaige Grosskreutz, all of whom were white men protesting the Kenosha, Wisconsin, police shooting Jacob Blake, a Black man, some days earlier. Even though his possession of the weapon was a misdemeanor, Rittenhouse's violence made him a "cause célèbre across conservative media throughout late 2020," and he raised hundreds of thousands of dollars for his legal defense. Even some law enforcement officers and public officials cheered him on, like the officer from Virginia who donated to Rittenhouse's legal defense with the note, "God bless. Thank you for your courage. Keep your head up. You've done nothing wrong," and "Every rank-and-file police officer supports you. Don't be discouraged by actions of the political class of law enforcement leadership."[66] Rittenhouse's defenders focus on Kenosha's civil unrest; however, his actions highlight how some white gun owners cloak themselves in the "racially infused rhetoric of law and order," which has been deployed against people of color and others who challenge the status quo since the 1960s.[67]

Castile, Crawford, Roberson, and Bradford are just some of the many Black gun owners who are part of this recent history—they are too numerous to detail individually here. While none of this suggests that Black Americans are the only ones subjected to oversurveillance, racially charged policing has long been important to both the state apparatus and those white private citizens who see themselves as enforcers of their interpretation of the public peace. Throughout the antebellum era, the state and white citizens aligned themselves in the suppression and control of armed Black folks. The state legislatures, governors, and county courts set the parameters, and individual people and communities worked within them at the local level. In North Carolina, the General Assembly recognized the broad utility in Black laborers' gun use and made allowances for enslavers to harness their workers' armed labor and for free Black people use firearms for their own ends. However, these laws ensured that white citizens controlled and supervised their Black neighbors' access to guns. The presumptive policing of armed Black people has never been wholly about firearms, which many Americans have long uphold as the guarantor of liberty, or perhaps even seen as its material embodiment. Instead, it is often about how the state or powers that be *understand* firearms in nonwhite hands. How do Black Americans safely exercise this right, which has been so dangerously elusive at times?

While one can debate its causes and meaning, the United States has a glaring problem with gun violence, as is evidenced through its affliction with homicides, mass shootings, and suicides, the latter of which constitutes the largest proportion of gun fatalities. The country's racial dynamics have always been more complicated than a solely Black and white dynamic, but Black people's experiences are at the center of this book.[68] The reality of their firearm use is that it sometimes subjects them to additional dangers, dangers that are rooted in prejudgments and misperceptions and that cut right to the heart of inequality. What is a right, really, if its very exercise can subject a citizen to a deadly response from the state, the ostensible guarantor of those rights? This does not suggest that every Black gun owner faces deadly force in every interaction with the authorities or white civilians, or that Black people do not engage in violence with each other. That was not the case in the eighteenth or nineteenth centuries, nor is it today. However, the state and many white citizens' perception of and reaction to armed Black citizens is deeply rooted in this complicated history of surveillance and supervision by the state and other citizens who assume it as a duty. Hope is not lost, however—this persistently problematic approach to race and firearms can be addressed, like many of our nation's historic challenges, via an honest reckoning with the past and a commitment to a more equitable future.

Notes

Abbreviations

CLUM   William L. Clements Library, University of Michigan, Ann Arbor, MI
CSR   Colonial and State Records of North Carolina, Documenting the American South
HRB   Hargrett Rare Book and Manuscript Library, University of Georgia, Athens, GA
JLEC   Joyner Library Special Collections, East Carolina University, Greenville, NC
John M. Morehead Papers, NCDAH
       John M. Morehead Papers, North Carolina Governors' Papers, North Carolina
       Department of Archives and History, Raleigh, NC
NCDAH North Carolina Department of Archives and History, Raleigh, NC
NCLP   North Carolina Legislative Publications, Session Laws, 1777–present, accessed
       via North Carolina Digital Collections
RML   David M. Rubenstein Rare Book and Manuscript Library, Duke University,
       Durham, NC
RSFB   Loren Schweninger, ed., Race, Slavery, and Free Blacks, Ser. I, Petitions to
       Southern Legislatures, 1777–1867 (1999); and Ser. II, Petitions to Southern
       County Courts, 1775–1867 (2005), microfilm
SHC   Southern Historical Collection, Louis Round Wilson Library, University of
       North Carolina, Chapel Hill, NC
Thomas Bragg Letter Book, NCDAH
       Thomas Bragg Letter Book, January 1, 1855–February 28, 1857, North Carolina
       Governors' Papers, North Carolina Department of Archives and History,
       Raleigh, NC
Thomas Bragg Papers, NCDAH
       Thomas Bragg Papers, North Carolina Governors' Papers, North Carolina
       Department of Archives and History, Raleigh, NC
Tripp Papers, SHC
       William Henry Tripp and Araminta Guilford Tripp Papers, Southern
       Historical Collection, Louis Round Wilson Library, University of North
       Carolina, Chapel Hill, NC
WPA-LOC
       Works Progress Administration, Manuscript Division, Library of Congress

Introduction

1. B. Wood, *This Remote Part of the World*, 179–80, 236.

2. Merrens, *Colonial North Carolina*, 134–37; Inscoe, "Mountain Masters," 148, 155–56. Mines used enslaved workers in several capacities, including to blast away rock with explosives. See Forret, "Slave Labor in North Carolina's Antebellum Gold Mines."

3. Branch, *Fort Macon,* 5; Gabriel Johnston to the Board of Trade of Great Britain, April 4, 1749, in Saunders, *Colonial Records of North Carolina,* 4:922.

4. Connor, *History of North Carolina,* 1:265–66.

5. Jackson, *Force and Freedom,* 19.

6. Higginbotham, *In the Matter of Color,* 39; Berlin, *Generations of Captivity,* 55.

7. Eight other states, mostly in the South, passed legislation that regulated people's ability to carry concealed weapons, but these were not exclusively applied to people of color. These antebellum laws, coupled with the criminalization of dueling, were intended to reduce public violence. Cramer *Concealed Weapons Laws,* 2–3, 6, 116, 139–40.

8. NCLP, *Session Laws of North Carolina, 1831–1832* (Ch. XLIV, Sec. I), 34.

9. NCLP, *Session Laws of North Carolina, 1840–1841* (Ch. XXX, Sec. I), 61–62.

10. Franklin, *Free Negro in North Carolina, 1790–1860,* 35. Blu, *Lumbee Problem,* 45–48; Milteer, *Beyond Slavery's Shadow,* 8–9

11. NCLP, *Session Laws of North Carolina, 1860–1861* (Ch. XXXIV, Secs. I and II).

12. Citizenship was a fluid concept prior to the United States's Civil War. People expected and received different rights from their local, state, and national governments. As Eric Foner points out, voting and militia service were often understood as the markers of citizenship, although white women were excluded from both but were still understood to be citizens. In North Carolina, and most of the rest of the nation, people of color were not equal citizens to their white neighbors and could not enjoy the same rights and privileges. E. Foner, *Fiery Trial,* 93–94.

13. Jonathan A. Stanley to Gen. W. A. Blount, March 10, 1858, in Correspondence, 1837–1858, James Gray Blount Papers, NCDAH.

14. Weber, "The State, Its Basic Functions," 230–31; Weber, "Politics as a Vocation," 78.

15. Berlin, *Generations of Captivity,* 273–75; US Department of Commerce, *Negro Population, 1790–1915,* 57. Claudio Saunt's work on the connections between the dispossession of Indigenous people and American slavery is instrumental to understanding this national growth. He argues, among other points, that "both earned the support of northerners who were sympathetic to the cause of white supremacy and often personally invested in the oppressive policies; and both generated a vocal opposition in Congress that remained a minority, in part because the three-fifths compromise skewed representation in favor of the slave South." Enslavers "mocked and condemned anti-expulsion activists and abolitionists with equal contempt," though white Americans were ultimately united by the "common interest in acquiring land" but driven apart over the "westward expansion of the slave empire." Saunt, *Unworthy Republic,* 318–20.

16. US Department of Commerce, *Negro Population, 1790–1915,* 57. In the 1750s, Black people also constituted about a third of the colony's total population. Fischer, *Suspect Relations,* 149.

17. B. Wood and Tise, "Conundrum of Unfree Labor," 87.

18. Barth, "'Sinke of the America,'" 1–2; McIlvenna, *Very Mutinous People,* 51–52, 125.

19. Barth, "Sinke of America," 10–11, 17.

20. *Commercial Bulletin and Missouri Literary Register* (St. Louis, MO), May 29, 1835; *Emancipator and Republican* (Boston, MA), January 26, 1849; *Raleigh Register* (Raleigh, NC), September 8, 1849; *Plain Dealer* (Cleveland, OH), August 23, 1853; *Charleston Mercury*

(Charleston, SC), July 26, 1859; Cott et al., *Root of Bitterness*, 170; C. Jones, *Engendering Whiteness*, 131–32.

21. De Bow, *Industrial Resources, etc.*, 2:175. Despite these critiques, North Carolina did have a modest system of railroads; gold, lead, silver, and copper mines; sawmills to support its profitable lumber industry; cotton factories; and other industrial projects. Bolton, *Poor Whites of the Antebellum South*, 16–19, 35–36, 39–40.

22. Joseph Blocher explores how historically, local authorities's "geographic tailoring" created different firearm regulations for urban and rural jurisdictions, each of which had different experiences and needs. Blocher, "Firearm Localism," 85. Additional research in different locations could produce interesting comparative work.

23. There is an extensive literature about Black men's military service through the eighteenth and nineteenth centuries, but those studies, and their subject matter, are not within this project's scope.

24. A. Watson, "Consideration of European Indentured Servitude," 395; CSR, *Session Laws of North Carolina, 1715–1716* (Ch. 46, Sec. 6), 63.

25. P. Morgan, *Slave Counterpoint*, 389–91.

26. Giltner, *Hunting and Fishing in the New South*, 2, 21–23, 43, 47, 154–55.

27. See Cottrol and Diamond, "The Second Amendment"; Cottrol, "Public Safety and the Right to Bear Arms"; Cramer, *Armed America*; Cramer, *For the Defense of Themselves*; Halbrook, *That Every Man Be Armed*; and Winkler, *Gun Fight*.

28. Winkler, *Gun Fight*, 12.

29. Anderson, *Second*, 7–8, 125.

30. Higginbotham, *In the Matter of Color*, 38–40.

31. Stampp, *Peculiar Institution*, 90, 130; Blassingame, *Slave Community*, 200, 209.

32. Franklin and Schweninger, *Runaway Slaves*, 102–3; Paquette, "Social History Update," 684.

33. Jackson, *Force and Freedom*, 2, 103.

34. Forret, *Slave against Slave*, 68, 69.

35. Rothman also explains how free and enslaved people of color's military service aided both the British and United States's armies in the struggle over the Old Southwest, though I am less interested in the purely military applications of armed Black men's labor. Rothman, *Slave Country*, 103–5, 132, 139–46.

36. Ely, *Israel on the Appomattox*, 179–82.

37. Franklin, *Free Negro in North Carolina*, 78; Milteer, *North Carolina's Free People of Color*, 50, 51–53, 82–85.

38. Emberton, *Beyond Redemption*, 87–90, 104–5, 147–50, 165.

39. Krugler, *1919, the Year of Racial Violence*, 7, 198–99, 206–11.

40. Johnson, *Negroes and the Gun*, 13, 40–43, 51, 75, 80–81, 92–93.

41. Umoja, *We Will Shoot Back*, 6.

42. Umoja, *We Will Shoot Back*, 2, 6, 15–16, 115–18.

43. Hill, *Deacons for Defense*, 3, 35, 166; Cobb, *This Nonviolent Stuff'll Get You Killed*, 5, 125, 129.

44. Gallay, *Indian Slave Trade*, 65; McIlvenna, *Very Mutinous People*, 108, 152–54.

45. Milteer, *Beyond Slavery's Shadow*, 8–9.

46. Inscoe, "Mountain Masters," 143–45.

47. Waters, "Life beneath the Veneer," 27–28, 33, 224.

48. McCurry, *Confederate Reckoning*, 33–34.

Chapter 1

1. Edwards, *People and Their Peace*, 13, 26, 221–22, 238–39. Edwards explains that in the 1820s, North Carolina's lawmakers, lawyers, and judges increasingly used the language of rights, which focused on individuals—especially white men with property—at the expense of a local peace framework that was more amenable to subordinate actors in this legal system, like Black people. This was a process, however, and localism persisted because of the popular understanding that that the assembly's dictates were simply "laws generated in a different place—the state level" and were not superior to local institutions. Edwards, *People and Their Peace*, 13, 211–12.

2. *Raleigh Register, and North-Carolina Gazette* (Raleigh, NC), September 7, 1842. This phrase was part of a report from a meeting of the city's commissioners, who were concerned with the lax enforcement of the laws against enslaved workers's unsupervised meetings.

3. CSR, *Session Laws of North Carolina, 1741*, 64. The North Carolina Department of Archives and History has several bonds in its collections that represent the extant records but that are likely incomplete. Further, these are only from those New Hanover enslavers who chose to follow the law. As a class, they sometimes violated it without consequence. See Henry Watters's bond (February Term 1795); Ed Spearman's bond (September Term 1797); John F. Burgwin's bond (March Term 1805); John Poisson's bond (September Term 1805); Thomas Snead's bond (May Term 1809); William Cutlar's bond (May Term 1814); Ezekiel Lane's bond (May Term 1820); William Watts Jones's bond (May Term 1820); John R. London's bonds (both July Term 1821); Thomas Cowan's bond (July Term 1821); William Reston's bond (December Term 1822); Archibald Maclaine Hooper's bond (June Term 1825); William C. Lord's bond (April Term 1826); Frederick J. Swann's bond (June Term 1826); Archibald M. Hooper's bond (January Term 1826); Thomas J. Davis's bond (January Term 1829); Edward Pigford's bond (June Term 1830); William L. Ashe's bond (June Term 1841), all bonds in folder "Permission for Slaves to Carry Guns, 1795–1841," Records of Slaves and Free Persons of Color, 1786–1888, New Hanover County Records, NCDAH. See also Northampton County residents: William B. Lockhart's petition and bond (both June Term 1827); and Robert H. Weston's bond (June Term 1829), all documents in folder "Bonds for slaves to carry firearms, 1827, 1829, 1857," Miscellaneous Slave Records (1785–1861), Northampton County Records, NCDAH. Additionally, see the following Chowan County residents: Henderson Standin's bond (December Term 1797), in folder "1797"; Benjamin Brown's bond (March Term 1798), in folder "1798"; James Hathaway's petition and bond (both in March Term 1804), in folder "1804"; Henderson Standin's bond (September Term 1806), in folder "1806"; Samuel Treadwell's bond (June Term 1807), in folder "1807"; William Wright's petition (March Term 1830), in folder "1830"; Elisha Copeland's petition (undated December Term), in folder "No date," all folders in Miscellaneous Slave Records (1730–1861), Chowan County Records, NCDAH.

4. NCLP, *Session Laws of North Carolina, 1840–1841* (Ch. XXX, Sec. I), 61–62.

5. La Vere, *Tuscarora War*, 48–49. "Memorial from agents of Carolina and merchants trading with Carolina concerning military aid for the colony," in Saunders, *Colonial Records of North Carolina*, 2:201–2. North Carolina's tobacco planters also enslaved Indigenous people,

particularly in the late seventeenth and early eighteenth centuries, when "the African slave trade was only just gearing up in England's American colonies." Further, trade goods, including guns and ammunition, fueled wars between Indigenous nations and towns. Those who had access to European trade goods raided others for captives who could be sold or traded at Charles Town, South Carolina. La Vere, *Tuscarora War*, 51–53, 98–99; Perdue, *Native Carolinians*, 27. La Vere's research shows that prior to the gun trade, Indigenous captives were "merely a happenstance of war. But once English South Carolinians introduced a profit motive into it, Indians began making war for the purpose of taking captives, whom they then sold to the English." This led to "horror-filled years" for the Indigenous people in the region and many were sold off to sugar plantations in the English Caribbean. La Vere, *Tuscarora War*, 52.

6. Fischer, *Suspect Relations*, 7–8, 21, 25–26, 27; Hadden, *Slave Patrols*, 33.

7. Barth, "'Sinke of America,'" 10–12.

8. Barth, "'Sinke of America,'" 14–17. McIlvenna's *A Very Mutinous People*, offers an engaging narrative of early North Carolina that hinges on the notion that many of its early settlers were moving away from the restricting bureaucracy and social divisions of seventeenth-century Virginia, including the enslaved Africans and Indigenous people who fled.

9. Henry Purse's examination (December 1795), in folder "Inquests 1795, Coroners' Inquests 1782–1869" (broken series), Craven County Records, NCDAH.

10. CSR, *Session Laws of North Carolina*, 1715–1716 (Ch. 46, Sec. 9), 63–64.

11. Potter, *Office and Duty of a Justice of the Peace*, 167–68. The assembly compensated some of these citizens who were injured while pursuing armed enslaved people. In one instance, it did so under a militia law, even though the injured men were not serving at the time and they were mistakenly shot by other white men. As one scholar notes, these actions demonstrated a "recognition that the safety of all Whites in the county required such a reaction from the White population." Kaiser, "'Masters Determined to be Masters,'" 22–23.

12. *True Republican and Newbern Weekly Advertiser* (New Bern, NC), June 19, 1811.

13. One might argue that the assembly passed this 1729 law in a period where race had not yet overtaken class as the primary measure of fitness for inclusion in the body politic. Edmund Morgan's classic book, *American Slavery, American Freedom*, places the beginnings of this transformation in Nathaniel Bacon's 1676 rebellion in Virginia, although North Carolina made these changes more slowly than either Virginia or South Carolina, as demonstrated through distinctive legislation for both Black and white subordinate laborers and the creation of a slave code. For further reading see E. Morgan, *American Slavery, American Freedom*; and Hadden, *Slave Patrols*, 33–35.

14. Wood and Tise, "The Conundrum of Unfree Labor," 88, 90–91.

15. Barth, "'Sinke of America,'" 3; CSR, *Session Laws of North Carolina*, 1729 (Ch. 5, Sec. 7), 35–36.

16. Watson, "Impulse toward Independence," 318, 323; Hadden, *Slave Patrols*, 34; Halasz, *Rattling Chains*, 19–20.

17. Martin, *Public Acts*, 1:103–4.

18. Halasz, *Rattling Chains*, 19–20; CSR, *Session Laws of North Carolina*, 1729 (Ch. 5, Sec. 7), 35–36; CSR, *Session Laws of North Carolina*, 1741 (Ch. 24, Sec. 40), 64.

19. CSR, *Acts of the North Carolina General Assembly*, 1768 (Ch. 13, Secs. 1, 5, 8), 775–76.

20. Martin, *Public Acts*, 1:104.

21. Martin, *Public Acts*, 1:103–4.

22. Martin, *Public Acts*, 1:104.

23. Martin, *Public Acts*, 1:104.

24. Martin, *Public Acts*, 1:104.

25. Martin, *Public Acts*, 1:104. In 1794, the assembly modified this regulation and thereafter, patrollers were "entitled to receive the one half of the penalties recovered" for the infractions they halted. Rowan County, *Patrol Regulations*, 5.

26. Martin, *Public Acts*, 1:104.

27. Order for Jesse Benthall and others (September 1830), in folder "Slave patrol records No Date, 1837–1859," Miscellaneous Slave Record (1785–1861), Northampton County Records, NCDAH.

28. Hadden, *Slave Patrols*, 37. Dry's grandfather had been a South Carolina planter and his father had been a justice of the peace and militia captain in Brunswick Town, North Carolina. Dry, while a young militia captain himself, led a counterattack that helped to save the town from Spanish raiders in 1748. He rose to a colonelcy by 1754, was appointed collector of the port at Brunswick Town in 1761, served in the assembly from 1760 to 1762, and owned a large plantation. Schaw, *Journal of a Lady of Quality*, 314–15; and Cheney, *North Carolina Government, 1585–1979*, 46–48.

29. Jonathan Harvey's letter to the captains calling out the militia (June 1802), in folder "Insurrection Among Slaves 1802–1803" (Court Papers), Slave Records 1759–1864, Perquimans County Records, NCDAH.

30. Wood and Tise, "The Conundrum of Unfree Labor," 85–86; Hadden, *Slave Patrols*, 132; Franklin and Schweninger, *Runaway Slaves*, 92.

31. Martin, *Public Acts*, 1:104; Schweninger, *RSFB*, Ser. I, Craven County Petition, 1835, reel 7, frame 00020–23.

32. Thomas J. Davis's bond (January Term 1829), in folder "Permission for Slaves to Carry Guns, 1795–1841," Records of Slaves and Free Persons of Color, 1786–1888, New Hanover County Records, NCDAH.

33. Elisha Copeland's petition (undated December Term), in folder "No date," Miscellaneous Slave Records (1730–1861), Chowan County Records, NCDAH.

34. Thomas Hemmingway's bond (July 1819), in folder "Permit to Carry Firearms, 1819," Miscellaneous Records, 1786–1925, Brunswick County Records, NCDAH.

35. Henderson Standin's bond (December Term 1797), in folder "1797"; and Henderson Standin's bond (September Term 1806), in folder "1896," both folders in Miscellaneous Slave Records (1730–1861), Chowan County Records, NCDAH.

36. See William B. Lockhart's $500 bond in folder "Bonds for slaves to carry firearms, 1827, 1829, 1857," Miscellaneous Slave Records (1785–1861), Northampton County Records, NCDAH; and Frederick J. Swann's $400 bond, in folder "Permission for Slaves to Carry Guns, 1795–1841," Records of Slaves and Free Persons of Color, 1786–1888, New Hanover County Records, NCDAH.

37. Joseph Crecey's petition (January 1769), in folder "Permits to carry guns—1769, 1853, 1858," Miscellaneous Records, 1710–1933, Perquimans County Records, NCDAH.

38. *Acts of the North Carolina General Assembly, 1773* (Ch. 11), in W. Clark, *State Records of North Carolina*, 23:918.

39. CSR, *Acts of the North Carolina General Assembly, 1774* (Ch. 14, Secs. 2, 3), 966. "Long bullets" was a street bowling game that was often restricted in colonial towns. The bullets

were made of metal, wood, or stone and play sometimes lead to "divers [*sic*] Inconveniences." Struna, "Puritans and Sport," 18.

40. Rankin, *North Carolina Continentals*, 8–9; Bowman, "The Virginia County Committees," 322; Connor, *Cornelius Harnett*, 86.

41. Saunders, *Colonial Records of North Carolina*, 9:xxxii.

42. Harsanyi, *First Freedom*, 38. Minutes of the Wilmington Committee of Safety January 5, 1775–January 27, 1775, in Saunders, *Colonial Records of North Carolina*, 9:1108–12; Minutes of the Rowan County Committee of Safety September 23, 1774, in Saunders, *Colonial Records of North Carolina*, 9:1074.

43. Wilmington, NC, Safety Committee, *Proceedings of the Safety Committee*, 53, 64. Memorial from Nathaniel Rochester, William Johnston, and Ambrose Ramsey concerning a gun factory in Hillsborough, 1778; and North Carolina House of Commons Journal, October 28, 1779; both in W. Clark, *Colonial Records of North Carolina*, 13:345. Allen Jones to General Assembly, June 27, 1781, Joint Select Committee Reports and Papers, General Assembly Session Records, North Carolina Digital Collections, https://digital.ncdcr.gov /Documents/Detail/joint-papers-june-july-1781-joint-select-committee-reports-and -papers/836819?item=836973.

44. Letter from John Penn, Thomas Burke, and Allen Jones to Governor Richard Caswell, January 21, 1780, in W. Clark, *State Records of North Carolina*, 15:323.

45. Quarles, *Negro in the American Revolution*, 124. Minutes of the Bladen, Brunswick, Duplin, and Wilmington-New Hanover County Committees of Safety, June 20 to June 21, 1775, in Saunders, *Colonial Records of North Carolina*, 10:25. Wilmington, NC, Safety Committee, *Proceedings of the Safety Committee*, 31.

46. Charles II and Locke, *Two Charters Granted by King Charles IId*, 51; Barth, "Sinke of America," 17; Franklin, *Free Negro*, 102.

47. Wilmington Committee of Safety to Samuel Johnston, Esq., July 13, 1775, in Saunders, *Colonial Records of North Carolina*, 10:91. The commander at Fort Johnson was alleged to have "given encouragement to negroes to elope from their Masters and promised to protect them." Proceedings of the Safety Committee at Wilmington, July 20, 1775, in Saunders, *Colonial Records or North Carolina*, 10:112.

48. Proceedings of the Safety Committee at Wilmington, July 12, 1775, in Saunders, *Colonial Records or North Carolina*, 10:89.

49. Proceedings of the Safety Committee in Pitt County, July 8, 1775, in Saunders, *Colonial Records of North Carolina*, 10:87. North Carolinians also worried that the neighboring Cherokee might attack, as they did during the last few years of the Seven Years War. Further, some of them panicked that Lord Frederick North, the British prime minister, had given a "supply of Arms and Ammunition" to the Indigenous nations so that they might "attack us, and repeat the inhuman Cruelties of the last War, Ripping Infants from the wombs of their expiring mothers, roasting Christians to Death by a slow fire." Maass, "'All This Poor Province Could Do,'" 67, 70–71; Proceedings of the Safety Committee in Rowan County, August 1, 1773, in Saunders, *Colonial Records of North Carolina*, 10:135. See Maass's essay for further reading on the Seven Years War in the colony.

50. John Simpson to Richard Cogdell, July 15, 1775, in Saunders, *Colonial Records of North Carolina*, 10:94.

51. Simpson to Cogdell, July 15, 1775, in Saunders, *Colonial Records of North Carolina*, 10:95.

52. Jacobs, *Incidents in the Life of a Slave Girl*, 97–99.

53. Horton, *Free People of Color*, 151. White politicians were divided on Black men's voting, and even after their disenfranchisement, some of them continued to vote, particularly in local elections. Supporters argued that suffrage could maintain a gulf between free and enslaved Black people, but some opponents feared that it would eventually lead to Black justices and sheriffs or that it might further encourage enslaved people's desire for liberty. Others, like Richard Speight, took a partisan stance because Black voters did not support them or could be blamed for carrying elections for their rivals. Franklin, *Free Negro*, 13, 105–13, 120; North Carolina, *Journal of the Convention*, Art. I, Sec. 3, § 3; G. Johnson, *Ante-Bellum North Carolina*, 603–4; A. Watson, *History of New Bern and Craven County*, 207–8; *Greensborough Patriot* (Greensboro, NC), November 11, 1835; *Spectator* (New Bern, NC), November 6, 1835.

54. NCLP, *Session Laws of North Carolina*, 1779 (Ch. VII, Sec. I–IV), 280–81. The severity of the fines varied across place and time. In 1825, Lenoir County's patrollers who failed to act were fined $1.50 "for every such failure or neglect." Rutherfordton, Rutherford County, patrollers were fined five dollars in 1833, which notably doubled in 1840. After the 1840–41 legislative session, Murfreesboro, Hertford County, punished patrollers with a hefty twenty-dollar fine. In Raleigh, however, lax town watchmen and patrollers faced a paltry one-dollar penalty in 1856. NCLP, *Session Laws of North Carolina*, 1825 (Ch. LVII, Sec. IV), 40; NCLP, *Session Laws of North Carolina*, 1832–1833 (Ch. XLVIII, Sec. VIII), 48; NCLP, *Session Laws of North Carolina*, 1840–1841 (Ch. LVII, Sec. IV], 196–97; (Ch. LV, Sec. XI), 193; NCLP, *Session Laws of North Carolina, Private Laws*, 1856–1857 (Ch. XCVIII, Sec. XXXVII), 107.

55. Hadden, *Slave Patrols*, 72–73; NCLP, *Session Laws of North Carolina*, 1779 (Ch. VII Sec. II).

56. NCLP, *Session Laws of North Carolina*, 1779 (Ch. VII, Secs. III and II). These benefits were not always enough to make the work attractive. In 1828, eighty-three Lincoln County men petitioned the assembly that anyone "who dos [*sic*] not own any, nor wish to have any thing to do as respects the government or Discipline of the Negroes" should be exempt from patrol duties. On Lincoln County Petition, see Schweninger, *RSFB*, Ser. I, North Carolina, 1825, reel 6, frame 0083–87.

57. Rowan County, *Patrol Regulations for the County of Rowan*, 5.

58. Court order for commissions for Jordan L. Carrow and Zacheus Slade (February Term, 1830), in folder "Carrow and Slade commissioned to seize firearms found in possession of slaves—1830," Slaves and Free Negroes Bonds—Petitions, 1775–1861, Craven County Records, NCDAH. Slade served as the orderly sergeant for the Newbern Greys militia company in the early 1830s, and he kept track of the "muskets belonging to the state" in the aftermath of Nat Turner's uprising. He also served as the town sergeant, wherein he saw after municipal business, like the town pumps being in good order and enforcing the ordinances against people running their horses through the streets. *Newbern Sentinel* (New Bern, NC), June 3, 1831; *Newbern Spectator, and Literary Journal* (New Bern, NC), March 9, 1832; *Newbern Sentinel* (New Bern, NC), January 7, 1833; *Newbern Spectator, and Literary Journal* (New Bern, NC), October 19, 1832; *Newbern Sentinel* (New Bern, NC), September 14, 1831; *Newbern Spectator, and Literary Journal* (New Bern, NC), July 24, 1830; *Newbern Sentinel* (New Bern, NC), February 15, 1832; *Newbern Spectator, and Literary Journal* (New Bern, NC), June 1, 1832; July 6, 1832; March 15, 1833.

Carrow also stood in at times for John Gildersleeve, who ran a slave jail in New Bern from 1829 to about 1836. Gildersleeve bought and sold people in addition to jailing runaways until their enslavers reclaimed them. *Newbern Spectator, and Literary Journal* (New Bern, NC), April 27, 1832; *North Carolina Sentinel and Newbern Commercial, Agricultural and Literary Intelligencer* (New Bern, NC), October 5, 1831; *Newbern Spectator and Political Register* (New Bern, NC), August 14, 1835; and December 19, 1834; *Newbern Spectator, and Literary Journal* (New Bern, NC), April 23, 1831; April 25, 1829; August 30, 1828; *Newbern Spectator and Political Register* (New Bern, NC), May 20, 1836.

59. Rankin, *North Carolina Continentals*, 10; Josiah Martin to William Legge, June 30, 1775, in Saunders, *Colonial Records of North Carolina*, 10:43.

60. Rankin, *North Carolina Continentals*, 23–24. John Murray, "Proclamation by John Murray, Earl of Dunmore concerning martial law in Virginia, November 10, 1775," in Saunders, *Colonial Records of North Carolina*, 10:308–9; Gilbert, *Black Patriots and Loyalists*, 22. This does not suggest that the British were racial egalitarians. They drove some Black people out of their camps to die of exposure and killed some Black combatants after they had surrendered. Dann, *Revolution Remembered*, 240, 244; White, *Connecticut's Black Soldiers*, 28–29. Roth, *American Homicide*, 176.

61. Minutes of the New Bern Committee of Safety, August 2, 1775, in Saunders, *Colonial Records of North Carolina*, 10:138. Martin certainly understood that the colonies' Black populations were a potential obstacle for the rebels. While optimistically writing to Lord Dartmouth about the loyalists' prospects, he explained that, "tho [sic] Virginia and Maryland are both very populous, the Whites are greatly outnumbered by the Negroes, at least in the former, and in the latter they are a very great Proportion of the whole number of Inhabitants, a Circumstance that would facilitate exceedingly the Reduction of those Colonies who are very sensible of their Weakness arising from it." He added that in North Carolina "the Proportion of Blacks to Whites throughout the Province is very small" and concentrated in two or three southern counties, suggesting that the Black population's impact would be less pronounced than in the Chesapeake. Governor Josiah Martin to William Legge, Earl of Dartmouth, June 30, 1775, Henry Clinton Papers, Vol. 13, Fol. 21, CLUM.

62. Quarles, *Negro in the American Revolution*, 14. Crow, "Slave Rebelliousness," 84.

63. Quarles, *Negro in the American Revolution*, 111–12; Several of the Gentlemen, Merchants, and Traders of the City of London to King George III, October 11, 1775, in Dodsley, *Annual Register*, 267–68.

64. Schaw, *Journal of a Lady of Quality*, 199, 200–201.

65. Jean Blair to James Iredell, July 21, 1781, in Iredell, *Papers of James Iredell*, 2:266–67; William Caswell to Thomas Burke, September 4, 1781, in Clark, *State Records of North Carolina*, 22:592–93.

66. Morton, *American Revolution*, 80.

67. Newsome, "A British Orderly Book, 1780–1781: III," 296, 290; Newsome, "A British Orderly Book, 1780–1781: IV," 368.

68. Urwin, "'To Bring the American Army under Strict Discipline,'" 5. Charles Cornwallis to Henry Clinton, May 11, 1780, Henry Clinton Papers, Vol. 97, Fol. 37, CLUM.

69. Jean Blair to Hannah Iredell, May 10, 1781, in Iredell, *Papers of James Iredell*, 2:239.

70. Petition of George Merrick, December 3, 1791, Petitions (Miscellaneous), General Assembly Session Records, North Carolina Digital Collections; Resolution of George

Merrick's Petition, January 6, 1791, Petitions (Miscellaneous), General Assembly Session Records, North Carolina Digital Collections.

71. Newsome, "A British Orderly Book, 1780–1781: III," 296. Quarles, *Negro in the American Revolution*, 140–41.

72. Jean Blair to James Iredell, July 21, 1781, in Iredell, *Papers of James Iredell*, 2:266, North Carolina Digital Collections.

73. Jean Blair to James Iredell, July 21, 1781, in Iredell, *Papers of James Iredell*, 2:266.

74. Newsome, "A British Orderly Book, 1780–1781: III," 293, 296–97; Urwin, "To Bring the American Army under Strict Discipline,'" 5, 18. Jean Blair to Hannah Iredell May 10, 1781, in Iredell, *Papers of James Iredell*, 2:239.

75. Freeman, "North Carolina's Black Patriots," 3. The deposition of Wm. Griffin, March 18, 1784; petition of Ned Griffin, April 4, 1784; deposition of Col. James Armstrong; August 6, 1783, all in May 15: Senate bill to give Ned Griffin his freedom (petition and messages only), General Assembly Session Records, North Carolina Digital Collections.

76. Quarles, *Negro in the American Revolution*, 59–60, 183–84. Minutes of the North Carolina House of Commons, April 19–June 3, 1784, in Clark, *Colonial Records of North Carolina*, 19:507, 552, 609, 641, and 661. NCLP, *Acts of the North Carolina General Assembly, 1784* (Ch. LXX), in Clark, *State Records of North Carolina*, 24:639.

77. Smyth, *Tour in the United States of America*, 2:102.

78. Resolution in favor of William Bryan of Craven County, April 23, 1783, House Joint Resolutions: Apr. 21–30, General Assembly Session Records, North Carolina Digital Collections; Bryan had another enslaved man who was killed while fighting against "Rebel Slaves" though it is not clear from the record that these were related. North Carolina General Assembly, Minutes of the North Carolina House of Commons, April 18, 1783–May 17, 1783, in Clark, ed. *Colonial Records of North Carolina*, 19:258; Kay and Cary, *Slavery in North Carolina*, 73.

79. Berlin, *Generations of Captivity*, 111.

80. NCLP, *Session Laws of North Carolina, 1800* (Ch. XXVIII, Sec. I), 159.

81. G. Johnson, *Ante-Bellum North Carolina*, 600.

82. NCLP, *Session Laws of North Carolina, 1812* (Ch. I, Sec. I), 1; NCLP, *Session Laws of North Carolina, 1814* (Ch. I, Sec. VI), 3.

83. J. Taylor, *Revisal of the Laws of the State of North Carolina*, Ch. 1219, Sec. 1.

84. Hadden, *Slave Patrols*, 47.

85. Cramer, *Armed America*, 36–37. Some historians argue that militia duty was a tax on one's labor because, with few exceptions, all white men in their physically productive years were enrolled. Further, some scholars see the exemption of enslaved workers as a regressive tax and argue that they were barred not only for security reasons but also to prevent the enslaving elite from losing their laborers for the nearly two weeks of duty each year. Militia duty called white men away from their livelihoods, but enslavers's exempted workers continued to produce. Kay and Cary, *Slavery in North Carolina*, 60; and Dunkerly, *Redcoats on the Cape Fear*, 19.

86. NCLP, *Session Laws of North Carolina, 1830–1831* (Ch. CLVI, Secs. I, II, and III), 130–31. This regulation applied to Brunswick, Camden, Carteret, Craven, Currituck, Duplin, Hyde, Johnston, Jones, Lenoir, New Hanover, Onslow, Sampson, Tyrrell, and Wayne Counties. NCLP, *Session Laws of North Carolina, 1830–1831* (Ch. CLVI, Sec. I), 130.

87. NCLP, *Session Laws of North Carolina, 1840–1841* (Ch. XXX, Sec. I), 61–62.

88. On Craven County Petition, see Schweninger, *RSFB*, Ser. I, North Carolina, 1835, reel 7, frame 00022.

89. Willis Herring's petition (August Term 1841), in folder "Petition of Willis, a free man of color, to use a gun, 1841," Slaves and Free People of Color, n.d., 1783–1869, Wayne County Records, NCDAH; "Benajah Herring [Newhope District, Wayne County, North Carolina]," 1840 United States Federal Census database, population schedule, p. 207, image 904, Ancestry.com.

90. On Benajah Herring's petition, see Schweninger, *RSFB*, Ser. II, Part D, North Carolina, 1823, reel 2, frames 00077–79.

91. "Willis Herring [Newhope District, Wayne County, North Carolina]," 1840 United States Federal Census database, population schedule, p. 207, image 904, Ancestry.com.

92. For Craven County petition, see Schweninger, *RSFB*, Ser. I, North Carolina, 1828, reel 6, frame 00241. White North Carolinians wanted other hunting regulations that would have limited Black people's ability to take game. In 1791, fifty petitioners from Wilkes County petitioned the assembly to consider prohibiting the use of dead falls and "Dog Traps" in their county, as they were "very Distructive things Amongst stock & Dogs." Antebellum hunting was complicated, while one could hunt without a gun, deadfalls were useful for those who could only commit limited time to it. See Petition of the Inhabitants of Wilkes, n.d. 1791, Petitions [Miscellaneous], General Assembly Session Records, North Carolina Digital Collections.

93. For Craven County Petition, see Schweninger, *RSFB*, Ser. I, North Carolina, 1828, reel 6, frame 00241. North Carolina, *Journal of the Convention*, Art. I, Sec. 3, § 3.

94. *State v. James Woods*, jury presentment (undated); and jury presentment (June Term 1858), both in folder "Criminal Actions Concerning Slaves and Free Persons of Color, 1840–1849" (broken series), Criminal Actions Concerning Slaves and Free Persons of Color, 1840–1868, Craven County Records, NCDAH. On Craven County Petition, see Schweninger, *RSFB*, North Carolina, 1828, reel 6, frame 00241. Woods was probably a mixed-race day laborer in his late forties who, along with his wife, Penny, had seven children to provide for. The Woodses held $300 in real estate and another $100 in personal estate. "James Woods" [Richardsons, Craven County, North Carolina], 1860 United States Federal Census, population schedule, p. 44, image 14, Ancestry.com.

95. The assembly had prohibited free people from trading with enslaved workers since the colonial era, but firearms were not a stated concern. A 1715 law barred subordinate laborers from selling their masters's goods for their own benefit, as did another passed in 1826. The latter again made no mention of guns in an otherwise exhaustive list of banned crops, raw materials, tools, and liquor. CSR, *Session Laws of North Carolina, 1715–1716*; and NCLP, *Session Laws of North Carolina, 1826* (Ch. XIII, Sec. I), 7.

96. NCLP, *Session Laws of North Carolina, 1828–29* (Ch. XXXII, Secs. I, II, and III), 19.

97. North Carolina, *Journals of the Senate and House of Commons . . . 1830–31*, 131–32. This busy legislative session also debated free Black people's colonization to Liberia, enslaved workers hiring their own time, intermarriage between "free negroes and free persons of colour, and white persons and slaves," banning enslaved workers from meeting at night and limiting daytime assemblies to those under supervision, expanding the punishments for "harboring or maintaining runaway slaves," allowing sheriffs to sell captured runaways who were unclaimed, limiting free Black preachers' engagement with enslaved folks, free Black

people's ability to peddle, and modifying the slave patrol regulations. North Carolina, *Journals of the Senate and House of Commons . . . 1830–31*, 135, 136, 137, 138, 179, and 200.

98. William L. Ashe's bond (June Term 1841), in folder "Permission for Slaves to Carry Guns, 1795–1841," Records of Slaves and Free Persons of Color, 1786–1888, New Hanover County Records, NCDAH.

99. On Craven County Petition, see Schweninger, *RSFB*, Ser. I, North Carolina, 1828, reel 6, frame 00241; and *RSFB*, Ser. I, North Carolina, 1835, reel 7, frames 00021–22.

100. On Craven County Petition, see Schweninger, *RSFB*, Ser. I, North Carolina, 1835, reel 7, frames 00020–23.

101. NCLP, *Session Laws of North Carolina, 1831–1832* (Ch. XLIV, Sec. I), 34; G. Johnson, *Ante-Bellum North Carolina*, 555. Richard C. Rohrs explains that Walker's *Appeal in Four Articles* had a more profound effect on white North Carolinians than Turner did, and lead to a host of strict laws against free Black folks, including those that kept them from selling goods outside of their own county unless they were licensed, kept them from marrying white or enslaved people, barred them from teaching enslaved workers to read or write, and kept them from gambling with slaves. Rohrs, "Free Black Experience," 619.

102. Cecelski, *Fire of Freedom*, 10–11. Franklin, *Free Negro*, 66–67; *North Carolina Free Press* (Halifax, NC), September 7, 1830.

103. Franklin, *Free Negro*, 67–70.

104. G. Johnson, *Ante-Bellum North Carolina*, 516.

105. *North Carolina Sentinel and Newbern Commercial, Agricultural and Literary Intelligencer* (New Bern, NC), November 2, 1831. Patrol order, in folder "Patrol Records, 1830," Gates County Miscellaneous Records, 1780–1912, Gates County Records, NCDAH.

106. Joseph B. Hinton to John Gray Blount, December 20, 1830, in Blount, *John Gray Blount Papers*, 4:546.

107. Joseph B. Hinton to John Gray Blount, December 23, 1830, in Blount, *John Gray Blount Papers*, 4:547.

108. Hinton to Blount, December 23, 1830, in Blount, *John Gray Blount Papers*, 4:547–48.

109. Hinton to Blount, December 23, 1830, in Blount, *John Gray Blount Papers*, 4:548.

110. Hinton to Blount, December 23, 1830, in Blount, *John Gray Blount Papers*, 4:548.

111. Aptheker, *Negro Slave Revolts*, 50; Kaye with Downs, *Nat Turner, Black Prophet*, 76–81, 190–91; Genovese, *Roll, Jordan, Roll*, 593–95.

112. Raper, "The Effects of David Walker's Appeal," 49, 54–56; *Daily National Journal*, September 10, 1831.

113. Col. S. Whitaker to Governor Montford Stokes, September 15, 1831, #296; and Carter Jones to Stokes, September 17, 1831, #309; both in Montford Stokes Letter Book, North Carolina Governors' Papers, NCDAH; *Richmond Enquirer*, September 20, 1831; *Daily National Intelligencer*, September 19, 1831; *Vermont Chronicle*, September 30, 1831; Raper, "The Effects of David Walker's Appeal," 64; *Republican Citizen and State Advertiser*, September 23, 1831; Sadler "Dr. Stephen Graham's Narration," 364. "Mr. Usher" might have been Isaac Scott, who petitioned the legislature almost twenty years later for relief, "in consideration of his having ferreted out and exposed the conspiracy in 1831" in New Hanover County. *Daily Register* (Raleigh, NC) January 19, 1851.

114. Sadler, "Dr. Stephen Graham's Narration," 364. J. Borland to Governor Montford Stokes, September 18, 1831, #313–15, in Governor Montford Stokes Letter Book, NCDAH;

Vermont Chronicle, September 30, 1831; *United States' Telegraph* (Washington, DC), September 19, 1831; *Newbern Spectator, and Literary Journal* (New Bern, NC), September 23, 1831.

115. *Richmond Enquirer* (Richmond, VA), September 20, 1831; *Raleigh Register, and North-Carolina Gazette* (Raleigh, NC), September 22, 1831; October 6, 1831; *Observer and Telegraph* (Hudson, OH), September 29, 1831; *United States' Telegraph* (Washington, DC), September 19, 1831; *Carolina Observer* (Fayetteville, NC), October 12, 1831.

116. *North Carolina Spectator and Western Advertiser* (Rutherfordton, NC), October 1, 1831; *Carolina Observer* (Fayetteville, NC), October 12, 1831; *Raleigh Register, and North-Carolina Gazette* (Raleigh, NC), October 13, 1831. Forret, "Antebellum Gold Mines," 154–59.

117. NCLP, *Session Laws of North Carolina, 1831–1832* (Ch. XLIV, Sec. I), 34.

118. NCLP, *Session Laws of North Carolina, 1831–1832* (Ch. XLIV, Sec. I), 34; Johnson, *Ante-Bellum North Carolina*, 555.

119. *Journal* (Charlotte, NC), November 16, 1831; *Republican Citizen and State Advertiser* (Frederick, MD), September 23, 1831; Raper, "The Effects of David Walker's Appeal," 66–68, 70, 72.

120. Roth, *American Homicide*, 230.

121. Raper, "The Effects of David Walker's Appeal," 59–61. The president of the University of North Carolina requested firearms from Raleigh, as did sixty-six of his students who formed a volunteer militia company. University of North Carolina President Joseph Caldwell to Montford Stokes, September 17, 1831, #306; and University of North Carolina Students to Montford Stokes, September 17, 1831, #307, both in Montford Stokes Letter Book, NCDAH. This was not the only example of students at the University of North Carolina willing to use arms to maintain their slave system. Early in 1864, the Orange County sheriff, who was apparently low on manpower during the Civil War, called on thirty students to assist in breaking up "a camp of run away Negroes." Henry Armand London, who participated in the raid, explained to his sister that they were successful in "capturing the camp with all its contents, taking 7 prisoners and wounding one, without a man of us scratched." Henry London to Lilla London, February 16, 1864, Folder 868-Z, Henry Armand London Papers, SHC.

White men in the towns of Colerain, Edenton, Elizabeth City, Enfield, Fayetteville, Elizabeth City, Greensboro, Louisburg, Murfreesboro, Oxford, Scots Neck, Tarboro, Wadesboro, Warrenton, Williamsboro, and Wilmington applied for arms, as did others in Bertie, Gates, Halifax, Hyde, Johnston, Martin, Nash, New Hanover, Northampton, and Pitt Counties. See, among others, John B. Baker to Governor Montford Stokes, August 23, 1831, #250; Col. S. Whitaker to Stokes, August 26, 1831, #259; Fayetteville Magistrate of Police J. W. Wright to Stokes, August 26, 1831, #261; Maj. Gen. M. T. Hawkins to Stokes, August 26, 1831, #263; Commissioners of the Town of Wilmington to Stokes, September 14, 1831, #292; Commissioners of Louisburg to Stokes, September 15, 1831, #294; Bertie County Citizens' Committee to Stokes, August 31, 1831, #267, and September 16, 1831, #299; Halifax Magistrate of Police Edward B. Freeman and Capt. Jesse A. Simmons to Stokes September 16, 1831, #302; Capt. Jesse A. Simmons to Stokes, September 16, 1831, #303; J. Borland to Stokes, September 18, 1831, #313–315; Judge R. Strange to Stokes, September 19, 1831, #321; Major R. J. Yancey Jr. to Stokes, September 20, 1831, #328; Capt. M. T. Waddill Jr. to Stokes, September 20, 1831, #331; Thomas L. Singleton to Stokes, September 21, 1831, #332; Capt. Edward Morecock to Stokes, September 21, 1831, #334; Thomas Cox to Stokes, September 22, 1831, #336; Officers of the Williamsboro Greys to Stokes, September 25, 1831, #338; Col. Benjamin Watson to Stokes,

September 25, 1831, #340; H. Blount to Stokes, September 27, 1831, #342; Seth Peebles and others to Adjutant General of the North Carolina Militia Beverly V. Daniel, September 27, 1831, #344; Robert Williams to Stokes, September 29, 1831, #346; Gen. McDonald to Daniel, October 1, 1831, #350; B. H. Stammers to Stokes, October 3, 1831, #353; Gen. William Gregory to Daniel, October 5, 1831, #359; New Hanover Citizens' Committee to Stokes, October 14, 1831, #370; Capt. William W. Cherry to Stokes, October 15, 1831, #374; and Capt. John S. Smallwood to Stokes, October 10, 1831, #378, all in Montford Stokes Letter Book, NCDAH.

122. Charles Lockhart Pettigrew to Ebenezer Pettigrew, December 29, 1830, Addition of 2016, Pettigrew Family Papers, SHC.

123. Charles Lockhart Pettigrew to Ebenezer Pettigrew, December 29, 1830, Addition of 2016, Pettigrew Family Papers, SHC.

124. Officers of the Raleigh Guards to Governor John Motley Morehead, May 29, 1844, in folder "Correspondence, Petitions, etc., May 1, 1844–May 30, 1844," John M. Morehead Papers, NCDAH. Keeping safety in mind and wary that firearms sometimes ended up in the hands of those whom the state did not want armed, the officers of the Raleigh Guard noted that if they received new weapons, "our old muskets shall be returned and disposed of in such manner as your Excellency may order." Officers of the Raleigh Guards to Governor John Motley Morehead, May 29, 1844, in folder "Correspondence, Petitions, etc., May 1, 1844–May 30, 1844," John M. Morehead Papers, NCDAH.

125. William H. Bayne to John Motley Morehead, December 3, 1844, in folder "Correspondence, Petitions, etc., December 1, 1844–December 30, 1844," John M. Morehead Papers, NCDAH.

126. White North Carolinians's concerns about their militia's preparedness were exacerbated by these threats, but this anxiety extended into the 1840s and 1850s as well. Officers of the Raleigh Guards to Governor John Motley Morehead, May 29, 1844, in folder "Correspondence, Petitions, etc., May 1, 1844–May 30, 1844"; and William H. Bayne to John Motley Morehead, December 3, 1844, in folder "Correspondence, Petitions, etc., December 1, 1844–December 30, 1844," both in John M. Morehead Papers, NCDAH. Col. Robert G. Rankin to Governor David Settle Reid, August 15, 1856, in folder "Correspondence, Petitions, etc., August 1, 1851–August 31, 1851," David Settle Reid Papers, North Carolina Governors' Papers, NCDAH; New Bern citizens to Governor Thomas Bragg, December 15, 1856; and New Bern Committee of Conference to Bragg, December 19, 1856, both in folder "Correspondence, Petitions, etc., December 1, 1856–December 27, 1856," Thomas Bragg Papers, North Carolina Governors' Papers, NCDAH).

127. A. Watson, *Wilmington, North Carolina, to 1861*, 128–29. Franklin, *Free Negro*, 73.

128. G. Johnson, *Ante-Bellum North Carolina*, 601. Virginia banned free Black people's weapons use five months after Turner's rebellion. The justices of the peace lost the power to permit enslavers to arm their workers, and the county courts could no longer license free Black people. Virginia, *Acts Passed at a General Assembly . . . 1831* (Ch. XXII, Secs. 4), 21. In December 1831, Maryland passed a gun license requirement for free Black people. It also banned the sale of liquor or weapons to any Black person unless he or she had a license if free or "written authority" from an overseer if enslaved. See Cramer, *For the Defense of Themselves*, 74. Maryland, *Laws Made and Passed . . . 1832* (Ch. 323, Sec. 6). Delaware restricted its free Black population's gun use in 1832 after a heavy petition campaign by its white residents. Thereafter the legislature required them to apply for licenses that relied on at least five white men as character witnesses. Delaware, *Laws of the State of Delaware* (Ch. CLXXVI, Secs. 1, 2),

208–9. On Newcastle County Petition, see Schweninger, *RSFB*, Ser. 1, Delaware, 1831, reel 2, frames 0280–82. In 1833 Georgia followed Virginia's model and made it illegal for free Black residents "to own, use, or carry fire arms of any description whatever." Georgia, *Acts of the General Assembly . . . 1833* (Ch. "Persons of Colour," Secs. 7 and 8), 228. In 1834, Tennessee abolished its free Black residents's gun rights via constitutional reform. Since 1796, the state constitution had broadly acknowledged that "freemen" could keep arms "for their common defence," but this was constricted to "free *white* men." Cramer, *For the Defense of Themselves*, 59–60. By contrast, North Carolina's 1835 constitutional convention did not change Black people's gun rights even though it disenfranchised free Black men. North Carolina, *Journal of the Convention*, Art. I, Sec. 3, § 3. Despite this post-Turner ripple of anti-Black gun laws there is some evidence that the trend may have started earlier. Florida repealed an 1828 license law and removed free Black firearm rights six months *before* Turner's revolt. Florida, *Acts of the Legislative Council . . . 1827–8* (Ch. "An Act Concerning Slaves, Free Negroes and Mulattoes," Secs. 9, 10, and 11), 100–10.

129. Genovese, *Roll, Jordan, Roll*, 31; Cottrol and Diamond, "The Second Amendment," 336.

130. Stewart, *Holy Warriors*, 22–23, 45. While this 1830s wave of abolitionists was more aggressive, many North Carolina enslavers were also irritated by the Quakers's earlier efforts. For example, in 1793, Tyrrell County jurors presented "certain persons . . . of the Quaker persuasion" had "Accustomd themselves to liberate Their Negrows to the great Injury of their Neighbours and the Community at large" and further, that "they hold Out to the Negrows the Idea of liberty And Infranchisement And the Negroes prosesd with Such Ideas Conduct themselves in Such A Manner that property is unsafe and—Precarious and the lives of the Citizens is at Stake." The jurors added that, "Risings Amongst the Negroes Have bin frequently threatened" and that the authorities who should check them were powerless to do so, as they thought it "safer to Wink at Crimes then to Come forward in the punishment of them." This left the jurors worried, as they believed that "Numbers of Negroes are Armed and Stand in Open defiance of the law Frequently attacking the Whites with Impunity." The jurors were hopeful for "some law that may Prevent measures not Only highly Injurious to the liberty and property but Which May one day prove highly dangerous and Fatel." Tyrrell County jurors, jury presentment [October Session 1793], in folder "Criminal actions concerning slaves and free people of color, 1793, 1814–1825," Records of Slaves and Free Persons of Color, 1793–1868, N. D., Tyrrell County Records, NCDAH.

131. Newman, *Transformation of American Abolitionism*, 113; Garrison, *Thoughts on African Colonization*, iv; Genovese, *Roll, Jordan, Roll*, 84; Stauffer, *Black Hearts of Men*, 27.

132. *North-Carolina Free Press* (Tarborough, NC), September 6, 1831.

133. Douglass, *Life and Times of Frederick Douglass*, 238; De Witt, *Life, Trial and Execution of Capt. John Brown*, 94. John Anthony Copeland Jr. and his uncle Lewis Sheridan Leary were from Fayetteville, Cumberland County, but had relocated to Oberlin, Ohio, in 1854. Leary was killed in the fighting at Harpers Ferry, and Copeland was captured by the authorities and later executed. Their family was of multiracial Melungeon ancestry. Horton and Horton, *Slavery and the Making of America*, 163, 165; Hashaw, *Children of Perdition*, 47–48; Lubet, *"Colored Hero" of Harper's Ferry*, 72, 74.

134. *Raleigh Register, and North-Carolina Gazette* (Raleigh, NC), October 13, 1831; Ashe, *Biographical History of North Carolina*, 3:387; Franklin, *Free Negro*, 78; North Carolina *Journals of the Senate and House of Commons . . . 1850–'51*, 534, 635.

135. North Carolina, *Public Laws of the State of North-Carolina, 1858–'59*, Ch. 10; NCLP, *Session Laws of North Carolina, 1860–1861* (Ch. XXXIV, Secs. I and II).

136. On Craven County Petition, see Schweninger, *RSFB*, Ser. I, North Carolina, 1835, reel 7, frames 00021–22; and G. Johnson, *Ante-Bellum North Carolina*, 519. See Johnson's appendix for an assessment of Craven County's demographics in 1835 and a statistical analysis of the petitioners.

137. For Craven County Petition, see Schweninger, *RSFB*, Ser. I, North Carolina, 1835, reel 7, frames 00021–22.

138. For Halifax County Petition, see Schweninger, *RSFB*, North Carolina, Ser. I, 1840, reel 7, frame 0120–23.

139. By the War of 1812, the assembly amended the militia laws to prevent officers from enrolling free people of color, except as musicians. Prior to this conflict, the laws had vaguely ordered the enrollment of "all freemen and indentured servants, citizens of this State or of the United States" who were between eighteen and forty-five years of age. This was reversed in 1814 by another amendment which again declared that officers could enroll free Black men as long as they were sure to "designate by proper columns the free persons of colour from the rest of the militia." Within a decade the assembly made a final change and again limited free Black militiamen to musician positions. NCLP, *Session Laws of North Carolina, 1800* (Ch. XXVIII, Sec. I); NCLP, *Public Laws of North Carolina, 1860–1861* (Ch. XXIV, Sec. I); NCLP, *Session Laws of North Carolina,1812* (Ch. I., Sec. I); NCLP, *Session Laws of North Carolina, 1814* (Ch. I, Sec. VI); and J. Taylor, *Revisal of the Laws of the State of North Carolina* (Ch. 1219, Sec. 1).

140. *Greensborough Patriot* (Greensboro, NC) January 12, 1841.

141. NCLP, *Session Laws of North Carolina, 1840–1841* (Ch. XXX, Sec. I), 61–62; H. Jones, *Reports of Cases at Law . . . 1858–1859*, 6:448–49.

142. H. Jones, *Reports of Cases at Law . . . 1858–1859*, 448–49.

143. Jackson, *Force and Freedom*, 98–99.

144. On Beaufort County Petition, see Schweninger, *RSFB*, Ser. I, North Carolina, 1851, reel 7, frame 0374.

145. *Tri-Weekly Commercial* (Wilmington, NC), March 6, 1851.

146. On Beaufort County Petition, see Schweninger, *RSFB*, Ser. I, North Carolina, 1851, reel 7, frame 0374.

147. Franklin, *Free Negro*, 78. On Robeson County Petition, see Schweninger, *RSFB*, Ser. I, North Carolina, 1856, reel 7, frames 0493–97. These Robeson County concerns appear to have been hyperlocal: seven of the ten petitioners shared either the Baxley or Brown surname.

148. *Raleigh Register, and North-Carolina Gazette* (Raleigh, NC), September 6, 1842.

Chapter 2

1. Johnson, *Negroes and the Gun*, 41.

2. NCLP, *Session Laws of North Carolina, 1777* (Ch. 22, Secs. II, III, and IV), 245.

3. On New Hanover County petition, see Schweninger, *RSFB*, Ser. I, North Carolina, 1791, reel 4, frames 0183–87.

4. *Carolina Observer* (Fayetteville, NC), December 9, 1824.

5. *Carolina Observer* (Fayetteville, NC), December 9, 1824.

6. Browning, "Visions of Freedom," 73.

7. *Carolina Sentinel* (New Bern), August 10, 1822.

8. *Raleigh Register, and North-Carolina Gazette* (Raleigh, NC), October 24, 1828.

9. *Albany Advertiser* (Albany, NY), December 11, 1816. The swamps had long been a refuge for outlaws, not just runaways. During the Revolution, some loyalists who were "committing depredations" were identified as "outlying men" who were "well acquainted with every swamp and secret place to Harbour in." A "notorious outlyer Tory and Plunderer" could wreak havoc on a community, which heightened local terror during the war. See Petition of Duplin, Wayne, and Dobbs Counties, May 1784, Joint Standing Committees: Committee on Propositions and Grievances May 13–26: Reports and Papers, General Assembly Session Records, North Carolina Digital Collections; Resolution in favor of Josiah Bunn, April, 1783, House Joint Resolutions: Apr. 21–30, General Assembly Session Records, North Carolina Digital Collections.

10. Memorial of Henry Taylor, October/November 1795, Session of November–December, 1795: Joint Committee Reports, General Assembly Session Records, North Carolina Digital Collections.

11. Memorial of Henry Taylor, General Assembly Session Records, North Carolina Digital Collections.

12. Yellin, "Incidents Abroad," 159. *Raleigh Register, and North-Carolina Weekly Advertiser* (Raleigh, NC), April 26, 1811.

13. *Tarborough Southerner* (Tarboro, NC), October 15, 1859; *Tarboro Mercury* (Tarboro, NC), November 9, 1859. Hamlet was overzealous in this work; in April 1861, he was charged with murdering Azariah, a man enslaved by Col. H. Faison. While pursuing a runaway in Northampton County, Hamlet and his dogs came across Azariah, who was riving timber for his enslaver. Hamlet or his dogs mistook him for the runaway and the dogs attacked. Azariah ran to an overseer "who refused his protection" and then tried get back to his enslaver's house. Hamlet killed him before he got there. The newspaper correspondent was not sure if Azariah was killed "by dogs or by a gun," but Hamlet fled the state and Governor John W. Ellis offered a $200 reward for his capture. The hunter had become the hunted. *State Journal* (Raleigh, NC), April 10, 1861; *Weekly Raleigh Register* (Raleigh, NC), April 10, 1861).

14. *Albany Advertiser* (Albany, NY), December 11, 1816; *Raleigh Register, and North-Carolina Weekly Advertiser* (Raleigh, NC), March 28, 1811.

15. Watson, *Wilmington*, 35; *Wilmington Centinel* (Wilmington, NC), August 13, 1788.

16. CSR, *Session Laws of North Carolina, 1715–1716* (Ch. 46, Sec. 11), 64.

17. *North Carolina Sentinel* (New Bern, NC), May 2, 1829. "Ch. J. Nelson" [Craven County, North Carolina], 1830 US Federal Census database, population schedule, p. 149, Ancestry.com; "William S. Blackledge" [Craven County, North Carolina], 1830 US Federal Census database, population schedule, p. 120, Ancestry.com.

18. *North Carolina Sentinel* (New Bern, NC), May 2, 1829.

19. *North Carolina Sentinel* (New Bern, NC), May 2, 1829.

20. Potter, *Office and Duty of a Justice of the Peace*, 153.

21. *Newbern Sentinel* (New Bern, NC), August 18, 1827.

22. *Carolina Federal Republican* (New Bern, NC), April 26, 1817; *North Carolina Sentinel* (New Bern, NC), March 3, 1827; *Carolina Sentinel* (New Bern, NC), August 18, 1827. *North*

Carolina Sentinel (New Bern, NC), May 2, 1829; *Fayetteville Observer* (Fayetteville, NC), February 23, 1860; January 27, 1862; and December 12, 1864.

23. Durant Hatch to Ebenezer Pettigrew, December 22, 1821, in Pettigrew, *Pettigrew Papers* 2:26; "Durant Hatch" [Craven County, North Carolina], 1820 US Federal Census database, population schedule, p. 145, Ancestry.com.

24. Hatch to Pettigrew, December 22, 1821, in Pettigrew, *Pettigrew Papers*, 2:26.

25. Hatch to Pettigrew, December 22, 1821, in Pettigrew, *Pettigrew Papers* 2:26.

26. Weber, "Politics as a Vocation," 78.

27. *Raleigh Register, and North-Carolina Gazette* (Raleigh, NC), October 24, 1828.

28. Edwards, *People and Their Peace*, 83.

29. *Trenton Federalist* (Trenton, NJ), May 24, 1824; *Daily National Intelligencer* (Washington, D.C.), May 21, 1824; *Carolina Observer* (Fayetteville, NC), June 17, 1824; *Star, and North Carolina State Gazette* (Raleigh, NC), May 14, 1824. Another newspaper reported that there was only one trader and that "being unarmed, he and a part of his negroes fled for their lives." *Western Carolinian* (Salisbury, NC), May 18, 1824.

30. *Star, and North Carolina State Gazette* (Raleigh, NC), May 14, 1824; *Trenton Federalist* (Trenton, NJ), May 24, 1824.

31. *Trenton Federalist* (Trenton, NJ), May 24, 1824. Sheriff's inquisition (September 1812), in folder "Inquests 1811–1819" (broken series), Coroners' Inquests 1782–1869 (broken series), Craven County Records, NCDAH. Elias, his wife, Isabella, and their child were enslaved by Bogg. Someone brutally murdered Isabella, and while Elias was suspected, the investigation was inconclusive. Isabella's body was found in a field on another person's property, and the sheriff and his jury of inquest concluded that "she has been dead about seven days" as her body has been disturbed by a number of scavenging animals. She also had "some marks of violence on her throat supposed to be cut by a knife." Bogg swore that Elias told him that he, "had suffered a great deal for her, and that if he could not enjoy her, no other person should"; Bogg stated further that Elias added that "if Isabella's child was not sold whenever he was + to the same person that it should do no person any good." Sheriff's inquisition, September 1812, Craven County Records, NCDAH.

32. *State v. Francis Lytle Jr.*, Lytle Johnson's affidavit (October 3, 1822); and *State v. Francis Lytle Jr.*, jury presentment against (November Term 1817), both in folder "Criminal Actions Concerning Slaves and Free People of Color 1822–1838," Records of Slaves and Free Persons of Color, Criminal Action Papers, 1788–1869, Randolph County Records, NCDAH.

33. *Star, and North Carolina State Gazette* (Raleigh, NC), May 14, 1824; June 18, 1824.

34. *Raleigh Register, and North-Carolina State Gazette* (Raleigh, NC), February 10, 1824. While initially only Jack and Jim were charged with stealing twenty pounds of bacon and twenty pounds of beef from John B. Baker's house, the presentment for their breaking jail listed Willis and Elisha as well. See *State v. Jack + Jim* [undated], jury presentment, Gates County; *State v. Willis, Jim, Jack, + Elisha* [Spring Term 1824], jury presentment, Gates County, both in folder "Criminal Acton Concerning Slaves, 1824," Slave Records, n.d., 1783–1867, Gates County Records, NCDAH.

35. *Raleigh Register, and North-Carolina State Gazette* (Raleigh, NC), February 10, 1824; *Carolina Observer* (Fayetteville, NC), February 19, 1824; June 17, 1824; *Star, and North Carolina State Gazette* (Raleigh, NC), February 13, 1824; June 18, 1824. These men lived a dangerous life: Jack also had "several shot wounds" on his body. *Carolina Observer* (Fayetteville, NC),

June 17, 1824; *Argus* (Frankfort, KY) March 10, 1824. One newspaper noted that the "marks of the shot are fresh in one of Jim's thighs," indicating that Cross shot him shortly before the men killed him. *Carolina Observer* (Fayetteville, NC) June 17, 1824.

36. *Raleigh Register, and North-Carolina State Gazette* (Raleigh, NC), February 10, 1824; February 13, 1824; and *State v. Jim, Jack + Elisha* [undated], jury presentment, Gates County in folder "Criminal Action Concerning Slaves, 1824," Slave Records, n.d., 1783–1867, Gates County Records.

37. *Argus* (Frankfort, KY) March 10, 1824; *Richmond Enquirer* (Richmond, VA) February 17, 1824. Jim shot Cross, and probably cut him, but the grand jurors took two passes at Jack and Elisha on accessory charges. Ultimately, Jack was not charged, but Elisha was. *State v. Negro Jim, Jack + Elisha* [Spring Term 1824], jury presentment, Gates County; *State v. Jim, Jack + Elisha* [undated], jury presentment, Gates County, both in folder "Criminal Action Concerning Slaves, 1824," Slave Records, n.d., 1783–1867, Gates County Records.

38. *Raleigh Register, and North-Carolina State Gazette* (Raleigh, NC), February 10, 1824; *Star, and North Carolina State Gazette* (Raleigh, NC), February 13, 1824; *Richmond Enquirer* (Richmond, VA), February 17, 1824; *Star, and North Carolina State Gazette* (Raleigh, NC), May 14, 1824. Gilliam enslaved thirty-nine people, including Willis, until he sold him to Whitfield and Tomkins. The records are convoluted, but I suspect that Willis was Jim's brother. If he had been even loosely connected to Cross's murder, that might explain Gilliam selling him out of state via the coffle and offering the large reward. *Carolina Observer* (Fayetteville, NC), June 17, 1824; *Star, and North Carolina State Gazette* (Raleigh, NC), May 14, 1824; "Henry Gillam" [Gates County, North Carolina], 1830 US Federal Census database, population schedule, p. 86, Ancestry.com.

39. *Star, and North Carolina State Gazette* (Raleigh, NC), June 18, 1824; *Hampden Journal and Advertiser* (Springfield, MA), June 23, 1824; *Carolina Observer* (Fayetteville, NC), June 17, 1824. Other reports indicated that the fugitives had hoped to get to New York City. *Hampden Journal and Advertiser* (Springfield, MA), June 23, 1824; *Raleigh Register, and North-Carolina State Gazette* (Raleigh, NC), June 11, 1824.

40. *Carolina Observer* (Fayetteville, NC), June 17, 1824; *Raleigh Register, and North Carolina State Gazette* (Raleigh, NC), November 19, 1824.

41. Inquest over Sampson, a slave (March 1833), in folder "Coroners' Inquests, 1830–1839" (broken series), Miscellaneous Records, 1781–1922, Randolph County Records, NCDAH; "John K. Armstead" [Regiment 1, Randolph County, North Carolina], 1830 US Federal Census database, population schedule, p. 4, Ancestry.com.

42. *Fayetteville Observer* (Fayetteville, NC), July 24, 1849.

43. Ebenezer Pettigrew to William Shepard, in Pettigrew, *Pettigrew Papers*, 2:466–67; *Newburyport Herald* (Newburyport, MA), September 27, 1814.

44. *New England Palladium* (Boston, MA), September 27, 1814; Ebenezer Pettigrew to William Shepard, in Pettigrew, *Pettigrew Papers*, 2:467; *Weekly Visiter* (Kennebunk, ME), October 12, 1814.

45. *Raleigh Register, and North Carolina State Gazette* (Raleigh, NC), June 27, 1823; "Henry Culpepper" [Camden County, North Carolina], 1820 US Federal Census database, population schedule, p. 34, image 38, Ancestry.com. Other men experienced multiple attempts on their lives. Joshua Edwards, an enslaver near Fayetteville, drove his cart one night and had an enslaved woman walking ahead of him with a lantern to light the way. In the darkness,

someone came up behind him and fired a shotgun into his back, blasting a hand-sized hole in his body. Edwards had, "twice before within a year or two, been shot at in the same neighborhood." Initially, it was not clear who killed him, but about two weeks after the shooting, one of the men Edwards enslaved was "taken up ... on suspicion of being the murderer" and confessed. *North Carolina Spectator and Western Advertiser* (Rutherfordton, NC), December 3, 1830; "Joshua Edward" [Cedar Creek, Cumberland County, North Carolina], 1830 US Federal Census database, population schedule, p. 78, image 3, Ancestry.com; *Carolina Observer* (Fayetteville, NC), November 18, 1830; November 25, 1830.

46. *Baltimore Patriot and Mercantile Advertiser* (Baltimore, MD), August 29, 1823; *State v. Willoughby Foreman et al.*, unsigned petitioner to Governor Gabriel Holmes, August 1, 1824, General Assembly Session Records (Nov. 1824–Jan. 1825), NCDAH. I am indebted to Chris Meekins at the NCDAH for pointing me toward the *State v. Foreman* documents.

47. *Raleigh Register, and North Carolina State Gazette* (Raleigh, NC), August 29, 1823.

48. Cook-Bell, *Running from Bondage*, 139; G. Johnson, *Ante-Bellum North Carolina*, 46. Culpepper's brother, Thomas, also lived in Norfolk County, Virginia. In 1811, he fatally injured a man in a fight at a store in Camden County, NC, where Henry and their brother Archibald lived. The fight started when another man "was heard to give Henry the lye"; but Thomas broke it up. A second man, without provocation, then began pushing Henry and calling out "damn my soul Culpepper, if you shall not fight here." Thomas tried to keep the peace but finally fought the aggressor and smashed a brick into his head. The man later died, though it is unclear whether this was from the brick or because of his friends clumsily probing the wound after the fight. *Republican Argus* (Northumberland, PA), May 15, 1811.

49. *State v. Willoughby Foreman et als*, jury presentment (Fall Term 1823), General Assembly Session Records, NCDAH.

50. *State v. Willoughby Foreman et als*, jury presentment (Fall Term 1823), General Assembly Session Records, NCDAH.

51. *State v. Willoughby Foreman et als*, jury presentment (Fall Term 1823), General Assembly Session Records, NCDAH.

52. Franklin and Schweninger, *Runaway Slaves*, 86. For a deeper look at the communities in and around the Great Dismal Swamp, see Nevius, *City of Refuge*.

53. "Willoughby Foreman" [Norfolk, Virginia], 1830 US Federal Census database, population schedule, p. 122, image 133, Ancestry.com.

54. J. Taylor, *Revisal of the Laws of the State of North Carolina*, Ch. 1164, Sec. 2, 3, and 4. The sections in this law are mislabeled—there are two Section 2s. The one referenced here is the second of these.

55. J. Taylor, *Revisal of the Laws of the State of North Carolina*, Ch. 1164, Sec. 2, 3, and 4. Again, the sections in this law are mislabeled—there are two Section 2s. The one referenced here is the second of these. Taylor, *Revisal of the Laws of the State of North Carolina*, Ch. 1230, Sec. 1.

56. Weld, *American Slavery As It Is*, 14–15; Kaye, *Joining Places*, 133–36.

57. *Raleigh Register, and North-Carolina State Gazette* (Raleigh, NC), July 20, 1824.

58. Richard M. Lewis and other Bladen County residents to Governor Thomas Bragg, August 25, 1856, in Correspondence, Petitions, etc., August 1, 1856–August 31, 1856, Bragg Papers, NCDAH.

59. *Fayetteville Observer* (Fayetteville, NC), October 28, 1851.

60. *Fayetteville Observer* (Fayetteville, NC), October 28, 1851. For further reading on white Southerners's equation of abolitionism and emancipation with slave rebellion, see Rugemer, "Black Atlantic."

61. *Weekly Raleigh Register* (Raleigh, NC), May 18, 1859. "J. R. J. Daniel" [Eastern Division, Halifax County, North Carolina], 1860 US Federal Census database, population schedule, p. 404, image 189, Ancestry.com; "J. R. J. Daniel" [Eastern Division, Halifax County, North Carolina], 1860 US Federal Census database, slave schedule, p. 42, Ancestry.com.

62. *Weekly Raleigh Register* (Raleigh, NC), May 18, 1859.

63. *Fayetteville Observer* (Fayetteville, NC), June 4, 1850; *Raleigh Register* (Raleigh, NC), June 5, 1850; *State v. Dick, a slave*, jury presentment and coroner's inquests (both Spring Term 1850), in folder "Criminal Actions Concerning Slaves, 1816 1824, 1838–1856," Records of Slaves and Free Persons of Color, 1786–1888, New Hanover County Records, NCDAH; "Sam'l R. Potter" [Wilmington, New Hanover County, North Carolina], 1850 US Federal Census database, population schedule, p. 426B, image 527, Ancestry.com.

64. The records are somewhat unclear on the particulars of Annette and Dick's relationship, but the murder was likely a domestic dispute. Historians have argued that Southern society had a high level of interpersonal violence that was often visible in its domestic spaces. Wyatt-Brown, *Southern Honor*, 366–67. For further reading on the subject, see Forret, *Slave against Slave*; and Foster, *Rethinking Rufus*, chs. 6 and 3, respectively.

65. *Fayetteville Observer* (Fayetteville, NC), June 11, 1850.

66. William L. Ashe's bond, New Hanover County Records, NCDAH. This was an example of localized application of the law—the state legislature had banned enslaved people's firearm use in the early 1830s, though the New Hanover County Court continued to permit it. NCLP, *Session Laws of North Carolina, 1831–1832* (Ch. XLIV, Sec. I), 34.

67. Olmsted, *Cotton Kingdom*, 97.

68. *Alexandria Gazette* (Alexandria, VA), September 20, 1855; *Columbian Register* (New Haven, CT), October 6, 1855.

69. *Fayetteville Observer* (Fayetteville, NC), September 24, 1855; *North-Carolina Star* (Raleigh, NC), September 19, 1855.

70. *Fayetteville Observer* (Fayetteville, NC), September 24, 1855.

71. *Daily Register* (Raleigh, NC), October 6, 1855; *Fayetteville Observer* (Fayetteville, NC), October 8, 1855.

72. Edwards, *People and Their Peace*, 129–31; Genovese, *Roll, Jordan, Roll*, 33–34.

73. *Raleigh Register, and North-Carolina Gazette* (Raleigh, NC), September 5, 1843.

74. Coroner's report on Rigdon Lewis (January 1841), in folder "Inquests 1840–1849," Coroners' Inquests, 1782–1869 (broken series), Craven County Records, NCDAH. Court order for the Children of Tom Lewis (May Term 1839); John M. Harget indenture certificate for Rigdon Lewis (August 14, 1839); and James M. Harget apprentice bond for Rigdon Lewis (August 14, 1839), all in folder "Apprentice Bonds and Records, 1839," Apprentice Bonds and Records, 1832–1840, Craven County Records. The 1840 census, which named only the head of household, shows Harget's household consisting of himself, five "free colored" males between ten and thirty-five years of age, and thirteen enslaved people. While Manly ostensibly could have been a white laborer hired after the 1840 census, he was probably, like Rigdon Lewis, one of the "free colored persons" working for Harget. See "John M. Hargett" [South

Side Neuse River, Craven County, North Carolina], 1840 US Federal Census database, population schedule, image 19, Ancestry.com.

75. *Spectator* (New Bern, NC), May 3, 1839.

76. Coroner's report on Rigdon Lewis (January 1841), and Inquest over Rigdon Lewis (undated), both in folder "Inquests 1840–1849," Coroners' Inquests, 1782–1869 (broken series), Craven County Records, NCDAH.

77. Coroner's report on Rigdon Lewis (January 1841), and Inquest over Rigdon Lewis (undated).

78. Inquest over Rigdon Lewis (undated).

79. Unrelatedly, in the same newspaper that described this alleged theft from the theater, "a Negro man" found another "small pocket Pistol" and turned it into the Gazette's office, where the owner could retrieve it after paying for the advertisement "and rewarding the finder." *Wilmington Gazette* (Wilmington, NC) January 27, 1807. The stories do not appear to be related, as the stolen pistol's description suggests a finely crafted and easily recognizable weapon.

80. *Daily Journal* (Wilmington, NC), December 20, 1864.

81. For further reading on the illegal trade between enslaved folks and poor white people, see Forret, *Race Relations at the Margins*.

82. "P. K. Dickinson" [Wilmington, New Hanover County, North Carolina], 1840 US Federal Census database, population schedule, p. 7, image 20, Ancestry.com; *Raleigh Register, and North-Carolina Gazette* (Raleigh, NC), February 13, 1844.

83. *Raleigh Register, and North-Carolina Gazette* (Raleigh, NC), February 13, 1844. Children enjoyed recreational gun use through the eighteenth and nineteenth centuries. In 1773, the assembly passed a law to prevent "idle and disorderly Persons, as well as Slaves, and Children under Age" from firing guns in New Bern's streets. In 1841, the *Wilmington Chronicle*'s editors watched as three armed boys who all appeared to be under ten years of age walked past the newspaper's office. The newspapermen criticized the boys's parents for not heeding "the hundred and hundreds of warnings of fatal accidents from the use of firearms by children." During the Civil War, Beaufort County's William Tripp made plans to buy his son Josephus a gun when the boy was also ten years old. CSR, *Session Laws of North Carolina, 1773* (Ch. 19, Secs. 11 and 12), 918; *Fayetteville Observer* (Fayetteville, NC), June 30, 1841; William Tripp to Araminta Tripp, January 30, 1863, Folder 4, Tripp Papers, SHC.

84. *Daily Progress* (New Bern, NC), July 1, 1861.

85. NCLP, *Session Laws of North Carolina, 1831–1832* (Ch. XLIV, Sec. I), 34; NCLP, *Session Laws of North Carolina, 1860–1861* (Ch. XXXIV, Secs. I and II).

86. Stephen Evans petition (May Term 1854), in folder "Petition of Stephen Evans, a free man of color, to hunt with a gun, 1854," Slaves and Free People of Color, n.d., 1783–1869, Wayne County Records, NCDAH.

87. *People's Press* (Salem, NC), August 3, 1855. Some of the newspapers covering this shooting went even further in their critique. For instance, one ended with, "We have been astonished at the inattention of parents in regard to their children carrying fire-arms, and are also astonished that more accidents do not occur." *North Carolina Standard* (Raleigh, NC) August 1, 1855. Further, accidents like these created a marketing opportunity for gun manufacturers. The Young America Target Pistol Manufacturing Company, based in New Haven, Connecticut, advertised a new device, "designed for young men and boys who wish to enjoy the exciting sport or firing at a target, at the most trifling expense, and without any

danger of accident." The pistol was loaded and fired via a "common Fire Cracker, which forms a complete cartridge, and will carry a ball ten or fifteen paces with the same precision as the ordinary pistol, but not with sufficient force to do any serious damage." Interestingly, this company also saw an opportunity in Southern culture. It explained that, since the United States "is a shooting nation, the Young Americans must and will learn the art by which our independence was secured" and that their new target pistol "is exactly in time, and must meet with universal sale among our youth of the South and West." They retailed for twenty-five cents. *Tri-Weekly Commercial* (Wilmington, NC), September 17, 1857.

88. *North State Whig* (Washington, NC), January 22, 1851; *North-Carolina Star* (Raleigh, NC), February 1, 1851.

89. *North Carolina Standard* (Raleigh, NC), January 29, 1851. Wheeler, *Historical Sketches of North Carolina*, 1:209, 212.

90. *North Carolina Standard* (Raleigh, NC), February 1, 1851.

91. Court records often valued the firearms that enslaved people used in crimes at five shillings, which would have been worth less than two dollars in the 1850s, although this may not have reflected the weapons actual value. Also consider that in 1860, the Montgomery County Court appraised a stolen pistol at one dollar. These were inexpensive but should not be read as an indication of poor quality. Consider that in 1850, one could buy, through legal channels, a new single barreled shotgun for as little as $3.50. *Mississippian* (Jackson, MS), January 19, 1849; *Evening Post* (New York, NY), June 11, 1860; *State v. Malcolm B. Stuart,* jury presentment (Fall Term 1860), Montgomery County Criminal Action Papers, 1860–1863, NCDAH; H. F. Clark and Company, *Clark's Illustrated Treatise,* 52. Further, one could buy a bag of shot for under two dollars and powder ran for about eight cents for a half pound. Bryant Bennett Ledger, vol. 1, c. 1, 1851–1868, pp. 22, 29, Bryant Bennett Papers, 1767–1902 and undated, RML.

92. *Raleigh Register, and North-Carolina Gazette* (Raleigh, NC), February 13, 1844.

93. *Massachusetts Spy* (Worcester, MA), February 24, 1858; *New England Farmer* (Boston, MA), February 20, 1858.

94. *Tarborough Southerner* (Tarboro, NC), September 25, 1858.

95. *Tarborough Southerner* (Tarboro, NC), September 25, 1858; *Weekly Raleigh Register* (Raleigh, NC), September 29, 1858; *Lowell Daily Citizen and News* (Lowell, MA), October 12, 1858.

96. "William Goodman" [Washington County, North Carolina], 1860 US Federal Census database, population schedule, p. 309, image 11, Ancestry.com; *Weekly Raleigh Register* (Raleigh, NC), September 29, 1858; *Lowell Daily Citizen and News* (Lowell, MA), October 12, 1858.

97. *State v. Angus Campbell,* jury presentment (Fall Term 1854), in folder "Criminal Action Papers Concerning Slaves," Slave Records, Richmond County Records, NCDAH; "Angus Campbell" [Richmond County, North Carolina], 1860 US Federal Census database, population schedule, p. 194, image 386, Ancestry.com.

98. *State v. Charles Hamburg,* Dianah Bohnstedt's affidavit (June Term 1854), in Criminal Action Papers, New Hanover County Records, NCDAH; Forret, *Race Relations at the Margins,* 100–101.

99. *State v. Charles Hamburg,* Bohnstedt's affidavit, NCDAH.

100. John Gray Account Book, 1856: April 21, May 6, 14, June 27, 1856; Philip Northern Bray Account Books, 1856–1918, SHC.

218 Notes to Chapter 2

101. John Gray Account Book, 1856: April 21, June 20, SHC. Other enslaved did this shopping as well, like Aron and Daniel, who picked up nails for their enslavers (May 10 and July 22, 1856); other patrons sent family members to make purchases on their accounts. The unnamed wives of Henry Besley, William Frost, Malica Dudley, and Jilery Morse made purchases on their husbands's accounts (March 22 and April 17, 1856); and Jonathan B. Lindsey and Thomas Mercer both sent their sons (April 4, April 21, and May 27, 1856). There were at least three women named Mary Doxey living in Currituck County at the time, who were married to William Doxey, John Doxey, and Zachariah Doxey. All of these Doxey men were enslavers and neither household has any white members listed as Beasley, which further suggests that he was in fact an enslaved man. "William Doxey" and "Mary Doxey" [Tull's Creek District, Currituck County, North Carolina], 1850 US Federal Census database, population schedule, p. 173; "John Doxey" and "Mary Doxey" [Moyock District, Currituck County, North Carolina], 1850 US Federal Census database, population schedule, p. 168; "Zachariah Doxey" and "Mary Doxey" [Poplar Branch District, Currituck County, North Carolina], 1850 US Federal Census database, population schedule, p. 200; "John Doxey," "William Doxey," and "Zachariah Doxey" [Currituck County, North Carolina], 1850 US Federal Census database, slave schedule, all on Ancestry.com.

102. Forret, *Race Relations*, 100.

103. Forret, *Race Relations*, 89; Colyer, *Brief Report of the Services Rendered*, 20.

104. Bynum, *Unruly Women*, 47; Cecil-Fronsman, *Common Whites*, 80–81, 82. These economic and social interactions between lower class Black and white North Carolinians were common enough that they continued to draw comments from historians at the turn of the century, who argued that free people of color in the "country districts" were "usually . . . on terms of friendship with that other class of incompetents, the 'poor whites'" and that these groups sometimes "lived on terms of sexual intimacy." Bassett, *Slavery in the State of North Carolina*, 43.

105. On James Graham's Petition (Lincoln County), see Schweninger, *RSFB*, Ser. I, North Carolina, 1851, reel 7, frame 0382.

106. Abolitionist and reformer Richard Henry Dana Jr. explicitly linked flogging with racial subordination in his account of his earlier life at sea. When Dana's captain threatened to whip another sailor, the white man protested that he was "no negro slave." The captain responded with "I'll make you one . . . I'll teach you all who is master aboard!" In a separate incident the captain beat another sailor and taunted the rest of the crew, yelling at them, "You see your condition! . . . you didn't know what I was! Now you know what I am! I'll make you toe the mark, every soul of you, or I'll flog you all, fore and aft, from the boy up! You've got a driver over you! Yes, *a slave-driver,—a nigger-driver!* I'll see who'll tell me he isn't a NIGGER slave!" Dana, *Two Years before the Mast*, 102–6, 110–11. Dana was influenced by his abolitionism, but his disdain for the whip would have resonated with many other sailors. Yet it was not universal. When the navy abolished flogging in 1850, a Wilmington newspaper argued that "four fifths of the 'Old Salts' themselves" opposed the change, as "but for the 'Catting' of Skulks, all the work would have to be done by honest Sailors. There are others who deserve the lash in this world, and 'tis mistaken humanity to let them escape—the rod was made for the fool's back." *Weekly Commercial* (Wilmington, NC) October 4, 1850. While not specifically racialized, this attitude reflected the view that violence was acceptable against *all* subordinates, not just those who were enslaved.

107. Bolton, *Poor Whites of the Antebellum South*, 65, 50–51, 204n.

108. Federal Writers' Project, *Born in Slavery*, Vol. 11, North Carolina Narratives, pt. 1, 113 (David Blount), WPA-LOC.

109. Hadden, "South Carolina's Grand Jury Presentments," 89, 91.

110. *State v. Michael Wilder, State v. Dick*, and *State v. Pompey*, all on jury presentment (December Term 1816), in folder "1816, Criminal Actions Concerning Slaves, 1767–1829," Chowan County Records, NCDAH. It appears as if Jack was not actually charged on this presentment. The court was more concerned with Wilder's insufficient mastery than Jack's actions.

111. Court order to hold Jacob and Anthony in custody, in folder "Slave Record-Warrant for jailing slaves Jacob and Anthony, 1812," Miscellaneous Records, 1740–1940, Rowan County Records, NCDAH.

112. The deposition of Bob, n.d., in folder "Slaves and Persons of Color, 1802–1818," Miscellaneous Records, 1740–1940, Rowan County Records, NCDAH. "Antony" was listed as "Anthony" on this document.

113. Proceedings of the Safety Committee at Wilmington, August 17, 1775, in Saunders, *Colonial Records of North Carolina*, 10:158–59; Wood, *This Remote Part of the World*, 239. For conversations about the scarcity of gunpowder, see Saunders, *Colonial Records of North Carolina*, 10:23, 157, 370, 387, 470, 516, 536.

114. *State v. Michael Wilder; State v. Dick, State v. Pompey*, all on jury presentment (December Term 1816), in folder "1816, Criminal Actions Concerning Slaves, 1767–1829," Chowan County Records, NCDAH.

115. Grand jury report (November 23, 1853), in folder "1853, Slave Records 1830–1867" (broken series), Beaufort County Records, NCDAH.

116. Grand jury report (November Term 1832), in folder "Apprentice Bonds and Records, 1832," Apprentice Bonds and Records, 1832–1840, Craven County Records, NCDAH; Grand jury report (June Term 1853), in folder "Grand jury reports and presentments, 1848–1871," Miscellaneous Records, n.d., 1756–1945, New Hanover County Records, NCDAH.

117. *Cape-Fear Recorder* (Wilmington, NC), May 16, 1832. Bryan ran advertisements for several weeks until at least the middle of July but it is not clear if he ever recovered the firearms . . . or the flute. *Cape-Fear Recorder* [Wilmington, NC), July 11, 1832.

118. A. Warner to William Craig[?] (June 19, 1802), in folder "Insurrection among Slaves 1802–1803" (Court Papers), Slave Records 1759–1864, Perquimans County Records, NCDAH.

119. *State v. Michael Wilder, State v. Dick*, and *State v. Pompey*, all on jury presentment, December Term 1816, in folder "1816, Criminal Actions Concerning Slaves, 1767–1829," Chowan County Records, NCDAH.

120. John D. Whitford to Governor Thomas Bragg, January 15, 1855, Thomas Bragg Letter Book, pp. 24–25, NCDAH.

121. New Bern Committee of Conference to Thomas Bragg, December 19, 1856, in folder "Correspondence, Petitions, etc., December 1, 1856–December 27, 1856," Thomas Bragg Papers, NCDAH.

122. John D. Whitford to Governor Thomas Bragg, January 15, 1855, Thomas Bragg Letter Book, pp. 24–25, NCDAH.

123. R. W. Haywood to Governor Thomas Bragg, January 23, 1855, Thomas Bragg Letter Book, pp. 25–26, NCDAH.

124. Kaiser, "'Masters Determined to be Masters,'" 37. The federal government's weapons allotments could be substantial. Consider that in 1840, the United States Army's Ordnance Office notified North Carolina's governor that it was planning to send "about 650 Muskets" to the Old North State for the upcoming year. In 1859, Governor John W. Ellis requested some "two thousand long range rifles with bayonets attached" from Secretary of War John B. Floyd. He did not receive a speedy reply, and he repeated his request, adding that if the government could not supply the arms, Floyd should order the federal Arsenal in Fayetteville to "alter such guns as we have so as to make them more useful." In mid-January, the Ordnance Department finally sent about three hundred model 1856 rifles with sword bayonets, but this would not do. Ellis again asked the War Department to order the Fayetteville Arsenal to alter "1500 rifles + 3000 muskets from the flint + steel to the percussion lock" and to rifle the barrels of another thousand muskets to increase their effective range. Lt. Col. G. Talcott to Governor Edward B. Dudley, December 8, 1840, in folder "Correspondence, Petitions, etc., December 1, 1840–December 31, 1840," in Edward B. Dudley Papers, North Carolina Governors' Papers, NCDAH. Governor John W. Ellis to Secretary of War John B. Floyd, December 10, 1859, p. 159; December 23, 1859, p. 162; H. K. Craig to Governor John W. Ellis, January 17, 1859, p. 179; Governor John W. Ellis to Col. H. K. Craig, January 14, 1860, p. 173; and Governor John W. Ellis to Secretary of War John B. Floyd, December 23, 1859, p. 178, all in John W. Ellis Letter Book, 1859–1861, North Carolina Governors' Papers, NCDAH.

125. Governor Thomas Bragg to the North Carolina General Assembly, January 24, 1855, Thomas Bragg Letter Book, pp. 26–27, NCDAH.

126. The committee was primarily concerned with the influx of enslaved Black railroad workers, who they feared would spend the Christmas holiday in New Bern. Aside from the poorly secured arms, they worried that their town could be easily razed, as it was "chiefly composed of wood buildings, which are very compactly arranged." In the event of arson, the "destruction of our town would be inevitable, and the lives of almost defenseless women and children would be almost to the mercy of savage Africans." New Bern Committee of Conference to Bragg, December 19, 1856, in folder "Correspondence, Petitions, etc., December 1, 1856–December 27, 1856," Thomas Bragg Papers, NCDAH.

127. John D. Whitford to Governor Thomas Bragg, January 15, 1855, Thomas Bragg Letter Book, pp. 24, NCDAH.

128. Summary of Sampson's crimes, December 17, 1791, Petitions (Miscellaneous), General Assembly Session Records, North Carolina Digital Collections, https://digital .ncdcr.gov/Documents/Detail/petitions-miscellaneous/806881?item=807156. Houseman petitioned the legislature to "consider his deplorable situation as the parent of a numerous family" who was then "far advanced in life" and who relied on Sampson's labor. He added that Sampson had been tried and executed before Houseman knew of the charges, and he was therefore "deprived of making any defence in his behalf." Memorial of John Houseman, December 31, 1791, Petitions (Miscellaneous), General Assembly Session Records, North Carolina Digital Collections, https://digital.ncdcr.gov/Documents/Detail /petitions-miscellaneous/806881?item=807148.

129. *Raleigh Register and North Carolina Gazette* (Raleigh, NC), October 21, 1814.

130. Resolution of Robert Rowan, May 2, 1780, Senate Joint Resolutions: April 27—May 4, https://digital.ncdcr.gov/Documents/Detail/senate-joint-resolutions-april-27-may -4/816878?item=816944 ; Commission for William Locke, November 10, 1779, House Joint Resolutions: October 19—November 10, 1779, https://digital.ncdcr.gov/Documents /Detail/house-joint-resolutions-october-19-november-10/874481?item=874594; Resolution

for Robert Rowan, November 10, 1779, House Joint Resolutions: October 19–November 10, 1779, https://digital.ncdcr.gov/Documents/Detail/house-joint-resolutions-october-19 -november-10/874481?item=874606; all in General Assembly Session Records, North Carolina Digital Collections.

131. Governor Thomas Bragg to the North Carolina General Assembly, January 24, 1855, Thomas Bragg Letter Book, pp. 26–27, NCDAH.

132. W. A. Blount Sr. to E. Stanly, March 1858, in Correspondence, 1837–1858, James Gray Blount Papers, NCDAH. Blount was one of the wealthiest men in Beaufort County, with $40,000 in real estate and another $125,000 in personal estate. "W. A. Blount" [Chocowinity, Beaufort County, North Carolina], 1860 US Federal Census database, population schedule, p. 74, Ancestry.com. His son, William A. Blount Jr., also lived in the neighborhood and appears in the fifth chapter of this book.

133. W. A. Blount Sr. to E. Stanly, March 1858, in folder "Correspondence, 1837–1858," James Gray Blount Papers, NCDAH.

134. W. A. Blount Sr. to E. Stanly, March 1858; and Jonathan A. Stanley to Gen. W. A. Blount, March 10, 1858, both letters in folder "Correspondence, 1837–1858," James Gray Blount Papers, NCDAH. "W. A. Blount" [Washington, Beaufort County, North Carolina], 1860 US Federal Census database, population schedule, p. 204, Ancestry.com. "E. Stanly" was almost certainly Edward Stanly, a prominent North Carolina politician who relocated to California for a number of years before returning when Lincoln appointed him military governor of North Carolina in 1862. His absence would explain his nephew managing his local affairs. *Weekly Standard* (Raleigh, NC), November 22, 1848; January 24, 1855; *North State Whig* (Washington, NC), December 3, 1851; January 19, 1853; *Raleigh Register* (Raleigh, NC), July 9, 1851; Steve Miller, *North Carolina Unionists*, 115.

135. W. A. Blount Sr. to E. Stanly, March 1858.

136. H. Jones, *Reports of Cases at Law . . . 1858–1859*, 6:71. Some enslaved men created a personal code of ethics that was rooted in honor but tailored to function within the confines of enslavement. They were dissatisfied with their position, but historians have argued that some of them nevertheless felt "obliged by their condition to labor for their owner" and that "given their predicament, there was an honorable way of surviving it, and it was their duty to find that way and live it." Nathan Huggins explains that this was not the enslaved men's adherence to the biblical charge that they obey their enslavers but instead their inward focus on the performance of one's duty. At times, they protected enslavers's property or passed up opportunities to flee. These decisions were complicated and often pragmatic. Huggins might have focused more on the threats that enslaved laborers faced for failing to meet their enslavers's expectations, but his point is nevertheless compelling. Huggins, *Black Odyssey*, 234–35, 236–37.

137. Jones, *Reports of Cases at Law . . . 1858–1859*, 6:59.

Chapter 3

1. NCLP, *Session Laws of North Carolina, 1831–1832* (Ch. XLIV, Sec. I), 34; NCLP, *Session Laws of North Carolina, 1840–1841* (Ch. XXX, Sec. I), 61–62; NCLP, *Session Laws of North Carolina, 1860–1861* (Ch. XXXIV, Secs. I and II).

2. NCLP *Acts of the North Carolina General Assembly, 1785* (Ch. XXVIII, Secs. I, III, and IV), 749–50.

3. This vermin requirement covered Bladen, Brunswick, Burke, Caswell, Dobbs, Duplin, Franklin, Granville, Jones, Lincoln, Mecklenburg, Montgomery, New Hanover, Onslow,

Richmond, Rowan, Rutherford, Sampson Surry, Tyrrell, Wake, Warren, and Wilkes Counties. NCLP, *Acts of the North Carolina General Assembly, 1785* (Ch. XXVIII, Sec. III), 750; *North Carolina Christian Advocate* (Raleigh, NC), June 4, 1857.

4. For these recorded bounties, see various bounties in folder "Bounties for scalps of wolves and wild cats," n.d., 1762–1786, Granville County Records, NCDAH. Notably, some of these predators were passively shot via carefully rigged contraptions. When writing about colonial Virginians, Robert Beverley explained that "for Wolves they make Traps, and set Guns bated in the Woods, so that when he offers to seize the Bate, he pulls the Trigger, and the Gun discharges upon him." Beverley, *History and Present State of Virginia*, 73. Henry to William S. Pettigrew, June 13, 1857, Folder 202, Pettigrew Family Papers, 1776–1926, SHC.

5. *North-Carolinian* (Fayetteville, NC), January 16, 1841; *Western Democrat* (Charlotte, NC), August 9, 1859. In 1779, Bute County was divided into Warren and Franklin Counties, and Tryon County was divided into Lincoln and Rutherford Counties. CSR, *Acts of the North Carolina General Assembly, 1779* (Ch. 19, Sec. 3), 227–28; (Ch. 23, Sec. 2), 236. *North-Carolina Star* (Raleigh, NC), October 7, 1846; *Raleigh Register* (Raleigh, NC), December 4, 1847; *Weekly Ad Valorem Banner* (Raleigh, NC), April 25, 1861; *Fayetteville Semi-Weekly Observer* (Fayetteville, NC), June 18, 1857; Micajah Gainey bear bounty (July 1801), in folder "Bounty on Wild Animals, 1798–1802," Miscellaneous Records, 1779–1939, Richmond County Records, NCDAH; Ned Howard wolf bounty (May 1779), in folder "Bounties for scalps of wolves and wild cats," n.d., 1762–1786, Granville County Records, NCDAH.

6. CSR, *Acts of the North Carolina General Assembly, 1769* (Ch. 3, Secs. 1, 2, 3), 784. This law was repealed about twenty years later. See CSR, *Acts of the North Carolina General Assembly, 1788* (Ch. 11, Sec. 1), 958.

7. John F. Burgwin and Thos. F. Davis's bond (March Term 1805), in folder "Permission for slaves to carry guns, 1795–1841," New Hanover County Records, NCDAH. Federal Writers' Project, *Born in Slavery*, Vol. 11, North Carolina Narratives, pt. 2, 418 (Alex Woods), WPA-LOC.

8. Proctor, *Bathed in Blood*, 149.

9. Hadden, *Slave Patrols*, 37; A. Watson, *Wilmington*, 8; Minutes of the North Carolina Governor's Council, May 20–23, 1741, in Saunders, *Colonial Records of North Carolina*, 4:593–94, http://docsouth.unc.edu/csr/index.html/document/csr04-0176; Powell, *North Carolina through Four Centuries*, 75; Holles Newcastle to Governor Gabriel Johnston, October 31, 1744, in Clark, *State Records of North Carolina*, 11:593–94, http://docsouth.unc.edu/csr/index.html/document/csr11-0032.

10. Thomas Person, wild cat bounty (April 1765); and Charles Eaton, wolf bounty (May 1771), both, in folder "Bounties for scalps of wolves and wildcats," n.d., 1762–1786 (broken series), in Miscellaneous Records, 1722, 1747–1920, Granville County Records, NCDAH.

11. John F. Burgwin and Thos. F. Davis's bond (March Term 1805), in folder "Permission for slaves to carry guns 1795–1841," New Hanover County Records, NCDAH. Willis Herring's petition (August Term 1841), in folder "Petition of Willis, a free man of color, to use a gun, 1841," Slaves and Free People of Color, n.d., 1783–1869, Wayne County Records, NCDAH; "Benajah Herring" [Newhope District, Wayne County, North Carolina], 1840 US Federal Census database, p. 207, image 904, Ancestry.com.

12. Willis Herring's petition (August Term 1841), in folder "petition of Willis, a free man of color, to use a gun, 1841," Slaves and Free People of Color, n.d., 1783–1869, Wayne County

Records, NCDAH; "Benajah Herring" [Newhope District, Wayne County, North Carolina], 1840 US Federal Census, page 207, image 904, Ancestry.com.

13. J. Taylor, *Revisal of the Laws of the State of North Carolina*, Ch. 1164, Sec. 2, 3, and 4.

14. *Carolina Observer* (Fayetteville, NC), December 9, 1824.

15. John Swann's bond (January 1819), in folder "Permit to Carry Firearms, 1819," Miscellaneous Records, 1786–1925, Brunswick County Records, NCDAH.

16. H. Jones, *Reports of Cases at Law . . . 1858–1959*, 6:57–58. Even as late as 1860, other laborers loaded and stocked merchandise, including firearms, in their enslaver's stores. See Inscoe, "Mountain Masters," 158.

17. H. Jones, *Reports of Cases at Law . . . 1858–1859*, 6:57.

18. H. Jones, *Reports of Cases at Law . . . 1858–1859*, 6:58.

19. H. Jones, *Reports of Cases at Law . . . 1858–1859*, 6:58.

20. Tushnet, *Slave Law in the American South*, 33–34. Ruffin's point was that if workers had recourse from their enslavers's orders or punishments, his or her authority would be constantly eroded.

21. H. Jones, *Reports of Cases at Law . . . 1858–1859*, 6:71.

22. Genovese, *Roll, Jordan, Roll*, 48.

23. *Carolina Watchman* (Salisbury, NC), August 17, 1844. Like Harry during the Civil War, some Black North Carolinians's performed firearm-adjacent labor. While the exact nature of his work is not clear, an enslaved man whom a Union officer described as a "good mechanic and highly intelligent man" worked in the Confederate rifle factories near Raleigh, until he forged a pass and escaped. This was part of a longer wartime trend of coercing Black laborers into the war effort. During the Revolutionary War, for instance, some were put to work making gun stocks. Colyer, *Brief Report of the Services Rendered*, 29–30; Freeman, "North Carolina's Black Patriots," 31.

24. Starobin, "Privileged Bondsmen and the Process of Accommodation," 59, 61–62.

25. William Tripp to Araminta Tripp, October 9, 1861; January 5, 1863; March 21, 1863, Folder 4, Tripp Papers, SHC.

26. On New Hanover County Petition, see Schweninger, *RSFB*, Ser. I, North Carolina, 1791, reel 4, frame 00185.

27. NCLP, *Session Laws of North Carolina, 1777* (Ch. 22, Secs. II, III, and IV), 245.

28. *State v. Willoughby Foreman et al.*, unsigned petitioner to Governor Gabriel Holmes, August 1, 1824, in folder "Miscellaneous Correspondence (Nov. 1824–Jan. 1825)," General Assembly Session Records, November 1824–January 1825, NCDAH.

29. Jacobs, *Incidents in the Life*, 7–8, 104; T. Jones, *Experience of Rev. Thomas H. Jones*, 212.

30. Jay, *Miscellaneous Writings on Slavery*, 457. The Manumission Society had some successes in the mid-1820s, when North Carolina enslavers manumitted a few thousand people and one of their members was elected to the state senate. See Woodson, "Freedom and Slavery in Appalachian America," 142–43.

31. Jacobs, *Incidents in the Life*, 104.

32. Federal Writers' Project, *Born in Slavery*, Vol. 11, North Carolina Narratives, pt. 1, 141 (W. L. Bost).

33. Lane, *Narrative of Lunsford Lane*, 10–13, 21–22. Frederick Douglass's time in Baltimore taught him that neighbors's scrutinizing eyes encouraged urban enslavers to take better care of the people they enslaved. He noted that "every city slaveholder is anxious to have it known

of him, that he feeds his slaves well; and it is due to them to say, that most of them do give their slaves enough to eat. There are, however, some painful exceptions to this rule." Douglass, *Narrative of the Life*, 35. If Raleigh's enslavers behaved similarly to those in Baltimore, Smith's callousness was probably exceptional, which made it more impactful.

34. Lane, *Narrative of Lunsford Lane*, 9–10, 15–16.

35. Federal Writers' Project, *Born in Slavery*, Vol. 11, pt. 2, 418 (Alex Woods).

36. Proctor, *Bathed in Blood*, 157; Federal Writers' Project, *Born in Slavery*, Vol. 11, pt. 2, 418 (Alex Woods); W. Johnson, *Soul by Soul*, 19.

37. Federal Writers' Project, *Born in Slavery*, Vol 11, North Carolina Narratives, pt. 2, 225 (George Rogers).

38. Federal Writers' Project, *Born in Slavery*, Vol 11, North Carolina Narratives, pt. 2, 110 (Maggie Mials).

39. *Raleigh Register, and North-Carolina Gazette* (Raleigh, NC), July 29, 1828. The *Raleigh Register* listed him as "Cooley Wiggins," but this was likely a nickname or a mistake on the part of the editor. The census recorded a Claiborne Wiggins living with his wife and four young children in the area. "Claiborne Wiggins" [Bufalloe District, Wake County, North Carolina], 1830 US Federal Census database, population schedule, p. 424, Ancestry.com.

40. *Star, and North-Carolina Gazette* (Raleigh, NC), July 30, 1819; *Laws of the State of North-Carolina, Enacted in the Year 1817* (Ch. XXVI. Secs. I and II), 25, https://digital.ncdcr.gov/Documents/Detail/laws-of-the-state-of-north-carolina-enacted-in-the-year-1817/4229985; *Newbern Sentinel* (New Bern, NC), June 8, 1828.

41. *Newbern Sentinel* (New Bern, NC), May 31, 1828; *Carolina Federal Republican* (New Bern, NC), February 22, 1817; *Raleigh Register, and North-Carolina Gazette* (Raleigh, NC), July 29, 1828.

42. Weber, "Politics as a Vocation," 3–4; *Newbern Sentinel* (New Bern, NC), May 31, 1828; Stephen Miller, "Recollections of Newbern Fifty Years Ago," 351.

43. *Carolina Federal Republican* (New Bern, NC), February 22, 1817; *Raleigh Register, and North-Carolina Gazette* (Raleigh, NC), July 29, 1828.

44. Stephen Evans petition (May Term 1854), in folder "Petition of Stephen Evans, a free man of color, to hunt with a gun, 1854," Slaves and Free People of Color, n.d., 1783–1869, Wayne County Records, NCDAH.

45. *Raleigh Register, and North-Carolina Gazette* (Raleigh, NC), July 29, 1828.

46. *Daily Herald* (Wilmington, NC), December 3, 1859.

47. *Raleigh Register, and North-Carolina Gazette* (Raleigh, NC), November 1, 1825.

48. *State v. Negro Lizzy/State v. Negro Eliza*, jury presentment (March Term 1823); and William Gaston's affidavit (April 15, 1823); both in folder "Criminal Actions Concerning Slaves and Free People of Color, 1823–1826," Criminal Actions Concerning Slaves and Free Persons of Color, 1781–1839, Craven County Records, NCDAH. White North Carolinians sought to maintain a fair court system—the law and social custom built a two-tiered system that rested on inequality and there was generally little need for the courts to rig it further. As James W. Ely Jr. and David J. Bodenhamer have argued, the institution of enslavement "may not have dulled the region's legal sensibilities." Bodenhamer and Ely, "Regionalism and the Legal History of the South," 19.

During the winter of 1816, the Chowan County court's grand jurors petitioned the court about "an act of injustice" against a "Man of Colour" who was fined thirty-two pounds and ten pence for "an infringement of the Laws . . . when one of the Magistrates of the County for a similar offence was only fined £4." Further, in 1858, an enslaved man named Peter shot and killed his overseer during an escape attempt. The sheriff raised a posse to capture him, "dead or alive," but local editors wrote that "although the impulse to take swift vengeance on the murderer is almost irrepressible, we yet trust that the law may be suffered to take its course, and thus, we think, the example will be made more impressive, and the sanctity of the law remain inviolate." Peter was captured and despite the "outrage" against him, the editors believed that he "had as fair a trial as a man could have, and the advantage of able counsel" and that the proceedings, which sentenced him to the gallows, were "all quiet and respectful." Grand jurors petition December 13, 1816, in folder "Criminal Actions Concerning Slaves and Free People of Color, 1767–1829," Chowan County Records, NCDAH; *Wilmington Journal* (Wilmington, NC), March 22, 1858; April 23, 1858.

49. William Gaston to Susan Jane Gaston, May 7, 1823. William Gaston Papers, 1744–1950, SHC.

50. Coroner's report on Bob, a slave (November 1855), in folder "Coroners' Inquests—1855," Coroners' Inquests, 1768–1880 (broken series), New Hanover County Records, NCDAH; *Daily Herald* (Wilmington, NC), November 12, 1855.

51. *Democratic Press* (Raleigh, NC), May 28, 1859.

52. "Samuel Rogers" [District 4, Martin County, North Carolina], 1860 US Federal Census database, slave schedule, p. 11, Ancestry.com.

53. *Newbern Spectator, and Political Register* (New Bern, NC), January 2, 1835.

54. *New Era and Commercial Advertiser* (New Bern, NC), November 9, 1858; *Daily Progress* (New Bern, NC), November 10, 1858; *Semi-Weekly Standard* (Raleigh, NC), November 16, 1858; "Elijah Cuthbert" [15th Ward, City of New Bern, Craven County, North Carolina], 1860 US Federal Census database, population schedule, p. 39, Ancestry.com; Alex Taylor's examination (November 1858), and N. M. Chadwick's examination (November 1858), both in folder "Inquests 1850–1859" (broken series), Coroners' Inquests 1782–1869 (broken series), Craven County Records, NCDAH.

55. Coroner's report on Dinah, a negro woman slave (November 1858), in folder "Inquests 1850–1859" (broken series), Coroners' Inquests 1782–1869 (broken series), Craven County Records, NCDAH. The newspaper's graphic recounting of Dinah's tragic death is unsettling, but this sensationalist reporting was not rooted in her race or enslavement, however. Mid-nineteenth century newspapers often reported on murders and accidents in dramatic ways, even those involving white people's disfigurements or deaths, as one can see via other examples in this book.

56. *Weekly Raleigh Register* (Raleigh, NC), April 20, 1859. Murphy could not be traced through the 1860 census but in 1850, he enslaved thirty-one people—this young woman was part of a substantial community. "James L. Murphy" [Craven County, North Carolina], 1850 US Federal Census database, slave schedule, p. 697, Ancestry.com.

57. *Raleigh Register, and North-Carolina Gazette* (Raleigh, NC), December 21, 1841.

58. *Raleigh Register, and North-Carolina Gazette* (Raleigh, NC), February 2, 1844. While not common, this sort of accident did happen at times. In November 1857, two white men died in similar manners as their firearms catastrophically malfunctioned and sent the loads into the men's heads. *Fayetteville Observer* (Fayetteville, NC), November 16, 1857.

59. *Fayetteville Observer* (Fayetteville, NC), November 16, 1857. Inquest over Alexander, a slave (October 1854), in folder "Coroner's Inquests 1832–1871," Miscellaneous Records, 1786–1925, Brunswick County Records, NCDAH.

60. *American Advocate* (Kinston, NC), April 14, 1859; *Iredell Express* (Statesville, NC), March 30, 1860; *North Carolina Standard* (Raleigh, NC), August 14, 1858. Children were often the victims of these accidents, shooting themselves or their friends with firearms that had been left unattended. *Charlotte Democrat* (Charlotte, NC), January 22, 1856; *Tri-Weekly Commercial* (Wilmington, NC), July 24, 1855.

61. J. Taylor, *Revisal of the Laws of the State of North Carolina,* Ch. 1219, Sec. 1; North Carolina, *Journal of the Convention,* Art. I, Sec. 3, § 3; Franklin, *Free Negro,* 120. This chapter is focused on the first half of the nineteenth century, but more scholarship is needed on the colonial era constructions of Black manhood. These men were not completely unfettered but they had more opportunities than their sons and grandsons would later enjoy.

62. Willis Herring's petition (August Term 1841), in folder "Petition of Willis, a free man of color, to use a gun, 1841," Slaves and Free People of Color, n.d., 1783–1869, Wayne County Records, NCDAH; "Benajah Herring" [Newhope District, Wayne County, North Carolina]," 1840 US Federal Census.

63. Proctor, *Bathed in Blood,* 55–57.

64. Natchez, Mississippi's William Johnson, a free man of color who was an avid hunter, owned an impressive collection of firearms and enjoyed hunting with both his Black and white friends, his sons, and his apprentices. Davis and Hogan, *Barber of Natchez,* 69–72, 76.

65. Proctor, *Bathed in Blood,* 55–57; Olmsted, *Journey in the Seaboard Slave States,* 348–49.

66. Proctor, *Bathed in Blood,* 53–54.

67. Bumppo, "Deerhunt in North Carolina"; Cooper, *Last of the Mohicans,* 35.

68. Federal Writers' Project, *Born in Slavery,* Vol 11, North Carolina Narratives, pt. 1, 242 (W. Solomon Debnam). "Thomas R. Debnam" [Cross Roads, Wake County, North Carolina], 1850 US Federal Census database, population schedule, p. 148A, image 300, Ancestry. com; "A. R. Hodge" [North Eastern Division, Wake County, North Carolina], 1860 US Federal Census database, population schedule, p. 437, image 441, Ancestry.com.

69. Proctor, *Bathed in Blood,* 52–53.

70. The commonplace occurrence of these hunting and target shooting trips make them difficult to trace in the historical record—they oftentimes only appear when someone was accidentally injured. For instance, in 1843, a seventeen-year-old white Virginian named George Walker brought an enslaved person on a target shooting excursion that was noteworthy only because Walker stepped in front of his companion while "the negro boy" was firing at a target. He "received the contents of the gun in the back of his head" and later died from the injuries. If the target shooting trip had not become "another of those dreadful accidents resulting from the careless use of fire-arms," it would never have entered the historical record. *Raleigh Register, and North-Carolina Gazette* (Raleigh, NC), September 5, 1843.

71. NCLP, *Session Laws of North Carolina, 1840–1841* (Ch. XXX, Sec. I), 61–62. The laws addressing the state's agent to the Cherokee Nation and the chairman of the board of superintendents for the state's common schools exclusively referred to potential officeholders via masculine pronouns. The law did not specifically mandate that a man fill the office of Cherokee agent, but societal expectations and the patriarchal society in which few women commanded the resources for the required $100,000 bond assured that this would be so. The same was true for the chairman of the board of superintendents. Public school legislation dictated that "three men" needed to be elected for the district level "school committee," but the superintendent position was not gender specific. NCLP, *Session Laws of North Carolina,*

1840–1841 (Ch. IV, Secs. I–V), 7–9; and (Ch. VII, Secs. II, VI, and VIII), 11, 13. The firearm law was exceptional in its clear inclusion of both men and women.

72. Bynum, *Unruly Women*, 7.

73. D. G. White, *Ar'n't I a Woman?*, 120. This was not just about agricultural labor, but about hard work generally. McCurry explains that "women's work in the fields, although customary, was customarily ignored and even denied. A collusive silence surrounded one of the labor practices that most clearly distinguished yeoman farms from plantations, that set yeoman wives and daughters apart from their planter counterparts, that dangerously eroded the social distinctions between free women and slaves, and that cut deeply into the pride of men raised in a culture of honor." McCurry, *Masters of Small Worlds*, 80–81.

74. Helper, *Compendium of the Impending Crisis of the South*, 299.

75. McCurry, *Masters of Small Worlds*, 80–81; Helper, *Compendium of the Impending Crisis of the South*, 181–82.

76. D. G. White, *Ar'n't I a Woman?*, 13–14; Foner and James Branham, *Lift Every Voice*, 227–28.

77. For additional reading on the differences in Black and white women's cultures in the Slave South specifically, see Glymph, *Out of the House of Bondage*. Glymph emphasizes white women's roles in the violent enforcement of the slave system's racial hierarchy and the ways that they relied on Black women's labor to maintain their elite status.

78. D. G. White, *Ar'n't I a Woman*, 120; Federal Writers' Project, *Born in Slavery*, Vol 11, North Carolina Narratives, pt. 2, 407 (Plaz Williams). Williams took pride in this work. She explained, "I worked in de fiel's like a man an' I liked it too." After emancipation, some Black women continued to undertake this physically demanding labor. William George Hinton noted that he and his sister worked for a white farmer, whose land their family lived on. He did not comment on his own work but noted that his sister "plowed like a man" for the white farmer. Federal Writers' Project, *Born in Slavery*, Vol 11, North Carolina Narratives, pt. 1, 439 (Robert Hinton); Hudson, *To Have and to Hold*, 33.

79. Fraser, "Negotiating Their Manhood," 76.

80. "John Chapman [Swift Creek, Craven County, North Carolina]," 1860 US Federal Census database, population schedule, p. 233, Ancestry.com; *The Times: A Southern Literary and Family Paper* (Greensboro, NC), September 22, 1860; "Julia Chapman," "Noah Chapman," and "Abraham Jackson" [Swift Creek, Craven County, North Carolina], 1860 US Federal Census database, population schedule, p. 102, Ancestry.com.

81. *The Patriot* (Greensborough, NC), September 20, 1860.

82. *Daily Progress* (New Bern, NC), November 27, 1860; *Greensborough Patriot* (Greensboro, NC), September 20, 1860.

83. Minutes of the North Carolina House of Commons, April 18, 1783–May 17, 1783, in Clark, *State Records of North Carolina*, 19:258; *Newbern Daily Progress* (New Bern, NC), August 9, 1862.

84. Henry Armand London Diary, Vol. 2 (1864–1877), July 30, 1864, and "expenses," Folder 868-Z, Henry Armand London Papers, 1862–1877, 1887, SHC.

85. *Daily Journal* (Wilmington, NC), March 4, 8, 11, 12, 1864; *Daily Progress* (Raleigh, NC), July 25, 1864.

86. *Daily Progress* (Raleigh, NC), July 25, 1864.

87. *Daily Progress* (Raleigh, NC), July 25, 1864.

Chapter 4

1. Berlin, *Slaves without Masters*, 218; Franklin, *Free Negro*, 224.

2. R. Taylor, *Free Negro in North Carolina*, 5.

3. Franklin, *Free Negro*, 224–25.

4. Milteer, *North Carolina's Free People of Color*, 25; Franklin, *Free Negro*, 22.

5. Franklin, *Free Negro*, 20–28. The 1830 law still allowed enslavers to manumit laborers via their wills. Wood and Tise, "The Conundrum of Unfree Labor," 94–95; Franklin, *Free Negro*, 222. There was a great deal of hostility towards free Black laborers in some trades, notably mechanics. White mechanics wrote a few petitions to the assembly during the antebellum era seeking to limit Black participation in the trade. Franklin, *Free Negro*, 138–39.

6. *Session Laws of Virginia, 1831* (Ch. XXII, Sec. 4), 21; Cramer, *For the Defense of Themselves*, 59–60, 74. *Session Laws of Maryland, 1831*, Ch. 323, Sec. 6; *Session Laws of Delaware, 1833* (Ch. CLXXVI, Secs. 1, 2, 3, and 4), 180–82; *Session Laws of Georgia, 1833* (Ch. "Persons of Colour," Secs. 7 and 8), 228; Franklin, *Free Negro*, 51.

7. Petition in support of Benjamin and George Morgan in (November Term 1841) folder "Petitioners Request that Guns be Returned to Benjamin and George Morgan, 1841," Slaves and Free Negroes Bonds—Petitions, 1775–1861, Craven County Records, NCDAH. The signatories all lived in Craven County's South Side District, as did the Morgans. Four of the white men were enslavers: Beasley enslaved two people, Carmon three, Harris forty-three, and Simmons fifteen. There were two John Harrises on the census, one a planter and the other a free Black man. The planter was likely the petitioner, as no other Black people signed on. Palmer does not appear on the 1840 census, as it only recorded the heads of households by name. He was about twenty years old in 1840 and probably still lived with family or an employer. Petition in support of Benjamin and George Morgan in (November Term 1841) folder "Petitioners Request that Guns be Returned to Benjamin and George Morgan, 1841," Slaves and Free Negroes Bonds—Petitions, 1775–1861, Craven County Records, NCDAH; "Benjamin Morgan," "John Ferrand," "John Harris," and "Burton Carmon" [South Side Neuse River, Craven County, North Carolina], 1840 US Federal Census database, population schedule, p. 75, image 786, Ancestry.com; "William Simmons" and "James M. Beasley" [South Side Neuse River, Craven County, North Carolina], 1840 US Federal Census database, population schedule, p. 81, image 798, Ancestry.com.

8. *Western Democrat* (Charlotte, NC), September 1, 1857.

9. Edwards, *People and Their Peace*, 113.

10. Petition in support of Benjamin and George Morgan (November Term 1841), in folder "Petitioners Request that Guns be Returned to Benjamin and George Morgan, 1841," Slaves and Free Negroes Bonds—Petitions, 1775–1861; *State v. Ben Morgan*, jury presentment (June Term 1850); Morgan's recognizance bond (September Term 1850); and writ of capias (September Term 1850), all in folder "Criminal Actions Concerning Slaves and Free Persons of Color, 1850–1852," Criminal Actions Concerning Slaves and Free Persons of Color, 1840–1868, Craven County Records, NCDAH.

11. For Craven County Petition, see Schweninger, *RSFB*, Ser. I, North Carolina, 1828, reel 6, frame 0240–0243.

12. For Craven County Petition, see Schweninger, *RSFB*, Ser. I, North Carolina, 1835, reel 7, frame 00022; on Halifax County Petition, see Schweninger, *RSFB*, Ser. I, North Carolina, 1840, reel 7, frame 00121.

13. *North Carolina Standard* (Raleigh, NC), January 22, 1851. For Beaufort County Petition, see Schweninger, *RSFB*, Ser. I, North Carolina, 1851, reel 7, frame 0374. The 1851 petitioners' view that guns encouraged "slothful and idle habits" in Beaufort County's free people of color was inseparable from white citizens' concerns about armed maroons, who problematically helped themselves to farms and smokehouses in their neighborhood.

14. North Carolina, *Journals of the Senate and House of Commons ... 1850–'51*, 534, 635, 902.

15. NCLP, *Session Laws of North Carolina, 1860–1861* (Ch. XXXIV, Secs. I and II); Franklin, *Free Negro*, 224.

16. For Beaufort County Petition, see Schweninger, *RSFB*, Ser. I, North Carolina, 1851, reel 7, frames 0336–0340.

17. For Halifax County Petition, see Schweninger, *RSFB*, Ser. I, North Carolina, 1840, reel 7, frames 0120–0123; for Sampson County Petition, see Schweninger, *RSFB*, Ser. I, North Carolina, 1852, reel 7, frames 0404–10; for Duplin County Petition, see Schweninger, *RSFB*, Ser. I, North Carolina, 1861, reel 7, frames 0327–31.

18. William Calvin petition [undated], in folder "Permits to Carry Guns, no date, 1855," Records of Slaves and Free Persons of Color, Criminal Acts, 1788–1869, Randolph County Records, NCDAH; *Hillsborough Recorder* (Hillsborough, NC), March 13, 1845.

19. Edwards, *People and Their Peace*, 101–2, 112–13, 123, 126.

20. Petition of Wm. Walden and Sons, in folder "Mulattoes (Waldens) Petition to Use Firearms, 1842," Records of Slaves and Free Persons of Color, Crim Act, 1788–1869, Randolph County Records, NCDAH; "Anderson Walden" and "John C. Walden" [South Division, Randolph County, North Carolina], 1840 US Federal Census database, population schedule, p. 57, image 120, Ancestry.com; "William Walden" [Northern Division, Randolph County, North Carolina], 1840 US Federal Census database, population schedule, p. 117, image 240, Ancestry.com; "William Walden" [South Division, Randolph County, North Carolina], 1840 US Federal Census database, population schedule, p. 56, image 118, Ancestry.com; "Stanford Waldon" [Southern Division, Randolph County, North Carolina], 1850 US Federal Census database, population schedule, p. 88B, image 182, Ancestry.com.

21. "Anderson Walden" and "John C. Walden" [South Division, Randolph County, North Carolina], 1840 US Federal Census database, population schedule, p. 57, image 120, Ancestry.com; "William Walden" [Northern Division, Randolph County, North Carolina], 1840 US Federal Census database, population schedule, p. 117, image 240, Ancestry.com; "William Walden" [South Division, Randolph County, North Carolina], 1840 US Federal Census database, population schedule, p. 56, image 118, Ancestry.com; "Stanford Waldon" [Southern Division, Randolph County, North Carolina]," 1850 US Federal Census database, page 88B, image 182, Ancestry.com.

22. *State v. William Walden*, 1841; and *State v. Anderson Walden*, 1842, both in folder "Criminal Actions Concerning Slaves and Free People of Color, 1841–1858," Records of Slaves and Free Persons of Color, Crim Act, 1788–1869, Randolph County Records, NCDAH.

23. Recommendation of Wm Walden + Sons, in folder "Mulattoes (Waldens) Petition to Use Firearms, 1842," Records of Slaves and Free Persons of Color, Crim Act, 1788–1869, Randolph County Records, NCDAH.

24. "William Macon" and "Thomas Moffitt," [South Division, Randolph County, North Carolina], 1840 US Federal Census database, population schedule, p. 81, image 168; "John R. Brown [Northern Division, Randolph County, North Carolina]," 1840 US Federal Census database, population schedule, p. 95, image 196; "Thomas Macon," "William Brown," "John

Brady," "William Brady," "John D. Brown, Esq.," and "Levi B. Branson" [Northern Division, Randolph County, North Carolina], 1840 US Federal Census database, population schedule, p. 57, image 120; "John Rains" and "Jeremiah Bray" [South Division, Randolph County, North Carolina], 1840 US Federal Census database, population schedule, p. 56, image 118; "Tidance Lane" [Northern Division, Randolph County, North Carolina], 1840 US Federal Census database, population schedule, p. 101, image 208; "Matthias Bray" [Northern Division, Randolph County, North Carolina], 1840 US Federal Census database, population schedule, p. 105, image 216; "Henry Dorsett" [Northern Division, Randolph County, North Carolina], 1840 US Federal Census database, population schedule, p. 117, image 240; "James Gilliland" [Chatham County, North Carolina], 1840 US Federal Census database, population schedule, p. 154; "Brazil H. Hicks" [Upper Regiment, Chatham County, North Carolina], 1850 US Federal Census database, population schedule, p. 429B, image 337, all on Ancestry.com.

25. Recommendation of Wm Walden + Sons, NCDAH.

26. White men's support for the free Black applicant's character was unsurprisingly formulaic. Consider the four white men who backed Wayne County's Stephen Evans in 1854. They explained that they had known him for two years and knew nothing against his character. Similarly, the five white men who signed William Calvin's undated Randolph County petition noted he was "a very inoffensive man, of good moral character, + sober industrious habits." Stephen Evans's petition [May Term 1854], in folder "Petition of Stephen Evans, a free man of color, to hunt with a gun, 1854," Slaves and Free People of Color, n.d., 1783–1869, Wayne County Records, NCDAH; Letter in support of William Calvin [n.d.], in folder "Permits to Carry Guns, no date," 1855, Records of Slaves and Free Persons of Color, Criminal Acts, 1788–1869, Randolph County Records, NCDAH.

27. Houston, Blaine, and Mellette, *Maxwell History and Genealogy*, 427; *Southern Citizen* (Asheboro, NC), February 7, 1840; Kernodle, *Lives of Christian Ministers*, 148–49.

28. *State v. William Walden*, scire capias (November 1841); and *State v. William Walden*, recognizance bond (December 1841), both in folder "Criminal actions concerning slaves and free persons of color 1841–1858" (broken series), Criminal Actions, 1788–1869, Miscellaneous, C-S, n.d., 1825–1887, Randolph County Records, NCDAH.

29. *John R. Brown v. Thomas Macon*, promissory note from William Walden and John Rains to Samuel Brown, senior (May 1839); and scire facias for John Rains and Thomas Macon (May 1843), both in in folder "1839" (all the folders in this box are labeled "1839"— this is the second from the front), Randolph County Civil Action Papers, 1839, Randolph County Records, NCDAH.

30. Many of these white men knew each other quite well. Consider that in 1838, Hicks and Branson were codefendants in a debt case, and J. D. Brown signed one of their summons as a justice of the peace. Lane was the justice for another summons. *Joab Parks & the Use of William Edwards v. Brazil Hicks + Levi B. Branson*, scire facias for Brazil Hickes and Levi B. Branson (September 1838); and scire facias for Brazil H. Hicks and Levi B. Branson, January 1839, both in folder "1839" (all the folders in this box are labeled "1839"—this is the last from the front), Randolph County Civil Action Papers, 1839, Randolph County Records, NCDAH.

Lane, Dorsett, and J. D. Brown served together on the county's school committee in 1840. *Southern Citizen* (Asheboro, NC), February 7, 1840. Later, Branson and Rains were sued for nonpayment of a jointly held debt. See *Joseph Staly v. Levi Branson and John Rains*, scire facias for Levi Branson and John Rains (May 1840), in folder "1840" (all the folders are labeled "1840"—this is the last from the front), Randolph County Civil Action Papers, 1840, Randolph County Records, NCDAH.

In 1841, J. D. Brown testified on Branson's behalf, as did W. Brown. See *Jacob B. Lineberg v. Levi Branson*, scire facias for John Lambert, George Gough, and John D. Brown (February 1839], in folder, "1841" (there are three folders labeled "1841"—this is the second]; and *Jacob B. Lineberg v. Levi Branson*, scire facias for William Wool and William Brown (March 1840) in folder, 1841 (there are three folders labeled "1841"—this is the last from the front]), Randolph County Civil Action Papers, 1840–1841, Randolph County Records, NCDAH. Moffitt testified on Lane's behalf for a debt case that reached the state's supreme court. Iredell, *Reports of Cases at Law . . . 1841–1842*, 2:254–55.

In 1842, J. Brady testified on one of J. D. Brown's cases. Lane was summoned in another. See *John D. Brown v. Thos. Wilson*, scire facias for John Brady (February 1842); and *John D. Brown v. Thomas Wilson and Stanford Causey*, scire facias for Tidance Lane (April 1842), both in folder "1842" (all of the folders are labeled "1842"—these are in the sixth from the front), Randolph County Civil Action Papers, 1842, Randolph County Records, NCDAH. J. R. Brown sued Lane and another debtor. See *John R. Brown v. Tidance Lane & Garrit Lane*, scire facias for Tidance Lane and Garrit Lane [April 1842], in folder "1842" (all of the folders in this box are labeled "1842"—this is the fifth from the front), Randolph County Civil Action Papers, 1842, Randolph County Records, NCDAH). Macon, as "one of the acting justices of the peace," heard of Nathan W. Cox's complaint that Branson owed him money. See *Nathan W. Cox v. Levi B. Branson*, lien on Branson's property (May 7, 1842), in folder "1842" (all of the folders are labeled "1842"—this is the second from the front), Randolph County Civil Action Papers, 1842, Randolph County Records, NCDAH. Lane was also summoned to testify in a case wherein Branson was the plaintiff. J. Brady was also summoned. See *Susanah Needham + Others v. L. B. Branson + Others*, scire facias for Tid Lane (September 1842), in folder "1842." Finally, it appears that Branson's land adjoined Rains's and J. D. Brown's land. See *Stephen Hinshaw v. Eli Hickes, Brazel H. Hickes, and Levi B. Branson*, scire facias for Eli Hickes, Brazel H. Hickes, and Levi B. Branson (September 1840), in folder "1842" (all the folders are labeled "1842"—this is the second from the front), Randolph County Civil Action Papers, 1842, Randolph County Records, NCDAH.

31. "Right Pettiford" [Craven County, North Carolina], 1850 US Federal Census database, population schedule, p. 362A, image 288, Ancestry.com. Rose Pettifer and her husband also each put up fifty dollars to ensure that Israel Pettifer, likely a relative but probably not a son, as he was not mentioned with her other children in her will, would appear before the county court to answer his indictment. Israel added $100 of his own. See *State v. Wright Pettiford*, jury presentment (December Term 1849) and recognizance bond (February 1850), both in folder "Criminal Actions Concerning Slaves and Free People of Color, 1840–1849," Criminal Actions Concerning Slaves and Free Persons of Color, 1840–1868, Craven County Records, NCDAH; Rose Pettifer's will, in Craven County Record of Wills, 1840–1868, NCDAH).

32. *State v. Thomas Fenner*, jury presentment (June Term 1851); and Thomas Fenner's bond (December Term 1851), both in folder "Criminal Actions Concerning Slaves and Free Persons of Color, 1851–1856," Criminal Actions Concerning Slaves and Free Persons of Color, 1840–1868, Craven County Records, NCDAH. Nearby households of Fenners included those headed by the twenty-five-year-old farmer Jacob, thirty-year-old Samuel,

and fifty-five-year-old farmer Joseph. "Thomas Fenner," "John Fenner," and "Jacob Fenner" [Craven County, North Carolina], 1850 US Federal Census database, population schedule, p. 317A, image 196; "Joseph Fenner" [Craven County, North Carolina], 1850 US Federal Census database, population schedule, p. 316B, image 195; "Samuel Fenner" [Craven County, North Carolina], 1850 US Federal Census database, population schedule, p. 317A, image 196, all on Ancestry.com.

33. *State v. John Godette*, jury presentment (June Term, 1851); *State v. Will Godette*, jury presentment against William Godette (June Term 1851); *State v. James Gaudet*, jury presentment (Fall Term 1851); and *State v. William Godette*, recognizance bond (August 1851), all in folder "Criminal Actions Concerning Slaves and Free Persons of Color, 1851–1856," Criminal Actions Concerning Slaves and Free Persons of Color, 1840–1868, Craven County Records, NCDAH. "John Godet" [Craven County, North Carolina], 1850 US Federal Census database, population schedule, p. 307B, image 177, Ancestry.com; and "William Godett" [Craven County, North Carolina], 1850 US Federal Census database, population schedule, p. 311A, image 184, Ancestry.com.

34. *State v. James Godette*, recognizance bonds (one from April 1852 and and one n.d.), jury presentment (Fall Term 1851), and writs of capias (June 1851, and Spring Term 1852), all in folder "Criminal Actions Concerning Slaves and Free Persons of Color, 1840–1868," Craven County Records, NCDAH. "James Godett" [Craven County, North Carolina], 1850 US Federal Census database, population schedule, p. 311A, image 184, Ancestry.com; "Joshua Taylor" [Craven County, North Carolina], 1850 US Federal Census database, population schedule, p. 311B, image 185, Ancestry.com.

35. Franklin, *Free Negro*, 224. Individuals, often paired together, were typically bound for $50 or $100 each on bonds which totaled around $150 or $200. The Craven County records are useful for exploring these. For examples, see *State v. George Bragg*, scire capias (March 1855); *State v. Rove Chance*, scire capias (April 1852); *State v. William Cully*, scire capias (April 1852); *State v. Thomas Fenner*, scire capias (December 1851); *State v. Richard Garner*, scire capias (June Term 1858); *State v. Selvester B. Gaskins*, scire capias (March 1858); *State v. James Gaudett*, scire capias (April 1858); *State v. Elijah George*, scire capias (September 1858); *State v. Zachariah Johnson*, scire capias (March 1850); *State v. David Manly*, scire capias (March 1858); *State v. Jesse Mitchell*, scire capias (March 1851); *State v. William Mitchell*, scire capias (March 1851); *State v. Frederick Moore*, scire capias (March 1855); *State v. Ben Morgan*, scire capias (September 1850); *State v. Frank Pettiford*, scire capias (March 1850); *State v. Israel Pettiford*, scire capias (March 1850); *State v. George Robertson*, scire capias (March 1852); and *State v. Irwin Tyre*, scire capias (December 1851), all in folder "Criminal Actions Concerning Slaves and free Persons of Color, 1840–1849" (broken series), Criminal Actions Concerning Slaves and Free Persons of Color, 1840–1868, Craven County Records, NCDAH).

36. *State v. Jacob Fender*, scire capias (September 1858), in folder "Criminal Actions Concerning Slaves and free Persons of Color, 1840–1849" (broken series), Criminal Actions Concerning Slaves and Free Persons of Color, 1840–1868, Craven County Records, NCDAH.

37. *State v. John Godette* (October Term 1842); and *State v. Farnifold Moore* (March Term 1855), both in Craven County State Docket, 1840–1855, Court of Pleas and Quarter Sessions, NCDAH. *State v. George Bragg*, jury presentment (December Term 1854); and *State v. Thomas Fenner*, jury presentment (June Term 1851), both in folder "Criminal Actions Concerning Slaves and free Persons of Color, 1840–1849" (broken series), Criminal Actions Concerning Slaves and Free Persons of Color, 1840–1868, Craven County Records, NCDAH.

38. *State v. Joseph Banton* (December Term 1850) Craven County State Docket, 1847–1859, Court of Pleas and Quarter Sessions, NCDAH; *State v. Ben Banton* and *State v. Jesse Mitchell,* both in (December Term 1850) Craven County State Docket, 1847–1859, Court of Pleas and Quarter Sessions, NCDAH. "Benjamin Banton" [Craven County, North Carolina], p. 362B, image 289; and "Jesse Mitchell" [Craven County, North Carolina], both in 1850 United States Federal Census database, Ancestry.com.

39. NCDL, *Acts Passed by the General Assembly . . . 1831–32,* 11, https://digital.ncdcr.gov /Documents/Detail/acts-passed-by-the-general-assembly-of-the-state-of-north-carolina -1831-1832/1955766?item=2079344; Edwards, *People and Their Peace,* 72. Milteer, *North Carolina's Free People of Color,* 184.

40. *State v. George Bragg,* handwritten jury presentment and summons; and *State v. George Bragg,* jury presentment (both December Term 1854), both in folder "Criminal Actions Concerning Slaves and Free Persons of Color, 1840–1868," Craven County Records, NCDAH.

41. Gatlin, the son of a financially comfortable ferryman, was not prosecuted. *State v. George Bragg,* handwritten jury presentment and summons; and *State v. George Bragg,* jury presentment (both December Term 1854), both in "Criminal Actions Concerning Slaves and Free Persons of Color, 1840–1868," Craven County Records, NCDAH. "George Gatlin [Craven County, North Carolina]," 1850 US Federal Census database, population schedule, p. 316A, image 194, Ancestry.com.

42. "John Bragg" and "George "Bragg" [New Bern, Craven County, North Carolina], 1850 US Federal Census database, population schedule, p. 277B, image 177, Ancestry.com; *State v. George Bragg,* jury presentment (December Term 1854) and recognizance bond (March 1855), both in folder "Criminal Actions Concerning Slaves and Free Persons of Color, 1840–1868," Craven County Records, NCDAH; "Charles Stanley [New Bern, Craven County, North Carolina]," 1850 US Federal Census database database, population schedule, p. 295A, image 152, Ancestry.com.

Stanly's recently deceased father, John Carruthers Stanly, a free "dark-skinned mulatto," was a respected barber, landlord, and enslaving planter who had blood ties to one of North Carolina's elite political families. He had also been, before some financial reversals in his later years, one of the wealthiest men in Craven County. At his peak, Stanly held one hundred and twenty-seven people in bondage and was worth nearly $70,000. Schweninger, "John Carruthers Stanly and the Anomaly," 159, 161, 165, 170, 171, 182; Bishir, *Crafting Lives,* 45, 70–71; Franklin, *Free Negro,* 140.

43. Schweninger, "John Carruthers Stanly and the Anomaly," 159, 161, 165, 170; Bishir, *Crafting Lives,* 45, 70–71; Franklin, *Free Negro,* 140. At his financial peak, Stanly held one hundred and twenty-seven people in bondage and was worth nearly $70,000, which was an extraordinary fortune for any person in antebellum North Carolina. Schweninger, "John Carruthers Stanly," 171, 182; "Charles Stanley [New Bern, Craven County, North Carolina]," 1850 US Federal Census database database, population schedule, p. 295A, image 152, Ancestry.com; Bishir, *Crafting Lives,* 140, 261–63.

44. Bishir, *Crafting Lives,* 130; *State v. George Bragg,* jury presentment (December Term 1854), recognizance bond (March 1855), and writ of capias (September 1856), all in folder "Criminal Actions Concerning Slaves and Free Persons of Color, 1840–1868," Craven County Records, NCDAH.

45. Bishir, *Crafting Lives,* 123, 140.

46. Bishir, *Crafting Lives,* 10–11.

47. For further study of these family groups, see *State v. Daniel Keese*, jury presentment (December Term 1849); *State v. William Keese*, jury presentment (December Term 1849); *State v. John Moore*, jury presentment (December Term 1849); *State v. Nathan Moore*, jury presentment (December Term 1849); *State v. Baker Moore*, jury presentment (December Term 1849); *State v. Stephen Moore*, jury presentment (December Term 1849); *State v. Alfred Moore*, jury presentment (December Term 1849); *State v. Banton Moore*, jury presentment (December Term 1849); *State v. Frank Pettiford*, jury presentment (December Term 1849); *State v. Israel Pettiford*, jury presentment (December Term 1849); *State v. Rose Pettiford*, jury presentment (September Term 1849); and *State v. Wright Pettiford*, jury presentment (December Term 1849), all in folder "Criminal Actions Concerning Slaves and Free Persons of Color, 1840–1849" (broken series). See also *State v. William Mitchell*, jury presentment (December Term 1850); and *State v. Jesse Mitchell*, jury presentment (December Term 1850), both in folder "Criminal Actions Concerning Slaves and Free Persons of Color, 1850–1852." *State v. William Cully Jr.*, jury presentment (Fall Term 1851); *State v. William Cully Sr.*, jury presentment (Fall Term 1851); *State v. John Godette*, jury presentment (June Term, 1851); *State v. Will Godette*, jury presentment (June Term 1851); and *State v. James Gaudet*, jury presentment (Fall Term 1851), all in folder "Criminal Actions Concerning Slaves and Free Persons of Color, 1851–1856." All three of these folders can be found in Criminal Actions Concerning Slaves and Free Persons of Color, 1840–1868, Craven County Records, NCDAH.

48. White citizens petitioned the assembly for several anti-Black measures in this era. These demonstrated their desire to restrict free people of color in various way, including taxes on "negro mechanics" to discourage competition with white men and colonization to Liberia, "the Abolition and Free Soil States," or "the far West." Others complained that the licensing law was ineffective and that free Black people were a threat to white people's livestock and a negative influence on enslaved laborers. Some free Black people—who were able to—packed up and headed to the North and Midwest rather than face these increased restrictions. For Beaufort County Petition, see Schweninger, *RSFB*, Ser. I, North Carolina, 1850, reel 7, frames 0336–40, 0327–31; and *RSFB*, Ser. I, North Carolina, 1851, reel 7, frames 0371–74. For Sampson County Petition, see Schweninger, *RSFB*, Ser. I, North Carolina, 1852, reel 7, frames 0404–10. Bishir, *Crafting Lives*, 98, 136–45.

49. "Inaugural Address of David S. Reid," in Reid, *Papers of David S. Reid*, 1:275–76.

50. "Allen Keys," "Daniel Keys," and "William Keys" [Craven County, North Carolina], 1850 US Federal Census database, population schedule, p. 346B, image 257, Ancestry.com. *State v. Daniel Keese*, jury presentment (December Term 1849); and *State v. William Keese*, jury presentment (December Term 1849), both in folder "Criminal Actions Concerning Slaves and Free Persons of Color 1840–1849" (broken series), Craven County Records, NCDAH.

51. *State v. Edmund Hill*, scire capias (Fall Term 1859); and *State v. Abner Hill*, scire capias (Fall Term 1859); both in folder "Criminal Actions Concerning Slaves and Free People of Color, 1856–1861," Tyrrell County Records, NCDAH. "Dempsey Bray" [Tyrrell County, North Carolina], p. 18; "Franklin Phelps" [Tyrrell County, North Carolina], p. 69; "Abner Hill" [Tyrrell County, North Carolina], and "Edmund Hill" [Tyrrell County, North Carolina], p. 70, all in 1860 US Federal Census database, population schedule, Ancestry.com. "Franklin Phelps" [Tyrrell County, North Carolina], 1860 US Federal Census database, slave schedule, Ancestry.com. One of the other Hill brothers, nineteen-year-old William,

was also a shingle maker, and there were also white men practicing the trade in their neighborhood. "Burton Cahoon" and "Franklin Cahoon" [Tyrrell County, North Carolina], 1860 US Federal Census database, population schedule, p. 70, Ancestry.com; "Ludford Cohoon [Tyrrell County, North Carolina]," 1850 US Federal Census database, population schedule, p. 361, Ancestry.com; "Lodford Cohoon [Pasquotank County, North Carolina]," 1860 US Federal Census database, population schedule, p. 46, Ancestry.com; Sawyer, *America's Wetland*, 114–15; *State v. Abner Hill*, jury presentment (October Term 1850), in folder "Criminal Actions Concerning Slaves and Free Persons of Color, 1851–1856," Criminal Actions Concerning Slaves and Free Persons of Color, 1840–1868, Tyrrell County Records, NCDAH.

52. *State v. Thomas Fender*, jury presentment; and *State v. Jacob Fender*, jury presentment (both June Term 1858), both in folder "Criminal Actions Concerning Slaves and Free Persons of Color, 1851–1856," Criminal Actions Concerning Slaves and Free Persons of Color, 1840–1868, Craven County Records, NCDAH; "Thomas Fenner" and "Jacob Fenner [Gooding's District, Craven County, North Carolina]," 1860 US Federal Census database, population schedule, p. 14, Ancestry.com.

53. *State v. Thomas Fender*, recognizance bond; and *State v. Jacob Fender*, recognizance bond (both September 1858), both in folder "Criminal Actions Concerning Slaves and Free Persons of Color, 1851–1856," Criminal Actions Concerning Slaves and Free Persons of Color, 1840–1868, Craven County Records, NCDAH.

54. *State v. Wright Pettiford*, scire facias for James G. Gaskins and Joseph Gaskins (December 1849); *State v. Rose Pettiford*, scire facias for Arthur Ipock and John P. Ipock (December 1849); *State v. Frank Pettiford*, scire facias for Edward Ipock, Arthur Gaskins, and Daniel Simmons (December 1849); and *State v. Israel Pettiford*, scire facias for Edward Ipock (December 1849), all in folder "Criminal Actions Concerning Slaves and Free Persons of Color 1840–1849" (broken series), Criminal Actions Concerning Slaves and Free Persons of Color, 1840–1868, Craven County Records, NCDAH.

55. "Rose Pettiford," "Right Pettiford," "Lazarus Ipock," and "James G. Gaskins" [Craven County, North Carolina], 1850 US Federal Census database, population schedule, p. 362A, image 288; "Joseph Gaskins" [Craven County, North Carolina], 1850 US Federal Census database, population schedule, p. 377B, image 319; "Arthur Gaskins" [Craven County, North Carolina], 1850 US Federal Census database, population schedule, p. 378A, image 320; "Israel Pettiford" and "Francis Pettiford" [Craven County, North Carolina], 1850 US Federal Census database, population schedule, p. 346B, image 257; "Arthur Ipock" [Craven County, North Carolina], 1850 US Federal Census database, population schedule, p. 347A, image 258, all on Ancestry.com. Methodologically, it is difficult to understand households's spatial relationships solely via the census records, but I am reading the order in which the households were recorded to reflect some rough proximity.

56. To further complicate these ties between the Ipock and Pettifer families, in May of 1848, Elizabeth Ipock swore an oath that Benjamin Spellman, a free Black man from Beaufort County, was the child's father. The Craven County Court tried to coordinate with the Beaufort County sheriff to take him into custody and ensure that he appeared to answer the charges, but the sheriff could not find him despite several writs over the course of a year. By 1850, Spellman was no longer so elusive: The census shows him as a laborer in the household of Selinah Campen, a white woman in Beaufort County. See writ of capias, in *State v. Elizabeth Ipock* (April 1848); examination of Elizabeth Ipock, in *State [ex relation] Eliz. Ipock v. Benj*

Spellman (May 1848]; and writ of capias, in *State v. Benj'a Spellman* [free negro] (July 1848, January 1849, April 1849, July 1849), all in folder "Bastardy Bonds and Records, 1848–1849," Bastardy Bonds and Records 1846–1878 (broken series), Craven County Records, NCDAH; "Benjamin Spellman" and "Selinah Campen" [South Creek District, Beaufort County, North Carolina], 1850 US Federal Census database, population schedule, p. 432, Ancestry.com.

57. "Right Pettiford" [Craven County, North Carolina], 1850 US Federal Census database, population schedule, p. 362, Ancestry.com; "Peggy Dove," "Eliz. Ipock," and "Emeline Ipock" [New Berne, Craven County, North Carolina], 1850 US Federal Census database, population schedule, p. 582, Ancestry.com. Another Black woman, thirty-six-year-old Elizabeth Hanks, also lived in Dove's house, and it is unclear whether she was a boarder or a relative. See "Eliz. Hanks" [New Berne, Craven County, North Carolina], 1850 US Federal Census database, population schedule, p. 582, Ancestry.com.

58. Jury presentment, in *State v. Wright Pettiford, Elizabeth Ipock* (September Term 1849), in folder "Bastardy Bonds and Records, 1848–1849"; writ of capias, in *State v. Wright Pettiford, Elizabeth Ipock* (February Term 1850), in folder "Bastardy Bonds and Records, 1850–1859," Bastardy Bonds and Records 1846–1878 (broken series), Craven County Records, NCDAH.

59. *State v. John Moore*, jury presentment (December Term 1849), and scire facias for James Harrington and James Toler Jr. (December 1849); *State v. Nathan Moore*, jury presentment (December Term 1849), and scire facias for James Harrington and James Toler Jr. (December 1849); *State v. Baker Moore*, jury presentment (December Term 1849); *State v. Stephen Moore*, jury presentment (December Term 1849) and scire facias for James Harrington and James Toler Jr. (December 1849); *State v. Alfred Moore*, jury presentment (December Term 1849); and *State v. Banton Moore*, jury presentment (December Term 1849), all in folder "Criminal Actions Concerning Slaves and Free Persons of Color 1840–1849" (broken series), Criminal Actions Concerning Slaves and Free Persons of Color 1840–1868, Craven County Records, NCDAH.

60. James Tolar Jr., apprentice bond for John Moore (March 15, 1836); James Tolar Jr., indenture certificate for John Moore (November 15, 1836); James Tolar Sr., apprentice bond for Nathan Moore (November 15, 1836); and James Tolar Sr., indenture certificate for Nathan Moore (November 15, 1836), all in folder "Apprentice Bonds and Records, 1836," Apprentice Bonds and Records, 1832–1840, Craven County Records.

61. Charles Tolar, apprentice bond for Alfred Moore (August 16, 1837); Charles Tolar, indenture certificate for Alfred Moore (August 16, 1837); Charles Tolar, apprentice bond for Joel Moore (August 16, 1837); and Charles Tolar, indenture certificate for Joel Moore (August 16, 1837), all in folder "Apprentice Bonds and Records, 1837," Apprentice Bonds and Records, 1832–1840, Craven County Records.

62. "Stephen Moore" [Craven County, North Carolina], 1850 US Federal Census database, population schedule, p. 376A, image 316; "James Herington" [Craven County, North Carolina], 1850 US Federal Census database, population schedule, p. 377A, image 318; "James Toler Sr." "William Toler," and "John Moore" [Craven County, North Carolina], 1850 US Federal Census database, population schedule, p. 376B, image 317, all on Ancestry.com.

63. Iredell, *North Carolina Reports*, 30:188–89. While Lane was only transporting this pistol, other enslaved people carried them at work, even after the state banned this practice. An enslaved New Hanover County man named Bruce was cutting wood when his pistol,

which he had tucked in his pocket, accidentally fired and mortally wounded him. See Inquest over Bruce, a slave [August 1857], in folder "Coroners' Inquests—1857," Coroners' Inquests, 1768–1880 [broken series], New Hanover County Records.

64. Catterall, *Judicial Cases Concerning American Slavery*, 123. Iredell, *North Carolina Reports*, 30:189.

65. H. Jones, *Reports of Cases at Law . . . 1858–1859*, 6:71.

66. Edwards, *People and Their Peace*, 102.

67. Franklin, *Free Negro*, 191.

68. Franklin, *Free Negro*, 131; NCLP, *Session Laws of North Carolina, 1830–1831* (Ch. VII, Secs. I–II), 11; NCLP, *Session Laws of North Carolina, 1831–1832* (Ch. XXVII, Sec. I), 24. The law also required at least seven justices to approve the evidence of a petitioning peddlers's good character, which itself could have been an insurmountable obstacle. NCLP, *Session Laws of North Carolina, 1831–1832* (Ch. XXVII, Sec. I), 24. Additionally, in 1852, the state legislature came close to completely barring free people of color from peddling anywhere within the state. See Franklin, *Free Negro*, 132.

69. NCLP, *Session Laws of North Carolina, 1855* (Ch. XLIV, Sec. XVII), 108.

70. Franklin, "Free Negro in the Economic Life," 53.

71. Franklin, *Free Negro*, 224. Further, free Black North Carolinians often had little money, which meant that they were often unable to pay fines. As such, the assembly legislated in 1831 that the sheriff would then, "hire out the free person of color, so convicted, to any person, who will pay the fine for his services, for the shortest space of time." Franklin, *Free Negro*, 88–89; Swaim, *North Carolina Justice*, 460.

72. Iredell, *Reports of Cases at Law . . . 1844–1845*, 6:251.

73. Rohrs, "Free Black Experience," 620–21. Kellogg was likely the multiracial wheelwright with $1,500 in property on the 1850 census. His status played a role in his experiences—the town commissioners thought highly enough of his skills to occasionally hire him for public work. "William Kellogg" [Wilmington, New Hanover County, North Carolina], 1850 US Federal Census database, population schedule, p. 891, Ancestry.com; *The Commercial* (Wilmington, NC), January 5, 1850; *Wilmington Journal* (Wilmington, NC), December 24, 1852.

74. De Bow, *Seventh Census of the United States*, 302–3. Using Ancestry.com, records for the following individuals were found in the 1850 US Federal Census database, population schedule, for Craven County, North Carolina: "Benjamin Banton," p. 362B, image 289; "Richd Brown," p. 319B, image 201; "Ezekiel Chance," "Loftin Chance," and "Rufus Chance," p. 308A, image 178; "William Cully," p. 311B, image 185; "John Fenner" and "Thomas Fenner," p. 317A, image 196; "James Godett" and "William Godett," p. 311A, image 184; "John Godet," p. 307B, image 177; "Elijah George" and "Theopilus George," p. 318B, image 199; "George Lewis," p. 318A, image 198; "Willis Lewis," p. 320A, image 202; "Benjamin Morgan," p. 327B, image 219; "Richd Morris," p. 312A, image 186; "Richd Morris Jr.," p. 315A, image 192; "Francis Pettiford" and "Israel Pettiford," p. 346B, image 257; "Right Pettiford," p. 362A, image 288; "George Robeson," page 315A, image 192; and "Jacob Wiggins" and "John R. Wiggins," p. 378A, image 320. "Free Negroes licensed to Keep fire arms" (list), "Free Negroes licensed to carry guns 12 Months" (list), and "The licenses authorizing free Negroes to carry fire arms are for one year" (list), all in folder "Lists of Free Negroes licensed to keep guns, 1851–1854," Slaves and Free Negroes Bonds—Petitions, 1775–1861, Craven County Records, NCDAH.

75. The average numbers of licensees were tabulated using the 392 free Black men on the 1850 census who were between fifteen and sixty-nine years of age. The actual population varied each year but was stable enough over the period to be reliably used here.

76. *State v. Mack Rankin*, jury presentment (1858), in folder "Slaves and Persons of Color, 1842–1858," Miscellaneous Records, 1740–1940, Rowan County Records, NCDAH; *State v. Blake Robbins*, jury presentment (Fall Term 1850), in folder "Slave Papers Civil and Criminal 1850–1859," Slave Records 1739–1864, Perquimans County Records, NCDAH.

77. Craven County Court of Pleas and Quarter Sessions, Minute Book, 1850–1851, p. 83, NCDAH.

78. *State v. John Harriss*, Judge J. Shepherd's report (Spring Term 1859), in folder "Criminal Actions Concerning Slaves and Free Persons of Color, 1859," Criminal Actions Concerning Slaves and Free Persons of Color, 1840–1868, Craven County Records, NCDAH; H. Jones, *Reports of Cases at Law . . . 1858–1859*, 6:448–49.

79. *State v. John Harriss*, Judge J. Shepherd's report (Spring Term 1859), in folder "Criminal Actions Concerning Slaves and Free Persons of Color, 1859," Criminal Actions Concerning Slaves and Free Persons of Color, 1840–1868, Craven County Records, NCDAH); H. Jones, *Reports of Cases at Law . . . 1858–1859*, 6:448–49.

80. H. Jones, *Reports of Cases at Law . . . 1858–1859*, 6:449.

81. H. Jones, *Reports of Cases at Law . . . 1858–1859*, 6:449. In January 1812, Lot Battle placed a notice in the newspaper to complain of the "considerable damage" that he suffered from persons "Hunting, Cutting Timber and in other ways trespassing on his lands." He warned off future trespassers under penalty of the law. The following year, S. Springs and John Lord posted a notice against people hunting, oystering, fishing, or "landing their boats" on land for which they were administrators. In 1814, Lemuel Cotton placed a notice in the *Edenton Gazette* in which he complained that some Edenton residents had, "without liberty or license, taken upon themselves the authority to hunt, drive, pillage, and ransack the neighboring woods, to the great damage of the inhabitants." He added that most of the "adjacent land-holders from the many injuries they have received in their Stock, &c" had already posted against trespassers. In 1832, seven Cumberland County residents forbade "all persons from trespassing on our lands, for the purpose of hunting, gaming, or otherwise, with dogs or guns, by night or by day, under such penalties as the law directs" via a joint advertisement. This was part of some white citizens's growing desire to protect their private property from public use, but it did not develop into a regulation of white people's firearm use, or their mobility, because they were not seen as a threat to the larger community's interest in the same way that people of color were. *Carolina Federal Republican* (Newbern, NC), January 4, 1812; *Wilmington Gazette* (Wilmington, NC), October 2, 1813; *Edenton Gazette* (Edenton, NC), February 18, 1812; *Carolina Observer* (Fayetteville, NC), March 20, 1832.

82. Gross, *What Blood Won't Tell*, 41.

83. Catterall, *Judicial Cases*, 132.

84. Iredell, *Reports of Cases at Law . . . 1848–1849*, 9:384–85. W. Jordan, *White Over Black*, 168.

85. W. Jordan, *White over Black*, 168; Iredell, *Reports of Cases at Law . . . 1848–1849*, 9:384–85, 385. Unsurprisingly, none of these women were listed by name in the *Reports of Cases at Law*.

86. Franklin, *Free Negro*, 35–37.

87. Iredell, *North Carolina Reports . . . 1848–1949*, 265–66. The legal precedent of the "fourth generation inclusive" comes from at least as early as 1777, when it was used to distinguish

"all negroes, Indians, mulattoes, and all persons of mixed blood, descended from negro and Indian ancestors to the fourth generation inclusive" as being "incapable in law to be witnesses in any case whatsoever, except against each other." Before this change, the restrictions extended through to the third generation. See W. Clark, ed., *State Records of North Carolina*, 24:47; and 25:283, 445.

88. Iredell, *North Carolina Reports . . . 1848–1849.* The 1840 census lists the roughly sixty-year-old Dempsey as the head of a household with his wife and six dependents, all of whom were listed as "free colored persons." A decade later, Dempsey's only listed housemate was twenty-six-year-old Zacheus Dempsey, and both men were listed as "mulattos." If Dempsey's wife was legally defined as a free person of color, his children would have been unable to claim whiteness in the same manner that he had attempted. "Whitmill Dempsy" [Bertie County, North Carolina], 1850 US Federal Census database, population schedule, p. 7B, image 20, Ancestry.com.

89. Milteer, *North Carolina's Free People of Color*, 82; Catterall, *Judicial Cases*, 209–10.

90. H. Jones, *North Carolina Reports . . . 1857–58*, 50:25.

91. H. Jones, *Reports of Cases at Law . . . 1857–1858*, 5:12.

92. The trial records noted that "a negro is almost entirely known by his external marks, for example, his colour, his kinky hair, his thick lips . . . the nearer the defendant approached the appearance of a negro in these marks he was consequently by so much the farther from a white person." In antebellum trials "evidence" was given on the defendants's personal appearance, how they comported themselves, as well as how other people treated them. Gross, *What Blood Won't Tell*, 41. See especially the chapters titled "The Common Sense of Race" and "Performing Whiteness."

93. Moore, *History of North Carolina*, 110–11; H. Jones, *North Carolina Reports*, 50:26. If Justice Person sat on Dempsey's trial he might have ruled in his favor, if he accepted that Dempsey had a white female ancestor in each previous generation going back to his great-great-grandparents.

94. H. Jones, *Reports of Cases at Law*, 50:14–15.

95. H. Jones, *North Carolina Reports*, 50:28–29; Milteer, *North Carolina's Free People of Color*, 82–83; *Fayetteville Weekly Observer* (Fayetteville, NC), January 25, 1858. The court noted that there was a difference between a "free negro" and a "free person of color," although these terms were often used interchangeably. All "free negroes" were "free people of color" but not every "free person of color" was a "free negro." Under this framework, the laws directed at free Black people did not necessarily apply to every "free person of color." This tangle of legal and racial identities illustrates how convoluted racial constructions were, even within the constructed racial hierarchy that enslavers built their society on.

96. Catterall, *Judicial Cases*, 226; H. Jones, *North Carolina Reports*, 50:256.

97. H. Jones, *North Carolina Reports* 50:257.

98. Bynum, *Unruly Women*, 41; H. Jones, *North Carolina Reports*, 50:258.

99. J. Taylor, *Revisal of the Laws of the State of North Carolina*, Ch. 1219, Sec. 1; Iredell, *Reports of Cases at Law . . . 1844–1945*, 6:251. Free Black North Carolinians could vote from 1691 until 1715, when the assembly banned them, and then again after the state's constitution was ratified in 1776. The constitution was amended in 1835 when, as Harry Watson explains, many states which had "maintained a complex gradation of political rights based on economic class" came to "impose a radical legal dichotomy based on race and sex." Other historians have noted that some of these free Black property holders continued to do so, and others

were "indignant" when their ballots were refused. H. Watson, *Liberty and Power*, 52–53; Barth, "'Sinke of America,'" 17; Franklin, *Free Negro*, 13, 105–13, 120; Potter, *Laws of the State of North-Carolina*, 1:46; North Carolina, *Journal of the Convention*, Art. I, Sec. 3, § 3; Dodge, "Free Negroes of North Carolina," 22.

100. Franklin, "The Free Negro in the Economic Life," 51–52; Devereux, *Cases Argued and Determined*, 4:220, 343.

101. Moore, *History of North Carolina*, 37, 110; Iredell, *Reports of Cases at Law ... 1844–1845*, 6:252.

102. Iredell, *Reports of Cases at Law ... 1844–1845*, 6:250. Carole Emberton highlights how "the fact that black men were barred from militia duty and restricted in their personal possession of firearms led Taney" to his decision on Black people's rights. Emberton, *Beyond Redemption*, 108.

103. Howard, *Report of the Decision*, 33, 36, 59. During the debates over free Black North Carolinians's voting rights, some opponents argued that "free persons of colour never were considered as citizens, and no one has a right to vote but a citizen." *Newbern Spectator and Political Register* (New Bern, NC), July 3, 1835.

104. Devereux and Battle, *Reports of Cases at Law ... 1838–1839*, 3–4:25.

105. Basdill Thomas Petition (May 24, 1841), in folder "Petition to possess firearms, 1841," Miscellaneous Records, 1769–1929, n.d., Edgecombe County Records, NCDAH. Two of Thomas's supporters, both of whom were white men, can be reliably traced via historical records. William R. Dupree was involved with the Edgecombe County Democratic Party, attending conventions in the late 1830s. He was also likely the "W. R. Dupree," who would have been known locally for his poetry; he penned a patriotic poem, "July the 4th, 1776," which was published in the newspaper about five months after Thomas's application. R. T. Eagles was also active in the Democratic Party, attending a convention in 1841. *Weekly Standard* (Raleigh, NC), March 20, 1839; *Weekly Standard* (Raleigh, NC), May 1, 1839; *Tarboro' Press* (Tarboro, NC), October 2, 1841; *Tarboro' Press* (Tarboro, NC), November 27, 1841.

106. Basdill Thomas Petition (May 24, 1841), in folder "Petition to possess firearms, 1841," Miscellaneous Records, 1769–1929, n.d., Edgecombe County Records, NCDAH.

107. Iredell, *Reports of Cases, 1844–1845*, 250, 253.

108. For Sampson County Petition, see Schweninger, *RSFB*, Ser. I, North Carolina, 1852, reel 7, frames 0404–10.

109. Milteer, *North Carolina's Free People of Color*, 82–83.

110. Franklin, *Free Negro*, 101.

Chapter 5

1. Hal Jones to Cadwallader Jones, January 6, 1861, folder 1B, Cadwallader Jones Papers, 1847–1925, SHC.

2. Bynum, *Unruly Women*, 117.

3. In October 1861, Gen. D. H. Hill called on Craven County enslavers to provide one quarter of their slaves for two weeks of labor on New Bern's defenses. They were so unenthusiastic that Hill's troops threatened to "enforce the requisition," if necessary. Edgecombe County residents were more amenable. "Though less exposed to invasion than Craven" they quickly replied to the general's request and exceeded his quota. *Carolina Observer* (Fayetteville, NC), October 21, 1861.

4. C. J. Cowles to Brother A., November 8, 1863, #654–55, Letter Book K, Calvin J. Cowles Papers, NCDAH; Oakes, *Freedom National*, 402. Enslavers were worried about how the state would treat conscripted workers, as well. The adjutant and inspector general explained that "every effort will be made to induce contentment in the slaves" and that discipline would be "considerate and mild for minor offenses." There was also a mechanism to remove any overseer "who is guilty of cruelty towards them." This was a concern for some enslavers—the *Fayetteville Observer*'s editors reported that they had "unquestionable information from one of the truest men of this county" that a man he enslaved, who had been "conscripted for the work on the defences in this State," had been so badly mistreated that he vowed he would never go back, even if the state authorities killed him. *Western Democrat* (Charlotte, NC), December 13, 1864; *Fayetteville Observer* (Fayetteville, NC), December 29, 1864.

5. NCLP, *Session Laws of North Carolina, 1860–1861* (Ch. XXXIV, Secs. I and II); Franklin, *Free Negro*, 224; NCLP, *Session Laws of North Carolina, 1831–1832* (Ch. XLIV, Sec. I), 34.

6. NCLP, *Session Laws of North Carolina, First Extra Session 1861* (Ch. XIV, Sec. I), 103–4; North Carolina, *Revised Code of North Carolina*, 458.

7. NCLP, *Session Laws of North Carolina, First Extra Session 1861* (Ch. XVIII, Secs. I, II, and III), 107–8.

8. *Daily Register* (Raleigh, NC), July 17, 1861; *Carolina Watchman* (Salisbury, NC), July 4, 1861; *Hillsborough Recorder* (Hillsborough, NC), October 2, 1861. The ban on shooting within the town limits had earlier precedents. People fired guns on "days of public rejoicing" in the era, and this was common enough that it became noteworthy when merrymakers were not shooting. In 1850, Greensboro's David Franklin Caldwell wrote to his son that "our Christmas has been more than usually silent, comparatively little firing of Guns or pistols." The sound of gunfire was part of the background in larger towns, too, even during the war. On Christmas Day, 1865 the Confederate headquarters in Wilmington had to issue a general order to "positively prohibit" revelers from shooting in the town's limits, as "such firing will be looked upon as false alarm." David F. Caldwell to one of his sons, December 27, 1850, folder 4, David Franklin Caldwell Papers, SHC; *Elizabeth-City Star and North Carolina Eastern Intelligencer* (Elizabeth City, NC), February 18, 1832; *Daily North Carolinian* (Wilmington, NC), January 13, 1865.

9. *Daily Progress* (New Bern, NC), August 13, 1861.

10. *Newbern Weekly Progress* (New Bern, NC), August 13, 1861; Rankin, *Continentals*, 8–9; Bowman, "The Virginia County Committees of Safety," 322; Saunders, *Colonial Records of North Carolina*, 9:xxxii; *Carolina Watchman* (Salisbury, NC), July 4, 1861.

11. *Daily Register* (Raleigh, NC), July 17, 1861.

12. Court payment receipt (January Term 1862), in folder "Lenoir County Court Records 1849–1864," Box 2, Waite and Leone Hines Collection, NCDAH.

13. J. S. R. Burwell to George W. Burwell, August 12, 1864, Series 1, Folder 7, George W. Burwell Papers, SHC.

14. *Semi-Weekly Standard* (Raleigh, NC), December 29, 1860; *Fayetteville Semi-Weekly Observer* (Fayetteville, NC), December 27, 1860; John W. Owen to Benson S. Owen, December 20, 1860, in folder "Letters (1859–1862)," A. G. Owen Collection, NCDAH. Larkins's father was William S. Larkins, a New Hanover farmer with real and personal estate worth over $30,000. He also enslaved nineteen people. "Wm. S. Larkins" [New Hanover County, North Carolina], 1860 US Federal Census database, population schedule, p. 904, image

406, Ancestry.com; "Wm. S. Larkins" [New Hanover, North Carolina], 1860 United States Census, slave schedule, Ancestry.com.

15. John W. Owen to Benson S. Owen, December 20, 1860, A. G. Owen Collection, NCDAH; *Daily Herald* (Wilmington, NC), December 27, 1860; Watson, *Wilmington*, 135; William H. Anthon to John W. Ellis, December 10, 1860, in Ellis, *Papers of John W. Ellis*, 2:528n.

16. Enoch Sawyer to unknown (May 10, 1802), in folder "Insurrection among Slaves 1802–1803 (Court Papers)," Slave Records 1759–1864, Perquimans County Records, NCDAH.

17. *Wilmington Journal* (Wilmington, NC), December 27, 1860; John W. Owen to Benson S. Owen, December 20, 1860, A. G. Owen Collection, NCDAH; *Semi-Weekly Standard* (Raleigh, NC), December 29, 1860; William H. Anthon to John W. Ellis, December 10, 1860, in Ellis, *Papers of John W. Ellis*, 2:528–29.

18. *Wilmington Journal* (Wilmington, NC), January 3, 1861; *Daily Herald* (Wilmington, NC), December 27, 1860. The editors also applauded Anthon and Greeley for alerting Governor Ellis to the potential conspiracy, noting that "we ought to give even the Devil his dues." *Wilmington Journal* (Wilmington, NC), January 3, 1861.

19. *Semi-Weekly Standard* (Raleigh, NC), December 29, 1860.

20. *Newbern Weekly Progress* (New Bern, NC), January 8, 1861.

21. "W. A. Blount" [Chocowinity, Beaufort County, North Carolina], 1860 US Federal Census database, population schedule, p. 439, image 437, Ancestry.com. Major William A. Blount's father and namesake also lived in Chocowinity, but was sometimes referred to without rank, although he had attained the rank of general and would have been listed by that honorific, if any. He appears in this second chapter of this work. Cowper, "Sketch of the Life of Judge William B. Rodman," 212; *Weekly Raleigh Register* (Raleigh, NC), June 24, 1857); Federal Writers' Project, *Born in Slavery*, Vol 11, North Carolina Narratives, pt. 1, 113 (David Blount).

22. David Blount remembered the Major as a kind man but his own family life, or lack thereof, suggests otherwise. The Major did not permit his bondpeople to marry and he had one older woman raise all of the enslaved children. As a result, Blount and his brother Johnnie "ain't neber knowed who our folkses wuz." Federal Writers' Project, *Born in Slavery*, Vol 11, North Carolina Narratives, pt. 1, 112–13 (David Blount).

23. Federal Writers' Project, *Born in Slavery*, Vol 11, North Carolina Narratives, pt. 1, 113–14 (David Blount).

24. Federal Writers' Project, *Born in Slavery*, Vol 11, North Carolina Narratives, pt. 1, 114–15 (David Blount).

25. Federal Writers' Project, *Born in Slavery*, Vol 11, North Carolina Narratives, pt. 1, 110 (David Blount); J. G. Hamilton, *History of North Carolina*, 3:21–22; Oakes, *Freedom National*, 208–9. The federal government's early policies did not permit Union troops to interfere with enslaved North Carolinians but by March 1862, those who fled to Gen. Ambrose Burnside's lines found that he would hire them for wages and provide rations. The prospect of ten dollars per month for men and four dollars for women, plus food, was an attractive inducement. Oakes, *Freedom National*, 210, 327.

26. Araminta Tripp Diary, May 16, 1857, Folder 19, Tripp Papers, SHC; William Tripp to Araminta Tripp, January 7, 1862, Folder 4, Tripp Papers, SHC.

27. Joseph B. Morgan to Patrick Morgan, January 28, 1863, Morgan Family Civil War Papers, 1862–1864, Manuscript Collection, VMIA.

28. Joseph B. Morgan to Patrick Morgan, May 16, 1864, Morgan Family Civil War Papers, VMIA.

29. Lee Barfield to Maggie Barfield, February 25, 1864. Typescript of Letterbooks, 1863–1864, 113, in the Barfield Family Collection, HRB. The origin of the name "buffalo" is unclear. It initially applied to the local men who joined the First North Carolina Union Volunteers, whom the Confederates despised, but it was extended to other Unionists. For more on this, see Browning, "'Little Souled Mercenaries'?," 337–40.

30. Tristrim L. Skinner to Eliza Skinner, May 21, 1862, Skinner Family Papers, 1705–1900, SHC; Lee Barfield to Maggie Barfield, February 26, 1863, Typescript of Letterbooks, 1862–1863, 4, Barfield Family Collection, HRB. Tripp's brother, Benjamin, lived nearby—his household was listed directly next to Blount Jr's on the census. See "William A. Blount" [Chocowinity, Beaufort County, North Carolina], 1860 US Federal Census database, population schedule, p. 439, Ancestry.com.

31. *Carolina Observer* (Fayetteville, NC), August 4, 1862. This newspaper article also noted the "stampede" of 100 enslaved Camden County residents and another 500 from Currituck County who fled to the Union lines in Virginia, where "the Yankees find plenty of dirty work" for them. *Carolina Observer* (Fayetteville, NC), August 4, 1862.

32. For Herford County Petition, see Schweninger, *RSFB*, Ser. I, North Carolina, 1861, reel 7, frames 0608–10.

33. Matthews, *Public Laws of the Confederate States of America . . . 1862*, Ch. XLV, Sec. 1. While the law was heavily criticized by some Confederate soldiers and civilians, it did not exempt a substantial number of men from military service. Woodward, *Marching Masters*, 48–52.

34. "Wm. H. Tripp" [Durham's Creek, Beaufort County, North Carolina], 1860 US Federal Census database, p. 423, image 405, Ancestry.com; Barrett, *North Carolina as a Civil War Battleground*, 78; William Tripp to Araminta Tripp, December 11, 1863; May 16, 1863, Folder 4, Tripp Papers, SHC; *Wilmington Journal* (Wilmington, NC), December 17, 1863; Ulysses S. Grant to Henry W. Halleck, January 19, 1864, in Grant, *Ulysses S. Grant*, 1044.

35. William Tripp to Araminta Tripp, May 30, 1863, Folder 4, Tripp Papers, SHC; Manning, "Order of Nature," 110.

36. "Wm. H. Tripp" and "Araminta Tripp" [Durham's Creek, Beaufort County, North Carolina], 1860 US Federal Census database, population schedule, p. 423, image 405, Ancestry. com; Barrett, *North Carolina as a Civil War Battleground*, 78; Manning, "Order of Nature," 110; *Fayetteville Observer* (Fayetteville, NC), December 17, 1863; William Tripp to Araminta Tripp, October 9, 1861, March 15, 1862, December 11, 1863, May 16, 1863, May 30, 1863, Folder 4, Tripp Papers, SHC.

37. McMillen, *Southern Women*, 118. 134; Campbell, "Cultural Politics of Memory"; "Wm. H. Tripp" [Durham's Creek, Beaufort County, North Carolina], 1860 US Federal Census database, population schedule, p. 423, image 405, Ancestry.com; "Wm. H. Tripp" [Richland Township, Beaufort County, North Carolina], 1870 US Federal Census database, population schedule, p. 116, Ancestry.com. For further reading on the challenges that Southern women faced see Faust, *Mothers of Invention*, ch. 2.

38. *Fayetteville Observer* (Fayetteville, NC), December 17, 1863; William Tripp to Araminta Tripp, October 9, 1861, March 21, 1863, Folder 4, Tripp Papers, SHC.

39. William Tripp to Araminta Tripp, January 5, 1863, Folder 4, Tripp Papers, SHC.

40. *New York Times* (New York), November 3, 1864. The price of bacon rose from $0.33 per pound in 1862 to $7.50 by 1865. A bushel of wheat climbed from $3 to $50, and a barrel of flour from $8 to $500. In 1865, salt could sell for $70 a bushel and coffee for $100 per pound. In consequence, people made coffee substitutes from "okra, burnt wheat and sweet potatoes." Lefler and Newsome, *North Carolina*, 434; *New York Times*, December 3, 1861.

41. Stephen Dodson Ramseur to David Poindexter Ramseur, January 28, 1864, in Ramseur, *Bravest of the Brave*, 195–96.

42. J. G. R. Hamilton, *History of North Carolina*, 3:23; *Carolina Observer* (Fayetteville, NC), January 18, 1863; June 9, 1862.

43. *Carolina Observer* (Fayetteville, NC), April 21, 1862. Union troops carried off or destroyed a range of items on the Southern home front. In Jones County they relieved planter Richard Oldfield of all his horses, mules, cows, sheep, and hogs and then "ransacked his house, unlocking every door, trunk and drawer, tearing every thing to pieces, carried off butter, sucked eggs, took the lock off his gun, scattered his powder and carried off his shot, and finally insulted his wife." On the eve of the war Oldfield had $70,000 of real and personal property and enslaved nearly sixty people."R. Oldfield" [Oak District, Jones County, North Carolina], 1860 US Federal Census database, population schedule, p. 482, image 413, Ancestry.com; *Carolina Observer* (Fayetteville, NC), April 21, 1862.

44. William Tripp to Araminta Tripp, March 15, 1862; March 20, 1862; October 14, 1862; November 13, 1862, Folder 4, Tripp Papers, SHC. Tripp's request that Roden prevent people from taking his property highlights some of the cruelty of the system. In the years before the war, Tripp had allowed Roden to raise a hog but when it was butchered, the enslaver took half of the meat for himself. Araminta Tripp Diary, November 17, 1858, Folder 19, Tripp Papers, SHC.

45. William Tripp to Araminta Tripp, January 5, 1863, Folder 4, Tripp Papers, SHC.

46. William Tripp to Araminta Tripp, January 5, 1863, Folder 4, Tripp Papers, SHC. Tripp probably wanted Roden to "hide the gun in his house" because it had been illegal since the 1830s for enslavers to arm their workers. NCLP, *Session Laws of North Carolina, 1831–1832* (Ch. XLIV, Sec. I), 34.

47. Levine, *Confederate Emancipation*, 150–51; Manning, *What This Cruel War Was Over*, 50–51, and 85. James Oakes makes the case that the Lincoln administration's war aims included both national reunion *and* the destruction of slavery from the outset. See Oakes, *Freedom National*; William Tripp to Araminta Tripp, December 28, 1863, Folder 4, Tripp Papers, SHC.

48. William Tripp to Araminta Tripp, January 5, 1863; November 13, 1862, Folder 4, Tripp Papers, SHC.

49. William Tripp Diary, February 25, 1860; March 10, 1860; March 16, 1860; June 30, 1860, Folder 22, Tripp Papers, SHC; and William Tripp Diary, May 14, 1858, July 27, 1858, Folder 21, Tripp Papers, SHC.

50. William Tripp Diary, January 4, 1854, Folder 20, Tripp Papers, SHC; William Tripp Diary, February 13, 1860, March 5, 1860, March 13, 1860, Folder 22, Tripp Papers, SHC; "Harman Blango" [Durhams Creek, Beaufort County, North Carolina], 1860 US Federal Census database, population schedule, p. 845, Ancestry.com; "Rhodan Moore" [Richland Township, Beaufort County, North Carolina], 1870 US Federal Census database, population schedule, p. 48, Ancestry.com.

51. William Tripp Diary, May 3, 1857, June 15, 1857, September 16, 1857, October 24, 1857, Folder 21, Tripp Papers, SHC.

52. "Noah D. Guilford," and "Rebecka Guilford" [Washington, Beaufort County, North Carolina], 1850 US Federal Census database, population schedule, p. 834, Ancestry.com; William Tripp Diary, July 14, 1857, Folder 21, Tripp Papers, SHC.

53. William Tripp Diary, August 7, 1858, August 8, 1858, August 9, 1858, October 24, 1857, Folder 21, Tripp Papers, SHC; William Tripp Diary, October 8, 1854, Folder 20, Tripp Papers, SHC; "Israel Moore" [Durhams Creek, Beaufort County, North Carolina], 1860 US Federal Census database, population schedule, p. 842, Ancestry.com; William Tripp Diary, May 1, 1858, Folder 21, Tripp Papers, SHC.

54. William Tripp Diary, August 1, 1857, September 22, 1857, October 4, 1858, October 5, 1858, Folder 21, Tripp Papers, SHC; Araminta Tripp Diary, October 9, 1857; February 17, 1858, Folder 19, Tripp Papers, SHC.

55. Jury presentment (December Term 1860), in folder "1860"; and Jury presentment (Spring Term 1861), and jury presentment (March Term 1861), both in folder "1861–1867" (broken series), all three documents in Slave Records 1830–1867 (broken series), Beaufort County, NCDAH; William Tripp to Araminta Tripp, November 13, 1862, Folder 4, Tripp Papers, SHC.

56. For further reading on Black people's impact on the Southern home front, see Manning, *What This Cruel War Was Over*.

57. "Wm. H. Tripp," [Durham's Creek, Beaufort County, North Carolina], 1860 US Federal Census database, population schedule, p. 423, image 405, Ancestry.com; W. H. Tripp accounts with Joseph Potts, January, 1858, Box 1, Folder E, William H. and Araminta Guilford Tripp Papers, 1849–1911, JLEC. Enslavers and their bondpeople sometimes grew up together and had complicated interpersonal relationships. These relationships could also be misconstrued by enslavers. A "negro boy," held by a young planter, fatally shot his enslaver and feigned ignorance until some neighbors interrogated him and drew a confession. The newspaper opined, "what renders this act the more extraodinary is that the boy had been brought up in the family with his young master, and might be supposed to have contracted an attachment for him." He apparently shot his enslaver to escape "being punished for some offense." It is difficult to deduce the depth of William Tripp and Roden's relationship, or even how long they knew each other. Regardless, one should remember Jane Turner Censer comment that, "planters' racism and slaves' chattel status combined to encourage emotional distance between master and slave." *Star* (Raleigh, NC), November 2, 1809; Censer, *North Carolina Planters and Their Children*, 141.

58. William Tripp to Araminta Tripp, December 28, 1863, Folder 4, Tripp Papers, SHC; McCurry, *Confederate Reckoning*, 238, 239.

59. Browning, *Shifting Loyalties*, 96, 88.

60. McCurry, *Confederate Reckoning*, 250.

61. Araminta Tripp Diary, December 3, December 15, 1857, Folder 19, Tripp Papers, SHC.

62. William Tripp to Araminta Tripp, August 5, 1864, Folder 4, Tripp Papers, SHC. Mars, a man Tripp enslaved and brought on his deployment, told Tripp that he was opposed to serving in the United States Army. When Mars returned to Fort Fisher after a visit back to the Tripp farm, he told his enslaver that the federal troops were conscripting white and Black North Carolinians, and that he "would die in jail before he would go into the service." William Tripp to Araminta Tripp, January 21, 1863, Folder 4, Tripp Papers, SHC.

63. William Tripp to Araminta Tripp, January 21, 1863, Folder 4, Tripp Papers, SHC; Lee Barfield to Maggie Barfield, February 21, 1863, Typescript of Letterbooks, 1862–1863, 42, Barfield Family Collection, HRB.

64. *Western Democrat* (Charlotte, NC), February 7, 1865.

65. William Tripp to Araminta Tripp, May 30, 1863; August 11, 1863; May 16, 1863, Folder 4, Tripp Papers, SHC.

66. William Tripp to Araminta Tripp, May 16, 1863, Folder 4, Tripp Papers, SHC.

67. *North Carolina Standard* (Raleigh, NC), January 22, 1851.

68. *The Weekly Standard* (Raleigh, NC), October 12, 1864.

69. William Tripp to Araminta Tripp, November 25, 1864, Box 1, Folder A, William H. and Araminta Guilford Tripp Papers, 1849–1911, JLEC. This camp labor came with opportunities for Louis and Mars. In a letter to his wife, Tripp included a few words about Mars, noting that "I suppose he does not want to come home . . . he had rather stay here than at home. Mars has more money than I have, and makes all he wishes to make I don't think he can have less now than 5 or 6 hundred dollars besides he has a fat hog that will sell for 8 or 9 hundred dollars." Mars co-owned this hog with Louis, and its value should be understood in context of the Confederacy's breathtaking inflation. Tripp also added that "Mars is a great soap maker and sells a great deal." William Tripp to Araminta Tripp, November 20, 1864, Folder 4, Tripp Papers, SHC. Mars undertook this business in addition to the labor that Tripp demanded of him—despite his entrepreneurial savvy he was still enslaved. Nevertheless, camp life and the wartime economy provided Mars with greater opportunities than he previously had.

70. Jimerson, *Private Civil War*, 56, 57n; William Calder to Phila Calder, October 29, 1862, Correspondence, 1825–1886, Calder Family Papers, SHC.

71. Federal Writers' Project, *Born in Slavery*, Vol 11, North Carolina Narratives, pt. 1, 288 (Tempie Herndon Durham); Iobst, *Bloody Sixth*, 29, 33.

72. J. M. Worth to Governor Henry T. Clark, June 12, 1862, # 342, Henry T. Clark Letter Book, Part I, North Carolina Governors' Papers, NCDAH. In recognition of this labor's importance, the assembly authorized the salt commissioner to give the recruited or impressed free men of color the "rations and pay of soldiers." This equal pay for white soldiers and free Black laborers is particularly poignant because of the Union Army's initially unequal pay for its Black soldiers. Further emphasizing the importance of salt, the white men at the works were exempted from military duty. North Carolina, *Ordinances and Resolutions* (No. 18, Secs. 1 and 3), 151, 152. For further reading on salt see Lonn, *Salt as a Factor in the Confederacy*; and Powell, *North Carolina through Four Centuries*, 355.

73. Milteer, *North Carolina's Free People of Color*, 194. An officer in the Third North Carolina Regiment demonstrated this view of Black labor—he advertised in a newspaper for "a free negro man, as a waiting man" and added that "Good wages will be paid." *Daily Journal* (Wilmington, NC), April 12, 1862. *Georgia Weekly Telegraph* (Macon, GA) April 3, 1861; Milteer, *North Carolina's Free People of Color*, 2.

74. *Weekly Raleigh Register* (Raleigh, NC), October 16, 1861; *Raleigh Register* (Raleigh, NC), October 23, 1861.

75. *Daily Bulletin* (Charlotte, NC), April 18, 1862; Iredell, *Reports of Cases at Law . . . 1844–1845*, 6:250; *Weekly Raleigh Register* (Raleigh, NC), October 16, 1861.

76. Stephen Dodson Ramseur to David Poindexter Ramseur, April 30, 1864, in Ramseur, *Bravest of the Brave*, 214–15. It is not clear how Ramseur calculated these sums, but the

Confederate Congress' "act to increase the efficiency of the army by the employ of free negroes and slaves," which was approved in mid-February 1864, dictated eleven dollars per month. *Daily Journal* (Wilmington, NC), October 27, 1864.

77. Franklin, *Free Negro*, 93–94; H. Jones, *Reports of Cases at Law . . . 1859–1860*, 7:52–55. Further, in the fall of 1860, Tom, a man enslaved by Jonathan Hall, shot and killed a white man named Alexander Baily at Hall's farm. The coroner's inquest determined that "Tom shot him in self defence." Coroner's report on Alexander Baily (November 1860), in folder "Coroners' Reports—1860–1869" (broken series), Coroners' Inquests, 1794–1892, n.d. (broken series), Perquimans County Records, NCDAH.

78. Singleton, *Recollection of My Slavery Days*, 7–8; "Samuel Hyman" [New Bern, Craven County, North Carolina], 1860 US Federal Census database, population schedule, p. 53, image 108, Ancestry.com; Gerard, *Last Battleground*, 153, 155–56.

79. Singleton, *Recollection of My Slavery Days*, 7–8.

80. *Fayetteville Observer* (Fayetteville, NC), June 30, 1862.

81. Colyer, *Brief Report of the Services Rendered*, 26, 14–15.

82. E. Jordan, *Black Confederates and Afro-Yankees*, 225.

83. Kenzer, *Enterprising Southerners*, 28–29; *Durham Herald-Sun* (Durham, NC), October 8, 1939.

84. Milteer, *Beyond Slavery's Shadow*, 233.

85. *Semi-Weekly Standard* (Raleigh, NC), August 10, 1861.

86. *Semi-Weekly Standard* (Raleigh, NC), August 3, 1861.

87. Gallagher, *Confederate War*, 83–85; Faust, *Mothers of Invention*, 60.

88. Reidy, "Armed Slaves," 276.

89. There is an extensive body of work on African-descended men's military service for European empires throughout the Americas, which spanned from the earliest colonial incursions until the turn of the twentieth century. For further study, see Herman Bennett, *Africans in Colonial Mexico: Absolutism, Christianity, and Afro-Creole Consciousness, 1570–1640* (Bloomington: Indiana University Press, 2003); Peter Blanchard, *Under the Flags of Freedom: Slave Soldiers and the Wars of Independence in Spanish South America* (Pittsburgh: University of Pittsburgh Press, 2008); Roger Buckley, *Slaves in Red Coats: The British West India Regiments, 1795–1815* (New Haven, CT: Yale University Press, 1979); Laurent Dubois, *Avengers of the New World: The Story of the Haitian Revolution* (Cambridge, MA: The Belknap Press of Harvard University Press, 2004); Ada Ferrer, *Insurgent Cuba: Race Nation, and Revolution, 1868–1898* (Chapel Hill: University of North Carolina Press, 1999); John D. Garrigus, "Catalyst of Catastrophe? Saint-Domingue's Free Men of Color and the Battle of Savannah, 1779–1782," *Revista/Review Interamericana* 22, nos. 1–2 (1992): 109–25; Alejandro J. Gomez-del-Moral, "Florida Fallen: The Cuban Negro Militia and the Loss of Spanish East Florida, 1812–1821," *Illes i Imperis* 12 (2009): 19–47; Hendrik Kraay, *Race, State, and Armed Forces in Independence-Era Brazil: Bahia, 1790s–1840s* (Stanford, CA: Stanford University Press, 2001); Jane Landers, *Black Society in Spanish Florida* (Urbana: University of Illinois Press, 1999); Philip D. Morgan and Andrew Jackson O'Shaughnessy, "Arming Slaves in the American Revolution," in *Arming Slaves: From Classical Times to the Modern Age*, edited by Christopher Leslie Brown and Philip D. Morgan (New Haven, CT: Yale University Press, 2006); John Gabriel Stedman, *Stedman's Surinam: Life in an Eighteenth-Century Slave Society*, edited by Richard Price and Sally Price (Baltimore, MD: Johns Hopkins University Press,

1992); Michele Reid, "Protesting Service: Free Black Response to Cuba's Reestablished Militia of Color," *Journal of Colonialism and Colonial History* 5, no. 2 (2004): 1–22; Matthew Restall, "Black Conquistadors: Armed Africans in Early Spanish America," *The Americas* 57, no. 2 (2000): 171–205; David Sartorius, "My Vassals: Free-Colored Militias and the Ends of Spanish Empire," *Journal of Colonialism and Colonial History* 5, no. 2 (2004), https://muse .jhu.edu/article/173274; Ben Vinson III, *Bearing Arms for His Majesty: The Free-Colored Militia in Colonial Mexico* (Stanford, CA: Stanford University Press, 2001); and Peter M. Voelz, *Slave and Soldier: The Military Impact of Blacks in the Colonial Americas* (New York: Garland Publishing, Inc., 1993).

90. Manning, *What This Cruel War Was Over*, 108–9; McCurry, *Confederate Reckoning*, 318, 320–25. It bears noting that initially, Black men were "invited to participate only as inferiors" and the government had to be pushed into offering equal treatment and pay for them. Kantrowitz, *More Than Freedom*, 282–84, 287–94.

91. William Tripp to Araminta Tripp, March 1, 1863, Folder 4, Tripp Papers, SHC. There were other enslavers who were clearly exasperated with the challenges the war presented.

92. *Fayetteville Observer* (Fayetteville, NC), October 24, 1864.

93. John A. Hedrick to Benjamin Sherwood Hedrick, September 7, 1862, Folder 26, Benjamin Sherwood Hedrick Papers, 1843–1890, SHC.

94. Derby, *Bearing Arms*, 162, 167, 168–69.

95. Browning, *Shifting Loyalties*, 96, 99, 133.

96. Myers, *Executing Daniel Bright*, 81.

97. Browning, *Shifting Loyalties*, 96.

98. Myers, *Executing Daniel Bright*, 76–78. Lee Barfield to Maggie Barfield, December 15, 1863, Typescript of Letterbooks, 1862–1863, 104, Barfield Family Collection, HRB. While far beyond the scope of this paper, "Wild's African Brigade" was engaged in counterinsurgent operations during which Wild ordered Confederate guerillas's houses and barns burned, took four women hostage, liberated perhaps as many as 2,500 enslaved people, and executed a man suspected of guerilla activity. Myers's book offers an interesting look at this period in North Carolina history.

99. *Fayetteville Observer* (Fayetteville, NC), December 28, 1863.

100. Redkey, "Henry McNeal Turner," 338–39; Blight, *Race and Reunion*, 147; Cullen, "'I's a Man Now,'" 496–97.

101. Browning, *Shifting Loyalties*, 97, 98; Cecelski, *Waterman's Song*, 180–81.

102. Cecelski, *Waterman's Song*, 180.

103. *Fayetteville Observer* (Fayetteville, NC), March 7, 1864. The newspaper's charge that the Union Army separated Black families via conscription, even if true, is deeply hypocritical when one considers the destruction that the antebellum interstate slave trade wrought on Black families. W. Johnson's *Soul by Soul* offers excellent coverage of this trade.

104. *Fayetteville Observer* (Fayetteville, NC), March 7, 1864. The *Fayetteville Observer* printed inflated casualty numbers: the official reports for enlisted men indicate that at Olustee, the Eighth United States Colored Infantry Regiment lost 48 killed, 180 wounded, and 72 missing; the Thirty-Fifth United States Colored Infantry Regiment (organized as the First North Carolina) had 20 killed, 123 wounded, 77 missing; and the Fifty-Fourth Massachusetts had 13 killed, 62 wounded, 8 missing. In total, there were about 600 killed, wounded, and missing Black soldiers. One of the Thirty-Fifth USCT's casualties was Lt. Col. William N. Reed, who might have been the "highest-ranking black line officer of the Union Army." He

was shot through the lungs during a charge and died shortly after Olustee. Baltzell, "The Battle of Olustee,", 220; Coffman, "'He Has Earned the Right of Citizenship,'" 78; Mildfelt and Schafer, *Abolitionist of the Most Dangerous Kind*, 252–53.

Tripp did not comment on Olustee but he agreed with the *Fayetteville Observer*'s sentiments. He told Araminta about the fighting at Petersburg, stating that "it was the first time Genl Lees army ha [*sic*] had to fight negro troops and it is said the carnage was awful. The negroes came through the breach crying no quarter and remember Ft. Pillow and they got no quarter." He explained that the Confederates "slaughtered them like sheep" at the Crater and only took some prisoner because Lee interfered to save them. William Tripp to Araminta Tripp, August 4, 1864, Folder 4, Tripp Papers, SHC. His accuracy in relaying how the Confederates responded to the Twenty-Eighth US Colored Troops at Petersburg is less important than his clear sentiments on the matter.

105. Dinson A. Caldwell to R. C. Caldwell and M. C. Caldwell (April 10, 1862), Folder B, Box 1, Robert C. Caldwell Collection, East Carolina University Digital Collections.

106. William Tripp to Araminta Tripp, March 1, 1863, November 16, 1864, Folder 4, Tripp Papers, SHC.

107. William Tripp to Araminta Tripp, March 1, 1863, Folder 4, Tripp Papers, SHC; *New York Times* (New York), December 3, 1861.

108. William Tripp to Araminta Tripp, March 5, 1863, Folder 4, Tripp Papers, SHC.

109. William Tripp to Araminta Tripp, February 8, 1863, Folder 4, Tripp Papers, SHC.

110. McPherson, *Battle Cry of Freedom*, 793, 793n; Manning, *Order of Nature*, 116; R. Reid, *Freedom for Themselves*, 156, 159.

111. William A. Biggs to Lucy Biggs, May 3, 1864, in folder "1864–1865," Asa Biggs Papers, RML; Federal Writers' Project, *Born in Slavery*, Vol 11, North Carolina Narratives, pt. 1, 439 (Robert Hinton).

112. The Fifty-Sixth North Carolina Infantry Regiment also rounded up deserters in Randolph, Wilkes, and Yadkin Counties during the autumn of 1863. Newsome, *Fight for the Old North State*, 22–230; Cecelscki, *Fire of Freedom*, 119–20; John Washington Graham to William A. Graham, March 13, 1864, in Graham, *Papers of William A. Graham*, 6:43; Newsome, *Fight for the Old North State*, 174–77, 212.

113. Federal Writers' Project, *Born in Slavery*, Vol 11, North Carolina Narratives, pt. 1, 160–62 (Fanny Cannady).

114. Maj. Gen. Patrick Cleburne to the Commanding General, Corps, Division, Brigade, and Regimental Commanders of the Army of Tennessee, January 2, 1864, in US War Department, *War of the Rebellion*, Ser. I, Volume 52, part II, 590–91. Some historians frame Cleburne's proposal as an exercise in Confederate nationalism, which trumped maintaining the institution of slavery. As Ian Bennington explains, for some Southerners, the "logic of Confederate nationalism, born in a defense of slavery, had paradoxically moved past that defense." Binnington, *Confederate Visions*.

115. Cleburne to the Army of Tennessee, January 2, 1864, in US War Department, *War of the Rebellion*, Ser. I, Vol. 52, part II, 590.

116. Cleburne to the Army of Tennessee, January 2, 1864, in US War Department, *War of the Rebellion*, Ser. I, Vol. 52, part II, 591.

117. Bradley, "'This Monstrous Proposition,'" 153. Gen. Joseph Eggleston Johnston to Lt. Gen. William Hardee, Major Generals Benjamin Cheatham, Thomas Hindman, Patrick Cleburne, Alexander Stewart, William H. T. Walker, Brigadier Generals William Bate and Patton

Anderson, January 31, 1864, in US War Department, *War of the Rebellion*, Ser. I, Vol. 52, part II, 608; Segars and Barrow, *Black Southerners in Confederate Armies*, 22. Jefferson Davis had the same thought, albeit in hindsight. Newspapers noted that as he awaited the bill authorizing Black soldiers, he worried that it might have been more effective if passed earlier in the war. *Hillsborough Recorder* (Hillsborough, NC), March 22, 1865. For more on the Confederacy's discussions on Black soldiers, see Levine, *Confederate Emancipation*.

118. Powell, *North Carolina through Four Centuries*, 300, 368–70; Manning, *Order of Nature*, 110–12, 118–19.

119. *Hillsborough Recorder* (Hillsborough, NC), February 8, 1865.

120. *Semi-Weekly Standard* (Raleigh, NC), December 20, 1864.

121. *Semi-Weekly Standard* (Raleigh, NC), December 20, 1864.

122. *Semi-Weekly Standard* (Raleigh, NC), December 20, 1864; Evans, *Confederate Military History*, 387; *Hillsborough Recorder* (Hillsborough, NC), October 21, 1863.

123. *Hillsborough Recorder* (Hillsborough, NC), February 8, 1865; Evans, *Confederate Military History*, 387; *Hillsborough Recorder* (Hillsborough, NC), October 21, 1863.

124. *Hillsborough Recorder* (Hillsborough, NC), February 8, 1865; Evans, *Confederate Military History*, 387.

125. *Hillsborough Recorder* (Hillsborough, NC), February 8, 1865; and October 21, 1863.

126. Spencer, *Last Ninety Days*, 119.

127. Only about 25 percent of North Carolinians were enslavers, but the state's legislators were far more likely to be. Historian Marc W. Kruman notes that in 1850, the state had a higher percentage of enslavers in its legislature than any of the other states that would later form the Confederacy. This dominance was nonpartisan: 81 percent of the Democrats and 84 percent of the Whigs were slaveholders. Further, while 22 percent of the Democrats and 31 percent of the Whigs were in the legal professions, 63.5 percent of Democrats and 46.5 percent of the Whigs worked in agriculture and of these, 36 percent of the Democrats and 37.5 percent of the Whigs were planters who enslaved twenty or more people. Kruman, *Parties and Politics*, 47, 49. The enslavers's political dominance carried over to the Old North State's secession convention, where one hundred of the one hundred and twenty-two delegates were enslavers and held on average, more than thirty laborers in bondage. That average is inflated by seven delegates who each enslaved more than 100 people (including two who enslaved over two hundred workers). Nevertheless, the median number of enslaved people held by the convention's delegates was still a substantial twenty-one, which set them apart from the vast majority of North Carolinians. Wooster, *Secession Conventions of the South*, 197–98.

128. In November 1864, Jefferson Davis told Congress, "I must dissent from those who advise a general levy and arming of slaves for the duty of soldiers" as he thought it "would scarcely be deemed wise or advantageous by any" as long as there were enough white men to fight. He added however that, "should the alternative ever be presented of subjugation or of the employment of the slave as a soldier, there seems no reason to doubt what should be our decision." Bradley, "Debate on Arming the Slaves," 159. In Davis's view, white soldiers were preferential to Black ones, but national survival was paramount.

129. NCLP, *Session Laws of North Carolina, 1865 Public Laws (adjourned session)* (Ch. XIII, Sec. I), 33.

130. NCLP, *Session Laws of North Carolina, 1865 Public Laws (adjourned session)* (Ch. XIII, Sec. I), 33. Many North Carolinians were following the national discussion closely. Lewis Hanes loaned a copy of Gen. Robert E. Lee's letter "on the subject of arming and freeing the

negroes" to a friend who then let Jonathan Worth borrow it. Hanes wanted the letter back because yet another interested person wanted to read it. It is not clear where Hanes initially acquired the letter, but he explained to Worth that he was "forbidden" from publishing it and requested that those who borrowed it respect that. Lewis Hanes to Jonathan Worth, February 20, 1865, in Worth, *Correspondence of Jonathan Worth*, 353.

131. *Fayetteville Observer* (Fayetteville, NC), March 9, 1865. US War Department, *War of the Rebellion*, Ser. IV, Vol. 3, 1191. North Carolina Congressmen Robert R. Bridgers, Thomas C. Fuller, John A. Gilmer, James M. Leach, James T. Leach, George W. Logan, James G. Ramsay, and William N. H. Smith opposed the legislation. The ninth district's Burgess S. Gaither was the only representative who voted for it. While he was a strong state's rights advocate and worried about "consolidated military despotism," he believed that the national government had the jurisdiction to arm the enslaved men in the Confederacy. *Western Democrat* (Charlotte, NC), August 23, 1864; Warner and Yearns, *Biographical Register of the Confederate Congress*, 93–94.

132. *New York Times* (New York), March 9, 1865.

133. *New York Times* (New York), March 9, 1865.

134. McPherson, *Battle Cry*, 793.

135. *North Carolina Standard* (Raleigh, NC), March 3, 1865; *Conservative* (Raleigh, NC), March 9, 1865; W. A. Graham to unknown recipient, in Spencer, *Last Ninety Days of the War*, 129.

136. McCurry, *Confederate Reckoning*, 347; Leonard, *Men of Color to Arms!*, 15–16.

137. Jimerson, *Private Civil War*, 118.

138. Howell Cobb to James A. Seddon, January 8, 1865, in US War Department, *War of the Rebellion*, Ser. IV, Vol. 3, 1009–10.

139. *Daily North Carolina Times* (New Bern, NC), June 2, 1865; William Tripp to Araminta Tripp, February 8, 1863, Folder 4, Tripp Papers, SHC; McPherson, *Battle Cry*, 793, 793n; Manning, *Order of Nature*, 116.

140. Nichols, *Story of the Great March*, 236–37.

141. Nichols, *Story of the Great March*, 237–38.

142. *Fayetteville Observer* (Fayetteville, NC), October 31, 1864.

143. Berlin, *Generations of Captivity*, 255–56; Cecelscki, *Fire of Freedom*, 80; Browning, *Shifting Loyalties*, 133; R. Reid, "Raising the African Brigade," 266.

144. Schneider, "Institution of Slavery in North Carolina," xii.

145. McPherson, *For Cause and Comrades*, 171–72. "Joseph F. Maids" [White Oak, Jones County, North Carolina], 1860 US Federal Census database, population schedule, Ancestry. com.

Epilogue

1. Browning, "Visions of Freedom and Civilization," 80.

2. *Morning Star* (Wilmington, NC), June 13, 1868.

3. Emberton, *Beyond Redemption*, 147.

4. Giltner argues that in the post war period, hunting became a "growing source of tension between elite whites and former slaves over free blacks' privilege, subsistence, and labor" and further became a venue to profits, as outsiders traveled to the region to hunt and fish. Giltner, *Hunting and Fishing in the New South*, 7, 137–38, 144.

5. North Carolina, *Public Laws of the State of North Carolina . . . 1861–'62–'63–'64, and one in 1859* (Ch. 40, Secs. 2, 15), 99, 104.

6. Federal Writers' Project, *Born in Slavery*, Vol. 11, North Carolina Narratives, pt. 2, 231 (Hattie Rogers), www.loc.gov/item/mesn112/.

7. *Journal of Freedom* (Raleigh, NC), October 7, 1865.

8. *Journal of Freedom* (Raleigh, NC), October 7, 1865; *New Berne Daily Times* (New Bern, NC), October 6, 1865; O'Hara, *Minutes of the Freedmen's Convention*, 17–18.

9. O'Hara, *Minutes of the Freedmen's Convention*, 18.

10. Milteer, *North Carolina's Free People of Color*, 215; Giltner, *Hunting and Fishing in the New South*, 52; Berlin, *Freedom*, 801–2.

11. William A. Graham to Jonathan Worth, January 26, 1866, in Worth, *Correspondence of Jonathan Worth*, 482.

12. Emberton, *Beyond Redemption*, 82; *Daily Herald* (Wilmington, NC), December 30, 1865; Chafe, *Lifting the Chains*, 12.

13. James B. McPherson to Susan Hardin McPherson, August 2, 1868, Hardin and McPherson Family Papers, HRB.

14. *Newbern Daily Times*, evening edition (New Bern, NC), May 26, 1866. For an additional example, see also *Daily Herald* (Wilmington, NC), January 12, 1866.

15. *Newbern Daily Times* (New Bern, NC), May 26, 1866.

16. Iredell, *Reports of Cases at Law . . . 1844–1845*, 6:250, 252; *Newbern Daily Times*, evening edition (New Bern, NC), May 26, 1866.

17. *Newbern Daily Times* (New Bern, NC), May 26, 1866.

18. *Newbern Daily Times* (New Bern, NC), May 26, 1866; *Wilmington Post* (Wilmington, NC), December 17, 1867.

19. *Daily Herald* (Wilmington, NC), January 24, 1866.

20. *Daily North Carolina Standard* (Raleigh, NC), June 8, 1865; *Wilmington Herald* (Wilmington, NC), October 31, 1865; *Daily Standard* (Raleigh, NC), January 13, 1866; *Daily Dispatch* (Wilmington, NC), February 24, 1866.

21. *Daily Dispatch* (Wilmington, NC), October 25, 1866; *Daily Sentinel* (Raleigh, NC), May 8, 1866.

22. *Daily Dispatch* (Wilmington, NC), October 25, 1866; *Daily Sentinel* (Raleigh, NC), May 8, 1866.

23. *Daily Sentinel* (Raleigh, NC), May 8, 1866.

24. *Newbern Daily Times* (New Bern, NC), January 20, 1866; *Daily Dispatch* (Wilmington, NC), November 14, 1866.

25. *Daily Standard* (Raleigh, NC), January 25, 1870; *Eagle* (Fayetteville, NC), January 20, 1870; *Morning Star* (Wilmington, NC), May 7, 1868. *Patriot and Times* (Greensboro, NC), January 28, 1869; *Daily Charlotte Observer* (Charlotte, NC), July 8, 1879; *Asheville Daily Citizen* (Asheville, NC), May 7, 1898.

26. *Tarboro' Southerner* (Tarboro, NC), September 24, 1868; *American* (Statesville, NC), October 11, 1869.

27. *New-Berne Daily Times* (New Bern, NC), August 19, 1869.

28. *Newbern Daily Journal of Commerce* (New Bern, NC), February 19, 1867; *Wilmington Post* (Wilmington, NC), December 17, 1867. The newspaper went further than suggesting that these criminals opposed "the Union cause," and charged that the "men who blacked their

faces" to commit depredations were Confederate veterans. *Daily North-Carolina Standard* (Raleigh, NC), January 28, 1868.

29. *Tri-Weekly Standard* (Raleigh, NC), May 5, 1866; *Fayetteville News* (Fayetteville, NC), May 8, 1866; *Tarboro' Southerner* (Tarboro, NC), June 30, 1870.

30. Zipf, "'Whites Shall Rule the Land or Die,'" 504; Rohrs, "The Free Black Experience," 619.

31. *Morning Star* (Wilmington, NC), April 23, 1868.

32. *Morning Star* (Wilmington, NC), April 10, 1868.

33. Zipf, "'Whites Shall Rule the Land or Die,'" 500, 534–25, 526.

34. North Carolina, *Constitution of the State of North-Carolina . . . 1868*, 37. Though this project is interested in the nonmilitary application of Black people's arms use, several scholars have examined Black militia units's importance to their communities during Reconstruction, as they could, at least in some instances, deter white people's aggressions and provide safeguards against abusive employers. Emberton, *Beyond Redemption*, 88–90.

35. North Carolina, *Constitution of the State of North-Carolina . . . 1868*, 27–28.

36. Beckel, *Radical Reform*, 64–65; Bradley David Proctor, "Whip Pistol, and Hood," 249; US Congress, Joint Select Committee, *TestimonyTaken*, 169.

37. *Daily Journal* (Wilmington, NC), April 19, 1868.

38. Federal Writers' Project, *Born in Slavery*, Vol. 11, North Carolina Narratives, pt. 1, 144–45 (W. L. Bost).

39. Proctor, "Whip, Pistol, and Hood," 1–3, 323–24; US Congress, Joint Select Committee, *Testimony Taken*, 15–16, 64, 74, 87–90. White extremists' rape and brutality against Black women during Reconstruction is an often underrecognized but important aspect of the era's violence. For further reading, see Rosen, *Terror in the Heart of Freedom*.

40. Proctor, "Whip, Pistol, and Hood," 213–14. US Congress, Joint Select Committee, *Testimony Taken*, 169.

41. Rosen, *Terror in the Heart of Freedom*, 180–82; Proctor, "Whip, Pistol, and Hood," 214, 214 n620; US Congress, Joint Select Committee, *Testimony Taken*, 138. While he cannot be traced in the 1870 census, Watts was still living in Cleveland County a decade later with his wife and nine children, four of whom would have been around at the time of the joint select committee's hearing. "Jonas Watts" [Township No 3, Cleveland County, North Carolina], 1880 US Federal Census database, population schedule, p. 494, image 22, Ancestry.com.

42. *Semi-Weekly Sentinel* (Raleigh, NC), August 22, 1868; *Wilmington Journal* (Wilmington, NC), August 28, 1868.

43. Frank and John were not the only Black men who rejected the Union League. Anderson Buxton, a "colored" man from Elizabethtown, announced his withdrawal from the organization in the newspaper, blasting it as controlling Black voters's political power, when he believed that their interests were more closely aligned with Southern white people. *Wilmington Journal* (Wilmington, NC), August 28, 1868.

44. Prather, *We Have Taken a City*, 34–35, 51–54, 57; Umfleet, *Day of Blood*, 22.

45. Honey, "Class, Race, and Power,", 169–70; Umfleet, *Day of Blood*, 38–44. For example, the *Wilmington Messenger* printed an anecdotal list of crimes from around the state in an effort to create a theme of Black violence. On the same page it complained that "we do not doubt that every negro in Wilmington who possesses a pistol or weapon of any kind, makes it his daily companion, and he is ready for 'a rucus' at any hour." In yet another report on this

page, it lamented the insults "black brutes" allegedly offered white women and noted that "these are the rascals that will precipitate a race war probably if any occurs." The stage was primed for violence. *Wilmington Messenger* (Wilmington, NC), November 4, 1898.

46. *County Union* (Dunn, NC), October 26, 1898.

47. *County Union* (Dunn, NC), October 26, 1898.

48. Prather, *We Have Taken a City*, 82–85, 96; *Semi-Weekly Messenger* (Wilmington, NC), November 8, 1898. At this speech, Tillman explained that in his native South Carolina, white people dominated despite being a minority and added that "he could not conceive anything short of idiocy" in white North Carolinians as to why they had not managed to do the same despite having a majority. *Fayetteville Observer* (Fayetteville, NC), October 22, 1898.

49. Umfleet, *Day of Blood*, 114, 183; *Semi-Weekly Landmark* (Statesville, NC), October 11, 1898; Prather, *We Have Taken a City*, 101.

50. Prather, *We Have Taken a City*, 95, 99. The story of the Wilmington massacre and municipal coup d'état is much bigger than can be told here. For further reading, see Prather, *We Have Taken a City*; Cecelski and Tyson, *Democracy Betrayed*; Umfleet, *Day of Blood*; and Zucchino, *Wilmington's Lie*.

51. Prather, *We Have Taken a City*, 98–105, 112–15, 119–30.

52. *Journal* (Winston-Salem, NC), November 10, 1898; Prather, *We Have Taken a City*, 119–20, 132–35, 137, 147–48; Umfleet, *Day of Blood*, 102–4, 113–19.

53. Corey Townsend, "Woman Who Called the Cops on Oakland, Calif., Family Becomes Viral Meme," *The Root*, May 15, 2018, www.theroot.com/woman-who-called-the-cops-on-oakland-family-becomes-vir-1826029582; Cydney Henderson, "Hampton Inn Worker Fired for Calling Cops on Black Guests; Police Open 'Internal Investigation,'" *USA Today*, June 30, 2020, www.usatoday.com/story/travel/news/2020/06/29/hampton-inn-employee-fired-calling-cops-black-family-pool/3281804001/; Maya Eliahou and Christine Zdanowicz, "A White Woman Allegedly Hit a Black Teen, Used Racial Slurs and Told Him to Leave a Pool. Then She Bit a Cop," *CNN*, June 29, 2018, www.cnn.com/2018/06/29/us/pool-patrol-paula-south-carolina-trnd/index.html; Luz Pena, "'I Am Deeply Sorry': Woman Who Called Police on San Francisco Man Stenciling 'Black Lives Matter' on His Property Apologizes," *ABC 7 Los Angeles*, June 14, 2020, https://abc7.com/society/woman-who-called-police-on-man-stenciling-blm-apologizes-/6247524/; Niraj Chokshi, "White Woman Nicknamed 'Permit Patty' Regrets Confrontation Over Black Girl Selling Water," *New York Times*, June 25, 2018, www.nytimes.com/2018/06/25/us/permit-patty-black-girl-water.html; Jonah E. Bromwich, "Amy Cooper, Who Falsely Accused Black Bird-Watcher, Has Charge Dismissed," *New York Times*, February 16, 2021, www.nytimes.com/2021/02/16/nyregion/amy-cooper-charges-dismissed.html; Cleve R. Wootson Jr., "A Black Yale Student Fell Asleep in Her Dorm's Common Room. A White Student Called Police," *Washington Post*, May 11, 2018, www.washingtonpost.com/news/grade-point/wp/2018/05/10/a-black-yale-student-fell-asleep-in-her-dorms-common-room-a-white-student-called-police/.

54. For Newcastle County Petition, see Schweninger, *RSFB*, Ser. I, Delaware, 1831, reel 2, frame 00281–82.

55. Goff et al. "Essence of Innocence," 526–45; T. Rees Shapiro, "Study: Black Girls Viewed as 'Less Innocent' Than White Girls,'" *Washington Post*, June 27, 2017, www.washingtonpost.com; Rebecca Epstein et al., "Childhood Interrupted: The Erasure of Black Girls' Childhood," Georgetown Law Center for Poverty and Inequality, 2017, www.law.georgetown.edu/poverty-inequality-center/wp-content/uploads/sites/14/2017/08

/girlhood-interrupted.pdf; Monica Rhor, "Pushed Out and Punished: One Woman's Story Shows How Systems Are Failing Black Girls," *USA Today*, May 14, 2019, www.usatoday.com /in-depth/news/nation/2019/05/13/racism-black-girls-school-discipline-juvenile -court-system-child-abuse-incarceration/3434742002/; A. J. Willingham, "Study: We Think Black Men Are Bigger Than White Men (Even When They're Not)," CNN, March 14, 2017, www.cnn.com/2017/03/13/health/black-men-larger-study-trnd/index.html; Skinner and Haas, "Perceived Threat"; Anderson, *Second*, 157–58; Bristow, *Steeped in the Blood of Racism*, 192.

56. WDTN.com Staff, "Memorial March, Vigil Held for John Crawford III," *WDTN-TV*, August 19, 2020, www.wdtn.com/news/a-conversation-for-change/memorial-march-vigil -held-for-john-crawford-iii/; Associated Press, "John Crawford III Case: Feds Announce No Charges for Officer in Fatal 2014 Shooting," *NBC News*, July 12, 2017, www.nbcnews.com /news/us-news/john-crawford-iii-case-feds-announce-no-charges-officer-fatal-n782091; Mark Gokavi, "Walmart: 911 Caller 'Intentionally Lied to Police' in Crawford Shooting," *Dayton Daily News*, June 13, 2019, www.daytondailynews.com; Jessie Balmert, "At Issue: Open Carrying Guns," *Bucyrus Telegraph Forum*, July 26, 2014, www.portclintonnewsherald .com.

57. WDTN.com Staff, "Memorial March, Vigil"; Associated Press, "John Crawford III Case"; Gokavi, "Walmart: 911 Caller."

58. Sharon LaFraniere and Mitch Smith, "Philando Castile Was Pulled Over 49 Times in 13 Years, Often for Minor Infractions," *New York Times*, July 16, 2016, www.nytimes.com /2016/07/17/us/before-philando-castiles-fatal-encounter-a-costly-trail-of-minor-traffic -stops.html.

59. BBC Staff, "Philando Castile Death: Police Footage Released," *BBC News*, June 21, 2017, www.bbc.com/news/world-us-canada-40357355; Mark Berman, "What the Police Officer Who Shot Philando Castile Said About the Shooting," *Washington Post*, June 21, 2017, www.washingtonpost.com/news/post-nation/wp/2017/06/21/what-the-police-officer -who-shot-philando-castile-said-about-the-shooting/.

60. Colby Itkowitz, "Guns Are All Over GOP Ads and Social Media, Prompting Some Criticism," *Washington Post*, May 31, 2022, www.washingtonpost.com/politics/2022/05/31 /republicans-guns-ads-posts/; Katie Glueck et al., "In More Than 100 G.O.P. Midterm Ads This Year: Guns, Guns, Guns," *New York Times*, May 25, 2022. January 12, 2024, www.nytimes.com/2022/05/25/us/politics/republicans-campaign-guns.html. While this is most often undertaken by Republican candidates, some Democrats have engaged in it as well, particularly those moderate or conservative Democrats who are running in competitive districts. Joe Perticone, "Democrats in Red States Have Started Using Guns in Campaign Ads," *Business Insider*, September 11, 2018, www.businessinsider.com /democrats-using-guns-in-campaign-ads-2018-9.

61. Emily Sullivan, "Police Fatally Shoot Black Security Guard Who Detained Shooting Suspect," *NPR*, November 13, 2018, www.npr.org/2018/11/13/667252788/police-fatally -shoot-black-security-guard-who-detained-suspected-shooter; Jim Williams, "One Year After Security Guard Jemel Roberson Was Shot Dead by Midlothian Police, Family Wants to Know Why Officer Hasn't Been Charged," *CBS Chicago*, November 11, 2019, https://chicago .cbslocal.com/2019/11/11/one-year-after-security-guard-jemel-roberson-was-shot-dead-by -midlothian-police-family-wants-to-know-why-officer-hasnt-been-charged/; Jermont Terry, "Family of Jemel Roberson, Security Guard Shot Dead by Midlothian Officer, Receives

$7.5M Settlement—but Mother Says Justice Hasn't Been Served," *CBS News Chicago*, July 13, 2022, www.cbsnews.com/chicago/news/family-of-jemel-roberson-security-guard-shot-dead-by-midlothian-officer-receives-7-5m-settlement/.

62. Eliott C. McLaughlin, "Family Sues Hoover, Alabama, and the Officer Who Killed Emantic Bradford Jr. at a Mall on Thanksgiving," *CNN*, November 25, 2019, www.cnn.com/2019/11/25/us/alabama-mall-shooting-lawsuit-hoover-emantic-bradford/index.html.

63. Noah, "Emantic Bradford Jr.'s Death"; Luke Darby, "Trevor Noah: 'The Second Amendment Is Not Intended for Black People,'" *GQ*, November 28, 2018, www.gq.com/story/trevor-noah-second-amendment-not-for-black-people.

64. Anderson, *Second*, 9, 161.

65. Justin McFarlin, "I'm a Licensed Gun Owner but I Haven't Carried in Years. Why? I'm Black and I'm Scared," *USA Today*, September 9, 2020, www.usatoday.com/story/opinion/policing/2020/09/09/guns-white-privilege-dangerous-for-black-veteran-like-me-column/5738354002/; Lois Beckett, "Armed Protesters Demonstrate Against Covid-19 Lockdown at Michigan Capitol," *Guardian*, April 30, 2020, www.theguardian.com/us-news/2020/apr/30/michigan-protests-coronavirus-lockdown-armed-capitol.

66. McFarlin, "I'm a Licensed Gun Owner"; Todd Richmond, "Kyle Rittenhouse, Charged in Kenosha Protest Shootings, Returns to Court," *NBC Chicago*, March 10, 2021, www.nbcchicago.com/news/local/kyle-rittenhouse-charged-in-kenosha-protest-shootings-returns-to-court/2458192/; Phil Helsel, "Kyle Rittenhouse, Charged with Killing 2 Kenosha Protestors, Extradited to Wisconsin," *NBC News*, October 20, 2020, www.nbcnews.com/news/us-news/kyle-rittenhouse-charged-killing-2-kenosha-protesters-extradited-wisconsin-n1245579; Brakkton Booker, "Kyle Rittenhouse, Accused Kenosha Killer, Won't Face Gun Charges In Illinois," *NPR*, October 14, 2020, www.npr.org/sections/live-updates-protests-for-racial-justice/2020/10/14/923643265/kyle-rittenhouse-accused-kenosha-killer-wont-face-gun-charges-in-illinois; Anderson, *Second*, 159–60; Jemima McEvoy, "Virginia Cop Fired after Donating $25 to Kyle Rittenhouse Defense with Note: 'You've Done Nothing Wrong,'" *Forbes*, April, 21, 2021, www.forbes.com/sites/jemimamcevoy/2021/04/21/virginia-cop-fired-after-donating-25-to-kyle-rittenhouse-defense-with-note-youve-done-nothing-wrong/; Jemina McEvoy, "Kyle Rittenhouse Defense Fund Raising Hundreds of Thousands of Dollars Ahead of His November Murder Trial," *Forbes*, June 21, 2021, www.forbes.com/sites/jemimamcevoy/2021/06/21/kyle-rittenhouse-defense-fund-raising-hundreds-of-thousands-of-dollars-ahead-of-his-november-murder-trial/. Much evidence of the support for Rittenhouse came from a data breach at the Christian crowdfunding site GiveSendGo, which released the emails associated with the donations. Without it, much of this support would have remained anonymous. Jason Wilson, "US Police and Public Officials Donated to Kyle Rittenhouse, Data Breach Reveals," *Guardian*, April 16, 2021, www.theguardian.com/us-news/2021/apr/16/us-police-officers-public-officials-crowdfunding-website-data-breach.

67. Associated Press, "Armed Bystanders Watch Floyd Protesters in Crown Point: 'They Have a Right to Do That,'" *Chicago Tribune*, June 5, 2020, www.chicagotribune.com; Adrian Horton, "Hundreds of Armed Counter-Protesters Confront Black Lives Matter Rally in Ohio," *Guardian*, June 18, 2020, www.theguardian.com/us-news/2020/jun/18/hundreds-armed-counter-protesters-confront-black-lives-matter-event-bethel-ohio; Russ Bynum,

"At RNC, GOP Echoes Racial Code of Nixon's 1968 Campaign," *AP News*, August 27, 2020, https://apnews.com; Bristow, *Steeped in the Blood*, 40–41, 52–55, 165, 191–92.

68. Anestis, *Guns and Suicide*, 42–44; Max Fisher and Josh Keller, "Why Does the US Have So Many Mass Shootings? Research is Clear: Guns," *New York Times*, November 7, 2017, www.nytimes.com/2017/11/07/world/americas/mass-shootings-us-international .html; Roni Caryn Rabin, "'How Did We Now Know?' Gun Owners Confront a Suicide Epidemic," *New York Times*, November 17, 2020, www.nytimes.com/2020/11/17/health /suicide-guns-prevention.html; Jacqueline Stenson, "Handgun Ownership Is a 'Major Risk Factor' for Suicide," *NBC News*, June 3, 2020, www.nbcnews.com/health/mental-health /handgun-ownership-major-risk-factor-suicide-n1223666.

Bibliography

Primary Sources

MANUSCRIPT AND MICROFILM COLLECTIONS

Georgia

Hargrett Rare Book and Manuscript Library, University of Georgia, Athens, GA
 Barfield Family Collection
  Typescript of Letterbooks, 1862–1863
  Typescript of Letterbooks, 1863–1864
 Hardin and McPherson Family Papers

Michigan

William L. Clements Library, University of Michigan, Ann Arbor, MI
 Henry Clinton Papers

North Carolina

David M. Rubenstein Rare Book and Manuscript Library, Duke University, Durham, NC
 Asa Biggs Papers
 Bryant Bennett Papers
Joyner Library Special Collections, East Carolina University, Greenville, NC
 Robert C. Caldwell Collection (East Carolina University Digital Collections)
 William H. and Araminta Guilford Tripp Papers, 1849–1911
Louis Round Wilson Library, University of North Carolina, Chapel Hill, NC
 Southern Historical Collection
  Benjamin Sherwood Hedrick Papers
  Cadwallader Jones Papers
  Calder Family Papers
  David Franklin Caldwell Papers
  George W. Burwell Papers
  Pettigrew Family Papers
  Phillip Northern Bray Account Books
  Skinner Family Papers
  William Henry Tripp and Araminta Guilford Tripp Papers
North Carolina Department of Archives and History, Raleigh, NC
 A. G. Owen Collection
  Unpublished County Records
   Civil Action Papers, Randolph County
   Coroners' Inquests, Craven County Records
   Coroners' Inquests, New Hanover County Records

Craven County Court of Pleas and Quarter Sessions Minutes
Criminal Action Papers, Craven County
Criminal Action Papers, Montgomery County
Criminal Action Papers, New Hanover County
Criminal Action Papers Concerning Slaves, Richmond County
Criminal Actions Concerning Slaves, Chowan County
Criminal Actions Concerning Slaves, Gates County
Criminal Actions Concerning Slaves and Free People of Color, Craven County
Criminal Actions Concerning Slaves and Free People of Color, New Hanover
Criminal Actions Concerning Slaves and Free People
    of Color, Randolph County
Criminal Actions Concerning Slaves and Free People of Color, Tyrrell County
General Assembly Session Records
Miscellaneous Records, Brunswick County Records
Miscellaneous Records, Randolph County Records
Miscellaneous Slave Records, Chowan Country
Miscellaneous Slave Records, Gates County
Miscellaneous Slave Records, Northampton County
Pasquotank County, State Docket, Court of Pleas and Quarter Sessions
Records of Slaves and Free Persons of Color, New Hanover County
Records of Slaves and Free Persons of Color, Wayne County
Richmond County, State Trial Docket, Superior Court
Slave Records, Perquimans County
Slaves and Free Negroes Bonds-Petitions, Craven County

Calvin J. Cowles Papers
James Gray Blount Papers
North Carolina Governors' Papers
  David Settle Reid Papers
  Edward B. Dudley Papers
  Henry T. Clark Papers
  John M. Morehead Papers
  John W. Ellis Papers
  Montford Stokes Papers
  Thomas Bragg Papers
Wait and Leone Hines Collection

Virginia
Virginia Military Institute Archives, the Virginia Military Institute, Lexington, VA
  Morgan Family Civil War Papers

Washington, DC
Library of Congress
  Works Progress Administration
    Federal Writers' Project
      Born in Slavery: Slave Narratives from the Federal Writers' Project, 1936 to 1938

Online Collections

Ancestry.com

1810 United States Federal Census [database online, www.ancestry.com/search /collections/7613/]

1820 United States Federal Census [database online, www.ancestry.com/search /collections/7734/]

1830 United States Federal Census [database online, www.ancestry.com/search /collections/8058/]

1840 United States Federal Census [database online, www.ancestry.com/search /collections/8057/]

1850 United States Federal Census [database online, www.ancestry.com/search /collections/8054/]

1860 United States Federal Census [database online, www.ancestry.com/search /collections/7667/]

1870 United States Federal Census [database online, www.ancestry.com/search /collections/7163/]

1880 United States Federal Census [database online, www.ancestry.com/search /collections/6742/]

Documenting the American South, University of North Carolina at Chapel Hill

Colonial and State Records of North Carolina, www.docsouth.unc.edu/csr /index.php/volumes

Colonial Records, 1622–1776 (vols. 1–10)

State Records 1776–1790 (vols. 11–22)

North Carolina Digital Collections (https://digital.ncdcr.gov)

North Carolina Legislative Publications

Session Laws, 1777–present, https://digital.ncdcr.gov/documents?filter_17 =Session%20laws--North%20Carolina&applyState=true

NEWSPAPERS AND PERIODICALS

Albany Advertiser (Albany, NY)

Alexandria Gazette (Alexandria, VA)

American (Statesville, NC)

American Advocate (Kinston, NC)

Argus (Frankfort, KY)

Asheville Daily Citizen (Asheville, NC)

Baltimore Patriot and Mercantile Advertiser (Baltimore, MD)

Carolina Federal Republican (New Bern, NC)

Carolina Observer (Fayetteville, NC)

Carolina Sentinel (New Bern, NC)

Carolina Watchman (Salisbury, NC)

Charleston Mercury (Charleston, SC)

Charlotte Democrat (Charlotte, NC)

City Gazette and Commercial Daily Advertiser (Charleston, SC)

Columbian Register (New Haven, CT)

Commercial Bulletin and Missouri Literary Register (St. Louis, MO)

County Union (Dunn, North Carolina)

Daily Bulletin (Charlotte, NC),

Daily Charlotte Observer (Charlotte, NC)

Daily Dispatch (Wilmington, NC)

Daily Herald (Wilmington, NC)

Daily Journal (Wilmington, NC)

Daily National Intelligencer (Washington, DC)

Daily National Journal (Washington, DC)

Daily North-Carolina Standard (Raleigh, NC)

Daily North Carolina Times (New Bern, NC)

Daily North Carolinian (Wilmington, NC)

Daily Progress (New Bern and Raleigh, NC)

Daily Register (Raleigh, NC)

Daily Sentinel (Raleigh, NC)

Daily Standard (Raleigh, NC)

Democratic Press (Raleigh, NC)

Eagle (Fayetteville, NC)

Edenton Gazette (Edenton, NC)

Elizabeth-City Star and North Carolina Eastern Intelligencer (Elizabeth City, NC)

Emancipator and Republican (Boston, MA)

Evening Post (New York, NY)

Fayetteville News (Fayetteville, NC)

Fayetteville Observer (Fayetteville, NC)

Fayetteville Semi-Weekly Observer (Fayetteville, NC)

Fayetteville Weekly Observer (Fayetteville, NC)

Greensborough Patriot (Greensboro, NC)

Hampden Journal and Advertiser (Springfield, MA)

Hillsborough Recorder (Hillsborough, NC)

Iredell Express (Statesville, NC)

Journal (Charlotte, NC)

Journal (Winston-Salem, NC)

Journal of Freedom (Raleigh, NC)

Lowell Daily Citizen and News (Lowell, MA)

Massachusetts Spy (Worcester, MA)

Mississippian (Jackson, MS)

Morning Star (Wilmington, NC)

Newbern Daily Journal of Commerce (New Bern, NC)

Newbern Daily Times (New Bern, NC)

New-Berne Daily Times (New Bern, NC)

Newbern Sentinel (New Bern, NC)

Newbern Spectator, and Literary Journal (New Bern, NC)

Newbern Spectator, and Political Register (New Bern, NC)

Newbern Weekly Progress (New Bern, NC)

Newburyport Herald (Newburyport, MA)

New England Farmer (Boston, MA)

New England Palladium (Boston, MA)

New Era and Commercial Advertiser (New Bern, NC)

New York Times (New York, NY)

North-Carolina Free Press (Tarborough, NC)

North Carolina Sentinel (New Bern, NC)

North Carolina Sentinel and Newbern Commercial, Agricultural and Literary Intelligencer (New Bern, NC)

North Carolina Spectator and Western Advertiser (Rutherfordton, NC)

North Carolina Standard (Raleigh, NC)

North-Carolina Star (Raleigh, NC)

North-Carolinian (Fayetteville, NC)

North State Whig (Washington, NC)

Observer and Telegraph (Hudson, OH)

Patriot and Times (Greensboro, NC)

People's Press (Salem, NC)

Plain Dealer (Cleveland, OH)

Raleigh Register (Raleigh, NC)

Raleigh Register, and North-Carolina State Gazette (Raleigh, NC)

Raleigh Register, and North-Carolina Weekly Advertiser (Raleigh, NC)

Republican Argus (Northumberland, PA)

Republican Citizen and State Advertiser (Frederick, MD)

Richmond Enquirer (Richmond, VA)

Semi-Weekly Landmark (Statesville, NC)

Semi-Weekly Messenger (Wilmington, NC)

Semi-Weekly Sentinel (Raleigh, NC)

Semi-Weekly Standard (Raleigh, NC)

Southern Citizen (Asheboro, NC)

Star (Raleigh, NC)

Star, and North Carolina State Gazette (Raleigh, NC)

State Journal (Raleigh, NC)

Tarboro Mercury (Tarboro, NC)

Tarboro' Press (Tarboro, NC)

Tarborough Southerner (Tarboro, NC)

The Times: A Southern Literary and Family Paper (Greensboro, NC)

Trenton Federalist (Trenton, NJ)

Tri-Weekly Commercial (Wilmington, NC)

Tri-Weekly Standard (Raleigh, NC)

True Republican and Newbern Weekly Advertiser (New Bern, NC)

United States' Telegraph (Washington, D.C.)

Vermont Chronicle (Bellows Falls, VT)

Watchman and Southron (Wilmington, NC)

Weekly Ad Valorem Banner (Raleigh, NC)

Weekly Commercial (Wilmington, NC)

Weekly Raleigh Register (Raleigh, NC)

Weekly Visiter (Kennebunk, ME)

Western Carolinian (Salisbury, NC)

Western Democrat (Charlotte, NC)

Wilmington Centinel (Wilmington, NC)

Wilmington Chronicle (Wilmington, NC)

Wilmington Herald (Wilmington, NC)

Wilmington Journal (Wilmington, NC)

Wilmington Messenger (Wilmington, NC)

Wilmington Post (Wilmington, NC)

BOOKS AND ARTICLES

Berlin, Ira, ed. *Freedom: A Documentary History of Emancipation, 1861–1867. Series II: The Black Military Experience*. New York: Cambridge University Press, 1982.

Beverley, Robert. *The History and Present State of Virginia, in Four Parts*. London: R. Parker, 1705.

Blassingame, John W., ed. *Slave Testimony: Two Centuries of Letters, Speeches, Interviews, and Autobiographies*. Baton Rouge: Louisiana State University Press, 1977.

Blount, John Gray. *John Gray Blount Papers*. Vol 4, *1803–1833*. Edited by David T. Morgan. Raleigh: North Carolina Department of Cultural Resources, 1982.

Bumpo, Natty [pseud.]. "A Deerhunt in North Carolina." *American Turf Register and Sporting Magazine* 4, no. 4 (1833): 305–6.

Catterall, Helen Tunncliff. *Judicial Cases Concerning American Slavery and the Negro*. Vol. 2. 1929. Reprint, New York: Negro Universities Press, 1968.

Charles II, and John Locke. *The Two Charters Granted by King Charles IId. To the Proprietors of Carolina. With the First and Last Fundamental Constitutions of that Colony* (London: Richard Parker, 1698.

Cheney, John L., Jr., ed. *North Carolina Government, 1585–1979: A Narrative and Statistical History*. Raleigh: North Carolina Department of the Secretary of State, 1981.

Clark, H. F., and Company. *Clark's Illustrated Treatise on the Rifle, Shot-Gun and Pistol*. Memphis, TN: H. F. Clark and Company, 1850.

Colyer, Vincent. *Brief Report of the Services Rendered by the Freed People of the United States Army in North Carolina: In the Pring of 1862 after the Battle of Newbern*. New York: V. Colyer, 1864.

Cott, Nancy F., Jeanne Boydston, Ann Braude, Lori D. Ginzberg, and Molly Ladd-Taylor, eds. *Root of Bitterness: Documents of the Social History of American Women*, 2nd ed. Boston: Northeastern University Press, 1996.

Dana, Richard Henry, Jr. *Two Years before the Mast and Twenty-Four Years After: A Personal Narrative*. London: Sampson Low, Son, and Marston, 1869.

Dann, John C., ed. *The Revolution Remembered: Eyewitness Accounts of the War for Independence*. Chicago: University of Chicago Press, 1999.

De Bow, James Dunwoody Brownson. *The Industrial Resources, etc., of the Southern and Western States*. Vol. 2. New Orleans: De Bow's Review, 1852.

De Bow, James Dunwoody Brownson. *The Seventh Census of the United States*. Washington, DC: Robert Armstrong, 1853.

Derby, W. P. *Bearing Arms in the Twenty-Seventh Massachusetts Regiment of Volunteer Infantry During the Civil War, 1861–1865*. Boston: Wright and Potter, 1883.

De Witt, Robert M. *The Life, Trial and Execution of Capt. John Brown: Being a Full Account of the Attempted Insurrection at Harper's Ferry, VA*. New York: Robert M. De Witt, Publisher, 1859.

Dodsley, J. *The Annual Register, or a View of the History, Politics, and Literature, for the Year 1775*. London: Edmund Burke, 1776.

Douglass, Frederick. *The Life and Times of Frederick Douglass, from 1817 to 1882, Written by Himself*. Edited by John Lobb. London: The Christian Age, 1882.

Douglass, Frederick. *Narrative of the Life of Frederick Douglass, an American Slave*. 1845. Reprint, New York: Signet Classic, 1968.

Foner, Philip S., and Robert James Branham, eds. *Lift Every Voice: African American Oratory, 1787–1900*. Tuscaloosa: University of Alabama Press, 1998.

Garrison, William Lloyd. *Thoughts on African Colonization: Or an Impartial Exhibition of the Doctrines, Principles and Purposes of the American Colonization Society; together with the Resolutions, Addresses and Remonstrances of the Free People of Color*. Boston: Garrison and Knapp, 1832.

Graham, William A. *The Papers of William A. Graham*. Vol. 6, *1864–1865*. Edited by Max R. Williams. Raleigh: State Department of Archives and History, 1976. https://digital.ncdcr.gov/Documents/Detail/papers-of-william-alexander-graham-1864-1865-v.6/2691378.

Grant, Ulysses S. *Ulysses S. Grant: Memoirs and Selected Letters*. Edited by Mary D. McFeely and William S. McFeely. New York: Library of America, 1990.

Helper, Hinton Rowan. *Compendium of the Impending Crisis of the South*. New York: A. B. Burdick, 1860.

Houston, Florence Wilson, Laura Cowan Blaine, and Ella Dunn Mellette. *Maxwell History and Genealogy*. Indianapolis, IN: Press of C. E. Pauley, 1916.

Iredell, James. *The Papers of James Iredell*. Vol. 2, *1778–1783*. Edited by Don Higginbotham. Raleigh: North Carolina Division of Archives and History, Department of Cultural Resources, 1976. www.archive.org/details/papersofjamesire1976ired.

Jacobs, Harriet. *Incidents in the Life of a Slave Girl, Written by Herself*. Edited by J. Maria Child. 1861. Reprint, New York: Signet Classic, 2000.

Jay, William. *Miscellaneous Writings on Slavery*. Boston: John P. Jewett, 1853.

Jones, Thomas H. *The Experience of Rev. Thomas H. Jones, Who Was a Slave for Forty-Three Years*. Edited William L. Andrews. 1885. Reprint, Chapel Hill: University of North Carolina Press, 2003.

Kernodle, Peter Jefferson. *Lives of Christian Ministers*. Richmond, VA: Central Publishing Company, 1909.

Lane, Lunsford. *The Narrative of Lunsford Lane, Formerly of Raleigh, N.C. Embracing an Account of His Early Life, the Redemption, by Purchase of Himself and Family from Slavery, and His Banishment from the Place of His Birth for the Crime of Wearing a Colored Skin*. 4th ed. Boston: Lunsford Lane, 1848.

Miller, Stephen F. "Recollections of Newbern Fifty Years Ago." In *Our Living and Our Dead*, Vol. 1. Edited by S. D. Pool. Raleigh, NC: Branch of the Southern Historical Society, 1874. https://digital.lib.ecu.edu/13575.

Nichols, George Ward. *The Story of the Great March from the Diary of a Staff-Officer*. London: Sampson Low, Son, and Marston, 1865.

Niles, H., ed. *Niles' Weekly Register*. 2nd ser., Vol. 11. Baltimore, MD: Franklin Press, 1823.

O'Hara, James E. *Minutes of the Freedmen's Convention, Held in the City of Raleigh, on the 2nd, 3rd, 4th, and 5th of October, 1866*. Raleigh, NC: Standard Book and Job Office, 1866.

Olmsted, Frederick Law. *The Cotton Kingdom: A Traveller's Observations on Cotton and Slavery in the American Slave States*, edited by Arthur M. Schlesinger. New York: Alfred A. Knopf, 1962.

Olmsted, Frederick Law. *A Journey in the Seaboard Slave States; with Remarks on Their Economy*. New York: Dix and Edwards, 1856.

Pettigrew, Ebenezer. *The Pettigrew Papers*. Vol. 2, *1819–1843*. Edited by Sarah McCulloh Lemmon. Raleigh, NC: State Department of Archives and History, 1988.

Ramseur, Stephen Dodson. *The Bravest of the Brave: The Correspondences of Stephen Dodson Ramseur*. Edited by George G. Kundahl. Chapel Hill: University of North Carolina Press, 2010.

Reid, David S. *The Papers of David S. Reid*. Vol. 1, *1829–1852*. Edited by Lindley S. Butler. Raleigh, NC: Department of Cultural Resources, Division of Archives and History, 1993.

Schaw, Janet. *Journal of a Lady of Quality: Being the Narrative of a Journey from Scotland, to the West Indies, North Carolina, and Portugal, in the Years 1774 to 1776*. Edited by Evaline W. Andrews and Charles M. Andrews. New Haven, CT: Yale University Press, 1922.

Singleton, William Henry. *Recollection of My Slavery Days*. Peekskill, NY: Highland Democrat, 1922. http://docsouth.unc.edu/neh/singleton/singleton.html.

Smyth, J. F. D. *A Tour in the United States of America: Containing an Account of the Present Situation of that Country*, Vol. 2. Dublin: T. Henshall, 1784.

Spencer, Cornelia P. *The Last Ninety Days of the War in North Carolina*. New York: Watchman Publishing Company, 1866. http://docsouth.unc.edu/true/spencer/spencer.html.

Stedman, John Gabriel. *Stedman's Surinam: Life in an Eighteenth-Century Slave Society*. 1806. Edited by Richard Price and Sally Price. Baltimore, MD: Johns Hopkins University Press, 1992.

Swaim, Benjamin. *The North Carolina Justice: Contains a summary statement of the statutes and common law of this state, together with the decisions of the supreme court, and all the most approved forms and precedents relating to the office and duty of a justice of the peace and other public officers, according to modern practice*. 2nd ed. Raleigh, NC: Henry D. Turner, 1846.

Walker, David. *Walker's Appeal in Four Articles; together with a Preamble, to the Coloured Citizens of the World*. Boston: David Walker, 1830. http://docsouth.unc.edu/nc/walker/walker.html.

Weld, Theodore Dwight. *American Slavery As It Is: Testimony of a Thousand Witnesses*. New York: American Anti-Slavery Society, 1839.

Wheeler, John H. *Historical Sketches of North Carolina, from 1584 to 1851*. Vol. 1. Philadelphia,: Lippincott, Grambo, 1851.

Worth, Jonathan. *The Correspondence of Jonathan Worth*. Vol 1. Edited by J. G. de Roulhac Hamilton. Raleigh, NC: Edwards and Broughton, 1909.

GOVERNMENT DOCUMENTS

Clark, Walter, ed. *The State Records of North Carolina*, Vol. 11. Winston, NC: M.I. and J. C. Stewart, 1895. https://docsouth.unc.edu/csr/index.php/document/csr11-es02.

Clark, Walter, ed. *The State Records of North Carolina*, Vol. 13. Winston, NC: M.F. and J.C. Stewart, 1896. https://docsouth.unc.edu/csr/index.php/document/csr13-es01.

Clark, Walter, ed. *The State Records of North Carolina*, Vol. 15. Goldsboro, NC: Nash Brothers, Book and Job Printers, 1898. https://docsouth.unc.edu/csr/index.php/document/csr15-es01.

Clark, Walter, ed. *The State Records of North Carolina*. Vol. 19. Goldsboro, NC: Nash Brothers, Book and Job Printers, 1901. https://docsouth.unc.edu/csr/index.php/document/csr19-es01.

Clark, Walter, ed. *The State Records of North Carolina*, Vol. 22. Goldsboro, NC: Nash Brothers, Book and Job Printers, 1907. https://docsouth.unc.edu/csr/index.php/document/csr22-es01.

Clark, Walter, ed. *The State Records of North Carolina*, Vol. 23. Goldsboro, NC: Nash Brothers, Book and Job Printers, 1904. https://docsouth.unc.edu/csr/index.php/document/csr23-es01.

Clark, Walter, ed. *The State Records of North Carolina*, Vol. 24. Goldsboro, NC: Nash Brothers, Book and Job Printers, 1905. https://docsouth.unc.edu/csr/index.php/document/csr24-es01.

Clark, Walter, ed. *The State Records of North Carolina*, Vol. 25. Goldsboro, NC: Nash Brothers, Book and Job Printers, 1906. https://docsouth.unc.edu/csr/index.php/document/csr25-es01.

Delaware. *Laws of the State of Delaware, from the sixteenth day of January, one thousand eight hundred and thirty, to the thirteenth day of February, one thousand eight hundred and thirty-five to which is prefixed the Amended Constitution of said State*. Vol. 8. Dover, DE: S. Kimmey, 1841. https://babel.hathitrust.org/cgi/pt?id=nyp.33433009080197&seq=9.

Devereux, Thomas P. *Cases Argued and Determined in the Supreme Court of North-Carolina, from December Term, 1833, to June Term, 1834*, Vol. 4. Raleigh, NC: Joseph Gales and Son, 1836.

Devereux Thomas P., and William H. Battle. *Reports of Cases at Law, Argued and Determined in the Supreme Court of North Carolina: From June Term, 1838, to December Term, 1839, Both Inclusive*, Vols. 3 and 4. Raleigh, NC: Turner and Hughes, 1840.

Ellis, John W. *The Papers of John W. Ellis*. Vol. 2, *1860–1861*. Edited by Noble J. Tolbert. Raleigh, NC: State Department of Archives and History, 1964.

Florida. *Acts of the Legislative Council of the Territory of Florida, Passed at Their 6th Session: 1827–8*. Tallahassee: Joseph D. Davenport, 1828. https://archive.org/details/actsoflegis28flor/page/n3/mode/2up.

Florida. *Acts of the Legislative Council of the Territory of Florida, Passed at Their Ninth Session, 1831*. Tallahassee: Gibson and Smith, 1831. https://archive.org/details/actsoflegis31flor/page/n3/mode/2up.

Georgia. *Acts of the General Assembly of the State of Georgia, Passed in Milledgeville, at an Annual Session in November and December 1833*. Milledgeville, GA: Polhill and Fort, 1834. https://www.google.com/books/edition/_/igY4AAAAIAAJ?hl=en&gbpv=1.

Howard, Benjamin C. *A Report of the Decision of the Supreme Court of the United States, and the Opinions of the Judges Thereof, in the Case of Dred Scott versus John F. A. Sandford. December Term, 1856*. New York: D. Appleton, 1857.

Iredell, James, Jr. *North Carolina Reports*. Vol. 30, *Cases at Law Argued and Determined by the Supreme Court of North Carolina. December Term, 1847 to August Term, 1848, Both Inclusive*. Edited by Walter Clark. 1849. Reprint, Raleigh, NC: E. M. Uzzell, 1909.

Iredell, James, Jr. *North Carolina Reports*. Vol. 31, *Cases at Law Argued and Determined in the Supreme Court of North Carolina. December Term, 1848 to June Term, 1849 (Both Inclusive)*. Annotated by Walter Clark. Raleigh, NC: E. M. Uzzell, 1909.

Iredell, James, Jr. *Reports of Cases at Law Argued and Determined in the Supreme Court of North Carolina, from December Term, 1841 to June Term, 1842, both inclusive*. Vol. 2. Raleigh, NC: Turner and Hughes, 1842.

Iredell, James, Jr. *Reports of Cases at Law Argued and Determined in the Supreme Court of North Carolina, from December Term, 1844, to June Term, 1845, Both Inclusive*. Vol. 6. Raleigh, NC: Turner and Hughes, 1845.

Iredell, James, Jr. *Reports of Cases at Law Argued and Determined in the Supreme Court of North Carolina, from December Term, 1848, to June Term, 1849, Both Inclusive*. Vol. 9. Raleigh, NC: Seaton Gales, 1849.

Jones, Hamilton C. *North Carolina Reports*. Vol. 50, *Cases at Law Argued and Determined in the Supreme Court of North Carolina From December Term, 1857, to August Term, 1858, Inclusive*. Edited by Walter Clark. 1859. Reprint, Raleigh, NC: E. M. Uzzell, 1905.

Jones, Hamilton C. *Reports of Cases at Law, Argued and Determined in the Supreme Court of North Carolina, from December Term, 1857 to August Term, 1858, Inclusive*. Vol. 5. Salisbury, NC: J. J. Bruner, 1858.

Jones, Hamilton C. *Reports of Cases at Law Argued and Determined in the Supreme Court of North Carolina from December Term, 1858, to August Term, 1859, Inclusive*. Vol. 6. Salisbury, NC: J. J. Bruner, 1859.

Jones, Hamilton C. *Reports of Cases at Law Argued and Determined in the Supreme Court of North Carolina From December Term, 1859, to August Term, 1860, Inclusive*. Vol. 7. Salisbury, NC: J. J. Bruner, 1860.

Martin, Francois-Xavier. *The Public Acts of the General Assembly of North-Carolina*, Vol. 1. Newbern, NC: Martin and Ogden, 1804.

Maryland. *Laws Made and Passed by the General Assembly of the State of Maryland, at a session begun and held at Annapolis, on Monday the 26th day of December, 1831 and ended on Wednesday the 14th day of March, 1832*. Annapolis: J. Hughes, 1832. https://babel.hathitrust.org/cgi/pt?id=osu.32437123281210&seq=5.

Matthews, James M., ed. *Public Laws of the Confederate States of America, Passed at the Second Session of the First Congress; 1862*. Richmond, VA: R. M. Smith, 1862.

Nash, Frederick, James Iredell, and William H. Battle. *The Revised Statutes of the State of North Carolina, Passed by the General Assembly at the Session of 1836–1837*. Vol 1. Raleigh, NC: Turner and Hughes, 1837.

Newsome, A. R., ed. "A British Orderly Book, 1780–1781: III." *North Carolina Historical Review* 9, no. 3 (July 1932): 273–98.

Newsome, A. R., ed. "A British Orderly Book, 1780–1781: IV." *North Carolina Historical Review* 9, no. 4 (October 1932): 366–92.

North Carolina. *Constitution of the State of North-Carolina, together with the Ordinances and Resolutions of the Constitutional Convention, Assembled in the City of Raleigh, Jan 14th, 1868.* Raleigh, NC: Joseph W. Holden, 1868. https://name.umdl.umich.edu /aey0617.0001.001.

North Carolina. *Journal of the Convention, Called by the Freemen of North-Carolina, to Amend the Constitution of the State, Which Assembled in the City of Raleigh.* Raleigh, NC: J. Gales and Son, 1835. https://docsouth.unc.edu/nc/conv1835/conv1835.html.

North Carolina. *Journal of the Senate of the General Assembly of the State of North-Carolina at its Session of 1858–'59.* Raleigh, NC: Holden and Wilson, 1859. https://digital.ncdcr .gov/Documents/Detail/journal-of-the-senate-of-the-general-assembly-of-the-state -of-north-carolina-at-its-1858-1859-session/2690523.

North Carolina. *Journals of the Senate and House of Commons of the General Assembly of the State of North Carolina at the Session of 1830–31.* Raleigh, NC: Lawrence and LeMay, 1831. North Carolina Department of Cultural Resources Digital Collections. https://digital.ncdcr.gov/Documents/Detail/journals-of-the-senate-and-house -of-commons-of-the-general-assembly-of-north-carolina-at-its-...-1830-1831 -session/2690581?item=2760372.

North Carolina. *Journals of the Senate and House of Commons, of the General Assembly of the State of North Carolina, at its Session of 1850–'51.* Raleigh, NC: Seaton Gales, 1851.

North Carolina. *Ordinances and Resolutions passed by the State Convention.* 1861–1862. Raleigh, NC: Syme and Hall, 1961. https://archive.org/details/ordinancesresolunort.

North Carolina. *Public Laws of the State of North-Carolina, Passed by the General Assembly at Its Session of 1854–55.* Raleigh, NC: Holden and Wilson, 1855. https://babel .hathitrust.org/cgi/pt?id=nc01.ark:/13960/t5t734x79&seq=7.

North Carolina. *Public Laws of the State of North-Carolina, Passed by the General Assembly, at Its Session of 1858–'9.* Raleigh, NC: Holden and Wilson, 1859. https://babel .hathitrust.org/cgi/pt?id=iau.31858018004949&seq=9.

North Carolina. *Public Laws of the State of North-Carolina, Passed by the General Assembly, at Its Session of 1860–'61.* Raleigh, NC: John Spelman, 1861. https://babel.hathitrust .org/cgi/pt?id=emu.000011334864&seq=5.

North Carolina. *Public Laws of the State of North Carolina, Passed by the General Assembly at the Sessions of 1861–'62–'63–'64, and one in 1859.* Raleigh, NC: Wm. E. Pell, 1866. https://babel.hathitrust.org/cgi/pt?id=umn.31951d02290165b&seq=5.

North Carolina. *Revised Code of North Carolina, Enacted by the General Assembly at the Session of 1854.* Edited by Bartholomew F. Moore and Asa Biggs. Boston: Little, Brown, 1855. http://www.archive.org/details/revisedcodeofnor1854nort.

Potter, Henry. *The Office and Duty of a Justice of the Peace, and a Guide to Sheriffs, Coroners, Clerks, and Constables, and other Civil Officers. According to the Laws of North-Carolina,* 2nd ed. Raleigh, NC: J. Gales and Son, 1828.

Potter, Henry, ed. *Laws of the State of North-Carolina: Including the Titles of Such Statutes and Parts of Statutes of Great Britain as Are in Force in Said State . . . : with Marginal Notes and References.* Vol. 1. Raleigh, NC: J. Gales, 1821.

Rowan County, *Patrol Regulations for the County of Rowan; Printed by Order of the County Court at August Term, 1825*. Salisbury, NC: Philo White, 1825.

Saunders, William L., ed. *The Colonial Records of North Carolina*. Vol. 2. Raleigh, NC: P. M. Hale, 1886.

Saunders, William L., ed. *The Colonial Records of North Carolina*, Vol. 4. Raleigh, NC: P. M. Hale, 1886.

Saunders, William L., ed. *The Colonial Records of North Carolina*. Vol. 9. 1890. Reprint, Wilmington, NC: Broadfoot Publishing, 1993.

Saunders, William L., ed. *The Colonial Records of North Carolina*. Vol. 10. Raleigh, NC: Josephus Daniels, 1890.

Taylor, John L. *A Revisal of the Laws of the State of North Carolina, Passed from 1821 to 1825 (both years inclusive) with Marginal Notes and References*. Raleigh, NC: J. Gales and Son, 1827.

United States Congressional Directories, 1789–1840. Edited by Perry M. Goldman and James Sterling Young. New York, NY; Columbia University Press, 1973.

US Congress, Joint Select Committee on the Condition of Affairs in the Late Insurrectionary States. *Testimony Taken by the Joint Select Committee to inquire into the Condition of Affairs in the Late Insurrectionary States: North Carolina*. Washington, DC: Government Printing Office, 1872.

US Department of Commerce, Bureau of the Census. *Negro Population, 1790–1915*. Washington, DC: Government Printing Office, 1918.

US Department of Commerce. *Fifteenth Census of the United States: 1830. Population*. Vol. 1, *Number and Distribution of Inhabitants*. Washington, DC: Government Printing Office, 1931.

US War Department. *The War of the Rebellion: A Compilation of the Official Records of the Union and Confederate Armies*. Ser. I, vol. 52, part II. Edited by George W. Davis, Leslie J. Perry, and Joseph W. Kirkley. Washington, D.C.: Government Printing Office, 1898.

US War Department. *The War of the Rebellion: A Compilation of the Official Records of the Union and Confederate Armies*. Ser. IV, vol. 3. Edited by Fred C. Ainsworth and Joseph W. Kirkley. Washington, D.C.: Government Printing Office, 1900.

Virginia, Commonwealth. *Acts Passed at a General Assembly of the Commonwealth of Virginia, Begun and Held at the Capitol in the City of Richmond, on Monday, the Fifth of December, in the Year of Our Lord, One Thousand Eight Hundred and Thirty-One, and of the Commonwealth, the Fifty-Sixth*. Richmond: Thomas Ritchie, 1832. https://babel.hathitrust.org/cgi/pt?id=uc1.a0001803196&seq=7.

Wilmington, NC, Safety Committee. *Proceedings of the Safety Committee: for the Town of Wilmington, N.C. from 1774 to 1776*. Raleigh, NC: Thomas Loring, 1844. https://hdl.handle.net/2027/loc.ark:/13960/t6nz8mj52.

MICROFILM

Schweninger, Loren, ed. *Race, Slavery, and Free Blacks*. Ser. I, *Petitions to Southern Legislatures, 1777–1867*. Bethesda, MD: University Publications of America, 1999. Microfilm.

Schweninger, Loren, ed. *Race, Slavery, and Free Blacks*. Ser. II, *Petitions to Southern County Courts, 1775–1867*. Bethesda, MD: University Publications of America, 2005. Microfilm.

Secondary Sources

BOOKS

Anderson, Carol. *The Second: Race and Guns in a Fatally Unequal America*. New York: Bloomsbury Publishing, 2023.

Anestis, Michael D. *Guns and Suicide: An American Epidemic*. New York: Oxford University Press, 2018.

Aptheker, Herbert. *Negro Slave Revolts in the United States, 1526–1860*. New York: International Publishers, 1939.

Arnold, Robert. *The Dismal Swamp and Lake Drummond, Early Recollections, Vivid Portrayal of Amusing Scenes*. Norfolk, VA: Green, Burke and Gregory, 1888.

Ashe, Samuel A'Court. *Biographical History of North Carolina from Colonial Times to the Present*. Vol. 3. Greensboro, NC: Charles L. Van Noppen, 1906.

Barrett, John Gilchrist. *North Carolina as a Civil War Battleground, 1861–1865*. Raleigh, NC: North Carolina Department of Cultural Resources, 1993.

Bassett, John Spencer. *Slavery in the State of North Carolina*. Baltimore, MD: Johns Hopkins Press, 1899.

Beckel, Deborah. *Radical Reform: Interracial Politics in Post-Emancipation North Carolina*. Charlottesville: University of Virginia Press, 2011.

Bederman, Gail. *Manliness and Civilization: A Cultural History of Race and Gender in the United States, 1880–1917*. Chicago: University of Chicago Press, 1995.

Berlin, Ira. *Generations of Captivity: A History of African-American Slaves*. Cambridge, MA: The Belknap Press of Harvard University Press, 2003.

Berlin, Ira. *Many Thousand Gone: The First Two Centuries of Slavery in North America*. Cambridge, MA: The Belknap Press of Harvard University Press, 1998.

Berlin, Ira. *Slaves Without Masters: The Free Negro in the Antebellum South*. New York: Vintage Books, 1976.

Binnington, Ian. *Confederate Visions: Nationalism, Symbolism, and the Imagined South in the Civil War*. Charlottesville: The University of Virginia Press, 2013.

Bishir, Catherine W. *Crafting Lives: African American Artisans in New Bern, North Carolina, 1770–1900*. Chapel Hill: University of North Carolina Press, 2013.

Black, Daniel P. *Dismantling Black Manhood: An Historical and Literary Analysis of the Legacy of Slavery*. New York: Garland Publishing, 1997.

Blanton, Deanne, and Lauren M. Cook. *They Fought Like Demons: Women Soldiers in the Civil War*. New York: Vintage Books, 2002.

Blassingame, John W. *The Slave Community: Plantation Life in the Antebellum South*. New York: Oxford University Press, 1979.

Blight, David W. *Race and Reunion: The Civil War in American Memory*. Cambridge, MA: The Belknap Press of Harvard University, 2001.

Blu, Karen I. *The Lumbee Problem: The Making of an American Indian People*. New York: Cambridge University Press, 1980.

Bolton, Charles C. *Poor Whites of the Antebellum South: Tenants and Laborers in Central North Carolina and Northeast Mississippi*. Durham, NC: Duke University Press, 1994.

Branch, Paul, Jr. *Fort Macon: A History*. Charleston, SC: Nautical and Aviation Publishing Company of America, 1999.

Bristow, Nancy K. *Steeped in the Blood of Racism: Black Power, Law and Order, and the 1970 Shootings at Jackson State College.* New York: Oxford University Press, 2020.

Browning, Judkin. *Shifting Loyalties: The Union Occupation of Eastern North Carolina.* Chapel Hill: University of North Carolina Press, 2011.

Bynum, Victoria E. *Unruly Women: The Politics of Social and Sexual Control in the Old South.* Chapel Hill: University of North Carolina Press, 1992.

Cecelski, David S. *The Fire of Freedom: Abraham Galloway and the Slaves' Civil War.* Chapel Hill: University of North Carolina Press, 2012.

Cecelski, David S. *The Waterman's Song: Slavery and Freedom in Maritime North Carolina.* Chapel Hill: University of North Carolina Press, 2001.

Cecelski, David S., and Timothy B. Tyson, eds. *Democracy Betrayed: The Wilmington Race Riot of 1898 and Its Legacy.* Chapel Hill: University of North Carolina Press, 1998.

Cecil-Fronsman, Bill. *Common Whites: Class and Culture in Antebellum North Carolina.* Lexington: University Press of Kentucky, 1992.

Censer, Jane Turner. *North Carolina Planters and Their Children.* Baton Rouge: Louisiana State University Press, 1984.

Chafe, William H. *Lifting the Chains: The Black Freedom Struggle Since Reconstruction.* New York: Oxford University Press, 2023.

Cobb, Charles E., Jr. *This Nonviolent Stuff'll Get You Killed: How Guns Made the Civil Rights Movement Possible.* Durham, NC: Duke University Press, 2016.

Connor, R. D. W. *Cornelius Harnett: An Essay in North Carolina History.* Raleigh, NC: Edwards and Broughton, 1909.

Connor, R. D. W. *History of North Carolina.* Vol. 1, *The Colonial and Revolutionary Periods, 1584–1783.* New York: Lewis Publishing, 1919.

Cook-Bell, Karen. *Running from Bondage: Enslaved Women and Their Remarkable Fight for Freedom in Revolutionary America.* New York: Cambridge University Press, 2021.

Cooper, J. Fenimore. *The Last of the Mohicans. A Narrative of 1757.* New York: D. Appleton, 1887.

Cramer, Clayton. *Armed America: The Remarkable Story of How and Why Guns Became as American as Apple Pie.* Nashville, TN: Nelson Current, 2006.

Cramer, Clayton. *Concealed Weapons Laws of the Early Republic: Dueling, Southern Violence, and Moral Reform.* Westport, CT: Praeger, 1999.

Cramer, Clayton. *For the Defense of Themselves and the State: The Original Intent and Judicial Interpretation of the Right to Keep and Bear Arms.* Westport, CT: Praeger, 1994.

Davis, Edwin Adams, and William Ransom Hogan. *The Barber of Natchez.* Baton Rouge: Louisiana State University Press, 1954.

Dunkerly, Robert. *Redcoats on the Cape Fear: The Revolutionary War in Southeastern North Carolina.* Jefferson, NC: McFarland and Company, 2012.

Edwards, Laura F. *The People and Their Peace: Legal Culture and the Transformation of Inequality in the Post-Revolutionary South.* Chapel Hill: University of North Carolina Press, 2009.

Ely, Melvin Patrick. *Israel on the Appomattox: A Southern Experiment in Black Freedom from the 1790s through the Civil War.* New York: Vintage Books, 2005.

Emberton, Carole. *Beyond Redemption: Race, Violence, and the American South after the Civil War.* Chicago: University of Chicago Press, 2013.

Evans, Clement Anselm, ed. *Confederate Military History*. Vol. 12. Atlanta: Confederate Publishing Company, 1899. https://archive.org/details/confedmilhist12evanrich.

Faust, Drew Gilpin. *Mothers of Invention: Women of the Slaveholding South in the American Civil War*. Chapel Hill: University of North Carolina Press, 1996.

Fischer, Kirsten. *Suspect Relations: Sex, Race, and Resistance in Colonial North Carolina*. Ithaca, NY: Cornell University Press, 2002.

Foner, Eric. *The Fiery Trial: Abraham Lincoln and American Slavery*. New York: W. W. Norton, 2010.

Foner, Eric. *Reconstruction: American's Unfinished Revolution, 1863–1877*. New York: Harper and Row, 1988.

Forret, Jeff. *Race Relations at the Margins: Slaves and Poor Whites in the Antebellum Countryside*. Baton Rouge: Louisiana State University Press, 2006.

Forret, Jeff. *Slave against Slave: Plantation Violence in the Old South*. Baton Rouge: Louisiana State University Press, 2015.

Franklin, John Hope. *The Free Negro in North Carolina, 1790–1860*. Chapel Hill: University of North Carolina Press, 1943.

Franklin, John Hope, and Loren Schweninger. *Runaway Slaves: Rebels on the Plantation*. New York: Oxford University Press, 1999.

Gallagher, Gary W. *The Confederate War: How Popular Will, Nationalism, and Military Strategy Could Not Stave off Defeat*. Cambridge, MA: Harvard University Press, 1997.

Gallay, Alan. *The Indian Slave Trade: The Rise of the English Empire in the American South, 1670–1717*. New Haven, CT: Yale University Press, 2002.

Genovese, Eugene. *Roll, Jordan, Roll: The World the Slaves Made*. New York: Vintage Books, 1976.

Gerard, Philip. *The Last Battleground: The Civil War Comes to North Carolina*. Chapel Hill: University of North Carolina Press, 2019.

Gilbert, Alan. *Black Patriots and Loyalists: Fighting for Emancipation in the War for Independence*. Chicago: University of Chicago Press, 2012.

Giltner, Scott E. *Hunting and Fishing in the New South: Black Labor and White Leisure after the Civil War*. Baltimore, MD: Johns Hopkins University Press, 2008.

Glymph, Thavolia. *Out of the House of Bondage: The Transformation of the Plantation Household*. New York: Cambridge University Press, 2008.

Gross, Ariela Julie. *What Blood Won't Tell: A History of Race on Trial in America*. Cambridge, MA: Harvard University Press, 2009.

Hadden, Sally E. *Slave Patrols: Law and Violence in Virginia and the Carolinas*. Cambridge, MA: Harvard University Press, 2001.

Halasz, Nicholas. *The Rattling Chains: Slave Unrest and Revolt in the Antebellum South*. New York: David McKay Company, 1966.

Halbrook, Stephen P. *That Every Man Be Armed: The Evolution of a Constitutional Right*. Albuquerque: University of New Mexico Press, 1984.

Hamilton, J. G. de Roulhac. *History of North Carolina*. Vol. 3, *North Carolina since 1860*. Chicago: Lewis Publishing, 1919.

Harsanyi, David. *First Freedom: A Ride through America's Enduring History with the Gun*. New York: Threshold Editions, 2018.

Hashaw, Tim. *Children of Perdition: Melungeons and the Struggle of Mixed America*. Macon, GA: Mercer University Press, 2006.

Higginbotham, A. Leon. *In the Matter of Color: Race and the American Legal Process; the Colonial Period*. New York: Oxford University Press, 1978.

Hill, Lance. *The Deacons for Defense: Armed Resistance and the Civil Rights Movement*. Chapel Hill: University of North Carolina Press, 2004.

Hinks, Peter P. *To Awaken My Afflicted Brethren: David Walker and the Problem of Antebellum Slave Resistance*. University Park: Pennsylvania State University Press, 1997.

Hoffert, Sylvia D. *A History of Gender in America*. Upper Saddle, NJ: Pearson Education, 2003.

Horton, James Oliver. *Free People of Color: Inside the African American Community*. Washington, DC: Smithsonian Institution Press, 1993.

Horton, James Oliver, and Lois E. Horton. *Slavery and the Making of America*. New York: Oxford University Press, 2005.

Hudson, Larry E., Jr. *To Have and to Hold: Slave Work and Family Life in Antebellum South Carolina*. Athens: University of Georgia Press, 1997.

Huggins, Nathan Irvin. *Black Odyssey: The African-American Ordeal in Slavery*. New York: Vintage Books, 1990.

Hunter, Tera W. *Bound in Wedlock: Slave and Free Black Marriage in the Nineteenth Century*. Cambridge, MA: The Belknap Press of Harvard University Press, 2017.

Iobst, Richard W. *The Bloody Sixth: The Sixth North Carolina Regiment, Confederate States of America*. Durham: North Carolina Confederate Centennial Commission, 1965. https://digital.ncdcr.gov/Documents/Detail/bloody-sixth-the-sixth-north-carolina -regiment-confederate-states-of-america/3404619?item=3418444.

Jackson, Kellie Carter. *Force and Freedom: Black Abolitionists and the Politics of Violence*. Philadelphia: University of Pennsylvania Press, 2019.

Jimerson, Randall C. *The Private Civil War: Popular Thought during the Sectional Conflict*. Baton Rouge: Louisiana State University Press, 1988.

Johnson, Guion Griffis. *Ante-Bellum North Carolina: A Social History*. Chapel Hill: University of North Carolina Press, 1937.

Johnson, Nicholas. *Negroes and the Gun: The Black Tradition of Arms*. Amherst, NY: Prometheus Books, 2014.

Johnson, Walter. *Soul by Soul: Life inside the Antebellum Slave Market*. Cambridge, MA: Harvard University Press, 1999.

Jones, Cecily. *Engendering Whiteness: White Women and Colonialism in Barbados and North Carolina, 1627–1865*. Manchester, UK: Manchester University Press, 2007.

Jordan, Ervin L., Jr. *Black Confederates and Afro-Yankees in Civil War Virginia*. Charlottesville: University Press of Virginia, 1995.

Jordan, Winthrop D. *White over Black: American Attitudes toward the Negro, 1550–1812*, 2nd ed. Chapel Hill: University of North Carolina Press, 1968.

Kantrowitz, Stephen. *More Than Freedom: Fighting for Black Citizenship in a White Republic, 1829–1889*. New York: Penguin Press, 2012.

Kay, Marvin L. Michael, and Lorin Lee Cary. *Slavery in North Carolina, 1748–1775*. Chapel Hill: University of North Carolina Press, 1995.

Kaye, Anthony E. *Joining Places: Slave Neighborhoods in the Old South*. Chapel Hill: University of North Carolina Press, 2007.

Kaye, Anthony E., with Gregory P. Downs. *Nat Turner, Black Prophet: A Visionary History*. New York: Farrar, Straus, and Giroux, 2024.

Kenzer, Robert C. *Enterprising Southerners: Black Economic Success in North Carolina, 1865–1915*. Charlottesville: University of Virginia Press, 1989.

Kinshasa, Kwando Mbiassi. *Black Resistance to the Ku Klux Klan in the Wake of the Civil War*. Jefferson, NC: McFarland and Company, 2006.

Krugler, David F. *1919, the Year of Racial Violence: How African Americans Fought Back*. New York: Cambridge University Press, 2015.

Kruman, Marc W. *Parties and Politics in North Carolina, 1836–1865*. Baton Rouge: Louisiana State University Press, 1983.

La Vere, David. *The Tuscarora War: Indians, Settlers, and the Fight for the Carolina Colonies*. Chapel Hill: University of North Carolina Press, 2013.

Lefler, Hugh Talmage, and Albert Ray Newsome. *North Carolina: The History of a Southern State*. Chapel Hill: University of North Carolina Press, 1954.

Leonard, Elizabeth D. *Men of Color to Arms!: Black Soldiers, Indian Wars, and the Quest for Equality*. New York: W. W. Norton, 2010.

Levine, Bruce. *Confederate Emancipation: Southern Plans to Free and Arm Slaves during the Civil War*. New York: Oxford University Press, 2006.

Lonn, Ella. *Salt as a Factor in the Confederacy*. Tuscaloosa: University of Alabama Press, 1965.

Lubet, Steven. *The "Colored Hero" of Harper's Ferry: John Anthony Copeland and the War Against Slavery*. New York: Cambridge University Press, 2015.

Manning, Chandra. *What This Cruel War Was Over: Soldiers, Slavery, and the Civil War*. New York: Vintage Books, 2007.

Marks, Stuart A. *Southern Hunting in Black and White: Nature, History, and Ritual in a Carolina Community*. Princeton, NJ: Princeton University Press, 1991.

McCurry, Stephanie. *Confederate Reckoning: Power and Politics in the Civil War South*. Cambridge, MA: Harvard University Press, 2010.

McCurry, Stephanie. *Masters of Small Worlds: Yeoman Households, Gender Relations, and the Political Culture of the Antebellum South Carolina Low Country*. New York: Oxford University Press, 1995.

McIlvenna, Noeleen. *A Very Mutinous People: The Struggle for North Carolina, 1660–1713*. Chapel Hill: University of North Carolina Press, 2009.

McMillen, Sally G. *Southern Women: Black and White in the Old South*. Arlington Heights, IL: Harlan Davidson, 1992.

McPherson, James M. *Battle Cry of Freedom: The Civil War Era*. New York: Oxford University Press, 1988.

McPherson, James M. *For Cause and Comrades: Why Men Fought in the Civil War*. New York: Oxford University Press, 1997.

Merrens, Harry Roy. *Colonial North Carolina in the Eighteenth Century: A Study in Historical Geography*. Chapel Hill: University of North Carolina Press, 1964.

Mildfelt, Todd, and David D. Schafer. *Abolitionist of the Most Dangerous Kind: James Montgomery and His War on Slavery*. Norman, OK: University of Oklahoma Press, 2023.

Miller, Steve M. *North Carolina Unionists and the Fight Over Secession*. Charleston, SC: The History Press, 2019.

Milteer, Warren Eugene, Jr. *Beyond Slavery's Shadow: Free People of Color in the South.* Chapel Hill: University of North Carolina Press, 2021.

Milteer, Warren Eugene, Jr. *North Carolina's Free People of Color, 1715–1885.* Baton Rouge: Louisiana State University Press, 2020.

Mintz, Sidney W., and Richard Price. *The Birth of African-American Culture: An Anthropological Perspective.* Boston: Beacon Press, 1976.

Moore, John W. *History of North Carolina: From the Earliest Discoveries to the Present Time.* Raleigh, NC: Alfred Williams, 1880.

Morgan, Edmund S. *American Slavery, American Freedom: The Ordeal of Colonial Virginia.* New York: W. W. Norton, 1975.

Morgan, Philip D. *Slave Counterpoint: Black Culture in the Eighteenth-Century Chesapeake and Lowcountry.* Chapel Hill: University of North Carolina Press, 1998.

Morton, Joseph C. *The American Revolution.* Westport, CT: Greenwood Press, 2003.

Myers, Barton A. *Executing Daniel Bright: Race, Loyalty, and Guerilla Violence in a Coastal Carolina Community, 1861–1865.* Baton Rouge: Louisiana State University Press, 2009.

Nevius, Marcus P. *City of Refuge: Slavery and Petit Marronage in the Great Dismal Swamp, 1763–1856.* Athens: University of Georgia Press, 2020.

Newman, Richard S. *The Transformation of American Abolitionism: Fighting Slavery in the Early Republic.* Chapel Hill: University of North Carolina Press, 2007.

Newsome, Hampton. *The Fight for the Old North State: The Civil War in North Carolina, January-May 1864.* Lawrence: University Press of Kansas, 2019.

Oakes, James. *Freedom National: The Destruction of Slavery in the United States, 1861–1865.* New York: W. W. Norton, 2013.

Perdue, Theda. *Native Carolinians: The Indians of North Carolina.* Raleigh, NC: Division of Archives and History, Department of Cultural Resources, 1985.

Powell, William S. *North Carolina through Four Centuries.* Chapel Hill: University of North Carolina Press, 1989.

Prather, H. Leon, Sr. *We Have Taken a City: Wilmington Racial Massacre and Coup of 1898.* Cranbury, NJ: Associated University Presses, 1984.

Proctor, Nicolas. *Bathed in Blood: Hunting and Mastery in the Old South.* Charlottesville: University Press of Virginia, 2002.

Quarles, Benjamin. *The Negro in the American Revolution.* 1961. Reprint, New York: W. W. Norton, 1973.

Raboteau, Albert J. *Slave Religion: The "Invisible Institution" in the Antebellum South.* 1978. New York: Oxford University Press, 2004.

Rankin, Hugh F. *The North Carolina Continentals.* Chapel Hill: University of North Carolina Press, 1971.

Reid, Richard M. *Freedom for Themselves: North Carolina's Black Soldiers in the Civil War.* Chapel Hill: University of North Carolina Press, 2008.

Rosen, Hannah. *Terror in the Heart of Freedom: Citizenship, Sexual Violence, and the Meaning of Race in the Postemancipation South.* Chapel Hill: University of North Carolina Press, 2009.

Roth, Randolph. *American Homicide.* Cambridge, MA: The Belknap Press of Harvard University Press, 2009.

Rothman, Adam. *Slave Country: American Expansion and the Origins of the Deep South.* Cambridge, MA: Harvard University Press, 2005.

Saunt, Claudio. *Unworthy Republic: The Dispossession of Native Americans and the Road to Indian Territory.* New York: W. W. Norton, 2020.

Sawyer, Roy T. *America's Wetland: An Environmental and Cultural History of Tidewater Virginia and North Carolina.* Charlottesville: University of Virginia Press, 2010.

Segars, J. H., and Charles Kelly Barrow, eds. *Black Southerners in Confederate Armies: A Collection of Historical Accounts.* Gretna, LA: Pelican Publishing, 2007.

Stampp, Kenneth M. *The Peculiar Institution: Slavery in the Ante-Bellum South.* New York: Alfred A. Knopf, 1978.

Stauffer, John. *The Black Hearts of Men: Radical Abolitionists and the Transformation of Race.* Cambridge, MA: Harvard University Press, 2001.

Stevenson, Brenda E. *Life in Black and White: Family and Community in the Slave South.* New York: Oxford University Press, 1996.

Stewart, James Brewer. *Holy Warriors: The Abolitionists and American Slavery.* Rev. ed. New York: Hill and Wang, 1996.

Sweet, James H. *Recreating Africa; Culture, Kinship, and Religion in the African-Portuguese World, 1441–1770.* Chapel Hill: University of North Carolina Press, 2003.

Taylor, Rosser H. *The Free Negro in North Carolina.* Chapel Hill: University of North Carolina Press, 1920. https://docsouth.unc.edu/nc/taylorrh/taylorrh.html.

Tushnet, Mark V. *Slave Law in the American South:* State v. Mann *in History and Literature.* Lawrence: University of Kansas Press, 2003.

Umfleet, LeRae Sikes. *A Day of Blood: The 1898 Wilmington Race Riot.* Raleigh, NC: North Carolina Office of Archives and History, 2009.

Umoja, Akinyele Omowale. *We Will Shoot Back: Armed Resistance in the Mississippi Freedom Movement.* New York: New York University Press, 2013.

Warner, Ezra J., and W. Buck Yearns. *Biographical Register of the Confederate Congress.* Baton Rouge: Louisiana State University Press, 1975.

Watson, Alan D. *A History of New Bern and Craven County.* New Bern, NC: Tryon Palace Commission, 1987.

Watson, Alan D. *Wilmington, North Carolina, to 1861.* Jefferson, NC: McFarland and Company, 2003.

Watson, Harry L. *Liberty and Power: The Politics of Jacksonian America.* New York: Noonday Press, 1990.

White, David O. *Connecticut's Black Soldiers, 1775–1783.* Guildford, CT: Globe Pequot, 1973.

White, Deborah Gray. *Ar'n't I a Woman?: Female Slaves in the Plantation South.* New York: W. W. Norton, 1985.

Winkler, Adam. *Gun Fight: The Battle over the Right to Bear Arms in America.* New York: W. W. Norton, 2011.

Wood, Bradford J. *This Remote Part of the World: Regional Formation in Lower Cape Fear, North Carolina, 1725–1775.* Columbia: University of South Carolina Press, 2004.

Wood, Peter H. *Black Majority: Negroes in Colonial South Carolina from 1670 through the Stono Rebellion.* New York: Alfred A. Knopf, Inc., 1974.

Woodward, Colin Edward. *Marching Masters: Slavery, Race, and the Confederate Army during the Civil War.* Charlottesville: University of Virginia Press, 2014.

Wooster, Ralph A. *The Secession Conventions of the South.* Westport, CT: Greenwood Press, 1976.

Wyatt-Brown, Bertram. *Southern Honor: Ethics and Behavior in the Old South.* New York: Oxford University Press, 1982.

Zucchino, David. *Wilmington's Lie: The Murderous Coup of 1898 and the Rise of White Supremacy.* New York: Atlantic Monthly Press, 2020.

JOURNAL ARTICLES AND BOOK CHAPTERS

Baltzell, George F. "The Battle of Olustee (Ocean Pond), Florida." *Florida Historical Society Quarterly* 9, no. 4 (1931): 199–223.

Barth, Jonathan Edward. "'The Sinke of the America': Society in the Albemarle Borderlands of North Carolina, 1663–1729." *North Carolina Historical Review* 87, no. 1 (2010): 1–27.

Battle, George Gordon. "The State of North Carolina v. Negro Will, a Slave of James S. Battle; a Cause Celebre of Ante-Bellum Time." *Virginia Law Review.* 6, no. 7 (1920): 515–30.

Blocher, Joseph. "Firearm Localism." *Yale Law Journal* 123, no. 1 (2013): 82–146.

Bodenhamer, David J., and James W. Ely, Jr. "Regionalism and the Legal History of the South." In *Ambivalent Legacy: A Legal History of the South*, edited by James W. Ely Jr. and David J. Bodenhamer, 3–29. Jackson: University Press of Mississippi, 1984.

Bowman, Larry. "The Virginia County Committees of Safety, 1774–1776." *Virginia Magazine of History and Biography* 79, no. 3 (1971): 322–37.

Bradley, Mark L. "'This Monstrous Proposition': North Carolina and the Confederate Debate on Arming the Slaves." *North Carolina Historical Review* 80, no. 2 (2003): 153–87.

Browning, Judkin Jay. "'Little Souled Mercenaries'? The Buffaloes of Eastern North Carolina during the Civil War." *North Carolina Historical Review* 77, no. 3 (2000): 337–63.

Browning, Judkin Jay. "Visions of Freedom and Civilization Opening before Them: African Americans Search for Autonomy during Military Occupation in North Carolina." In *North Carolinians in the Era of the Civil War and Reconstruction*, edited by Paul D. Escott, 69–100. Chapel Hill: University of North Carolina Press, 2008.

Campbell, Jacqueline Glass. "The Cultural Politics of Memory: Confederate Women and General William T. Sherman." In *The Civil War in Popular Culture: Memory and Meaning*, edited by Lawrence A. Kreiser Jr. and Randal Allred, 101–16. Lexington: University Press of Kentucky, 2014.

Cottrol, Robert J. "Public Safety and the Right to Bear Arms." In *The Bill of Rights in Modern America*, edited by David J. Bodenhamer and James W. Ely Jr., 73–97. Bloomington: Indiana University Press, 2008.

Cottrol, Robert J., and Raymond T. Diamond. "The Second Amendment: Toward an Afro-Americanist Reconsideration." *Georgetown Law Journal* no. 80 (1991): 309–61.

Cowper, Pulaski. "Sketch of the Life of Judge William B. Rodman." *North Carolina University Magazine* 2nd ser., vol. 13, no. 5 (1894): 209–24.

Crow, Jeffrey J. "Slave Rebelliousness and Social Conflict in North Carolina, 1775 to 1802." *William and Mary Quarterly*, 3rd ser., vol. 37, no. 1 (1980): 79–102.

Cullen, Jim. "'I's a Man Now.'" In *A Question of Manhood: A Reader in U.S. Black Men's History and Masculinity*. Vol. 1, *"Manhood Rights": The Construction of Black Male History and Manhood, 1750–1870*, edited by Darlene Clark Hine and Earnestine Jenkins, 489–501. Bloomington: Indiana University Press, 1999.

Dodge, David. "The Free Negroes of North Carolina." *Atlantic Monthly* 57 (1886): 20–30.

Forret, Jeff. "Slave Labor in North Carolina's Antebellum Gold Mines." In *North Carolina Historical Review* 76, no. 2 (1999): 135–62.

Franklin, John Hope "The Free Negro in the Economic Life of Ante-Bellum North Carolina." In *Free Blacks in America, 1800–1860*, edited by Bracey Meier Rudwick, 45–59. Belmont, CA: Wadsworth Publishing, 1971.

Fraser, Rebecca. "Negotiating Their Manhood: Masculinity amongst the Enslaved in the Upper South, 1830–1861." In *Black and White Masculinity in the American South, 1800–2000*, edited by Lydia Plath and Sergio Lussana, 76–94. Newcastle, UK: Cambridge Scholars Publishing, 2009.

Goff, Phillip Atiba, Matthew Christian Jackson, Brooke Allison Lewis Di Leone, Carmen Marie Culotta, and Natalie Ann DiTomasso. "The Essence of Innocence: Consequences of Dehumanizing Black Children." *Journal of Personality and Social Psychology* 106, no. 4 (2014): 526–45.

Hadden, Sally E. "South Carolina's Grand Jury Presentments: The Eighteenth-Century Experience." In *Signposts: New Directions in Southern Legal History*, edited by Sally E. Hadden and Patricia Hagler Minter, 89–109. Athens: University of Georgia Press, 2013.

Honey, Michael. "Class, Race, and Power in the New South: Racial Violence and the Delusions of White Supremacy." In *Democracy Betrayed: The Wilmington Race Riot of 1898 and Its Legacy*, edited by David S. Cecelski and Timothy B. Tyson, 163–84. Chapel Hill: University of North Carolina Press, 1998.

Inscoe, John. "Mountain Masters: Slaveholding in Western North Carolina." *North Carolina Historical Review* 69, no. 2 (1984): 143–73.

Lightner, David L., and Alexander M. Ragan. "Were African American Slaveholders Benevolent or Exploitative? A Quantitative Approach." *Journal of Southern History* 71, no. 3 (2005): 535–58.

Maass, John R. "'All This Poor Province Could Do': North Carolina and the Seven Years' War, 1757–1762." *North Carolina Historical Review* 79, no. 1 (2002): 50–89.

Manning, Chandra. "The Order of Nature Would Be Reversed: Soldiers, Slavery, and the North Carolina Gubernatorial Election of 1864." In *North Carolinians in the Era of the Civil War and Reconstruction*, edited by Paul D. Escott, 101–28. Chapel Hill: University of North Carolina Press, 2008.

Paquette, Robert L. "Social History Update: Slave Resistance and Social History." *Journal of Social History* 24, no. 3 (1991): 681–685.

Redkey, Edwin S. "Henry McNeal Turner: Black Chaplain in the Union Army." In *Black Soldiers in Blue: African American Troops in the Civil War Era*, edited by John David Smith, 336–60. Chapel Hill: University of North Carolina Press, 2002.

Reid, Richard. "Raising the African Brigade: Early Black Recruitment in Civil War North Carolina." *North Carolina Historical Review* 70, no. 3 (1993): 266–301.

Reidy, Joseph P. "Armed Slaves and the Struggles for Republican Liberty in the U.S. Civil War." In *Arming Slaves: From Classical Times to the Modern Age*, edited by Christopher Leslie Brown and Philip D. Morgan, 274–303. New Haven, CT: Yale University Press, 2006.

Rohrs, Richard C. "The Free Black Experience in Antebellum Wilmington, North Carolina: Refining Generalizations about Race Relations." *Journal of Southern History* 78, no. 3 (2012): 615–38.

Roth, Sarah N. "'How a Slave Was Made a Man': Negotiating Black Violence and Masculinity in Antebellum Slave Narratives." *Slavery and Abolition* 28, no. 2 (2007): 255–75.

Rugemer, Edward B. "The Black Atlantic and the Coming of the Civil War." *Journal of the Civil War Era* 2, no. 2 (2012): 179–95.

Sadler, Lynn Veach. "Dr. Stephen Graham's Narration of the 'Duplin Insurrection': Additional Evidence of the Impact of Nat Turner." *Journal of American Studies*, 12, no. 3 (December 1978): 359–67.

Schweninger, Loren. "John Carruthers Stanly and the Anomaly of Black Slaveholding." *The North Carolina Historical Review* 67, no. 2 (1990): 159–92.

Skinner, Allison L., and Ingrid J. Haas. "Perceived Threat Associated with Police Officers and Black Men Predicts Support for Policing Policy Reform." *Frontiers in Psychology* 7 (July 2016). https://doaj.org/article/4a4b1274ea1541f4ace108c00b8b7eeb.

Starobin, Robert S. "Privileged Bondsmen and the Process of Accommodation: The Role of Houseservants and Drivers as Seen in Their Own Letters." *Journal of South History* 5, no. 1 (1971): 46–70.

Struna, Nancy. "Puritans and Sport: The Irretrievable Tide of Change." *Journal of Sport History* 4, no. 1 (1977): 1–21.

Urwin, Gregory J. W., "'To Bring the American Army under Strict Discipline': British Army Foraging Policy in the South, 1780–81." *War in History* 26, no. 1 (2019): 4–26.

Watson, Alan D. "Impulse toward Independence: Resistance and Rebellion among North Carolina Slaves, 1750–1775." *Journal of Negro History* 63, no. 4 (1978): 317–28.

Weber, Max. "Politics as a Vocation." In *From Max Weber: Essays in Sociology*, edited by H. H. Gerth and C. Wright Mills, 77–128. Abingdon, UK: Routledge, 1991.

Weber, Max. "The State, Its Basic Functions, and Economic Foundations of Imperialism." In *Max Weber: Readings and Commentary on Modernity*, edited by Stephen Kalberg, 230–37. Malden, MA: Blackwell Publishing, 2005.

Wood, Bradford J., and Larry E. Tise, "The Conundrum of Unfree Labor." In *New Voyages to Carolina: Reinterpreting North Carolina History*, edited by Larry E. Tise and Jeffrey J. Crow, 85–109. Chapel Hill: University of North Carolina Press, 2017.

Woodson, Carter G. "Freedom and Slavery in Appalachian America." *Journal of Negro History* 1, no. 2 (1916): 132–50.

Yellin, Jean Fagan. "Incidents Abroad: Harriet Jacobs and the Transatlantic Movement." In *Women's Rights and Transatlantic Antislavery in the Era of Emancipation*, edited by Kathryn Kish Sklar and James Brewer Stewart, 158–72. New Haven, CT: Yale University Press, 2007.

Zipf, Karin L. "'The Whites Shall Rule the Land or Die': Gender, Race, and Class in North Carolina Reconstruction Politics." *Journal of Southern History* 65, no. 3 (1999): 499–534.

DISSERTATIONS, THESES, AND REPORTS

Coffman, Peter W. "'He Has Earned the Right of Citizenship': The Black Soldiers of North Carolina in the Civil War; a Comment on Historiography, Treatment, and Pensions." MA thesis, East Carolina University, Greenville, 2015.

Epstein, Rebecca, Jamilia J. Blake, and Thalia González. *Childhood Interrupted: The Erasure of Black Girls' Childhood.* Georgetown Law Center for Poverty and Inequality, 2017. www.law.georgetown.edu/poverty-inequality-center/wp-content/uploads/sites /14/2017/08/girlhood-interrupted.pdf.

Freeman, W. Trevor. "North Carolina's Black Patriots of the American Revolution." MA thesis, East Carolina University, Greenville, 2020.

Kaiser, John James. "'Masters Determined to be Masters': The Insurrectionary Scare in Eastern North Carolina." MA thesis, North Carolina State University, Raleigh, 2006.

Proctor, Bradley David. "Whip, Pistol, and Hood: Ku Klux Klan Violence in the Carolinas During Reconstruction." PhD diss., University of North Carolina, Chapel Hill, 2013.

Raper, Derris Lea. "The Effects of David Walker's Appeal and Nat Turner's Insurrection on North Carolina." MA thesis, University of North Carolina, Chapel Hill, 1969.

Schneider, Tracy Whittaker. "The Institution of Slavery in North Carolina, 1860–1865." PhD diss., Duke University, Durham, 1979.

Warlick, John Thomas, IV. "'What's Past is Prologue': North Carolina's Forgotten Black Code," MA thesis, University of North Carolina, Charlotte, 2020.

Waters, Darin J. "Life beneath the Veneer: The Black Community in Asheville, North Carolina from 1793 to 1900." PhD diss., University of North Carolina, Chapel Hill, 2012.

VIDEOS

Noah, Trevor. "Emantic Bradford Jr.'s Death and Why the Second Amendment Doesn't Apply to Black Men." *Daily Show*, YouTube, 5:30, November 27, 2018. www.youtube .com/watch?v=wWwQjH7T1.

General Index

abolition: arguments for, 109; and dispossession of Indigenous people, 196n15; support for, among sailors, 218n106

abolitionists, 145–46, 154; Southern attitudes toward, 125, 145–46, 149; and use of violence, 45–46, 47, 71–72, 145, 154

accidents, firearm, 57, 78, 101, 104–5, 225n58, 226n70, 236n63; and accessibility of guns, 73–76; and carelessness, 102–5; and children, 102, 103, 104, 105, 216n87, 226n60

Alabama, 6, 88, 191

Alamance County, 105

alcohol, 19, 32, 38, 67–68, 80, 100, 153, 205n95, 208n128

Appeal in Four Articles (Walker), 39–41, 206n101

Beaufort, NC, 1, 163

Beaufort County: Black community in, 153; government actions against free people of color, 40, 49, 117, 229n13; insurrection rumors in, 28; jail in, 84

Bertie County, 134, 207n121

Bladen County, 27, 28, 41, 54, 70–71, 88, 90, 93–94, 183, 221n3

bounties for wildlife, 90–91, 92, 222n4

Britain, 25, 28, 31; British Army, 29, 30–32

Brunswick County: arming slaves in, 53, 93; committee of safety in, 27, 28; court cases in, 136–37; hunting in, 107; maroons in, 57; militia in, 200n28; regulations in, 200n28, 204n86, 221n3; shooting accident in, 105; wildlife bounties in, 90–91

Buffaloes (North Carolina Unionists), 148, 243n29

Buncombe County, 14

Bureau of Refugees, Freedmen, and Abandoned Lands, 180–81, 183–84

Burke County, 43, 90, 93, 180, 221n3

Bute County, 91, 222n5

Cabarrus County, 180

Camden County, 67–68, 96, 204n86, 214n48, 243n31

Carteret County, 90, 91, 154, 183, 204n86

Caswell County, 90, 221n3

Catawba County, 97–98

Charlotte, NC, 26, 155

Chatham County, 120, 156, 186

children and teenagers: accessing firearms, 78–79, 80–81, 103–4, 216n83; during the Civil War, 150, 167, 171, 172; and conspiracy, 40–41, 145–47; as enforcers of the law, 111, 146–47, 207n121; firearm accidents, 75–76, 78, 103–4, 105, 216n83, 216n83, 226n60; free people of color, 114, 115, 118–20, 121–22, 123–24, 125, 128–29, 226n60, 239n88; as hunting companions, 107; licenses and the county courts, 115, 118, 119, 121–22, 123–24, 125; manumission of, 114; as perpetrators of violence, 77, 103; regulations about, 25–26, 185, 216n83; as victims of or witnesses to violence, 54, 74–76 78, 103,170, 186, 187, 190, 253n41, 253n41

Chocowinity, NC, 87, 242n21

Chowan County: arming slaves in, 23–25; Black Union soldiers in, 165; Cornwallis's Black auxiliaries near, 32; court cases in, 83, 84, 85; enslaved people's diets, 97; fines and penalties in, 225n48; illegal arms trade in, 83, 84, 85

Index of Names

www.ingramcontent.com/pod-product-compliance
Lightning Source LLC
Chambersburg PA
CBHW020333191225
37040CB00031B/263